ISNM 75:
International Series of Numerical Mathematics
Internationale Schriftenreihe zur Numerischen Mathematik
Série internationale d'Analyse numérique
Vol. 75

Edited by
Ch. Blanc, Lausanne; R. Glowinski, Paris;
G. Golub, Stanford; P. Henrici, Zürich;
H. O. Kreiss, Pasadena; A. Ostrowski, Montagnola;
J. Todd, Pasadena

Birkhäuser Verlag
Basel · Boston · Stuttgart

Multivariate Approximation Theory III

Proceedings of the Conference at the Mathematical Research Institute at Oberwolfach, Black Forest, January 20–26, 1985

Edited by

Walter Schempp
Karl Zeller

1985

Birkhäuser Verlag
Basel · Boston · Stuttgart

Editors

Prof. Dr. Walter Schempp
Lehrstuhl für Mathematik I
Universität Siegen
Hölderlinstrasse 3
D–5900 Siegen (FRG)

Prof. Dr. Karl Zeller
Mathematisches Institut
Universität Tübingen
Auf der Morgenstelle 10
D–7400 Tübingen (FRG)

Library of Congress Cataloging in Publication Data
Main entry under title:

Multivariate approximation theory III.
(International series of numerical mathematics ; vol. 75)
Proceedings of the Fourth International Symposium on Multivariate Approximation Theory.
English and German.
1. Approximation theory -- Congresses. 2. Functions of several real variables -- Congresses. I. Schempp, W. (Walter), 1938– . II. Zeller, Karl. III. International Symposium on Multivariate Approximation Theory (4th : 1985 : Oberwolfach Mathematical Research Institute) IV. Title: Multivariate approximation theory 3. V. Title: Multivariate approximation theory three. VI. Series.
QA297.5.M847 1985 511'.4 85–15645
ISBN 3-7643-1738-8

CIP-Kurztitelaufnahme der Deutschen Bibliothek

Multivariate approximation theory . . . :
proceedings of the conference at the Math.
Research Inst. at Oberwolfach, Black Forest.
– Basel ; Boston ; Stuttgart : Birkhäuser
3. January 20–26, 1985. – 1985.
(International series of numerical mathematics ; Vol. 75)
ISBN 3-7643-1738-8
NE: Mathematisches Forschungsinstitut ⟨Oberwolfach⟩; GT

Printed in Germany
ISBN 3-7643-1738-8

MS-SHK
MSMON

PREFACE

The Fourth International Symposium on Multivariate Approximation Theory was held at the Oberwolfach Mathematical Research Institute, Black Forest, W.-Germany, during the week of January 20 - 26, 1985. The preceding conferences on this topic were held in 1976, 1979, and 1982*. We were pleased to have more than 50 mathematicians from 13 countries in attendance. The program included 40 lectures. These Proceedings form a record of most of the papers presented at the Symposium.

The topics treated cover different problems on multivariate approximation such as polynomial approximation on simplices, multivariate splines (box-splines, dimension of spline spaces), blending methods, multivariate Hermite interpolation, data smoothing and surface representation, and multivariate summation methods.

We would like to thank the director of the Oberwolfach Mathematical Research Institute, Prof. Dr. M. Barner, and his staff for providing the facilities. Of the people who gave their time to help make this conference a success, we would like to mention in particular Prof. Dr. F.J. Delvos (Siegen), Dr. G. Baszenski (College Station, Texas), and Dipl.-Math. H. Nienhaus (Siegen). Finally, our thanks are due to Carl Einsele of Birkhäuser Publishers for his valuable cooperation.

May 1985

Walter Schempp
Siegen

Karl Zeller
Tübingen

Editors

---

*"Constructive Theory of Functions of Several Variables", Lecture Notes in Mathematics 571 (1977)
"Multivariate Approximation Theory", ISNM 51 (1979)
"Multivariate Approximation Theory II", ISNM 61 (1982)

CONTENTS

ZUR TAGUNG

Vom 20. bis 26. Januar 1985 fand im Mathematischen Forschungsinstitut Oberwolfach eine Tagung über "Mehrdimensionale konstruktive Funktionentheorie" statt. Sie wurde, wie schon die Oberwolfach-Tagungen gleichen Themas der Jahre 1976, 1979 und 1982 von den Herausgebern geleitet. Es nahmen insgesamt 54 Mathematiker an der Tagung teil, die aus China, der Deutschen Demokratischen Republik, England, Israel, Italien, den Niederlanden, Norwegen, Polen, Schottland, Schweden, Ungarn, den Vereinigten Staaten von Amerika und der Bundesrepublik Deutschland kamen.

Das Vortragsprogramm bestand aus 40 Vorträgen, in dessen Mittelpunkt Fragen der Darstellung, Approximation und numerischen Behandlung von Funktionen mehrerer Variablen standen. Als Schwerpunkte der Vorträge sind zu nennen

- Polynomapproximation über Simplices,
- Multivariate Splines (Box-Splines, Dimension von Spline-Räumen),
- Blending-Methoden,
- Mehrdimensionale Hermite-Interpolation,
- Glättung von Daten und Flächendarstellung,
- Mehrdimensionale Summierungsmethoden.

Die Tagung verlief in einer sehr freundlichen Atmosphäre, zu der die Gastfrendschaft und zuvorkommende Hilfe der Mitarbeiter des Oberwolfacher Instituts wesentlich beigetragen haben. Ihnen, den Vortragenden und Sitzungsleitern sei an dieser Stelle sehr herzlich gedankt.

Walter Schempp　　Karl Zeller
Siegen　　Tübingen

Tagungsleiter

LIST OF PARTICIPANTS

Lothar Bamberger, Mathematisches Institut der Universität München, Theresienstraße 39, D-8000 München 2, Fed. Rep. Germany

Günter Baszenski, Department of Mathematics, Center for Approximation Theory, Texas A & M University, College Station, Texas 77843-3368, U.S.A.

Jan Boman, Matematiska Institutionen, Stockholms Universitet, Box 6701, S-11385 Stockholm, Sweden

Bruno Brosowski, Fachbereich Mathematik der Johann-Wolfgang-Goethe-Universität, Robert-Mayer-Straße 6-10, D-6000 Frankfurt a. M. 1, Fed. Rep. Germany

Geng-zhe Chang, Department of Mathematics, University of Science and Technology of Hefei, Anhui, People's Republic of China

Charles K. Chui, Department of Mathematics, Center for Approximation Theory, Texas A & M University, College Station, Texas 77843-3368, U.S.A.

Zbigniew Ciesielski, Instytut Matematyczny, Polskiej Akademii Nauk, Oddzial w Gdansku, 81-825 Sopot, ul. Abrahama 18, Poland

Lothar Collatz, Institut für Angewandte Mathematik der Universität Hamburg, Bundesstr. 55, D-2000 Hamburg 13, Fed. Rep. Germany

Wolfgang Dahmen, Fakultät für Mathematik der Universität Bielefeld, Universitätsstraße, Postfach 8640, D-4800 Bielefeld 1, Fed. Rep. Germany

Franz-Jürgen Delvos, Lehrstuhl für Mathematik I der Universität Siegen, Hölderlinstraße 3, D-5900 Siegen, Fed. Rep. Germany

Hermann Engels, Lehrstuhl für Mathematik und Institut für Geometrie und Praktische Mathematik der Rheinisch-Westfälischen Technischen Hochschule Aachen, Templergraben 55, D-5100 Aachen, Fed. Rep. Germany

Willi Freeden, Institut für Reine und Angewandte Mathematik der Rheinisch-Westfälischen Technischen Hochschule Aachen, Templergraben 55, D-5100 Aachen, Fed. Rep. Germany

Manfred von Golitschek, Institut für Angewandte Mathematik und Statistik der Universität Würzburg, Am Hubland, D-8700 Würzburg, Fed. Rep. Germany

T.N.T. Goodman, Department of Mathematics, The University of Dundee, Dundee DDI 4HN, Scotland

Werner Haußmann, Fachbereich Mathematik der Universität Duisburg, Lotharstraße 65, D-4100 Duisburg 1, Fed. Rep. Germany

Richard Haverkamp, Institut für Angewandte Mathematik der Universität Bonn, Wegelerstraße 6, D-5300 Bonn 1, Fed. Rep. Germany

Gerhard Heindl, Fachbereich Mathematik der Universität Wuppertal, Gaußstraße 20, D-5600 Wuppertal 1, Fed. Rep. Germany

Klaus Höllig, Computer Sciences Department, University of Wisconsin-Madison, 1210 West Dayton Street, Madison, Wisconsin 53706, U.S.A.

Hans-Bernd Knoop, Fachbereich Mathematik der Universität Duisburg, Lotharstraße 65, D-4100 Duisburg 1, Fed. Rep. Germany

András Kroó, Mathematical Institute of the Hungarian Academy of Sciences, V. Reáltanoda u. 13-15, H-1364 Budapest, Hungary

Licia Lenarduzzi, Istituto per le Applicazioni della Matematica e dell'Informatica, Via L. Cicognara 7, I-20129 Milano, Italy

Dany Leviatan, School of Mathematical Sciences, Tel-Aviv University, Ramat Aviv, Israel

David Levin, School of Mathematical Sciences, Tel-Aviv University, Ramat Aviv, Israel

William Light, Department of Mathematics, Cartmel College, The University of Lancaster, Bailrigg, Lancaster LA1 4YL, England

Franz Locher, Fachbereich Mathematik und Informatik der Fernuniversität Hagen, Postfach 940, D-5800 Hagen, Fed. Rep. Germany

Alfred K. Louis, Fachbereich Mathematik der Universität Kaiserslautern, Erwin-Schrödinger-Straße, D-6750 Kaiserslautern, Fed. Rep. Germany

Eberhard Luik, Mathematisches Institut der Universität Tübingen, Auf der Morgenstelle 10, D-7400 Tübingen, Fed. Rep. Germany

Tom Lyche, Institutt for Informatikk, Universitetet I Oslo, P.O. Box 1080, 0316 Blindern, Oslo 3, Norway

Günter Meinardus, Fakultät für Mathematik und Informatik der Universität Mannheim, Seminargebäude A 5, D-6800 Mannheim, Fed. Rep. Germany

Holger Mettke, Sektion Mathematik der Technischen Universität Dresden, Mommsenstraße 13, DDR-8027 Dresden, GDR

Charles A. Micchelli, International Business Machines Corporation, Thomas J. Watson Research Center, P.O. Box 218 Yorktown Heights, New York 10598, U.S.A.

Hans Michael Möller, Fachbereich Mathematik und Informatik der Fernuniversität Hagen, Postfach 940, D-5800 Hagen, Fed. Rep. Germany

Ferenc Móricz, University of Szeged, Bolyai Institute, Aradi Vértanúk tere 1, H-6720 Szeged, Hungary

Manfred W. Müller, Universität Dortmund, Lehrstuhl Mathematik VIII, Postfach 500 500, D-4600 Dortmund 50, Fed. Rep. Germany

Helmut Nienhaus, Lehrstuhl für Mathematik I der Universität Siegen, Hölderlinstraße 3, D-5900 Siegen, Fed. Rep. Germany

Gerhard Opfer, Institut für Angewandte Mathematik der Universität Hamburg, Bundesstraße 55, D-2000 Hamburg 13, Fed. Rep. Germany

Pia Pfluger, Mathematisch Instituut, Universiteit van Amsterdam, Roetersstraat 15, NL-1018 WB Amsterdam, The Netherlands

Alfio Quarteroni, Istituto di Analisi Numerica del Consiglio Nazionale delle Ricerche, Palazzo dell'Università, Corso Carlo Alberto, 5, I-27100 Pavia, Italy

Heinz-Joachim Rack, Universität Dortmund, Abteilung Mathematik, Postfach 500 500, D-4600 Dortmund 50, Fed. Rep. Germany

Manfred Reimer, Lehrstuhl Mathematik III der Universität Dortmund, Postfach 500 500, D-4600 Dortmund 50, Fed. Rep. Germany

Robert Schaback, Institut für Numerische und Angewandte Mathematik der Universität Göttingen, Lotzestraße 16-18, D-3400 Göttingen, Fed. Rep. Germany

Walter Schempp, Lehrstuhl für Mathematik I der Universität Siegen, Hölderlinstraße 3, D-5900 Siegen, Fed. Rep. Germany

Rudolf Scherer, Institut für Praktische Mathematik der Universität Karlsruhe, Englerstraße 2, Postfach 6380, D-7500 Karlsruhe 1, Fed. Rep. Germany

Hans Joachim Schmid, Mathematisches Institut der Universität Erlangen-Nürnberg, Bismarckstraße 1 1/2, D-8520 Erlangen, Fed. Rep. Germany

Rita Schmidt, Hahn-Meitner-Institut für Kernforschung Berlin GmbH, Postfach 390128, Glienickerstraße 100, D-1000 Berlin 39 (Wannsee), Fed. Rep. Germany

Harold S. Shapiro, Matematiska Institutionen, Kungl. Tekniska Högskolan, S-100 44 Stockholm, Sweden

Xie-Chang Shen, Department of Mathematics, Peking University, Beijing, People's Republic of China

Burkhard Sündermann, Institut für Mathematik der Universität Dortmund, Postfach 500 500, D-4600 Dortmund 50, Fed. Rep. Germany

Manfred Tasche, Sektion Mathematik, Wilhelm-Pieck-Universität, Universitätsplatz 1, DDR-2500 Rostock, GDR

Hans-Joachim Töpfer, Mathematisches Institut der Universität Augsburg, Memmingerstraße 6, D-8900 Augsburg, Fed. Rep. Germany

Ren-Hong Wang, Department of Mathematics, Jilin University, Changchun, Jilin, People's Republic of China

Alistaire G. Watson, Department of Mathematical Sciences, University of Dundee, Dundee DD1 4HN, Scotland

Helmut Werner, Institut für Angewandte Mathematik der Universität Bonn, Wegelerstraße 6, D-5300 Bonn1, Fed. Rep. Germany

Karl Zeller, Mathematisches Institut der Universität Tübingen, Auf der Morgenstelle 10, D-7400 Tübingen 1, Fed. Rep. Germany

PROGRAM OF THE SESSIONS

Monday, January 21

8.50	K. Zeller:	Words of welcome
First morning session.		Chairman: K. Zeller
9.00	Z. Ciesielski:	Approximation by algebraic polynomials on a simplex
9.40	G.Z. Chang:	Convexity and diminishing properties of Bernstein polynomials over triangles
10.20	M. Reimer:	Abschätzung von Lagrange-Quadratsummen für die Sphäre mit Hilfe gewisser Eigenwerte
Second morning session.		Chairman: M.W. Müller
11.10	B. Sündermann:	Normen von Projektionen in mehreren Veränderlichen
11.50	W. Freeden:	Mehrdimensionale Euler'sche und Poisson'sche Summenformeln
First afternoon session.		Chairman: H.S. Shapiro
15.30	W.A. Light:	Projections on bivariate function spaces
16.10	K. Zeller:	Basic bivariate approximations
16.50	M. v. Golitschek:	Degree of best approximation by blending functions

Second afternoon session.		Chairman: W. Haußmann
17.30	H. Nienhaus:	Generalized Melkes-Interpolation
18.10	F.J. Delvos:	Intermediate blending

Tuesday, January 22

First morning session.		Chairman: G. Meinardus
9.00	L. Collatz:	Approximation von Funktionen mehrerer Veränderlicher mit gewissen Singularitäten
9.40	C.K. Chui:	Bivariate vertex splines
10.20	C.A. Micchelli:	Algebraic aspects of box splines
Second morning session.		Chairman: M. Reimer
11.10	W. Dahmen:	On the number of solutions to systems of linear diophantine equations and multivariate splines
11.50	P. Pfluger:	The dimension of $S_2^1(\Delta)$ in special cases
First afternoon session.		Chairman: B. Brosowski
15.00	K. Höllig:	Multivariate cardinal splines
15.40	R.H. Wang:	The dimension of bivariate spline spaces with general triangulation

16.20	G. Heindl:	Konstruktion und Anwendung (2- und 3-dimensionaler) quadratischer Spline-Funktionen
Second afternoon session.		Chairman: D. Leviatan
17.00	D. Levin:	Multidimensional reconstruction by by set-valued approximation
17.40	L. Lenarduzzi:	Approximation methods for experimental data and applications

Wednesday, January 23

First morning session.		Chairman: L. Collatz
9.00	W. Schempp:	CAWD (= Computer Aided Waveform Design)
9.40	T.N.T. Goodmann:	Shape preserving approximation
10.20	G. Opfer:	On certain minimal polynomials in complex domains
Second morning session.		Chairman: H. Werner
11.10	G.A. Watson:	The solution of generalized least squares problems
11.50	M. Tasche:	A collocation method for some elliptic boundary value problems

Thursday, January 24

First morning session.		Chairman: X. Shen
9.00	F. Móricz:	Cesàro summability of double orthogonal series
9.40	A. Kroó:	Unicity of best L_1-approximation
10.20	G. Baszenski:	n-th order blending with polynomial splines
Second morning session.		Chairman: M. Tasche
11.10	F. Locher:	Convergence of Hermite-Fejér interpolation via Korovkin's theorem
11.50	H.B. Knoop:	Hermite-Fejér und höhere Hermite-Fejér-Interpolation mit Randbedingungen
First Afternoon Session.		Chairman: G.Z. Chang
15.00	X.C. Shen:	The basis and moment problems of some systems of analytic functions
15.40	T. Lyche:	Knot insertion and discrete box splines
16.20	W. Haußmann:	Best harmonic L_1-approximants to subharmonic functions

Second afternoon session.		Chairman: C.K. Chui
17.00	A. Quarteroni:	Polynomial approximation theory and analysis of spectral methods
17.40	J. Boman:	Reconstruction of a function from its weighted line integrals

Friday, January 25

First morning session.		Chairman: Z. Ciesielski
9.00	H.S. Shapiro:	The Gram matrix of non-negative functions
9.40	L. Bamberger:	Interpolation in bivariate spline spaces
10.20	H.M. Möller:	Solutions of nonlinear equations by elimination
Second morning session.		Chairman: G.A. Watson
11.10	H.J. Rack:	On multivariate polynomial L_1-approximation to zero and related coefficient inequalities
11.50	E. Luik:	Cubature error bounds using degrees of approximation

International Series of
Numerical Mathematics, Vol. 75

INTERPOLATION IN BIVARIATE SPLINE SPACES

Lothar Bamberger

Mathematisches Institut, Universität München

1. Introduction

Interpolation has played a crucial role in the development of univariate spline theory [11]. However in two dimensions interpolation is only known when the degree of the splines is relatively large compared to the smoothness ([9]). Let Δ be a triangulation of a region $\Omega \subseteq \mathbb{R}^2$, $n, \mu \in \mathbb{N}_o$, and define

$$S_n^\mu(\Delta) := \{s \in C^\mu(\Omega) : s_{|D} \in \mathbb{P}_n \text{ for all triangles } D \text{ of } \Delta\},$$

where $\mathbb{P}_n$ denotes all polynomials of total degree n. Because of considerable difficulties in the investigation of arbitrary triangulations (see [10, 6]) we will concentrate on regular partitions, especially on $\Delta_{N,N}^{(1)}$, the triangulation of type 1 of the region $[0,N]^2$ with $N \in \mathbb{N}$.

Fig. 1

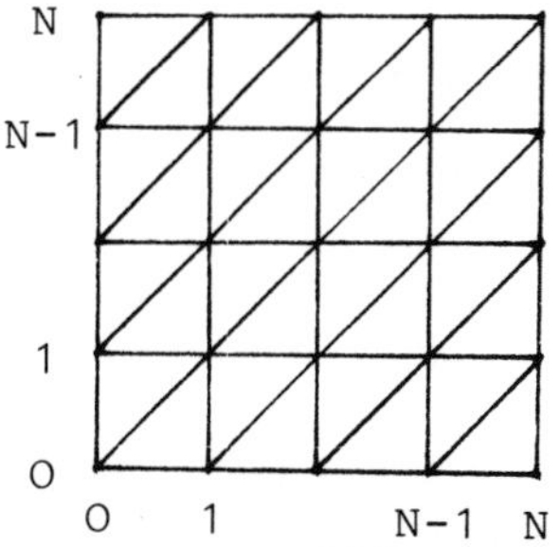

The triangulation $\Delta_{N,N}^{(1)}$

In this paper we will provide an interpolation scheme in

$$(S_3^1(\Delta_{N,N}^{(1)}))_h := \{s : I \times I \to \mathbb{R} \text{ with } s = \varphi(\tfrac{\cdot}{h}) \text{ and } \varphi \in S_3^1(\Delta_{N,N}^{(1)})\},$$

where $h = 1/N$ and $I = [0,1]$.

Figure 2 shows the splines B^1 and B^2 of minimum support in $S_3^1(\Delta_{N,N}^{(1)})$. The largeness of their

Fig.2.

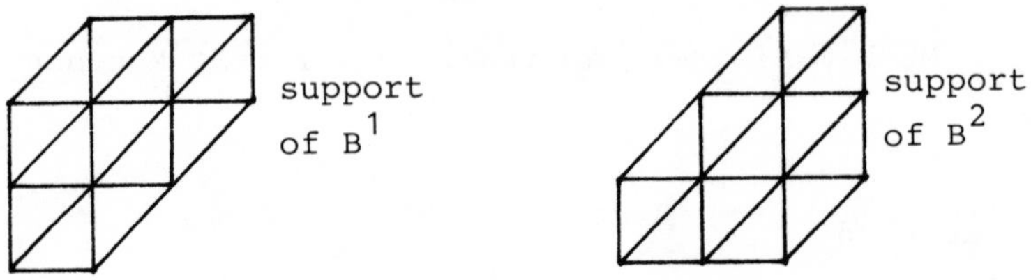

support reveals the dependence of data over a lot of triangles which does not admit local interpolation schemes like in the finite element method.

2. Bézier polynomials over triangles

If U,V, and $W \in \mathbb{R}^2$ are not located on a line each $z \in \mathbb{R}^2$ can be uniquely represented in the form

$$(2.1) \qquad z = uU + vV + wW \quad \text{with} \quad u + v + w = 1.$$

u,v and w are called <u>barycentric coordinates</u>. Now we define the <u>Bernstein polynomials</u> of degree $n \in \mathbb{N}_o$ by

$$(2.2) \qquad B^n_{i,j,k}(u,v,w) = \frac{n!}{i!j!k!} u^i v^j w^k \text{ for all } (i,j,k) \in J_n,$$

where $\quad J_n = \{(i,j,k) \in \mathbb{Z}^3 : 0 \leq i,j,k \ , \ i+j+k = n\}$.

They form a basis of $\mathbb{P}_n$, so that any $\overline{\Phi}_n \in \mathbb{P}_n$ can be uniquely written as

$$(2.3) \qquad \overline{\Phi}_n(z) = \Phi_n(u,v,w) = \sum_{(i,j,k)\in J_n} b_{ijk} \, B^n_{i,j,k}(u,v,w)$$

with the <u>Bézier ordinates</u> b_{ijk}. Then $\overline{\Phi}_n$ is called <u>Bézier polynomial</u>. For $(i,j,k) \in J_n$ let

(2.4) $$z_{ijk} = \frac{iU+jV+kW}{n},$$

and associate with it the Bézier ordinate b_{ijk}. We have

(2.5)
$$\begin{aligned}\overline{\Phi}_n(U) &= \Phi(1,0,0) = b_{n,o,o}\\ \overline{\Phi}_n(V) &= \Phi(0,1,0) = b_{o,n,o}\\ \overline{\Phi}_n(W) &= \Phi(0,0,1) = b_{o,o,n}\,.\end{aligned}$$

For a differentiable function f and $\xi \in \mathbb{R}^2 \setminus \{0\}$ we define the directional derivative of f with respect to ξ by

$$D_\xi f(z) = \lim_{t\to o} \frac{1}{t} f\,(z+t\xi), \quad z \in \mathbb{R}^2.$$

The directional derivatives of a Bézier polynomial Φ_n with respect to the edge directions are obtained by taking corresponding differences.

$$(D_{U-W}\Phi_n)(u,v,w) =$$

$$= n \sum_{(i,j,k)\in J_{n-1}} (b_{i+1,j,k}-b_{i,j,k+1})B^{n-1}_{i,j,k}(u,v,w)$$

(2.6) $$(D_{V-U}\Phi_n)(u,v,w) =$$

$$= n \sum_{(i,j,k)\in J_{n-1}} (b_{i,j+1,k}-b_{i+1,j,k})B^{n-1}_{i,j,k}(u,v,w)$$

$$(D_{V-W}\Phi_n)(u,v,w) =$$

$$= n \sum_{(i,j,k)\in J_{n-1}} (b_{i,j+1,k}-b_{i,j,k+1})B^{n-1}_{i,j,k}(u,v,w).$$

Because of (2.5) we get in the vertex U

(2.7) $$(D_{U-W}\overline{\Phi}_n)(U) = n(b_{n,o,o} - b_{n-1,o,1}).$$

From (2.6) and (2.5) we can deduce the mixed derivatives in a vertex.

(2.8) $(D_{V-U}D_{U-W}\overline{\Phi}_n)(U) = n(n-1)(b_{n-1,1,o}-b_{n-1,o,1}-b_{n-2,1,1}+b_{n,o,o})$.

Let us point out that the restriction of a bivariate Bézier polynomial to an edge leads to a univariate Bézier polynomial.

3. Interpolation for C^1-cubics on a three-direction mesh

Each spline function $s \in (S_3^1(\Delta_{N,N}^{(1)}))_h$ consists of $2N^2$ polynomials on the indicidual triangles. The Bézier points of the collection of all triangles are $\xi_{\ell,m} = \frac{1}{3}(\ell h, mh)$, $\ell, m = 0,\ldots,3N$ and the associated Bézier ordinates of s $a_{\ell,m}$, $\ell, m = 0,\ldots,N$. Note that common edges of two adjacent triangles share the same Bézier ordinates what is equivalent to the continuity of s. In oder to ensure C^1-continuity of s we must impose additional conditions on the $a_{\ell,m}$. Using (2.6) for the directional derivatives across the edge $\Gamma_{\ell,m} := \{(x, mh+x-\ell h) : x \in [\ell h, (\ell+1)h]\}$, $\ell, m = 0,\ldots,N-1$ it can be shown that the continuity of this derivative is equivalent to

(3.1a) $$a_{3\ell+i,3m+i-1} + a_{3\ell+i-1,3m+i} - a_{3\ell+i-1,3m+i-1} - a_{3\ell+i,3m+i} = 0, \quad i = 1,2,3.$$

For horizontal edges we get

(3.1b) $$a_{3\ell+i,3m+1} + a_{3\ell+i-1,3m-1} - a_{3\ell+i-1,3m} - a_{3\ell+i,3m} = 0,$$
$$i = 1,2,3, \quad \ell = 0,\ldots,N-1, \quad m = 1,\ldots,N-1$$

and for edges parallel to (0,1)

(3.1c) $$a_{3\ell+1,3m+i} + a_{3\ell-1,3m+i-1} - a_{3\ell,3m+i-1} - a_{3\ell,3m+i} = 0,$$
$$i = 1,2,3, \quad \ell = 1,\ldots,N-1, \quad m = 0,\ldots,N-1.$$

Conditions like these can be found in [8]. Also note that C^1-continuity induces by (2.6)

(3.2a) $$a_{3\ell+1,3m} - a_{3\ell,3m} = a_{3\ell,3m} - a_{3\ell-1,3m}, \quad \ell = 1,\dots,N-1, \quad m = 0,\dots,N$$

(3.2b) $$a_{3\ell,3m+1} - a_{3\ell,3m} = a_{3\ell,3m} - a_{3\ell,3m-1}, \quad \ell = 0,\dots,N, \quad m = 1,\dots,N-1.$$

To a given function $f \in C^2(I\times I)$ we want to construct the interpolating spline s fulfilling the following interpolation conditions ($D_{1,o} := \frac{\partial}{\partial x}$, $D_{o,1} := \frac{\partial}{\partial y}$, $D_{1,1} := \frac{\partial^2}{\partial x \partial y}$).

(3.3a) $$s(ih,jh) = f(ih,jh) \quad , \quad i,j = 0,\dots,N$$

(3.3b) $$D_{1,o}s(ih,jh) = D_{1,o}f(ih,jh) \quad , \quad i,j = 0,\dots,N$$

(3.3c) $$D_{o,1}s(ih,0) = D_{o,1}f(ih,0) \quad , \quad i = 0,\dots,N$$
$$D_{o,1}s(0,jh) = D_{o,1}f(0,jh) \quad , \quad j = 1,\dots,N$$

(3.3d) $$\lim_{\substack{x\to ih- \\ y\to o+}} D_{1,1}s(x,y) = D_{1,1}f(ih,0), \quad i = 1,\dots,N$$
$$\lim_{\substack{x\to o+ \\ y\to jh-}} D_{1,1}s(x,y) = D_{1,1}f(0,jh), \quad j = 1,\dots,N.$$

In order to get s we have to determine the $(a_{\ell,m})$ by either using the interpolation conditions (3.3) or the smoothness conditions (3.1) and 3.2).

<u>1.</u> First we want to determine a_{ij} for $i=0,\dots,3$, $j=0,1$. (3.3a), (3.3b) and (3.3c) give

(3.4a) $$a_{oo} = f(0,0), a_{1o} = a_{oo}+D_{1,o}f(0,0)h/3, \; a_{o1}=a_{oo}+D_{o,1}f(0,0)h/3.$$

Now (3.1a) leads to

(3.4b) $a_{11} = a_{1o} + a_{o1} - a_{oo}$.

Because of (3.3a), (3.3b) and (3.3d) we obtain by observing (2.7) and (2.8)

(3.4c) $a_{3o} = f(h,0)$, $a_{2o} = a_{3o} - D_{1,o}f(h,0)h/3$, $a_{31} = a_{3o} +$
$+ D_{o,1}f(h,0)h/3$, $a_{21} = a_{2o} + a_{31} - a_{3o} - D_{1,1}f(h,0)h^2/6$.

<u>2.</u> We want to determine a_{ij}, $i=0,\dots,3$, $j=3m-1,3m$ for given $m=1,\dots,N$ and assume that for $i=0,\dots,3$ and $0 \le j \le 3m-2$ the Bézier ordinates are already determined. From (3.3) we get

(3.5a) $a_{o,3m} = f(0,mh)$, $a_{o,3m-1} = a_{o,3m} - D_{o,1}f(0,mh)h/3$,
$a_{1,3m} = a_{o,3m} + D_{1,o}f(o,mh)h/3$, $a_{1,3m-1} = a_{o,3m-1} + a_{1,3m} -$
$- a_{o,3m} - D_{1,1}f(0,mh)h^2/6$, $a_{3,3m} = f(h,mh)$, $a_{2,3m} =$
$= a_{3,3m} - D_{1,o}f(h,mh)h^2/6$.

(3.2) induces

(3.5b) $a_{2,3m-1} = a_{1,3m-1} + a_{2,3m-2} - a_{1,3m-2}$,
$a_{3,3m-1} = a_{3,3m} + a_{2,3m-1} - a_{2,3m}$.

If $m<N$, we determine $a_{i,3m+1}$, $i=0,\dots,3$.
(3.2b) and (3.1b) provide

(3.5c) $a_{o,3m+1} = 2a_{o,3m} - a_{o,3m-1}$, $a_{i,3m+1} = a_{i-1,3m} +$
$+ a_{i,3m} - a_{i-1,3m-1}$, $i=1,2,3$.

Note that $a_{3,3m+1}$ can also be calculated by (3.2b) ($=2a_{3,3m} - a_{3,3m-1}$) but this is compatible with the previous computation.

3. Let $\ell=1,\dots,N-1$ be given and determine a_{ij}, $i=3\ell+1,\dots,3\ell+3$, $j=0,\dots,3$. Assume that we have already got a_{ij} for $i\leq 3\ell$ and $j=0,\dots,3$. (3.2a) and (3.1c) lead to

$$\text{(3.6a)}\quad a_{3\ell+1,0} = 2a_{3\ell,0}-a_{3\ell-1,0},\ a_{3\ell+1,i} = a_{3\ell,i}+ + a_{3\ell,i-1}-a_{3\ell-1,i-1},\quad i=1,2,3.$$

(3.3) provide

$$\text{(3.6b)}\quad a_{3\ell+3,0} = f((\ell+1)h,0),\quad a_{3\ell+2,0} = a_{3\ell+3,0}- -D_{1,0}f((\ell+1)h,0)h/3,\quad a_{3\ell+3,1} = a_{3\ell+3,0} + +D_{0,1}f((\ell+1)h,0)h/3,\ a_{3\ell+2,1} = a_{3\ell+3,1}+a_{3\ell+2,0}- -a_{3\ell+3,0}-D_{1,1}f((\ell+1)h,0)h^2/6,\quad a_{3\ell+3,3} = f((\ell+1)h,h), a_{3\ell+2,3} = a_{3\ell+3,3}-D_{1,0}f((\ell+1)h,h)h^2/6.$$

Because of (3.1a) we get

$$\text{(3.6c)}\quad a_{3\ell+2,2} = a_{3\ell+1,2}+a_{3\ell+2,1}-a_{3\ell+1,1}\ ,\ a_{3\ell+3,2} = = a_{3\ell+3,3}+a_{3\ell+2,2}-a_{3\ell+2,3}.$$

4. Now we have determined all a_{ij} with $i=0,\dots,3$ or $j=0,\dots,3$. Fix $\ell,m=1,\dots,N-1$ and assume that we have got all a_{ij} with $i\leq 3\ell$ or $j\leq 3m$. (3.1b) and (3.1c) provide

$$\text{(3.7a)}\quad a_{3\ell+i,3m+1} = a_{3\ell+i-1,3m}+a_{3\ell+i,3m}-a_{3\ell+i-1,3m-1},\ i=1,2,3,$$
$$a_{3\ell+1,3m+i} = a_{3\ell,3m+i}+a_{3\ell,3m+i-1}-a_{3\ell-1,3m+i-1},\ i=1,2,3.$$

Note that all possible computations of the Bézier ordinates are compatible. (3.3a) and (3.3b) give

$$\text{(3.7b)}\quad a_{3\ell+3,3m+3} = f((\ell+1)h,(m+1)h),\quad a_{3\ell+2,3m+3} = = a_{3\ell+3,3m+3}-D_{1,0}f((\ell+1)h,(m+1)h)h/3.$$

(3.1a) induces

(3.7c) $$a_{3\ell+2,3m+2} = a_{3\ell+1,3m+2}+a_{3\ell+2,3m+1}-a_{3\ell+1,3m+1},$$
$$a_{3\ell+3,3m+2} = a_{3\ell+3,3m+3}+a_{3\ell+2,3m+2}-a_{3\ell+2,3m+3}.$$

Now all a_{ij} are determined. Note that in (3.3d) we have limits because in $(S_3^1(\Delta_{N,N}^{(1)}))_h$ second derivatives are not continuous.

4. Numerical examples

For $N \in \mathbb{N}$ let s_N be the interpolating spline of a function f and

$$e(N) := \sup_{z\in[o,1]^n} |f(z)-s_N(z)|.$$

For $N_1 \neq N_2$ we can obtain the order of convergence numerically by

$$\alpha = \frac{\log(e(N_1)/e(N_2))}{\log(N_2/N_1)}.$$

Example 1: $f(x,y) = e^x$

N	e(N)	α
8	0.129 E-5	3.92
12	0.259 E-6	3.95
16	0.829 E-7	3.97
20	0.342 E-7	3.97
24	0.165 E-7	3.98

Example 2: $f(x,y) = 1/(y+1)$

N	e(N)	α
8	0.914 E-5	3.64
12	0.197 E-5	3.78
16	0.654 E-6	3.84
20	0.275 E-6	3.88
24	0.135 E-6	3.90

Example 3: $f(x,y) = \sin(x-y)$

N	e(N)	α
8	0.156 E-5	3.79
12	0.318 E-6	3.92
16	0.102 E-6	3.95
20	0.422 E-7	3.96
24	0.204 E-7	3.97

Example 4: $f(x,y) = x^2 y^2$

N	e(N)	α
8	0.259 E-3	2.82
12	0.798 E-4	2.91
16	0.343 E-4	2.94
20	0.178 E-4	2.95
24	0.103 E-4	2.96

Example 5: $f(x,y) = e^x y$

N	e(N)	α
8	0.330 E-4	2.62
12	0.106 E-4	2.80
16	0.464 E-5	2.87
20	0.243 E-5	2.90
24	0.143 E-5	2.92

Note that in the examples 1,2 and 3 the order of convergence is 4 whereas in 4 and 5 it is 3. This is due to the fact that the first three functions depend only on one variable corresponding to one of the three mesh directions. See [3] for the fact that the general order of approximation is only 3. A more detailed analysis of approximation properties will be given in a forthcoming work.

References

1. Barnhill, R.E., Farin, G.: C^1 quintic interpolation over triangles: two explicit representations. International journal for numerical methods in engineering 17, 1763-1778 (1981).

2. de Boor, C., DeVore, R., Höllig, K.: Approximation order from smooth bivariate pp functions. In [5], 353-357 (1983).

3. de Boor, C., Höllig, K.: Approximation order from bivariate C^1-cubics: a counterexample. Proc. Amer. Math. Soc. 85, 397-400 (1982).

4. de Boor, C., Höllig, K.: Bivariate box splines and smooth pp functions on a three-direction mesh. J. of Comp. and Applied Math. 9, 13-28 (1983).

5. Chui, Ch., Schumaker, L., Ward, J.M.(eds.): Approximation Theory IV. Academic Press (1983).

6. Chui, Ch., Wang, R.-H.: Multivariate spline spaces. J. of Math. Anal. and Applications 94, 197-221 (1983).

7. Dahmen, W., Micchelli, Ch.: Recent progress in multivariate splines. In [5], 27-122 (1983).

8. Farin, G.: Subsplines über Dreiecken. Dissertation, Braunschweig (1979).

9. Morgan, J., Scott, R.: A nodal basis for C^1 piecewise polynomials of degree $n \geq 5$. Math. Comput. 29, 736-740 (1975).

10. Morgan, J., Scott, R.: The dimension of the space of C^1 piecewise polynomials. Manuscript (1976).

11. Schultz, M.H., Varga, R.S.: L-splines. Numer.Math. 10, 345-369 (1967).

12. Schumaker, L.: On the dimension of spaces of piecewise polynomials in two variables. In: Multivariate Approximation Theory, Schempp, W., Zeller, K. (eds.) ISNM 51, Birkhäuser, Basel (1979).

Lothar Bamberger
Universität München
Mathematisches Institut
Theresienstraße 39
D-8000 München 2
Fed. Rep. Germany

International Series of
Numerical Mathematics, Vol. 75

n-th Order Polynomial Spline Blending

Günter Baszenski

Ruhr-Universität Bochum, Rechenzentrum
4630 Bochum 1, West Germany

currently
Department of Mathematics
Texas A & M University
College Station, Texas 77843-3368
USA

1. Introduction

The objective of this paper is to construct an n-th order Blending scheme based on univariate polynomial spline projectors. - Discrete Blending schemes have the general advantage of preserving an asymptotic interpolation error as compared to the corresponding tensor product interpolation but with a reduced number of data.

We construct a basis of certain tensor product B-splines for the Blending scheme and show how to compute the interpolating Blending spline efficiently. Representing the solution in terms of B-splines has certain advantages (de Boor [1]) such as efficient and stable evaluation by recursion, easily computable derivatives and integrals and so on.

Certain special cases of the described problem have already been treated in the literature: For $n = 1$ the Blending scheme degenerates to a tensor product, which is considered in several textbooks on splines. - Gordon [8] treated the discrete Blending scheme ($n = 2$) for cubic splines without introducing locally supported splines. He used cardinal splines (which are biorthogonal to $\lambda_i f = f(t_i)$) instead. - A locally supported basis for $n = 2$ and linear or cubic splines with homogeneous boundary conditions has been constructed by Cavendish/Gordon/Hall [4].

The structure of this paper is as follows: In the following section we introduce complete spline interpolation projectors and use them in the third section to construct the Blending projector. In the fourth section we solve the Blending interpolation problem and in the last two sections we discuss how to construct a basis for the blended spline function space and the representation of the interpolant in terms of those basis elements.

2. Univariate Complete Spline Interpolation

In this section we state some well known facts about univariate spline interpolation. We introduce spline spaces with respect to the uniform spacing h^k as follows:

2.1 Definition. Let $N, k, m \in \mathbf{N}; h = 1/N, 2m \leqslant N$.

a) We consider the knot sequences

$$t_i = \begin{cases} 0 & i = 1,\dots,2m \\ (i-2m)h^k & i = 2m+1,\dots,d_k \\ 1 & i = d_k+1,\dots,d_k+2m \end{cases}$$

where $d_k = 2m + N^k - 1$.

b) These knot sequences induce the $2m$-th order polynomial spline spaces

$$S_k = span\,\{N_{\mu k}(x) : \mu = 1,\dots,d_k\}$$

where

$$N_{\mu k}(x) = (t_{\mu+2m} - t_\mu)[t_\mu, \dots, t_{\mu+2m}](\cdot - x)_+^{2m-1}$$

are the corresponding normalized B-splines. –

Associated with S_k is the following so called complete interpolation scheme:

2.2 Proposition. Let the linear functionals λ_{ik} on $C^{m-1}[0,1]$ be defined by

$$\lambda_{ik} f = \begin{cases} D^{i-1} f(0) & i=1,\dots,m \\ f((i-m)h^k) & i=m+1,\dots,d_k-m \\ D^{i-d_k+m-1} f(1) & i=d_k-m+1,\dots,d_k \end{cases}.$$

Then the complete spline interpolation projectors $P_k : C^{m-1}[0,1] \to C^{m-1}[0,1]$ with range $im\ P_k = S_k$ and interpolation conditions $\Lambda P_k = span\ \{\lambda_{ik} : i=1,\dots,d_k\}$ are well defined.

We have

$$P_k f = \sum_{\mu=1}^{d_k} c_\mu N_{\mu k}(x)$$

where

$$\mathbf{A}^{(k)} \mathbf{c} = \mathbf{z} \tag{1}$$

with

$$\mathbf{A}^{(k)} = \left(\lambda_{ik} N_{\mu k}\right)_{\substack{i=1,\dots,d_k \\ \mu=1,\dots,d_k}}, \quad \mathbf{c} = \left(c_\mu\right)_{\mu=1,\dots,d_k} \quad \mathbf{z} = \left(\lambda_{ik} f\right)_{i=1,\dots,d_k} \quad . -$$

The matrix $\mathbf{A}^{(k)}$ is totally positive and banded. A decomposition of $\mathbf{A}^{(k)}$ and back substitution without pivoting yields accurate numerical results for (1) (see de Boor/Pinkus [3]).

The interpolation projectors $P_1, P_2, \dots$ are ordered in the following sense (this property will be essential for the Blending construction below):

2.3 Proposition. We have $P_{k_1}P_{k_2} = P_{k_2}P_{k_1} = P_{k_1}$ if $k_1 \leqslant k_2$. We write $P_{k_1} \leqslant P_{k_2}$. –

We have the following interpolation error estimate:

2.4 Proposition. (Swartz/Varga [13])
If $f \in C^{2m}[0,1]$ then

$$\| f - P_k f \|_\infty \leqslant K_m (h^k)^{2m} \| D^{2m} f \|_\infty$$

where the constant K_m is independent of the spacing h^k and of f. –

3. The Blending Interpolant

We want to apply spline interpolation to bivariate functions and therefore introduce parametric extensions P'_k, P''_l of the interpolation projectors P_k (see also Delvos/Schempp [7]).

3.1 Definition.
$P'_1, P'_2, \ldots, P''_1, P''_2, \ldots : C^{(m-1,m-1)}([0,1]^2) \to C^{(m-1,m-1)}([0,1]^2)$ are defined as

$$P'_k f(x,y) = (P_k f(\cdot,y))(x)$$
$$P''_l f(x,y) = (P_l f(x,\cdot))(y) \qquad (f \in C^{(m-1,m-1)}([0,1]^2),\ x,y \in [0,1]).$$

We have

$$P'_k f(x,y) = \sum_{\mu=1}^{d_k} c_\mu(y) N_{\mu k}(x)$$

with

$$\mathbf{A}^{(k)} \mathbf{c}(y) = \mathbf{z}(y)$$

$$\mathbf{c}(y) = \Big(c_\mu(y) \Big)_{\mu=1,\ldots,d_k}, \quad \mathbf{z}(y) = \Big(\lambda'_{ik} f \Big)_{i=1,\ldots,d_k}$$

where λ'_{ik} are parametric extensions of the functionals λ_{ik} given by

$$(\lambda'_{ik} f)(y) = \lambda_{ik} f(\cdot,y) \qquad (f \in C^{(m-1,m-1)}([0,1]^2),\ y \in [0,1]).$$

$P''_l f$ can be defined in a similar way. –

The parametrically extended projectors commute pairwise, more precisely we have:

3.2 Proposition.

$$P'_{k_1}P'_{k_2} = P'_{k_2}P'_{k_1} = P'_{k_1} \qquad (k_1 \leqslant k_2)$$
$$P''_{l_1}P''_{l_2} = P''_{l_2}P''_{l_1} = P''_{l_1} \qquad (l_1 \leqslant l_2)$$
$$P'_k P''_l = P''_l P'_k \ . –$$

3.3 Remark. $P'_k P''_l$ is the tensor product spline interpolation projector characterized by $im\ P'_k P''_l = S_k \otimes S_l$, $\Lambda(P'_k P''_l) = span\,\{\lambda'_{ik}\lambda''_{jl} : i=1,...,d_k,\ j=1,...,d_l\}$. –

The n-th order Boolean sum of these parametrically extended operators is defined as:

3.4 Definition. $B_n := P'_1 P''_n \oplus P'_2 P''_{n-1} \oplus \cdots \oplus P'_n P''_1$
with $A \oplus B := A + B - AB$. –

It is an interpolation projector with:

3.5 Proposition. (Gordon/Cheney [9])

$$im\ B_n = \sum_{k=1}^{n} im\ P'_k P''_{n+1-k} = \sum_{k=1}^{n} S_k \otimes S_{n+1-k}$$

and

$$\Lambda B_n = \sum_{k=1}^{n} \Lambda(P'_k P''_{n+1-k})$$

$$= span\,\{\lambda'_{ik}\lambda''_{j,n+1-k} : k=1,...,n,\ i=1,...,d_k,\ j=1,...,d_{n+1-k}\}. -$$

The following sum representations for B_n and its associated remainder projector are useful for practical computations. They can be proved algebraically using the commutativity and absorption properties stated in Proposition 3.2.

3.6 Theorem. (Delvos/Posdorf [6])

a) $$B_n = \sum_{k=1}^{n} P'_k P''_{n+1-k} - \sum_{k=1}^{n-1} P'_k P''_{n-k}$$

b) For a projector P let $\overline{P}$ denote the corresponding remainder projector given by $\overline{P}f = f - Pf$. The remainder projector of B_n is

$$\overline{B}_n = \overline{P}'_n + \overline{P}''_n - \sum_{k=1}^{n} \overline{P}'_k \overline{P}''_{n+1-k} + \sum_{k=1}^{n-1} \overline{P}'_k \overline{P}''_{n-k}\ . - \tag{2}$$

We can now prove the following error estimates for interpolation with B_n:

3.7 Corollary. For any $f \in C^{(2m,2m)}([0,1]^2)$ the estimate

$$\|\overline{B}_n f\|_\infty \leqslant K_m (h^n)^{2m} \left(\|D_x^{2m} f\|_\infty + \|D_y^{2m} f\|_\infty\right)$$
$$+ K_m^2 (h^n)^{2m} (n-1+nh^{2m})\, \|D_x^{2m} D_y^{2m} f\|_\infty$$

holds.

Proof. Let $f \in C^{(2m,2m)}([0,1]^2)$. From (2) we conclude that

$$\|\bar{B}_n f\|_\infty \leqslant \|\bar{P}'_n f\|_\infty + \|\bar{P}''_n f\|_\infty + \sum_{k=1}^{n} \|\bar{P}'_k \bar{P}''_{n+1-k} f\|_\infty + \sum_{k=1}^{n-1} \|\bar{P}'_k \bar{P}''_{n-k} f\|_\infty .$$

Using the univariate error estimates stated in Proposition 2.4 we get

$$\|\bar{P}'_n f\|_\infty \leqslant K_m (h^n)^{2m} \|D_x^{2m} f\|_\infty$$
$$\|\bar{P}''_n f\|_\infty \leqslant K_m (h^n)^{2m} \|D_y^{2m} f\|_\infty$$

and (since $D_x^{2m} \bar{P}''_l f(x,y) = \bar{P}''_l D_x^{2m} f(x,y)$)

$$\|\bar{P}'_k \bar{P}''_l f\|_\infty \leqslant K_m^2 (h^{k+l})^{2m} \|D_x^{2m} D_y^{2m} f\|_\infty . -$$

The above Corollary shows a characteristic feature of Boolean interpolation: Compared to a tensor product interpolant the same asymptotic error bound is attained by a reduced number of interpolation conditions. In particular we get for B_n and for $P'_n P''_n$:

3.8 Remark.

a) $$\|\bar{B}_n f\|_\infty \leqslant C_1 (h^n)^{2m} \quad (\|D_x^{2m} f\|_\infty + \|D_x^{2m} D_y^{2m} f\|_\infty + \|D_y^{2m} f\|_\infty)$$
$$\|\overline{P'_n P''_n} f\|_\infty \leqslant C_2 (h^n)^{2m} \quad (\|D_x^{2m} f\|_\infty + \|D_x^{2m} D_y^{2m} f\|_\infty + \|D_y^{2m} f\|_\infty)$$

b) $$dim\, \Lambda B_n = nN^{n+1} + (4m-n-1)N^n + (2m-1)^2$$
$$dim\, \Lambda(P'_n P''_n) = N^{2n} + (4m-2)N^n + (2m-1)^2 . -$$

4. Efficient Computation of the Blending Interpolant $B_n f$

To compute the Blending interpolant $B_n f$ efficiently we combine the sum representation of Theorem 3.6 with a result of de Boor [2] concerning the computation of tensor product interpolants:

4.1 Theorem. For $f \in C^{(m-1,m-1)}([0,1]^2)$ we have

$$B_n f(x,y) = \sum_{k=1}^{n} s_k(x,y) - \sum_{k=1}^{n-1} \tilde{s}_k(x,y)$$

with

$$s_k(x,y) = \sum_{\mu=1}^{d_k} \sum_{\nu=1}^{d_{n+1-k}} c_{\mu\nu}^{(k)} N_{\mu k}(x) N_{\nu,n+1-k}(y)$$
$$\tilde{s}_k(x,y) = \sum_{\mu=1}^{d_k} \sum_{\nu=1}^{d_{n-k}} \tilde{c}_{\mu\nu}^{(k)} N_{\mu k}(x) N_{\nu,n-k}(y) .$$

The coefficients $c_{\mu\nu}^{(k)}$ are determined by the two systems of linear equations

$$\mathbf{A}^{(k)}\,\mathbf{U} = \mathbf{Z}^{(k)}; \qquad \mathbf{A}^{(n+1-k)}\,(\mathbf{C}^{(k)})^t = \mathbf{U}^t$$

where

$$\mathbf{U} = \left(u_{\mu j}\right)_{\substack{\mu=1,\ldots,d_k \\ j=1,\ldots,d_{n+1-k}}}, \quad \mathbf{Z}^{(k)} = \left(\lambda'_{ik}\,\lambda''_{j,n+1-k}\,f\right)_{\substack{i=1,\ldots,d_k \\ j=1,\ldots,d_{n+1-k}}}, \quad \mathbf{C}^{(k)} = \left(c_{\mu\nu}^{(k)}\right)_{\substack{\mu=1,\ldots,d_k \\ \nu=1,\ldots,d_{n+1-k}}}.$$

Either system can be solved by one LU decomposition and repeated back substitution for the multiple right hand sides.

Similarly the coefficients $\tilde{c}_{\mu\nu}^{(k)}$ are determined by

$$\mathbf{A}^{(k)}\,\mathbf{V} = \tilde{\mathbf{Z}}^{(k)}; \qquad \mathbf{A}^{(n-k)}\,(\tilde{\mathbf{C}}^{(k)})^t = \mathbf{V}^t$$

with

$$\mathbf{V} = \left(v_{\mu j}\right)_{\substack{\mu=1,\ldots,d_k \\ j=1,\ldots,d_{n-k}}}, \quad \tilde{\mathbf{Z}}^{(k)} = \left(\lambda'_{ik}\,\lambda''_{j,n-k}\,f\right)_{\substack{i=1,\ldots,d_k \\ j=1,\ldots,d_{n-k}}}, \quad \tilde{\mathbf{C}}^{(k)} = \left(\tilde{c}_{\mu\nu}^{(k)}\right)_{\substack{\mu=1,\ldots,d_k \\ \nu=1,\ldots,d_{n-k}}}. \; -$$

We conclude this section with the outline of an algorithm which efficiently computes $B_n f$ in this way.

4.2 Algorithm. Assume that *decomp*(**A**) LU-decomposes a matrix **A** and that *solve*(**A**,**B**,**Z**) yields the solution **C** of $\mathbf{AU} = \mathbf{Z}$, $\mathbf{BC}^t = \mathbf{U}^t$ by back substitution. Then the following algorithm computes all coefficients $\mathbf{C}^{(1)}, \ldots, \mathbf{C}^{(n)}, \tilde{\mathbf{C}}^{(1)}, \ldots, \tilde{\mathbf{C}}^{(n-1)}$ of $B_n f$ as represented in the preceding Theorem. Each of the $\mathbf{A}^{(k)}$ is decomposed only once. Not more than two of the matrices $\mathbf{A}^{(k)}$ are needed simultaneously.

```
Ψ := decomp(A^(n));

for k from 1 to (n−1)÷2
do
   Φ := decomp(A^(k));
   C^(k) := solve(Φ,Ψ,Z^(k));
   C^(n+1−k) := solve(Ψ,Φ,Z^(n+1−k));
   Ψ := decomp(A^(n−k));
   C̃^(k) := solve(Φ,Ψ,Z̃^(k));
   C̃^(n−k) := solve(Ψ,Φ,Z̃^(n−k))
od;

if odd n
then C^(n÷2+1) := solve(Ψ,Ψ,Z^(n÷2+1))
```

else $\Phi := decomp(\mathbf{A}^{(n\div 2)})$;

$\mathbf{C}^{(n\div 2)} := solve(\Phi,\Psi,\mathbf{Z}^{(n\div 2)})$;

$\mathbf{C}^{(n\div 2+1)} := solve(\Psi,\Phi,\mathbf{Z}^{(n\div 2+1)})$;

$\tilde{\mathbf{C}}^{(n\div 2)} := solve(\Phi,\Phi,\tilde{\mathbf{Z}}^{(n\div 2)})$

fi . –

5. A Basis for $im\ B_n$

The representation of $B_n f$ in Theorem 4.1 is not in terms of a basis. In this section we give a method to choose a basis for $im\ B_n$ and in the next section we consider the problem of transforming $B_n f$ as derived in Theorem 4.1 into a basis representation. In particular we construct a basis which guarantees a numerically stable transformation.

5.1 Lemma. There exist $\mathbf{I}_q \subseteq \{1,\ldots,d_q\}$ $(q=1,...,n)$ such that $\bigcup_{q=1}^{k} \{N_{\mu q}(x) : \mu \in \mathbf{I}_q\}$ is a basis for $im\ P_k = S_k$ $(k=1,...,n)$.

Proof. Choose $\mathbf{I}_1 := \{1,\ldots,d_1\}$. Then $\{N_{1,1},\ldots,N_{d_{1,1}}\}$ is a basis for S_1. Since $S_1 \subseteq S_2$ we can exchange d_1 elements of $\{N_{1,2},\ldots,N_{d_{2,2}}\}$ against $\{N_{1,1},\ldots,N_{d_{1,1}}\}$ such that $\{N_{\mu 1} : \mu=1,...,d_1\} \cup \{N_{\mu 2} : \mu \in \mathbf{I}_2\}$ is a basis for S_2. Continuing this way we can establish the exsistence of $\mathbf{I}_3, \mathbf{I}_4,\ldots,\mathbf{I}_n$ with the required properties iteratively. –

5.2 Theorem. $\bigcup_{q=1}^{n} \bigcup_{r=1}^{n+1-q} \{N_{\mu q}(x)\, N_{\nu r}(y) : \mu \in \mathbf{I}_q,\ \nu \in \mathbf{I}_r\}$ is a basis for $im\ B_n$.

Proof. According to Proposition 3.5 and to the previous Lemma

$$\begin{aligned} im\ B_n &= \sum_{k=1}^{n} im\ P'_k P''_{n+1-k} \\ &= span \bigcup_{k=1}^{n} \bigcup_{q=1}^{k} \bigcup_{r=1}^{n+1-k} \{N_{\mu k}(x)\, N_{\nu r}(y) : \mu \in \mathbf{I}_q,\ \nu \in \mathbf{I}_r\} \\ &= span \bigcup_{q=1}^{n} \bigcup_{r=1}^{n+1-q} \{N_{\mu q}(x)\, N_{\nu r}(y) : \mu \in \mathbf{I}_q,\ \nu \in \mathbf{I}_r\}. \end{aligned}$$

The functions are linearly independent since they form a subset of

$$\bigcup_{q=1}^{n} \bigcup_{r=1}^{n} \{N_{\mu q}(x) N_{\nu r}(y) : \mu \in \mathbf{I}_q,\ \nu \in \mathbf{I}_r\}$$

which by Lemma 5.1 is a basis for $S_n \otimes S_n$. –

The obtained result can be modified to obtain bases of B_n whose elements have smaller support. We use the following elementary result from linear algebra:

5.3 Lemma. Let V, W be vector spaces of finite dimension with $V \subseteq W$.
Let $v_1, \ldots, v_m$ be a basis for V and $v_1, \ldots, v_m, w_1, \ldots, w_n$ be a basis for W.
Assume that $\tilde{v}_1, \ldots, \tilde{v}_m$ is a second basis for V.
Then $\tilde{v}_1, \ldots, \tilde{v}_m, w_1, \ldots, w_n$ is also a basis for W.

Proof. The matrices which transform $(v_1, \ldots, v_m)$ to $(\tilde{v}_1, \ldots, \tilde{v}_m)$ and $(v_1, \ldots, v_m, w_1, \ldots, w_n)$ to $(\tilde{v}_1, \ldots, \tilde{v}_m, w_1, \ldots, w_n)$ obviously have the same determinant. –

From Theorem 5.2 we can now deduce the following result:

5.4 Theorem.
a) If $n = 2l+1$ ($l \in N_o$) then

$$\bigcup_{k=1}^{l} \{N_{\mu k}(x)\, N_{\nu,n+1-k}(y) : \mu=1,\ldots,d_k;\ \nu\in \mathbf{I}_{n+1-k}\}$$
$$\cup \bigcup_{k=1}^{l} \{N_{\mu,n+1-k}(x)\, N_{\nu k}(y) : \mu\in \mathbf{I}_{n+1-k};\ \nu=1,\ldots,d_k\} \tag{3}$$
$$\cup \quad \{N_{\mu,l+1}(x)\, N_{\nu,l+1}(y) : \mu,\nu=1,\ldots,d_{l+1}\}$$

is a basis for *im* B_n.

b) If $n = 2l$ ($l \in N$) then

$$\bigcup_{k=1}^{l-1} \{N_{\mu k}(x)\, N_{\nu,n+1-k}(y) : \mu=1,\ldots,d_k;\ \nu\in \mathbf{I}_{n+1-k}\}$$
$$\cup \bigcup_{k=1}^{l} \{N_{\mu,n+1-k}(x)\, N_{\nu k}(y) : \mu\in \mathbf{I}_{n+1-k};\ \nu=1,\ldots,d_k\} \tag{4}$$
$$\cup \quad \{N_{\mu l}(x)\, N_{\nu,l+1}(y) : \mu=1,\ldots,d_l;\ \nu=1,\ldots,d_{l+1}\}$$

is a basis for *im* B_n.

Proof. Assume $n=2l+1$. Then

$$\bigcup_{q=1}^{n} \bigcup_{r=1}^{n+1-q} \{N_{\mu q}(x)\, N_{\nu r}(y) : \mu\in \mathbf{I}_q,\ \nu\in \mathbf{I}_r\}$$

$$= \bigcup_{r=l+2}^{n} \bigcup_{q=1}^{n+1-r} \{N_{\mu q}(x)\, N_{\nu r}(y) : \mu \in \mathbf{I}_q , \nu \in \mathbf{I}_r \}$$

$$\cup \bigcup_{q=l+2}^{n} \bigcup_{r=1}^{n+1-q} \{N_{\mu q}(x)\, N_{\nu r}(y) : \mu \in \mathbf{I}_q , \nu \in \mathbf{I}_r \}$$

$$\cup \bigcup_{q=1}^{l+1} \bigcup_{r=1}^{l+1} \{N_{\mu q}(x)\, N_{\nu r}(y) : \mu \in \mathbf{I}_q , \nu \in \mathbf{I}_r \} .$$

Applying Lemma 5.1 and Lemma 5.3 yields the result.
The case $n = 2l$ is proved in a similar way . —

5.5 Remark. Writing the interpolant $B_n f$ in terms of a basis of the form (3) or (4) gives a representation

$$B_n f(x,y) = \sum_{k=1}^{n} \sum_{\mu=1}^{d_k} \sum_{\nu=1}^{d_{n+1-k}} c^*_{\mu\nu}\, N_{\mu k}(x)\, N_{\nu, n+1-k}(y) .$$

Compared to the representation in Theorem 4.1 the number of parameters is reduced. Also, an evaluation of $B_n f(x,y)$ requires the computation of n instead of $2n-1$ tensor product splines only.

6. Choice of the Basis Elements to be Exchanged

In this section we develop an algorithm which determines a numerically suitable process for the basis exchange discussed in the previous section. The key to this algorithm is to write the B-splines $N_{\mu,l-1}$ as a linear combination of the $N_{\nu l}$ and to examine the coefficients occurring.

6.1 Lemma. (Jia [10])

a) $$N_{\mu,l-1}(x) = \sum_{\nu=1}^{d_l} \beta_{\mu l}(\nu)\, N_{\nu l}(x) \qquad (5)$$

with $\beta_{\mu l}(\nu) = (\tau_{\mu+2m} - \tau_\mu)\,[\tau_\mu, \ldots, \tau_{\mu+2m}]\,(\cdot - t_{\nu+1})_+ \cdots (\cdot - t_{\nu+2m-1})_+$
where

$$\tau_\mu = \begin{cases} 0 & \mu = 1, \ldots, 2m \\ (\mu - 2m)h^{l-1} & \mu = 2m+1, \ldots, d_{l-1} \\ 1 & \mu = d_{l-1}+1, \ldots, d_{l-1}+2m \end{cases}$$

and

$$t_\nu = \begin{cases} 0 & \nu = 1, \ldots, 2m \\ (\nu - 2m)h^{l} & \nu = 2m+1, \ldots, d_l \\ 1 & \nu = d_l+1, \ldots, d_l+2m \end{cases} .$$

b) We have $\beta_{\mu l}(\nu) \geqslant 0$. $\beta_{\mu l}(\nu)$ is positive if and only if one of the following conditions is satisfied:

$$1 \leqslant \mu \leqslant 2m, \qquad \mu \leqslant \nu \leqslant \mu N$$

or $\quad 2m+1 \leqslant \mu \leqslant d_{l+1}-2m, \qquad (\mu-2m)N+2m \leqslant \nu \leqslant \mu N$

or $\quad d_{l+1}-2m+1 \leqslant \mu \leqslant d_l, \qquad (\mu-2m)N+2m \leqslant \nu \leqslant \mu-N^{l-1}+N^l.$

c) $\quad \max\{\beta_{\mu l}(\nu) : \nu=1,\ldots,d_l\} \to M_\mu := \max\{N_{\mu,l-1}(x) : x \in [0,1]\} \quad (N \to \infty)$

and M_μ is independent of the spacing h^l. –

A characterization of the basis splines to be exchanged in order to obtain a numerically stable procedure is as follows:

6.2 Theorem. For $1 \leqslant \mu \leqslant d_{l-1}$ let $1 \leqslant k_\mu \leqslant d_l$ such that $\beta_{\mu l}(k_\mu) = \max\{\beta_{\mu l}(\nu) : \nu=1,\ldots,d_l\}$. Then

$$N_{k_\mu,l}(x) = \frac{1}{\beta_{\mu l}(k_\mu)} \{N_{\mu,l-1}(x) - \sum_{\nu \neq k_\mu} \beta_{\mu l}(\nu)\, N_{\nu l}(x)\}.$$

The coefficients satisfy

$$0 \leqslant \frac{\beta_{\mu l}(\nu)}{\beta_{\mu l}(k_\mu)} \leqslant 1$$

$$\frac{1}{\beta_{\mu l}(k_\mu)} > 1, \quad \frac{1}{\beta_{\mu l}(k_\mu)} \quad \text{is bounded for } h^l \to 0. –$$

This leads to the following algorithm for constructing $\mathbf{I}_l$:

6.3 Algorithm. The index set $\mathbf{I}_l \subseteq \{1,\ldots,d_l\}$ is obtained by deleting the following d_{l-1} elements from $\{1,\ldots,d_l\}$:

a) For $\mu = 2m,\ldots,d_{l-1}-2m+1$ delete the indices $\nu_\mu = N(\mu-m)+m$.

b) For $\mu = 2m-1, 2m-2,\ldots,1$ delete ν_μ determined by
$\beta_{\mu l}(\nu_\mu) = \max\{\beta_{\mu l}(\nu) \; : \; \mu \leqslant \nu < \nu_{\mu+1}\}$.

c) For $\mu = d_{l-1}-2m+2,\ldots,d_{l-1}$ delete ν_μ which is given by
$\beta_{\mu l}(\nu_\mu) = \max\{\beta_{\mu l}(\nu) \; : \; \nu_{\mu-1} < \nu \leqslant \mu-N^{l-1}+N^l\}$.

Discussion. For the B-splines $N_{\mu,l-1}(x)$ $(\mu=2m,\ldots,d_{l-1}-2m+1)$ (i. e. those which have simple knots only) it is not difficult to show that the largest coefficient in (5) occurrs for ν_μ where $N_{\nu_\mu,l}(x)$ and $N_{\mu,l-1}(x)$ have the same midpoint of support, which can be transformed into the condition given in step a). The mapping $\mu \to \nu_\mu$ is one-to-one.

The maxima in steps b), c) are taken only over a subset of the nonzero coefficients $\beta_{\mu l}(\nu)$ in order to enforce a one-to-one correspondence $\mu \rightarrow \nu_\mu$ (which might not be guaranteed if the number of additional knots, i. e. N is small). If N is sufficiently large we obtain the coefficients characterized in Theorem 6.2. —

7. Concluding Remarks

The concept of bivariate spline interpolation by Blending methods developed here can be extended in several ways. The results used in the construction exist also for non-uniform spacing, for other end conditions, and for more than two variables. Finally, the restriction to splines of even order is not essential.

Acknowledgements

I wish to thank Professors Schumaker and Utreras for several helpful discussions on the subject and Professors Delvos and Schempp for their interest in my work. I am greatly indebted to the A. v. Humboldt-Foundation for support of my studies and for providing funds to visit the conference.

References

[1] C. de Boor
Splines as Linear Combinations of B-Splines. A Survey.
In: Approximation Theory II. Eds.: G. G. Lorentz et al.
Academic Press, New York 1976, 1-47.

[2] C. de Boor
Efficient Computer Manipulation of Tensor Products.
ACM Transactions on Mathematical Software 5, No. 2 (1979), 173-182.

[3] C. de Boor, A. Pinkus
Backward Error Analysis for Totally Positive Linear Systems.
Numer. Math. 27 (1977), 485-490.

[4] J. C. Cavendish, W. J. Gordon, C. A. Hall
Ritz-Galerkin Approximations in Blending Function Spaces.
Numer. Math. 26 (1976), 155-178.

[5] F. J. Delvos
d-Variate Boolean Interpolation.
J. Approximation Th. 34 (1982), 99-114.

[6] F. J. Delvos, H. Posdorf
N-th Order Blending.
In: Spline Functions, Karlsruhe 1975. Eds.: K. Böhmer et al.
Springer, Berlin 1976, 53-64.

[7] F. J. Delvos, W. Schempp
The Method of Parametric Extension Applied to Right Invertible Operators.
Numer. Funct. Anal. and Optimiz. 6, No. 2 (1983), 135-148.

[8] W. J. Gordon
Distributive Lattices and Approximation of Multivariate Functions.
In: Approximation with Special Emphasis on Spline Functions,
Ed.: I. J. Schoenberg. Academic Press, New York 1969, 223-277.

[9] W. J. Gordon, E. W. Cheney
Bivariate and Multivariate Interpolation with Noncommutative Projectors.
In: Linear Spaces and Approximation. Eds.: P. L. Butzer, B. Sz.-Nagy.
ISNM 40, Birkhäuser, Basel 1977, 381-387.

[10] R. Q. Jia
Total Positivity of the Discrete Spline Collocation Matrix.
J. Approximation Th. 39 (1983), 11-23.

[11] M. H. Schultz
Spline Analysis.
Prentice-Hall, Englewood Cliffs 1973.

[12] L. L. Schumaker
Spline Functions: Basic Theory.
Wiley, New York 1981.

[13] B. Swartz, R. S. Varga
Error Bounds for Spline and L-Spline Interpolation.
J. Approximation Th. 6 (1972), 6-49.

International Series of
Numerical Mathematics, Vol. 75

THE LIMITS OF MULTIVARIATE CARDINAL SPLINES

Carl de Boor(1), Klaus Höllig(1,2) and
Sherman Riemenschneider(2)

In this note we characterize the limits of box-splines as their degree tends to infinity. Our results generalize classical theorems of I. J. Schoenberg [6,7].

Let T denote a set of vectors with integer components which span R^d. The centered box-spline $M : R^d \to R$ corresponding to T is defined by [1]

$$\int_{R^d} M(x)\varphi(x)dx := \int_{[-1/2,1/2]^T} \varphi\Big(\sum_{t\in T} y_t t\Big)dy, \quad \varphi \in C_0(R^d) \ . \tag{1}$$

Setting $\varphi(x) = \exp(-iyx)$ we see that the Fourier transform of M is given by

$$\hat{M}(y) = \prod_{t\in T} \frac{\sin(yt/2)}{yt/2} \tag{2}$$

which stresses the similarity to the univariate case. We denote by $S := \text{span}\{M(\cdot - j) : j \in Z^d\}$ the space of multivariate cardinal splines.

To state our main result we need some auxiliary notation. We denote by nT the set containing each vector in T with multiplicity n. From (2) we see that the corresponding box-spline M_n is obtained from M by n-fold convolution,

$$M_n = M * \cdots * M \ . \tag{3}$$

Finally we define the set

---

(1)Sponsored by the United States Army under Contract No. DAAG29-80-C-0041.

(2)Supported by National Science Foundation Grant No. DMS-8351187.

$$\Omega := \{x : |\hat{M}(x + 2\pi j)| < |\hat{M}(x)|,\ j \in Z^d\backslash 0\} . \qquad (4)$$

The set $\bar{\Omega}$ is a fundamental domain, i.e. its translates form an essentially disjoint partition of R^d.

Proposition.

$$\Omega \cap (\Omega + 2\pi j) = \emptyset,\ j \neq 0 ,$$

$$\bigcup_{j \in Z^d} (\bar{\Omega} + 2\pi j) = R^d .$$

As an example, Figure 1 shows the set Ω corresponding to the set $T = \{(1,0),(1,1),(0,1)\}$.

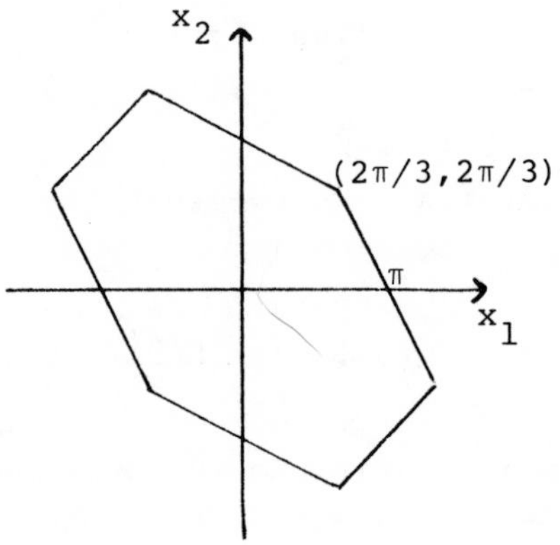

Figure 1

Theorem. <u>Assume that</u> $f \in L_2(R^d)$. <u>There exists a sequence of splines</u> $s_n = \Sigma_j a_{n,j} M_n(\cdot - j)$ <u>with</u> $a_n \in l_2(Z^d)$ <u>which converges to</u> f <u>in</u> $L_2(R^d)$ <u>if and only if</u> $\operatorname{supp} \hat{f} \subset \bar{\Omega}$.

In the univariate case s_n can be chosen as the cardinal interpolant ($f \in L_2$ and $\operatorname{supp} \hat{f} \subset \bar{\Omega} = [-\pi,\pi]$ implies that f is continuous). In several variables this is possible only in special cases [2,3]. We point out below further interesting differences from the univariate theory.

Remark 1. The set $\bar{\Omega}$ is in general not connected.

As an example consider the set $T = \{t_1,\ldots,t_p\}$ which contains all vectors with entries ± 1.

We claim that the hyperplanes $\{x : xt_\nu = 2\pi l\}$ with $l \in Z\backslash 0$ do not intersect $\mathrm{int}(\bar{\Omega})$. To see this let us assume that $xt_\nu = 2\pi jt_\nu \neq 0$ for some ν and $j \in Z\backslash 0$ and that $x \in \mathrm{int}(\bar{\Omega})$. There exists $y \in \mathrm{int}(\bar{\Omega})$ with

$$yt_\nu = 2\pi jt_\nu$$
$$yt \notin 2\pi Z,\ t \neq t_\nu .$$

Then for all z sufficiently close to y we have

$$\left|\frac{\hat{M}_n(z - 2\pi j)}{\hat{M}_n(z)}\right| = \prod_\mu \left|\frac{zt_\mu}{(z - 2\pi j)t_\mu}\right|^n \geq c\left|\frac{zt_\nu}{(z - 2\pi j)t_\nu}\right|^n > 1$$

which implies that $z \notin \Omega$.

From the above observation it follows that the boundary of the set $B := \{x : \Sigma_{\nu=1}^d |x_\nu| \leq 2\pi\}$ does not intersect $\mathrm{int}(\bar{\Omega})$. By the Proposition $\mathrm{vol}(\Omega) = (2\pi)^d$, and since $\mathrm{vol}(B) = (2\pi)^d 2^d/d!$ it follows that for large d the set $\bar{\Omega}$ cannot be connected.

Remark 2. The linear independence of the box-splines $M_n(\cdot - j)$, $j \in Z^d$ is in general not sufficient for the wellposedness of cardinal interpolation.

The wellposedness of cardinal interpolation is equivalent to the (strict) positivity of the characteristic polynomial

$$P_n(x) := \sum_j M_n(j)\exp(ijx) = \sum_j \hat{M}_n(x + 2\pi j) . \tag{5}$$

Let T consist of the unit vectors and the vector $(1,\ldots,1)$. By the result in [5] the corresponding box-splines are linearly independent. We claim that $P_n(x) < 0$ for $x = 2\pi(\lambda,\ldots,\lambda,-3/2)$ with $2\lambda = 3/(d - 2)$ and n,d sufficiently large. From (2) we see that $\hat{M}_n(x) < 0$ for n odd. Moreover,

$$\hat{M}_n(x + 2\pi j) = \hat{M}_n(x)\ \varepsilon(j)\Big(\prod_\nu \frac{xt_\nu}{(x + 2\pi j)t_\nu}\Big)^n \tag{6}$$

with $\varepsilon(j) \in \{-1,1\}$. With the above choice of the vectors t_ν,

$$a_j(x) := \prod_\nu \frac{xt_\nu}{(x + 2\pi j)t_\nu} \left(\prod_{\nu=1}^{d-1} \frac{\lambda}{\lambda + j_\nu} \right) \frac{-3/2}{-3/2 + j_d} \frac{\lambda}{\lambda + \Sigma_{\nu=1}^{d} j_\nu} .$$

It is easily seen that $|a_j(x)| < 1$ for $j \neq 0$ and λ sufficiently small. Moreover, $a_j(x) \leq (1 + c|j|)^{-1}$ for $|j|$ sufficiently large. Therefore it follows from (6) that

$$1 - \sum_{j \neq 0} |a_j(x)|^n > 0$$

for n sufficiently large. This mplies that $P_n < 0$.

The proof of the Proposition and the Theorem will be given in a forthcoming paper [4]. We will consider more generally the approximation properties of translates of functions M_n which are n-fold convolutions of an arbitrary continuous function with compact support. Our results for cardinal splines are a special case of this general theory.

REFERENCES

[1] C. de Boor and K. Höllig, B-splines from parallelepipeds, Mathematics Research Center Technical Summary Report #2320 (1982), J. d'Anal. Math. **42** (1982/83), 99-115.

[2] C. de Boor, K. Höllig and S. D. Riemenschneider, Convergence of bivariate cardinal interpolation, to appear in Constr. Approx.

[3] C. de Boor, K. Höllig and S. D. Riemenschneider, Bivariate cardinal interpolation by splines on a three direction mesh, to appear in Illinois J. Math.

[4] C. de Boor, K. Höllig and S. D. Riemenschneider, ms.

[5] R.-Q. Jia, Local linear independence of translates of a box spline, to appear in Constr. Approx.

[6] I. J. Schoenberg, Notes on spline functions. III, On the convergence of the interpolating cardinal splines as their degree tends to infinity, Israel J. Math. **16** (1973), 87-93.

[7] I. J. Schoenberg, Cardinal spline interpolation, SIAM, Philadelphia (1973).

International Series of
Numerical Mathematics, Vol. 75

LOCAL SMOOTHING FOR SCATTERED AND NOISY DATA

M. Bozzini, L. Lenarduzzi

We make use of local methods to estimate a function from experimental measures; we study the approximation error. For what deals the width of the local support, for a specific application, we formalize a criterium already found experimentally.

0. Introduction

Let us consider smoothing formulae of local type. A smoothing function is constructed from an assigned set of points in the hypothesis that they are given according to a deterministic law or at random and, in both cases, scattered on the domain D.

The values of the function we want to approximate can be given with good precision or, else, they can be noised.

In these hypothesis, in section 1 we study the statistical properties of a smoothing function obtained with local least squares scheme of the type which Lancaster and Salkauskas deal with in [6], while in section 2 we deal with the particular case of the weighted mean of the functional values.

1. General case

Let $f(\underline{x})$ be a smooth function defined on the domain $D \subset \mathbb{R}^k$. Let the values $\tilde{f}_i = f(\underline{x}_i) + e_i$ be measured at N points; e is the noise with the usual assumptions: $E(e_i)=0$, $\mathrm{cov}(e_i, e_j) = \sigma^2 \delta_{ij}$.

Let us indicate $\underline{t}$ a generic point of the domain D; we consider a bounded weight function $w_{\underline{t},R}(\underline{x})$ with one of the following forms depending on the geometrical shape of the support:

1° hypercubic support with edge 2R and centre at $\underline{t}$

$$w_{\underline{t},R}(\underline{x}) = \prod_{1}^{k} w\left(\frac{|t_i - x_i|}{R}\right) \qquad w \geq 0$$

2° hyperspheric support with radius R and centre at $\underline{t}$

$$w_{\underline{t},R}(\underline{x}) = w\left(\frac{\mathrm{dist}(\underline{t},\underline{x})}{R}\right) \qquad w \geqq 0$$

with the usual euclidean distance.

Let us call $B(\underline{t},R)$ the support of w and M_R the number of data enclosed in $B(\underline{t},R)$.

Let us call

$$Q_{\underline{t}}(\underline{x}) = \sum_{j \leq l} c_j q_j^t(\underline{t}-\underline{x}) \qquad j=(j_1,j_2,\ldots,j_k)$$

the polynomial of total degree l in terms of a basis obtained from

$$\left\{\prod_{r=1}^{k}(t_r-x_r)^{j_r},\ |j| \leqq l\right\}$$

and which is orthogonal respect to the weight w on the set $\{x_i\}$, that is to say:

$$<q_j^t, q_h^t> = \sum_{i=}^{N} w_{\underline{t},R}(\underline{x}_i)\, q_j^t(\underline{t}-\underline{x}_i)\, q_h^t(\underline{t}-\underline{x}_i) = 0 \text{ if } h \neq j$$

We call $\tilde{Q}_{\underline{t}}(\underline{x})$ the polynomial solution of the least squa res problem:

$$\min_{c_j} \sum_{1}^{N} w_{\underline{t},R}(\underline{x}_i)\,(Q_{\underline{t}}(\underline{x}_i) - \tilde{f}_i)^2 \qquad (0)$$

We use two different types of approximating functions depending on the current problem, taking into account what is in [6].

Case A

If the problem requires the evaluation of the function at a large number of points respect to the number N of assigned points, it can be suitable to make use of the following function:

$$m_N(\underline{t}) = \frac{\sum_{i=1}^{N} \varphi_{\underline{t}}(\underline{x}_i)\,\tilde{Q}_{\underline{x}_i}(\underline{t})}{\sum_{i=1}^{N} \varphi_{\underline{t}}(\underline{x}_i)} \qquad (1)$$

where the function $\varphi_{\underline{t}}(\underline{x})$ has support with the same geometry as w with parameter $R_1 \leqq R$ and is such that $m_N(\underline{x}_i) = \tilde{Q}_{\underline{x}_i}(\underline{x}_i)$.

One can choose $\varphi_{\underline{t}}(\underline{x})$ so that $m_N(\underline{t})$ has enough continuous derivatives on D.

The approximation defined with (1) has expected value:

$$E_e(m_N(\underline{t})) = \frac{\sum_1^N \varphi_{\underline{t}}(\underline{x}_i) E_e(\tilde{Q}_{\underline{x}_i}(\underline{t}))}{\sum^N \varphi_{\underline{t}}(\underline{x}_i)} \tag{2}$$

where $E_e \tilde{Q}_{\underline{x}_i}(\underline{t}) = \sum_{|j|\leq 1} c_j^* q_j^i(\underline{x}_i^1 - \underline{t})$ with c_j^* Fourier coefficients obtained from the true values f_i.

The variance is:

$$\sigma_e^2(m_N(\underline{t})) = \frac{\sigma^2}{(\sum_{r=1}^N \varphi_{\underline{t}}(\underline{x}_r))^2} \sum_{h=1}^N \left\{ \sum_{i=1}^N \varphi_{\underline{t}}(\underline{x}_i) \sum_{|j|\leq 1} \frac{w_{\underline{x}_i, R}(\underline{x}_r) q_j^i(\underline{x}_i - \underline{x}_h)}{\sum_{r=1}^N w_{\underline{x}_i, R}(\underline{x}_r) q_j^i(\underline{x}_i - \underline{x}_r)^2)} q_j^i(\underline{x}_i - \underline{t}) \right\}^2 \tag{3}$$

Case B

In the case we must evaluate the function at a number of points reduced respect to N or the number N of given points is very large (asymptotic sample) we prefer to make use of the function defined with the value taken by $\tilde{Q}_{\underline{t}}$ at $\underline{t}$, for each $\underline{t} \in D$.

$$m_N(\underline{t}) = \tilde{Q}_{\underline{t}}(\underline{t}) \tag{4}$$

Of course such function has the required degree of continuity when a suitable weight function w is chosen.

The random variable defined with (4) has expected value:

$$E_e(\tilde{Q}_{\underline{t}}(\underline{t})) = \sum_{|j|\leq 1} c_j^* q_j(\underline{0}) \tag{5}$$

with c_j^* Fourier coefficients from the values f_i.

The variance is:

$$\sigma_e^2(m_N(\underline{t})) = \sigma^2 \sum_{|i|\leq 1} \sum_{|j|\leq 1} q_i^t(\underline{0}) q_j^t(\underline{0}) \frac{\sum_{h=1}^N w_{\underline{t},R}^2(\underline{x}_h) q_i^t(\underline{x}_h - \underline{t}) q_j^t(\underline{x}_h - \underline{t})}{\sum_{h=1}^N w_{\underline{t},R}(\underline{x}_h) q_i^t(\underline{x}_h - \underline{t})^2) \sum_{h=1}^N w_{\underline{t},R}(\underline{x}_h) q_j^t{}^2(\underline{x}_h - \underline{t})} \tag{6}$$

In case of asymptotic sampling, that is to say as $N \to \infty$, $R \to 0$ so that $M_R \to \infty$ and under the assumption f is integrable, then

$$E_e(\tilde{Q}_{\underline{t}}) \simeq \frac{\sum_{h\leq 1} q_h(\underline{0}) \int_D w_{\underline{t},R} q_h^t f d\mu}{\int_D w (q_h^t)^2 d\mu} \tag{7}$$

Remark: in this case the $\{q_h^t\}$ are solution of the problem (O) in the continuous case.

μ is an assigned measure on D in the case of points given with a deterministic law or the normalized measure (probability) in the case this law is of random type. In the latter case M_R has the meaning of expected value $N\int_{B(\underline{t},R)} d\mu$ and (7) is true in the sense of stochastic convergence, because of Slutsky theorem [7].

The variance is:

$$\sigma_e^2(\tilde{Q}_{\underline{t}}(\underline{t})) \simeq \frac{\sigma^2}{N} \frac{\sum\limits_{i\leq l}\sum\limits_{j\leq l} q_i^t(\underline{0})\, q_j^t(\underline{0}) \int_D w^2_{\underline{t},R}\, q_i^t q_j^t d\mu}{\sqrt{\int_D w(q_i^t)^2 d\mu \int_D w(q_j^t)^2 d\mu}} \tag{8}$$

Error

A measure of the approximation error can be given, coherent with the fact we deal with a least squares approximation; it is the following one:

$$\mathrm{MSE} = E_x E_e (m(\underline{t})-f(\underline{t}))^2 = E_x(E_e(m(\underline{t}))-f(\underline{t}))^2 + E_x(\sigma_e^2(m)) \tag{9}$$

in case of random points or:

$$\mathrm{MSE} = E_e(m(\underline{t})-f(\underline{t}))^2 + \sigma_e^2(m) \tag{10}$$

in case of fixed points.

Asymptotic expansion for MSE

We assume we are in asymptotic conditions, $N\rightarrow\infty$, $R\rightarrow 0$ so that $M_R\rightarrow\infty$ and we use the approximating formula (4).

Let $\underline{t}$ be such that $B(\underline{t},R)$ is all contained in D. Let μ, distribution law of the $\underline{x}_i$, be differentiable and not vanishing near $\underline{t}$ and symmetric respect to $\underline{t}$. So M_R is linear function of R.

Let exist the Taylor expansion of f with centre at $\underline{t}$ till the desired order. We have the following asymptotic expansion

MSE defined by (9)

$$\mathrm{MSE} \simeq \frac{A_0}{M_R} + R^{2(l+1)} c_1 A_1 + \frac{\sigma^2 A_2}{M_R} \qquad \text{for } l \text{ odd} \tag{11a}$$

$$\mathrm{MSE} \simeq \frac{A_3}{M_R} + R^{2(l+2)} c_2 A_4 + \frac{\sigma^2}{M_R} A_5 \qquad \text{for } l \text{ even} \tag{11b}$$

where, of course, the expansion is in stochastic sense. The $\{A_i\}$ are positive constants: in particular A_2 and A_5 are functions of w and q_j only, while A_0, A_1, A_3, A_4 are functions of w, $\{q_j\}$ and f, so that their largeness depend on the dimension k; $c_1 = c_2 = 1$ if $B(\underline{t},R)$ is hyperspheric; $c_1 = (\sqrt{k})^{2(l+1)}$, $c_2 = (\sqrt{k})^{2(l+2)}$ if $B(\underline{t},R)$ is hypercubic.

Besides, we assume M_R constant with k and hence that N is an increasing function of k.

MSE defined by (10)

$$MSE \simeq R^{2(l+1)} c_1 A_1 + \frac{\sigma^2 A_2}{M_R} \quad \text{for } l \text{ odd} \qquad (12a)$$

$$MSE \simeq R^{2(l+2)} c_2 A_4 + \frac{\sigma^2 A_5}{M_R} \quad \text{for } l \text{ even} \qquad (12b)$$

The derivation for the one dimensional case is outlined in Appendix I.

From (11) (respectively (12)) we observe the consistency in MSE of the approximation.

The (11) (respectively 12)) gives an error measure as a function of R, width parameter of the support $B(\underline{t},R)$; the function has one minimum only and so it is possible, at least in theory, to determine R optimal.

Last, we observe that, in the hypothesis of $\underline{x}_i$ deterministic and no noise, the asymptotic expansion of the error of the model is:

$$|m(\underline{t})-f(\underline{t})| \simeq \begin{cases} \sqrt{A}\ R^{l+1} & \text{for } l \text{ odd} \qquad (13a) \\ \sqrt{A_4}\ R^{l+2} & \text{for } l \text{ even} \qquad (13b) \end{cases}$$

2. Particular case l=0

In the case l=0 the smoothing function of type B becomes

$$m_o(\underline{t}) = \frac{\sum w_{\underline{t},R}(\underline{x}_i)\tilde{f}_i}{\sum w_{\underline{t},R}(\underline{x}_i)} \qquad (14)$$

The smoothing function (14) has already been studied and applied [1], [2], [3], [4], [5].

In these papers, one can find convergence properties under various hypothesis on f (discontinuity, continuity of class C^r, $r \geq 0$) and applications in which it is evident that it is useful to choose R as a function of $\underline{t}$.

In asymptotic conditions and under the suitable hypothesis (see section 1), one has:

$$E_x E_e(m(\underline{t})) = f(\underline{t}) + \mathcal{O}(R^2) \qquad (15)$$

Because of its simple form, (14) has application in the

multivariable approximation problem in $\mathbb{R}^k$ with $k>20$. In such a problem it can be interpreted as the expected value of a random variable of discrete type whose values have probability $p_i=w_i/\sum w_h$ to happen.

Hence the random variable f has variance

$$V = \sum \tilde{f}_i^2 p_i - (\sum \tilde{f}_i p_i)^2 \tag{16}$$

for N fixed.

In the case of no noise and for a function f with uniformely bounded gradient we have seen in[2] that V increases as log k and so it is good to make use of (14) also in high dimensional spaces, as required in general in problems of nuclear physics.

Moreover, as observed in[2] , it is possible to give a criterium to determine the optimal value of R depending on the characteristic behaviour of V, as studied experimentally.

We notice that there is a complete theoretical explanation at least when N is large enough so that one can study the function $V=V(R)$ in its asymptotic form.

In fact, within the hypothesis that a suitable Taylor expansion exists, with centre at $\underline{t}$, and regular distribution, the most significant part of the expected value $E_x E_e(V)$ is:

$$E_x E_e(V) \simeq a_1 R^2 - \frac{a_2}{R^2} - \frac{b}{R^3} + \sigma^2 - \frac{\sigma^2 c_1}{M_R} \tag{17}$$

with a_1, b, c_1 positive constants and a_2 not positive constant.

From this expansion, we observe that the behaviour as a function of R is that one of an increasing function with a saddle point.

In the case the data are without noise, that is to say $\sigma^2=0$, the function can show in dependence on the value a_2, either a minimum or a saddle point.

In Appendix II we outline the derivation of (17)for the monodimensional case and uniform distribution.

Appendix I

Asymptotic expansion for MSE

We outline the proof for the one dimensional case for convenience. MSE has the form:

$$MSE= E_x E_e (m(\underline{t})-f(\underline{t}))^2 = E_x((E_e(m(\underline{t}))-f(\underline{t}))^2+\sigma_e^2(m))$$

For i=0,..,l and j=0,..,l one has in probability that

$$\sum w_{t,R}(x_h)q_i(t-x_h)q_j(t-x_h) \simeq M_R \int_{-a}^{a} w(y)q_i(t-yR)q_j(t-yR)\mu' dy$$

that we write in short notation:

$$M_R \int_E wq_i q_j d\mu$$

Expanding MSE and gathering the terms, one gets:

$$MSE \simeq \operatorname{var}_x \underbrace{\frac{\sum_{i=1}^{M_R}\left(\sum_j \dfrac{w\left(\frac{x_i-t}{R}\right)q_j(x_i)f_i}{\int_E wq_j^2 d\mu} - q_j(0)\right)}{M_R}}_{A} + \underbrace{\left(\sum_{j=0}^{l} \frac{\int_E wq_j f d\mu}{\int wq_j^2 d\mu} q_j(0)-f(t)\right)^2}_{B} +$$

$$+ \underbrace{\frac{\sigma^2}{M_R} \sum_{i=0}^{l} \sum_{j=0}^{l} \frac{q_i(0)q_j(0) \int_E w^2 q_i q_j d\mu}{\int_E wq_i^2 d\mu \int_E wq_j^2 d\mu}}_{C}$$

A is a term due to the randomness of the x_i. It is a term of $\frac{1}{M_R}$ size order because it is variance of the arithmetic mean from a population with finite variance

B contains the error of the model

C is variance of the estimator due to the noise and has $\frac{1}{M_R}$ size order

It is possible to explicit B making use of a Taylor expansion of f with centre at t. In fact:

$$\sum_{j=0}^{l} \frac{\int_E wq_j f d\mu}{\int_E wq_j^2 d\mu} q_j(0) = f(t)q_0(0)+f'(t)(c_{0,1}q_0(0)+q_1(0))+..\frac{f^{(l)}(t)}{l!}(c_{0,l}q_0(0)+..$$

$$c_{l-1,l}q_{l-1}(0)+q_l(0))+\frac{f^{(l+1)}(t)}{(l+1)!}(-q_{l+1}(0))+\frac{f^{(l+2)}(\eta)}{(l+2)!}(-q_{l+2}(0))$$

with $$c_{i,j}=\frac{\int_E wq_i(-Ry)^j d\mu}{\int_E wq_i^2 d\mu \int_E wq_j^2 d\mu}$$

The coefficients of $f'(t),..f^{(l)}(t)/(l)!$ vanishe as they are=to the values at O of the monomials $(-Ry)^j$ $j=1,..,l$; for l even the coeff cient of $f^{(l+1)}/(l+1)!$ vanishes because q_{l+1} is odd function; $q_j(O) \asymp R^j$. It follows that

$$\sum_{j=0}^{l} \frac{\int_E w q_j f d\mu}{\int_E w q_j^2 d\mu} q_j(O) \asymp R^{l+1} \text{ for } l \text{ odd, while } R^{l+2} \text{ for } l \text{ even;}$$

Remark: removing the hypothesis of randomness of the x_i, A disappears, while B and C remain in certainity.

<u>Appendix II</u>

Proof of the behaviour of the variance as a function of R, in the one dimensional case and uniform distribution, for convenience.

Let us subdivide the interval $I=[0,1]$ in subintervals with equal probabilities $P=1/n$, $0=t_1, t_2 .. t_n=1$.

Let be $(x_1, x_2, .., x_m)$ the sample with m large enough respect to n so that the number of the x_i in each subinterval is approximately constant.

For n large enough we can write:

$$m_o(t) \simeq \frac{1}{mR} \frac{\sum_{mR} \tilde{f}_i w_i}{\int_{-a}^{a} w}$$

or assuming the normalization of w, we write $m_o(t) \simeq 1/mR \sum \tilde{f}_i w_i$

For the generic x_i in $I_j=(t_j-1/2n, t_j+1/2n)$ and expandin the function f, we have

$$\tilde{f}(x_i)=e_i+f(t_j)+f'(t_j)(x_i-t_j)+O(1/n)^2 \text{ for } x_i \in I_j$$

Dropping the terms with exponent larger than one, one has:

$$E_x(V)=\Bigg\{\underbrace{\frac{1}{nR}\sum^{n} f_j^2 \int_{I_j} \frac{wdx}{n} - \Big(\frac{1}{nR}\sum f_j \int_{I_j}\frac{wdx}{n}\Big)^2}_{A}\Bigg\} - \Bigg\{\underbrace{\frac{1}{n^2R^2}\sum f_j^2 \int_{I_j} \frac{w^2dx}{n} - \frac{1}{n^2R^2}\sum f_j^2 \Big(\int_{I_j}\frac{wdx}{n}\Big)^2}_{B}\Bigg\} +$$

$$+\Bigg\{\frac{1}{nR}\sum \int_{I_j} f_j'^2 (x-t_j)^2 \frac{wdx}{n} - \overbrace{\Big(\frac{1}{nR}\sum \int_{I_j} f_j'(x-t_j)\frac{wdx}{n}\Big)^2}^{C}\Bigg\} - \Bigg\{\frac{1}{n^2R^2}\sum \overbrace{\int f_j'^2 (x-t_j)^2 \frac{w^2dx}{n}}^{D} +$$

$$-\frac{1}{n^2R^2}\sum \overbrace{\Big(\int f_j'(x-t_j)}\frac{wdx}{n}\Big)^2\Bigg\} + \frac{2}{n^2R^2}\Bigg\{\sum f_j \int_{I_j} f_j'(x-t_j) \overbrace{\frac{wdx}{n} - \sum f_j \int_{I_j} f_j'(x-t_j)}^{E} \frac{w^2dx}{n} -$$

$$-\sum\sum f_j \int_{I_j} \frac{w\,dx}{n} \int_{I_k} f_j'(x-t_k)\frac{w\,dx}{n} \Big\} + \sigma^2 - \underbrace{\frac{\sigma^2}{nR^2}\int_0 w\,dx}_{F}$$

A is a variance of the values $\{f(t_i)\}$

B gives a mean variation of the weights and can be more or less important depending on the used weight function

C gives the mean variation of difference between $f(x_j)$ and $f(t_j)$ respect to w

D is a variability of the function gw

E is an adjusting term

F is the term due to the noise

Let us consider the first part of the first term A and expand it in t_j; we have:

$$\frac{1}{R}\Big\{\frac{1}{n}\sum^n f_j^2 (w_j + w_j' \int_{I_j} \frac{(t_j - x)\,dx}{Rn} + \frac{1}{2} w_j'' \int_{I_j} \frac{(t_j-x)^2 dx}{R^2 n} + O\Big(\frac{1}{n^4 R^3}\Big)\Big\} \simeq$$

$$\frac{1}{R}\Big\{\int_0^1 f^2(s)\, w\Big(\frac{t-s}{R}\Big) ds + \frac{1}{2}\int_0^1 f^2(s)\, w''\Big(\frac{t-s}{R}\Big) \frac{1}{3n^2R^2} + O\Big(\frac{1}{n^4R^3}\Big)\Big\} \simeq$$

$$R^2 \Big\{ f'^2(t) \int_{-a}^{a} y^2 w(y)\,dy \Big\} - \frac{1}{6n^2R^2} \Big\{ f^2(t) \int_{-a}^{a} w''(y)\,dy \Big\} + O\Big(\frac{1}{n^2}\Big)$$

In analogue way for the remaining terms;we obtain as principal part:

$$\Big\{f^2(t) \underbrace{\int_{-a}^{a} y^2 w(y)\,dy}_{a_1}\Big\} R^2 - \Big\{\frac{1}{6n^2} f^2(t) \underbrace{\int_{-a}^{a} w''(y)\,dy}_{a_2} \Big\} \frac{1}{R^2} +$$

$$-\Big\{\frac{1}{n^3} f^2(t) \underbrace{\int_{-a}^{a} w'^2(y)\,dy}_{b} \Big\} \frac{1}{R^3} + \sigma^2 - \frac{\sigma^2}{nR} \underbrace{\int_{-a}^{a} w^2(y)\,dy}_{c_1}$$

The coefficient a_2 will be not positive for the usual bell-shaped weight function

References

1. M. Bozzini, L. Lenarduzzi:"Approssimazione multivariabile e riconoscimento di forme". Rendic. Ist. Lomb. 113 (1979)
2. M. Bozzini, L. Lenarduzzi:"Approximation of multivariable functions respect to random points less than 2^k, k dimension of space". Numer. Math 37 (1981)
3. M. Bozzini, F. De Tisi, L. Lenarduzzi:"An approximation method of the local type. Application to a problem of heart potential mapping". Computing 32 (1984)
4. Th. Gasser, H.G. Müller:"Kernel estimation of regression functions". Proceedings Heidelberg 1979. Lecture Notes in Math. 757
5. Th. Gasser, H.G. Müller and others:"Nonparametric regression analysis of growth curves". Annals of Statistics 12, n.1 (1984)
6. P. Lancaster, K. Salkauskas:"Surfaces generated by moving least squares methods". Math. Comp. 37 (1981)
7. M. Fisz:"Probability theory and mathematical statistics". J. Wiley eds. (1963)

Prof. Mira Bozzini, Istituto di Matematica dell'Università di Milano, via Saldini 50, 20133 Milano (Italy)

Dr. Licia Lenarduzzi, Istituto Applicazioni Matematica ed Informatica del C.N.R., via Cicognara 7, 20129 Milano (Italy)

International Series of
Numerical Mathematics, Vol. 75

CONVEXITY AND VARIATION DIMINISHING PROPERTY OF BERNSTEIN POLYNOMIALS OVER TRIANGLES

Geng-zhe Chang
Josef Hoschek

Abstract: Let $B^n(f;P)$ denote the Bernstein polynomials over triangle T and $\hat{f}_n$ denote the Bézier net associated with $B^n(f;P)$. A certain type of variations of $\hat{f}_n$ is introduced by GOODMAN quite recently. In the present paper the corresponding variation of $B^n(f;P)$ is defined by integration of the absolute value of the Laplacian of $B^n(f;P)$ over T. It is shown that the variation of $\hat{f}_n$ is always greater or equal to the variation of $B^n(f;P)$. The equality holds if and only if $\hat{f}_n$ is either convex (or concave) over T. The convexity of $\hat{f}_n$ implies the convexity of $B^n(f;P)$. As an application we receive a simple proof of a theorem due to CHANG and DAVIS.

1. INTRODUCTION

Let f be a set of n+1 real numbers, i.e., $f = \{f_0, f_1, \ldots, f_n\}$. The Bernstein polynomial associated with f is defined by

$$(1)\qquad B^n(f;x) := \sum_{i=0}^{n} f_i \binom{n}{i} x^i (1-x)^{n-i}, \qquad 0 \leqslant x \leqslant 1 .$$

It is easy to show that

$$\frac{d}{dx} B^n(f;x) = n \sum_{i=0}^{n-1} \Delta f_i \binom{n-1}{i} x^i (1-x)^{n-1-i},$$

$$(2)\qquad \frac{d^2}{dx^2} B^n(f;x) = n(n-1) \sum_{i=0}^{n-2} \Delta^2 f_i \binom{n-2}{i} x^i (1-x)^{n-2-i}$$

where Δ represents the forward difference operator, i.e., $\Delta f_i = f_{i+1} - f_i$, $i=0,1,\ldots,n-1$. Joining $\left(\frac{i-1}{n}, f_{i-1}\right)$ and $\left(\frac{i}{n}, f_i\right)$ by line segment for $i=1,2,\ldots,n$, a piecewise linear function, denoted by $\hat{f}_n(x)$, is obtained and is called the Bêzier polygon of $B^n(f:x)$.

From (2) we have

$$(3)\qquad \left|\frac{d^2}{dx^2} B^n(f;x)\right| \leqslant n(n-1) \sum_{i=0}^{n-2} |\Delta^2 f_i| \binom{n-2}{i} x^i (1-x)^{n-2-i}$$

Integrating on both sides of (3) we get

$$(4)\qquad \int_0^1 \left|\frac{d^2}{dx^2} B^n(f;x)\right| dx \leq n \sum_{i=0}^{n-2} |\Delta^2 f_i| \ .$$

We know that $\hat{f}_n(x)$ is convex (or concave) on [0,1] if and only if $\Delta^2 f_i \geq 0$ (or $\Delta^2 f_i \leq 0$) for $i=0,1,\ldots,n-2$, in this case we have from (2) that $B^n(f;x)'' \geq 0$ (or $B^n(f;x)'' \leq 0$). Hence it follows the following conclusions

(i) If $\hat{f}_n(x)$ is convex (or concave) on [0,1], then so is the Bernstein polynomial $B^n(f;x)$;

(ii) equality holds in (4) if and only if $\hat{f}_n(x)$ is either convex or concave on [0,1].

Now we turn our attention to Bernstein polynomials over triangles: Let T_1, T_2, T_3 be three vertices of a given triangle T which is called the domain triangle. It is known [1] that every point P of the plane of the triangle can be expressed uniquely by

$$(5)\qquad P = uT_1 + vT_2 + wT_3 \qquad \text{with} \qquad u + v + w = 1 \ .$$

(u,v,w) are called the barycentric coordinates of P with respect to the triangle T. We identify the point P with its barycentric coordinates and write P=(u,v,w). Barycentric coordinates of points inside or on the boundary of T are characterized by

$$u \geq 0, \quad v \geq 0, \quad w \geq 0 \ .$$

Let f be an arbitrarily given set containing (n+1)(n+2)/2 real numbers $f_{i,j,k}$, where i,j,k denote nonnegative integers such that i+j+k=n. We define

$$(6)\qquad B^n(f;P) := \sum_{i+j+k=n} f_{i,j,k}\, J^n_{i,j,k}(P)$$

where

$$(7)\qquad J^n_{i,j,k}(P) := \frac{n!}{i!j!k!} u^i v^j w^k \ ,$$

i+j+k=n, are called the Bernstein basis polynomials. $B^n(f;P)$ is called the n-th Bernstein polynomial of f over the triangle T. Geometrically (6) represents a triangular surface patch over T, so (6) is also called by experts in Computer Aided Geometric Design the Bernstein-Bézier triangular patch [1].

Some other terminologies from that field will be very helpful. f is called the set of Bêzier ordinates $f_{i,j,k}$ (i+j+k=n) for $B^n(f;P)$. If $f_{i,j,k}$ is erected over the corresponding point ($\frac{i}{n}, \frac{j}{n}, \frac{k}{n}$) in the domain triangle, a spatial point $F_{i,j,k}$ will be obtained. $F_{i,j,k}$ (i+j+k=n), are called the Bêzier points of $B^n(f;P)$.

Drawing a triangle with three points $F_{i+1,j,k}$, $F_{i,j+1,k}$, $F_{i,j,k+1}$ as its vertices, where i+j+k=n-1, a piecewise linear function $\hat{f}_n(P)$ over T is constructed and then is called the Bêzier net of $B^n(f;P)$. For n=3 a Bêzier net and the corresponding triangular patch are illustrated in figure 1.

Fig. 1: Bêzier net and corresponding patch over the triangle T

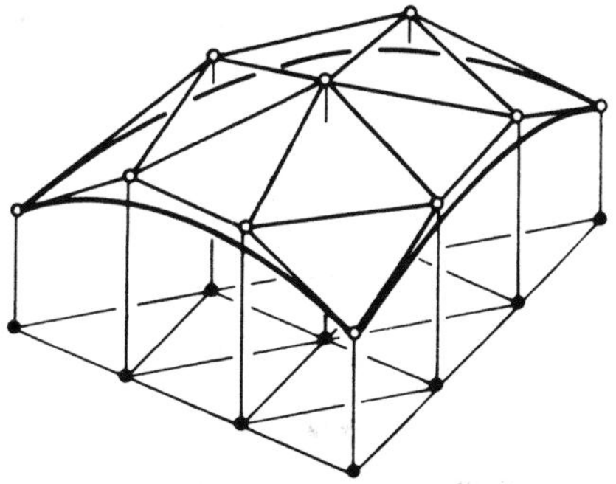

To obtain the analogue of (i), CHANG and DAVIS establish the following (see [2])

THEOREM 1. If $\hat{f}_n(P)$ is convex over T, then so is the Bernstein-Bêzier triangular patch $B^n(f;P)$.

We introduce three formal partial shift operators E_1, E_2 and E_3 by

$$E_1 f_{i,j,k} := f_{i+1,j,k} \; ; \quad E_2 f_{i,j,k} := f_{i,j+1,k} \; ; \quad E_3 f_{i,j,k} := f_{i,j,k+1}$$

(for i+j+k = n-1) and the abbrevations (for i+j+k = n-2)

$$D^1_{i,j,k} := (E_1-E_2)(E_1-E_3)f_{i,j,k} , \qquad D^2_{i,j,k} := (E_2-E_3)(E_2-E_1)f_{i,j,k} ,$$

$$D^3_{i,j,k} := (E_3-E_1)(E_3-E_2)f_{i,j,k} .$$

It has been shown that the convexity of $\hat{f}_n(P)$ over T is equivalent to the following inequalities (see [3])

$$D^{l}_{i,j,k} \geqslant 0 \quad , \quad l=1,2,3 \quad \text{and} \quad i+j+k = n-2 \ .$$

To extend the inequality (4) to the triangular Bernstein polynomials, quite recently T.N.T. GOODMAN defines

$$(8) \qquad V_1(g;T) := \iint_T (g_{xx}^2 + 2g_{xy}^2 + g_{yy}^2)^{1/2} \, dx \, dy$$

for function g which has continuous partial derivatives up to second order and

$$(9) \qquad V_1(\hat{f}_n;T) := \sum_{S=1}^{3} \sum_{i+j+k=n-2} V^{S}_{i,j,k}(\hat{f}_n)$$

for the piecewise linear function $\hat{f}_n$, in which

$$(10) \qquad V^{1}_{i,j,k}(\hat{f}_n) := \frac{|\hat{D}^{1}_{i,j,k}|\,|T_2T_3|^2}{2|T|} \quad ,$$

where $|T|$ denotes the area of the triangle T. Corresponding formulae hold for the variation $V^2_{i,j,k}(\hat{f}_n)$ and $V^3_{i,j,k}(\hat{f}_n)$. GOODMAN has proved in [4] that

$$(11) \qquad V_1[B^n(f;P);T] \leqslant V_1(\hat{f}_n;T).$$

It seems to the authors that (11) is not the proper generalization of (4) in sense that the equality in (11) does not occur for some convex $\hat{f}_n(P)$. For instance, we can see from the proof of lemma 1 in [4] that even for the convex Bézier net $\hat{f}_n$ for which $f_{n,o,o} = f_{o,n,o} = f_{o,o,n} = 1$ and $f_{i,j,k} = 0$, $i,j,k \neq n$, strict inequality holds in (11).

Main purpose of the present paper is to obtain a proper generalization of (4), i.e., to get a variation diminishing inequality similar to (11) in which the equality holds if and only if $\hat{f}_n(P)$ is either convex or concave over T.

2. REPRESENTATION OF LAPLACIAN $\Delta B^n(f)$

In order to obtain a generalization of (4), in present paper definition (8) is replaced by

$$(12) \qquad V_1^{*}(g;T) := \iint_T |\Delta g| \, dx \, dy = \iint_T \left| \frac{\partial^2 g}{\partial x^2} + \frac{\partial^2 g}{\partial y^2} \right| dx \, dy \ .$$

Definition (9) remains unchanged. It is clear that (12) is invariant under rotations. Definitions (8) and (12) coincide if

$$\frac{\partial^2 g}{\partial x^2} \quad \frac{\partial^2 g}{\partial y^2} \quad - \left(\frac{\partial^2 g}{\partial x \partial y}\right)^2 = 0.$$

In Euclidean 3-space, the previous equality implies that the Gaussian curvature of the surface $z = g(x,y)$ vanishes everywhere.

To calculate (12), we need a representation of the Laplacian for the Bernstein triangular polynomials.
The following lemma will be helpful.

LEMMA. Let A,B,C and a,b,c be real numbers.

Putting

$$D_a := A+a-b-c, \quad D_b := B+b-c-a, \quad D_c := C+c-a-b,$$

then the following bilinear form holds

$$(\xi,\eta,\zeta) \begin{pmatrix} A & c & b \\ c & B & a \\ b & a & C \end{pmatrix} \begin{pmatrix} \xi' \\ \eta' \\ \zeta' \end{pmatrix} = D_a\xi\xi' + D_b\eta\eta' + D_c\zeta\zeta'$$

for $\xi+\eta+\zeta = 0$ and $\xi'+\eta'+\zeta' = 0$.

<u>PROOF</u>. The following splitting is very clear

$$\begin{pmatrix} A & c & b \\ c & B & a \\ b & a & C \end{pmatrix} = \begin{pmatrix} D_a & Q & 0 \\ 0 & D_b & 0 \\ 0 & 0 & D_c \end{pmatrix} + \begin{pmatrix} b+c-a & c & b \\ c & c+a-b & a \\ b & a & a+b-c \end{pmatrix}.$$

For $\xi+\eta+\zeta = 0$ and $\xi'+\eta'+\zeta' = 0$ it follows that

$$(\xi,\eta,\zeta) \begin{pmatrix} b+c-a & c & b \\ c & c+a-b & a \\ b & a & a+b-c \end{pmatrix} \begin{pmatrix} \xi' \\ \eta' \\ \zeta' \end{pmatrix} = 0 .$$

hence we get the lemma by multiplication.

Note that the operator E_1, E_2 and E_3 commute, thus the Bernstein polynomial

(6) can be expressed very neatly in terms of those operators by

(13) $$B^n(f;P) = (uE_1 + vE_2 + wE_3)^n f_{o,o,o}$$

From (13), we have

(14)
$$\frac{\partial B^n(f;P)}{\partial u} = n(uE_1 + vE_2 + wE_3)^{n-1} E_1 f_{o,o,o} ,$$
$$\frac{\partial^2 B^n(f;P)}{\partial u^2} = n(n-1)(uE_1 + vE_2 + wE_3)^{n-2} E_1^2 f_{o,o,o} ,$$
$$\frac{\partial^2 B^n(f;P)}{\partial u \partial v} = n(n-1)(uE_1 + vE_2 + wE_3)^{n-2} E_1 E_2 f_{o,o,o}$$

and so on. Partial derivatives in (14) can be expressed explicitly by

(15)
$$\frac{\partial B^n}{\partial u} = n \sum_{i+j+k=n-1} E_1 f_{i,j,k} J^{n-1}_{i,j,k} (P)$$
$$\frac{\partial^2 B^n}{\partial u^2} = n(n-1) \sum_{i+j+k=n-2} E_1^2 f_{i,j,k} J^{n-2}_{i,j,k} (P) ,$$
$$\frac{\partial^2 B^n}{\partial u \partial v} = n(n-1) \sum_{i+j+k=n-2} E_1 E_2 f_{i,j,k} J^{n-2}_{i,j,k} (P)$$

respectively.

For calculation of Laplacian $\Delta B^n(f)$, we suppose that there already exists a rectangular coordinate system in the plane of the domain triangle and that T_i has (x_i, y_i) as its coordinates, i=1,2,3. Let P = (x,y). From (5) we have

(16) $$x = ux_1 + vx_2 + wx_3 \quad ; \quad y = uy_1 + vy_2 + wy_3 .$$

We obtain from (16) and (5) that

$$\frac{\partial u}{\partial x} = \frac{y_2-y_3}{2|T|}, \quad \frac{\partial v}{\partial x} = \frac{y_3-y_1}{2|T|}, \quad \frac{\partial w}{\partial x} = \frac{y_1-y_2}{2|T|}, \quad \frac{\partial u}{\partial y} = \frac{x_3-x_2}{2|T|}, \quad \frac{\partial v}{\partial y} = \frac{x_1-x_3}{2|T|}, \quad \frac{\partial w}{\partial y} = \frac{x_2-x_1}{2|T|} .$$

$$\frac{\partial u}{\partial x} + \frac{\partial v}{\partial x} + \frac{\partial w}{\partial x} = 0 , \qquad \frac{\partial u}{\partial y} + \frac{\partial v}{\partial y} + \frac{\partial w}{\partial y} = 0 .$$

Since
$$\frac{\partial B^n(f)}{\partial x} = \frac{\partial B^n}{\partial u}\frac{\partial u}{\partial x} + \frac{\partial B^n}{\partial v}\frac{\partial v}{\partial x} + \frac{\partial B^n}{\partial w}\frac{\partial w}{\partial x} ,$$

we have for the partial derivative of second order

$$(17)\qquad \frac{\partial^2 B^n(f)}{\partial x^2} = \left(\frac{\partial u}{\partial x} , \frac{\partial v}{\partial x} , \frac{\partial w}{\partial x} \right) H \begin{pmatrix} \frac{\partial u}{\partial x} \\ \frac{\partial v}{\partial x} \\ \frac{\partial w}{\partial x} \end{pmatrix} ,$$

where H is the 3×3 Hessian

$$H := \begin{pmatrix} \frac{\partial^2 B^n}{\partial u^2} & \frac{\partial^2 B^n}{\partial u \partial v} & \frac{\partial^2 B^n}{\partial u \partial w} \\ \frac{\partial^2 B^n}{\partial v \partial u} & \frac{\partial^2 B^n}{\partial v^2} & \frac{\partial^2 B^n}{\partial v \partial w} \\ \frac{\partial^2 B^n}{\partial w \partial u} & \frac{\partial^2 B^n}{\partial w \partial v} & \frac{\partial^2 B^n}{\partial w^2} \end{pmatrix} .$$

Similarly we get

$$\frac{\partial^2 B^n(f)}{\partial y^2} = \left(\frac{\partial u}{\partial y} , \frac{\partial v}{\partial y} , \frac{\partial w}{\partial y} \right) H \begin{pmatrix} \frac{\partial u}{\partial y} \\ \frac{\partial v}{\partial y} \\ \frac{\partial w}{\partial y} \end{pmatrix} .$$

By last two equations in (15) and its analogues, we receive

$$H = n(n-1) \sum_{i+j+k=n-2} \begin{pmatrix} E_1^2 f_{i,j,k}, & E_1 E_2 f_{i,j,k}, & E_1 E_3 f_{i,j,k} \\ E_2 E_1 f_{i,j,k}, & E_2^2 f_{i,j,k}, & E_2 E_3 f_{i,j,k} \\ E_3 E_1 f_{i,j,k}, & E_3 E_2 f_{i,j,k}, & E_3^2 f_{i,j,k} \end{pmatrix} J^{n-2}_{i,j,k}(P) .$$

(17) can be rewritten by the lemma as

$$(18)\qquad \frac{\partial^2 B^n(f)}{\partial x^2} = \frac{n(n-1)}{4|T|^2} \sum_{i+j+k=n-2} [D^1_{i,j,k} (y_2-y_3)^2 + D^2_{i,j,k} (y_3-y_1)^2 + D^3_{i,j,k} (y_1-y_2)^2] \, J^{n-2}_{i,j,k} (P) ,$$

$$(19)\qquad \frac{\partial^2 B^n(f)}{\partial y^2} = \frac{n(n-1)}{4|T|^2} \sum_{i+j+k=n-2} [D^1_{i,j,k} (x_3-x_2)^2 + D^2_{i,j,k} (x_1-x_3)^2 + D^3_{i,j,k} (x_2-x_1)^2] \, J^{n-2}_{i,j,k} (P) .$$

Adding up (18) and (19) side by side, we obtain the representation of the Laplacian

$$(20)\quad \Delta B^n(f) = \frac{n(n-1)}{4|T|^2} \sum_{i+j+k=n-2} (D^1_{i,j,k}|T_2T_3|^2 + D^2_{i,j,k}|T_3T_1|^2 + D^3_{i,j,k}|T_1T_2|^2) \cdot J^{n-2}_{i,j,k}(P) .$$

3. MAIN THEOREM

Now we can prove the main theorem of this paper.

THEOREM 2. Under assuptions of (9) and (12), the variation diminishing property for Bernstein triangular polynomials can be proved. We receive

$$(21)\qquad V_1^*[B^n(f);\, T] \leqslant V_1(\hat{f}_n;\, T)$$

with the equality if and only if $\hat{f}_n$ is either convex or concave.

PROOF. Since we have (see, for example, [1])

$$(22)\qquad \iint_T B^n(f;T)\, dx\, dy = \frac{2|T|}{(n+1)(n+2)} \sum_{i+j+k=n} f_{i,j,k} ,$$

upon applying (22) to $|\Delta B^n(f)|$, we obtain

$$V_1^*[B^n(f);\, T] = \iint_T |\Delta B^n(f)|\, dx\, dy \leqslant$$

$$\leqslant \frac{1}{2|T|} \sum_{i+j+k=n-2} [|D^1_{i,j,k}||T_2T_3|^2 + |D^2_{i,j,k}||T_3T_1|^2 + |D^3_{i,j,k}||T_1T_2|^2]$$

$$= V_1(\hat{f}_n;\, T)$$

by (9) and (10). Thus the inequality (21) has been established.

It remains to examine under what conditions the equality in (21) holds.

It is clear that if $\hat{f}_n$ is convex (concave) on T, then $D^S_{i,j,k} \geqslant 0$ ($D^S_{i,j,k} < 0$) for S=1,2,3 and i+j+k = n-2, and then we have $V_1^*[B^n(f);\, T] = V_1(\hat{f}_n;\, T)$; conversely, from the equality we can deduce that all $D^S_{i,j,k}$ should have same sign for S=1,2,3 and i+j+k = n-2. Hence $\hat{f}_n$ is either convex or concave.

This completes the proof of the main theorem.

4. APPLICATIONS

The techniques created in this contribution leads to a simple proof of the theorem 1 due to CHANG and DAVIS:

Similar to (17) we can find

$$(23)\qquad \frac{\partial^2 B^n}{\partial x \partial y} = \left(\frac{\partial u}{\partial x}, \frac{\partial v}{\partial x}, \frac{\partial w}{\partial x} \right) H \begin{pmatrix} \frac{\partial u}{\partial y} \\ \frac{\partial v}{\partial y} \\ \frac{\partial w}{\partial y} \end{pmatrix}$$

and then by the lemma (23) can be rewritten as

$$(24)\qquad \frac{\partial^2 B^n}{\partial x \partial y} = \frac{n(n-1)}{4|T|^2} \sum_{i+j+k=n-2} [D^1_{i,j,k} (x_3-x_2)(y_2-y_3) +$$

$$D^2_{i,j,k} (x_1-x_3)(y_3-y_1) + D^3_{i,j,k} (x_2-x_1)(y_1-y_2)] \, J^{n-2}_{i,j,k} (P) \, .$$

If $D^l_{i,j,k} \geqslant 0$ for $i+j+k = n-2$ and $l=1,2,3$, then we have by (18) and (19) that

$$(25)\qquad \frac{\partial^2 B^n}{\partial x^2} \geqslant 0 \, , \qquad\qquad \frac{\partial^2 B^n}{\partial y^2} \geqslant 0 \, .$$

By Cauchy-Schwarz inequality, it follows that

$$[\sum_{i+j+k=n-2} [D^1_{i,j,k}(x_3-x_2)(y_2-y_3)+D^2_{i,j,k}(x_1-x_3)(y_3-y_1)+D^3_{i,j,k}(x_2-x_1)(y_1-y_2)] J^{n-2}_{i,j,k}]^2$$

$$= [\sum_{i+j+k=n-2} [\sqrt{D^1_{i,j,k} J^{n-2}_{i,j,k}(x_3-x_2)} \sqrt{D^1_{i,j,k} J^{n-2}_{i,j,k} (y_2-y_3)} +$$

$$\sqrt{D^2_{i,j,k} J^{n-2}_{i,j,k}(x_1-x_3)} \sqrt{D^2_{i,j,k} J^{n-2}_{i,j,k} (y_3-y_1)} +$$

$$\sqrt{D^3_{i,j,k} J^{n-2}_{i,j,k}(x_2-x_1)} \sqrt{D^3_{i,j,k} J^{n-2}_{i,j,k} (y_1-y_2)}]^2$$

$$\leqslant (\sum_{i+j+k=n-2} [D^1_{i,j,k}(x_3-x_2)^2 + D^2_{i,j,k}(x_1-x_3)^2 + D^3_{i,j,k}(x_2-x_1)^2] \, J^{n-2}_{i,j,k}) \cdot$$

$$\cdot (\sum_{i+j+k=n-2} [D^1_{i,j,k}(y_2-y_3)^2 + D^2_{i,j,k}(y_3-y_1)^2 + D^3_{i,j,k}(y_1-y_2)^2] \, J^{n-2}_{i,j,k})$$

Hence we get

$$(26) \qquad \left(\frac{\partial^2 B^n}{\partial x \partial y} \right)^2 \leqslant \left(\frac{\partial^2 B^n}{\partial x^2} \right) \left(\frac{\partial^2 B^n}{\partial y^2} \right) .$$

This inequality implies that Gaussian curvature $K \geqslant 0$ and $B^n(f;P)$ is convex over T.

REFERENCES

[1] W. BOEHM, G. FARIN, J. KAHMANN: A survey of curve and surface methods in CAGD. Computer Aided Geometric Design **1**, 1-60 (1984).

[2] G. CHANG, P.J. DAVIS: The convexity of Bernstein Polynomials over triangles. J. Approxi. Theory **40**, 11-28 (1984).

[3] G. CHANG, Y.Y. FENG: A new proof for the convexity of Bernstein Polynomials over triangles. Chinese Annals of Mathematics, series B, **6**, 141-146 (1985).

[4] T.N.T. GOODMAN: Variation Diminishing Properties of Bernstein Polynomials on Triangles. (Preprint, Department of Mathematical Sciences, The University, Dundee DD1 4HN Scotland).

Prof. Geng-zhe Chang
University of Science and
Technology of China

Hefei, Anhui

The People's Republic of China

Visiting Scholar at
Department of Mathematics,
TH Darmstadt
Federal Republic of Germany

Prof. Dr. Josef Hoschek
Technische Hochschule Darmstadt, Fachbereich Mathematik
Schloßgartenstraße 7

D-6100 Darmstadt

International Series of
Numerical Mathematics, Vol. 75

The Dimensions of Bivariate Spline Spaces over Triangulations

Y. S. Chou[1] , Lo-Yung Su [2] and R. H. Wang[1]

1. Professor of Jilin University
2. University of Houston at Victoria

Let D be a polygon and Δ be a triangulation of D such that any vertex of a triangle does not lie in the interior (open line segment) of any edge of another triangle. Denoted by P_k, the collection of all polynomials with real coefficients and total degree k, that is, each $p \in P_k$ has the form

$$p(x,y) = \sum_{i=o}^{k} \sum_{j=0}^{k-i} C_{ij} x^i y^j ,$$

where C_{ij} are real numbers. A function S in $C^u(D)$ will be called a bivariate spline of degree (k,u) on the triangulation Δ , if the restriction of S to each triangle of this triangulation is in P_k. The collection of all these bivariate splines will be denoted by $S_k^u(\Delta) = S_k^u(\Delta ;D)$

A fundamental problem in theory of bivariate splines is to determine the dimension of the space $S_k^u(\Delta)$. This problem was first proposed by G. Strang (1974), where several conjectures were made. Later, Morgan and Scott (1975) have shown the exact dimension of $S_k^1(\Delta)$, where $k \geq 5$, and Δ is any given triangulation. Others inculde Wang (1979,1984), Schumaker (1979,1984), Farin (1979), Chui & Wang (1982,1983) have discussed the problem.

In this paper, we will give formulas for the dimensions of spaces $S_k^1(\Delta)$, where k=2,3,4 and Δ is any triangulation.

In order to present the results, we need the following lemmas.

----

1. Project supported by the Science Fundation of the Chinese Academy of of Sciences.

2. Project is supported by University of Houston-Victoria

Lemma 1 ([8]) Let Δ be any partition of D. The function S(x,y) is a bivariate spline belonging to $S_k^u(\Delta)$ if and only if for any interior edge, there exists a smoothing cofactor of the function S(x,y), and the function S(x,y) satisfies the global comformality condition

$$(1) \quad \sum_{i=1}^{N(Ar)} \{ l_{iAr}(x,y) \}^{u+1} \cdot Q_{iAr}(x,y) \equiv 0, \quad r=1,\dots,M.$$

Where $A_1, \dots, A_m$ are all interior vertices of Δ,

$$\Gamma_{iAr} : l_{iAr}(x,y) = 0, \quad i = 1,\dots,N(Ar)$$

are all interior edges, and $Q_{iAr}(x,y)$, (i=1, ...,N(Ar), r=1,...,M) is the smoothing cofactor of S(x,y) across Γ_{iAr} travelling along the counter-clockwise direction around Ar ([8]).

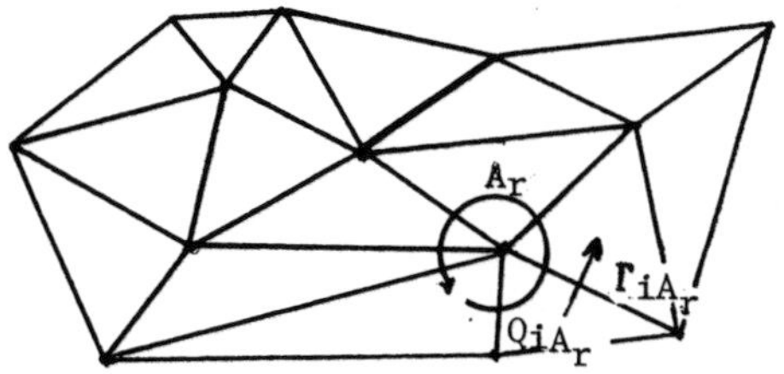

Lemma 2 ([9])

$$(2) \qquad \dim S_k^u(\Delta) = \binom{k+2}{2} + N\binom{k-u+1}{2} - \tau,$$

Where N is the number of all interior edges, and τ is the rank of coefficient matrix of linear equations determined by the global conformality condition (1). ([9])

Euler polyhedron formula:

Let be a triangulation with i interior vertices and β boundary vertices. Then the triangulation Δ has $2i+\beta-2$ triangles and $3i+2\beta-3$ edges.

Let $m_1, m_2, \ldots, m_n$ be distinct real numbers, and $V_k^u(n)$ be the vector space corresponding to the conformality condition at the origin 0:

$$V_k^u(n) := \{(q_1,q_2,\ldots,q_n) : \sum_{i=1}^{n} q_i(y)\,(x+m_i y)^{u+1} \equiv 0,\ q_1,\ldots,q_n \in P_{k-u-1}\},$$

where $0 \le u \le k-1$, and $x+m_i y=0$ $(i=1,\ldots,n)$ are the edges passing through origin 0.

$$d_k^u(n) := \dim V_k^u(n)$$

$$(3)\qquad d_k^u(n) = \tfrac{1}{2}\left(k-u-\left[\frac{u+1}{n-1}\right]\right)_+ \cdot \left\{(n-1)k-(n+1)u+(n-3) + (n-1)\left[\frac{u+1}{n-1}\right]\right\}$$

Schumaker ([5]) has given a formula for $d_k^u(n)$, and the above formula was rewritten by Chui & Wang ([1]).

According to formula (3), we have

$$d_2^1(n) = (n-3)_+$$

$$d_3^1(n) = \begin{cases} 0, & n=2 \\ 3(n-3)+2, & n=3 \end{cases}$$

$$d_4^1(n) = \begin{cases} 1, & n=2 \\ 6(n-2)+6, & n=3 \end{cases}$$

Let D be a region that be partitioned by irreducible algebraic curves and D_i, D_j be two adjancent cells of the partition Δ with common grid-segment $\Gamma_{ij}: l_{ij}(x,y)=0$. Let $S(x,y)$ be a function on Δ such that the restriction S on D_i and D_j be polynomials in P_k and be represented by $p_i(x,y)$

and $p_j(x,y)$ respectively.

Follow from Bezout's theorem in Algebraic Geometry, it is clear that $S(x,y) \varepsilon S_k^u(\overline{D_i U D_j})$ if and only if there exists $Q_{ij} \;\varepsilon\; P_{k-(u+1)\deg(l_{ij})}$ such that

$$p_i(x,y)-p_j(x,y) = l_{ij}(x,y)^{u+1} \cdot Q_{ij}(x,y)$$

We shall call $Q_{ij}(x,y)$ the smoothing cofactor of $S(x,y)$ across Γ_{ij} from D_j to D_i ([1] ,[8])

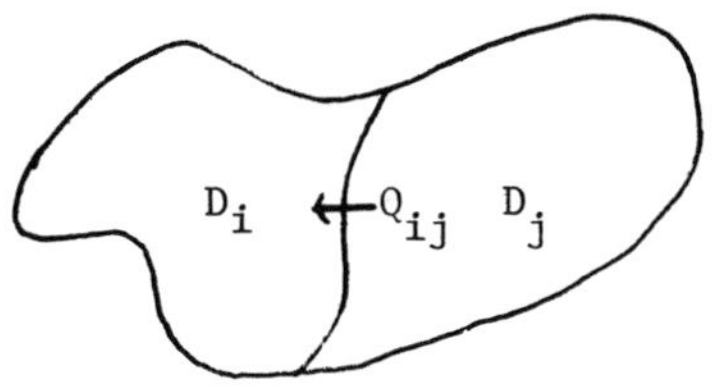

We called the partition Δ the cross-cut partition of the domain D, if Δ consists of straight lines crossing over D.

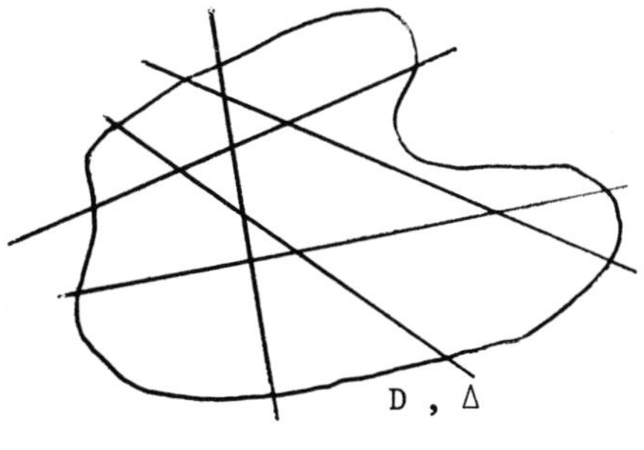

We cite a theorem from ([1]) that gives the dimension of the spline space over cross-cut partition.

Theorem Let D be a simply connected domain in R^2, and Δ_c is a cross-cut partition of D with L cross-cuts and V interior vertices $A_1,\dots,A_V$ in D such that n_i cross-cuts intersect at A_i, $i=1,\dots,v$. Then

$$\dim S_k^u(\Delta_c) = \binom{k+2}{2} + L\binom{k-u+1}{2} + \sum_{i=1}^{V} d_k^u(n_i),$$

where $0 \le u \le k-1$, and $d_k^u(n_i)$ is given by (3).

Proposition For any given triangulation Δ, there exists at any interior vertex, three edges on which the smoothing cofactors have not been fixed by the conformality conditions at other interior vertices.

Proof We shall present the proof by induction on the number of interior vertices. Let R(A) denote the polygon of the union of all triangles surrounding the interior vertex A.

$$R(A_1, A_2,\dots,A_r) = \bigcup_{i=1}^{r} R(A_i)$$

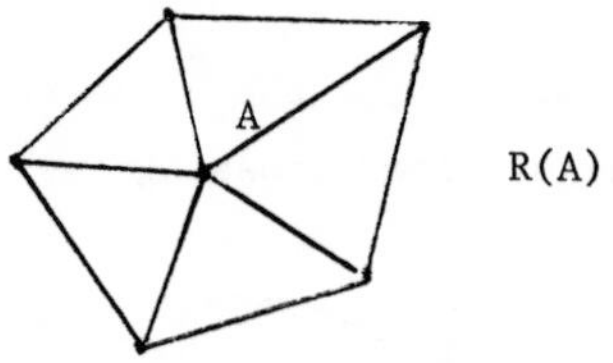

Observe that the proposition is obviously true when Δ has no interior vertex.

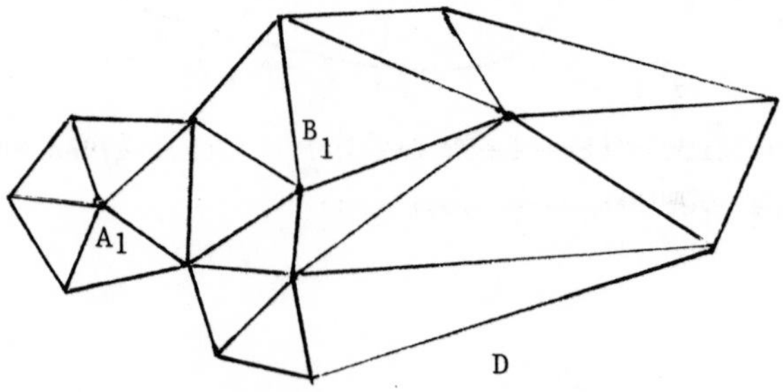

Now, we take any interior vertex A_1 of the triangulation Δ . It is clear that the proposition holds on the polygon $R(A_1)$. If all boundary vertices of $R(A_1)$ are boundary vertices of D, then we can take another vertex B_1 of the triangulation Δ , and repeat the above argument. Otherwise, we may take any interior vertex A_2 of the triangulation Δ that joints A_1 and then consider two cases,in each case we may take the three heavy lines:

1° When A_2 is a "convex" boundary vertex of $R(A_1)$,

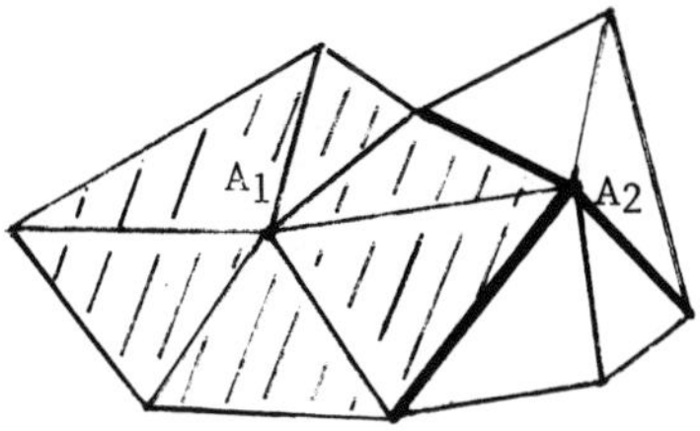

2° When A_2 is a "concave" boundary vertex of $R(A_1)$.

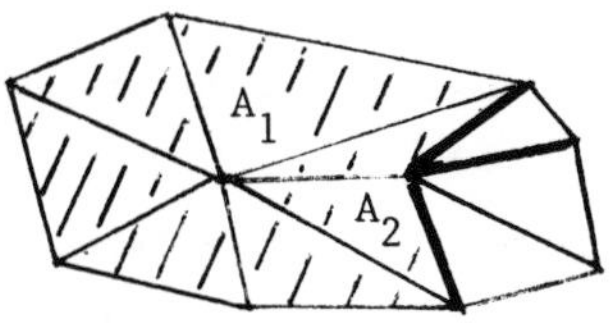

or

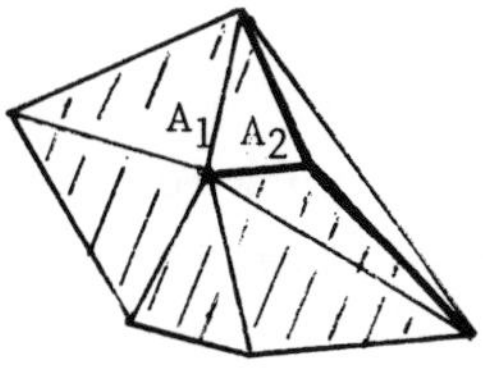

Using Euler formular, the polygon $R(A_1,A_2)$ has β +3 interior edges, where β is the number of all boundary vertices of $R(A_1,A_2)$, and $\beta > 3$. Hence the proposition still holds on $R(A_1,A_2)$. By the same token, we may conclude inductively from $R(A_1,\ldots,A_k)$ to $R(A_1,\ldots,A_k,A_{k+1})$. This summaries the proof of the proposition.

Now, we discuss the problem of dimension. According to Lemma 2 and Euler's formula,

$$(5) \qquad \dim S_k^1(\Delta) = \binom{k+2}{2} + (2\alpha + 3\delta + \beta - 3)\binom{k}{2} - \tau$$

where

β --- the number of all boundary vertices

δ --- the number of "singular" interior vertices for which the adjacent edges of each edge are collinear.

α --- the number of all non-singular interior vertices

τ --- the rank of the coefficient matrix of the linear equations determined by the global conformality condition (1).

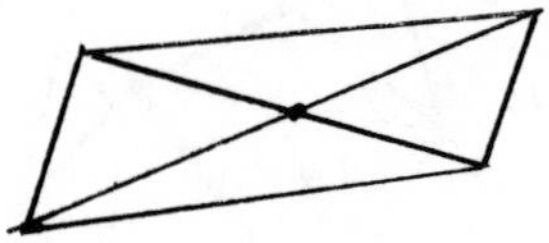

(local simple cross-cut)
"Singular" point

Using the proposition, τ is equal to the summation of all ranks of the coefficient matrix of the linear equations determined by the conformality condition corresponding to every interior vertex.
Note that for each singular vertex, there will be two edges on which their smoothing cofactors are free (when k=4, freedom will be 13). Therefore

$$(6) \qquad \tau = \begin{cases} 3\alpha + 2\delta, & \text{when } k=2 \\ 7\alpha + 6\delta, & \text{when } k=3 \\ 12\alpha + 11\delta, & \text{when } k=4. \end{cases}$$

Combining (5) and (6), we obtain

$$(7) \qquad \dim S_2^1(\Delta) = 3+\beta+\delta$$

$$(8) \qquad \dim S_3^1(\Delta) = 1+2\alpha+3\beta+3\delta$$

$$(9) \qquad \dim S_4^1(\Delta) = -3+6\alpha+6\beta+7\delta$$

For the space $S_2^1(\Delta)$, however, we found that there exist some singular cases.

Definition Denote by A the convex quadrilateral consists of two adjacent triangles of triangulation Δ. Consider a new triangulation $\bar{\Delta}$ produced by connecting another diagonal L_A of A.

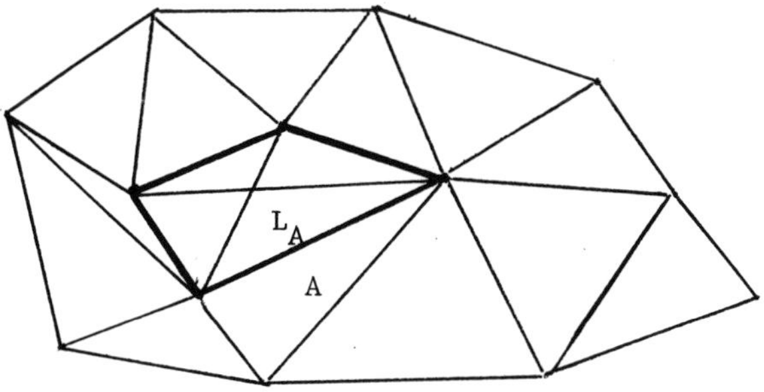

We will say that A has a guasi-singular vertex, if there is a so-called "local" triangulation (littler) $\Delta_1 \subset \bar{\Delta}$, such that any boundary edges of A is not the boundary edges of Δ_1, and the smoothing cofactors of the diagonal L_A of A are both vanishing.

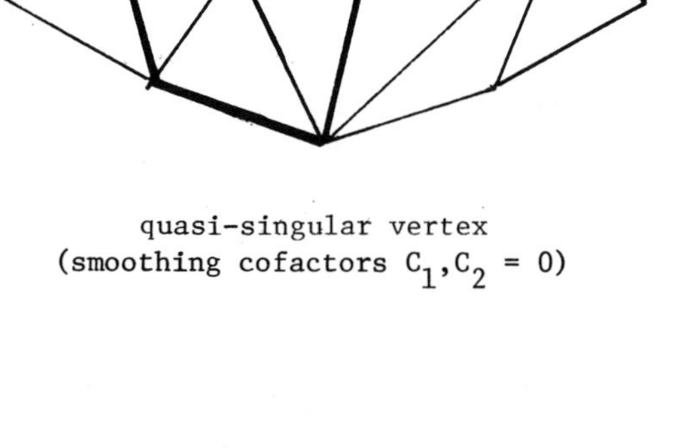

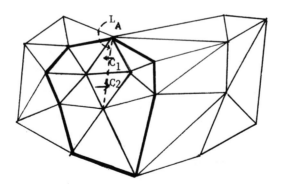

quasi-singular vertex
(smoothing cofactors $C_1, C_2 = 0$)

<u>Example 1</u> dim S_2^1=7, dim s_2^1=7, and C_1=C_2=0. (fig. a, Morgan-Scott, 1977)
So, Morgan-Scott's example has a quasi-singular vertex.

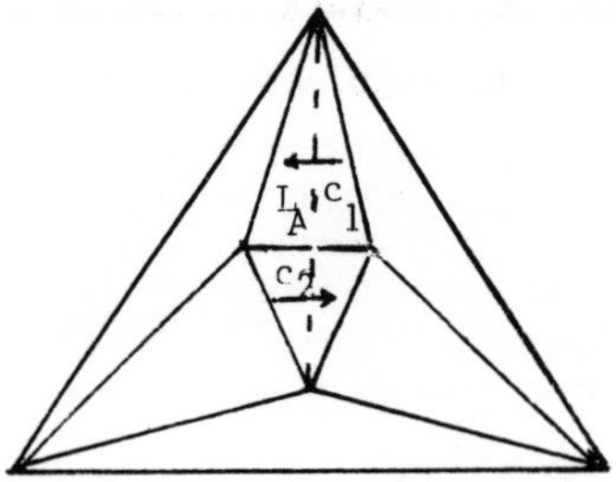

fig. a

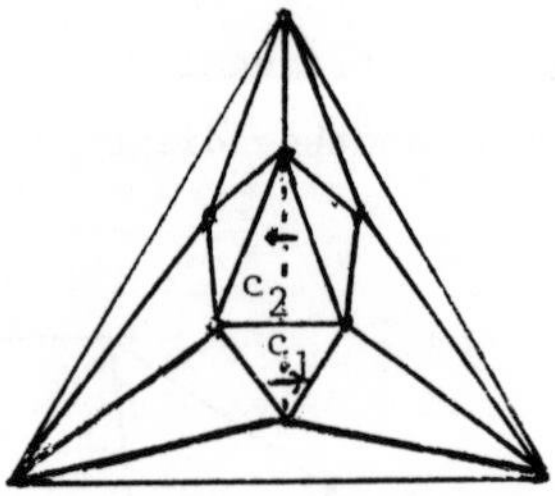

fig. b

<u>Example 2</u> dim $S_2^1(\Delta)$=7, dim $s_2^1(\bar{\Delta})$=7, and C_1=C_2=0. (fig. b)

In addition, we found other so-called "singular structures". They are different from the structures provided with a quasi-singular vertex:

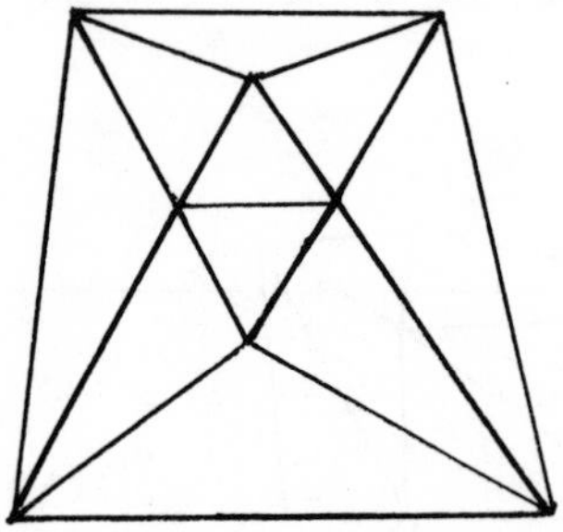

dim $S_2^1(\Delta_1)$ = 8

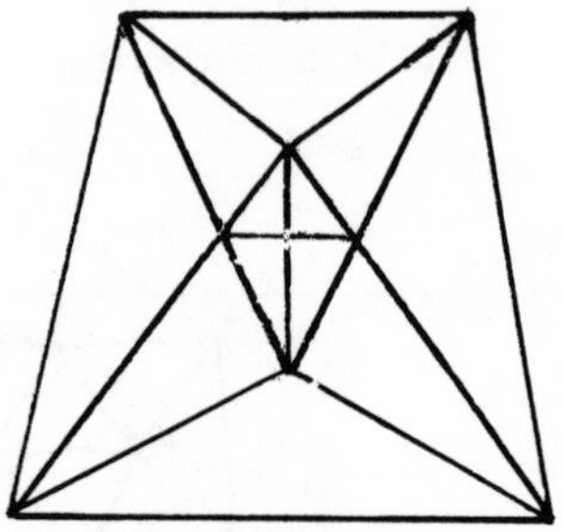

dim $S_2^1(\Delta_2)$ = 9

These singular structures do not satisfy the formula (7). Besides, there exist some nonsymmetrical triangulations that also contribute singularities. For example

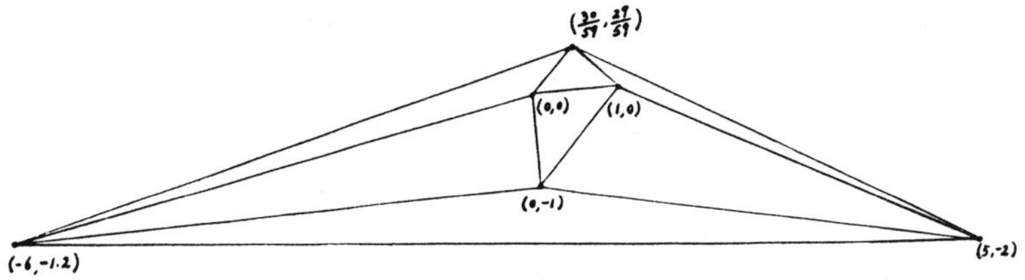

$$\dim S_2^1(\ \Delta\ ) = 7$$

In fact, for every Morgan-Scott like triangulation Δ (see fig.)

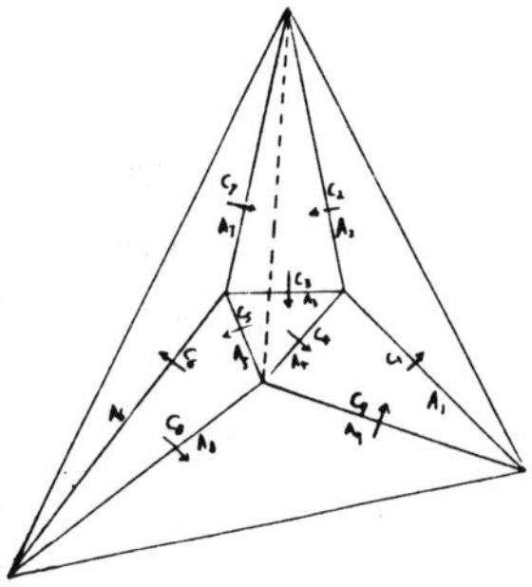

the dim $S_2^1(\ \Delta\ )=7$, if it satisfies the following condition

$$\begin{vmatrix} (A_5-A_7) & (A_5-A_6) & (A_4-A_2) & (A_4-A_1) \\ (A_5-A_8) & (A_5-A_9) & (A_4-A_8) & (A_4-A_9) \end{vmatrix} = 0$$

where A_i is the slope of respective line. From above, the formula (7) has to be modified into the following form:

$$(7') \qquad \dim S_2^1(\ \Delta\ ) = 3+\beta+\delta+\delta_q+\delta_s\ ,$$

where

Δ --- any given triangulation

β --- the number of all boundary vertices,

δ --- the number of all singular vertices,

δ_q --- the number of all quasi-singular vertices,

δ_s --- the sum of the additive dimensions produced by every singular structure.

The characterization of the singular structures is needed and it is left for future investigation. However we make an

Remark For the space $S_3^1(\Delta)$ and $S_4^1(\Delta)$, the quasi-singular vertices, and all singular structures that we have found in $S_2^1(\Delta)$ are vanishing.

References

1. Chui,C. K. and Wang, R. H. Multivariate splinespaces, J. Math. Analy. and Appl., 92(1983), 533-551.
2. Farin, G. Bezier Polynomials over Triangles and the construction of piecewise C^r-Polynomials.(to appear)
3. Morgan, J. and Scott, R. The dimension of the space of C^1-piecewise Polynomials, Unpublished manuscript.
4. Morgan and Scott, R. A nodal basis for C^1 piece polynomials of degree n 5, Math. Comp., 29(1975), 736-740.
5. Schumaker, L. L. On the dimension of spaces of piecewise polynomials in two variables, in: Multivariate Approximation Theory, ed. by W. Schempp and K. Zeller, ISBN 51, Birk hauser, Basel, (1979), 396-412.
6. Schumaker, L. L. Bounds on the dimension of multivariate piecewise polynomials, Rocky Mountain J.,(to Appear).
7. Strang, G. The dimension of piecewise polynomial spaces, and one-sided approximation, in: Lecture Notes in Mathematics, ed. by A. Dold etc., No.363(1974), 144-152.
8. Wang, R. H. The structural characterization and interpolation for multivariate splines, Acta Math. Sinica, 18(1975). 91-105.
9. Wang, R. H. On the analysis of multivariate splines in the case of arbitrary partition, Scientia Sinica, Math. I, 1979, 215-226.
10. Wang, R. H. The dimension and basis of spaces of Multivariate splines, Journal of Computational and Applied Mathematics, Vol. 12, No.1(1985). (in print).

International Series of
Numerical Mathematics, Vol. 75

On Bivariate Vertex Splines

C. K. Chui* and M. J. Lai

Department of Mathematics
Texas A&M University
College Station, TX 77843 USA

A vertex spline is one whose support contains exactly one interior vertex. Existence, construction, and approximation properties of bivariate vertex splines on triangulated regions are studied. Applications to interpolation and quasi-interpolation for unidiagonal triangulations are also discussed.

§1. Introduction

Suppose that we are given a triangulation Δ of a region D in the plane R^2 and are required to construct functions f whose restrictions to each triangular cell are bivariate polynomials of certain total degree so that they approximate the solution of a boundary value problem, say, or approximate and/or interpolate certain discrete data, we usually determine f as linear combinations of a certain basis $\{s_i\}$. In practice, it is most desirable, especially when finite element methods are used (cf. [6], p. 1129), that the supports of s_i are as small as possible, and in many situations, such as surface fitting problems, certain degree of smoothness is imposed on f. For instance, when continuous piecewise linear polynomials are used in the approximation problem, Courant basis elements [3] are usually chosen as the basis functions s_i.

It is clear that when higher degree polynomials are allowed, there is a better chance of achieving higher degree of smoothness and

*Supported by the U. S. Army Research Office under Contract No. DAAG 29-84-K-0154.

being able to construct s_i with smaller supports. However, although the smallest support is a single triangle, functions s_i with supports consisting of one or even two triangular cells are less useful since they, and any linear combination of them, have to vanish on all edges and vertices of the triangulation Δ. The smallest support without this "defect" is one which is a union of triangular cells sharing a common vertex as the only interior vertex of the support. We will call the basis functions with such supports vertex splines (or V-splines). Courant basis elements are certainly examples of V-splines. This paper is devoted to the study of existence, construction, and approximation properties of V-splines. Bézier representations of the polynomial pieces will be used, and a tool we develop to achieve our purposes efficiently is to express Taylor polynomials in terms of Bézier representations. This, together with the smoothing conditions, will be formulated in the next section. Existence theorems and characterizations in terms of areas of the appropriate triangles will be obtained in Section 3. The final section will be devoted to some important examples of V-splines, their applications to interpolation and quasi-interpolation, and the study of the order of approximation.

2. Preliminary results

Let $V_1 = (x_1,y_1)$, $V_2 = (x_2,y_2)$, and $V_3 = (x_3,y_3)$ be noncollinear points in the real plane R^2 and set

$$\delta = \begin{vmatrix} 1 & x_1 & y_1 \\ 1 & x_2 & y_2 \\ 1 & x_3 & y_3 \end{vmatrix}.$$

Then $\delta \neq 0$, and every point $X = (x,y)$ in R^2 can be expressed as

$$X = u_1V_1 + u_2V_2 + u_3V_3$$

where

$$u_1\delta = \begin{vmatrix} 1 & x & y \\ 1 & x_2 & y_2 \\ 1 & x_3 & y_3 \end{vmatrix}, \quad u_2\delta = \begin{vmatrix} 1 & x_1 & y_1 \\ 1 & x & y \\ 1 & x_3 & y_3 \end{vmatrix}, \quad u_3\delta = \begin{vmatrix} 1 & x_1 & y_1 \\ 1 & x_2 & y_2 \\ 1 & x & y \end{vmatrix}.$$

It is clear that $u_1 + u_2 + u_3 = 1$ independent of (x,y), and (u_1,u_2,u_3) is usually called the barycentric coordinate representation of X with respect to the closed triangular region $T(V_1,V_2,V_3)$ with vertices at V_1, V_2, V_3.

Let P_n be a polynomial with total degree at most n. Then P_n may be expressed as a <u>Taylor polynomial</u>

(1) $$P_n(x,y) = \sum_{i+j\leq n} c_{ij}(x - x_1)^i(y - y_1)^j,$$

where $0 \leq i,\ j \leq n$, or as a <u>Bézier polynomial</u>

(2) $$P_n(u_1,u_2,u_3) = \sum_{i_1+i_2+i_3=n} a_{i_1i_2i_3}\, \phi^n_{i_1i_2i_3}(u_1,u_2,u_3),$$

where $0 \leq i_1, i_2, i_3 \leq n$ and

(3) $$\phi^n_{i_1i_2i_3}(u_1,u_2,u_3) = \frac{n!}{i_1!i_2!i_3!} u_1^{i_1} u_2^{i_2} u_3^{i_3}.$$

Note that $0 \leq u_1, u_2, u_3 \leq 1$ so that $\phi^n_{i_1i_2i_3} \geq 0$ if and only if $X = (x,y)$ lies on the closed triangular region $T(V_1,V_2,V_3)$. It is convenient to arrange the <u>Bézier coefficients</u> $a_{i_1i_2i_3}$ of $P_n(u_1,u_2,u_3)$ in a triangular array as shown in Fig. 1. For the same polynomial P_n, we will give the relationship between its Taylor coefficients c_{ij} and Bézier coefficients $a_{i_1i_2i_3}$. First, we need the following notation. Let $A = (a_1,a_2)$ and $B = (b_1,b_2)$. The derivative of a function f along the directed line segment $B-A = (b_1-a_1,\ b_2-a_2)$ at A is

(4) $$(D_{B-A}f)(A) = \frac{d}{dt} f(A + t(B-A))\Big|_{t=0} .$$

It is clear that

(5) $$(D_{B-A}f)(A) = (b_1-a_1) \frac{\partial}{\partial x} f(A) + (b_2-a_2) \frac{\partial}{\partial y} f(A) .$$

If f is the Bézier polynomial $P_n(u_1,u_2,u_3)$ given by (2), then it is also clear that

(6) $$(D_{V_2-V_1}P_n)(u_1,u_2,u_3) = \left(\frac{\partial}{\partial u_2} P_n - \frac{\partial}{\partial u_1} P_n\right)(u_1,u_2,u_3) .$$

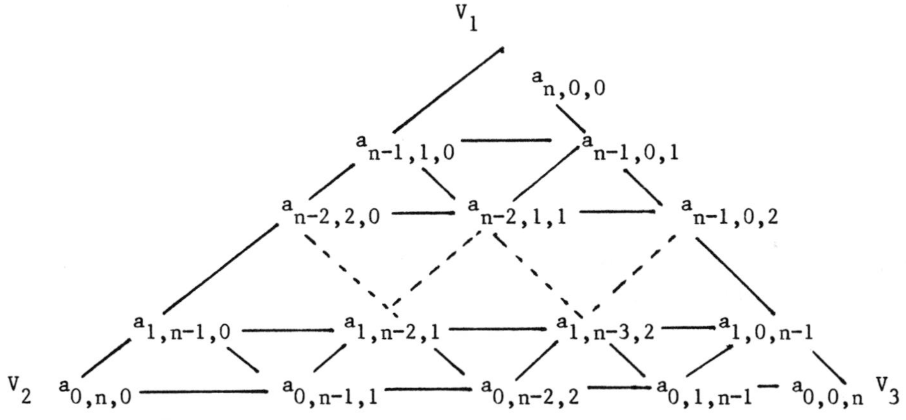

Fig. 1

Let Δ_{21}, Δ_{31}, and Δ_{32} be partial divided differences defined by

$$\Delta_{21}a_{i_1 i_2 i_3} = a_{i_1,i_2+1,i_3} - a_{i_1+1,i_2,i_3} ,$$

$$\Delta_{31}a_{i_1 i_2 i_3} = a_{i_1,i_2,i_3+1} - a_{i_1+1,i_2,i_3} ,$$

$$\Delta_{32}a_{i_1 i_2 i_3} = a_{i_1,i_2,i_3+1} - a_{i_1,i_2+1,i_3} .$$

Then (6) becomes

(7) $$(D_{V_2-V_1}P_n)(u_1,u_2,u_3) = n \sum_{i_1+i_2+i_3=n-1} \Delta_{21}a_{i_1i_2i_3}\phi^{n-1}_{i_1i_2i_3}(u_1,u_2,u_3).$$

As usual, we also use the notation $(D^i_{B-A}D^j_{C-A}f)(A) = D_{B-A}(D^{i-1}_{B-A}D^j_{C-A}f)(A) = (D^i_{B-A}D_{C-A}D^{j-1}_{C-A}f)(A)$ with $(D^0_{B-A}f)(A) = f(A)$. We have the following result.

THEOREM 1. Let f have continuous partial derivatives up to order n around V_1. Then the Taylor polynomial P_n of f at V_1 can be written as

(8) $$P_n(x,y) = P_n(u_1,u_2,u_3) =$$

$$\sum_{i_1+i_2+i_3=n} \sum_{t=0}^{i_2} \binom{i_2}{t} \sum_{s=0}^{i_3} \binom{i_3}{s} \frac{(n-s-t)!}{n!}\left(D^t_{V_2-V_1}D^s_{V_3-V_1}f\right)(V_1)\phi^n_{i_1i_2i_3}(u_1,u_2,u_3).$$

REMARK 1. If $P_n(x,y)$ has the Taylor representation at $V_1 = (x_1,y_1)$ given by (1), then it is clear that

(9) $$\left(D^t_{V_2-V_1}D^s_{V_3-V_1}P_n\right)(V_1)$$

$$= \sum_{k=0}^{t+s} \sum_{i+j=k} \binom{t}{i}\binom{s}{j}(x_2-x_1)^i(y_2-y_1)^{t-i}(x_3-x_1)^j(y_3-y_1)^{s-j}k!(t+s-k)!c_{k,t+s-k}.$$

Hence, the Bézier coefficients can be expressed in terms of the Taylor coefficients at a vertex of the triangular region.

Proof of Theorem 1. We will use induction on the degree n. For $n = 0$, (8) is trivially true. Let $Q_{n-1}(x,y)$ be the Taylor polynomial of total degree $n-1$ of $(D_{V_2-V_1}f)(x,y)$ at V_1, and assume that (8) holds for $Q_{n-1}(x,y)$ with f replaced by $D_{V_2-V_1}f$. Let $R_n(x,y)$ be the polynomial on the right-hand side of (8) then $R_n(V_1) = R_n(1,0,0) = f(V_1)$, and by (7),

$$(D_{V_2-V_1}R_n)(x,y)$$

$$= n \sum_{i_1+i_2+i_3=n-1} \Delta_{21}\Big(\sum_{t=0}^{i_2}\binom{i_2}{t}\sum_{s=0}^{i_3}\binom{i_3}{s}\frac{(n-s-t)!}{n!}(D^t_{V_2-V_1}D^s_{V_3-V_1}f)(V_1)\Big)$$

$$\cdot\ \phi^{n-1}_{i_1i_2i_3}(u_1,u_2,u_3)\ .$$

We first note that

$$n\Delta_{21}\Big(\sum_{t=0}^{i_2}\binom{i_2}{t}\sum_{s=0}^{i_3}\binom{i_3}{s}\frac{(n-s-t)!}{n!}(D^t_{V_2-V_1}D^s_{V_3-V_1}f)(V_1)\Big)$$

$$= \sum_{t=0}^{i_2+1}\binom{i_2+1}{t}\sum_{s=0}^{i_3}\binom{i_3}{s}\frac{(n-s-t)!}{(n-1)!}(D^t_{V_2-V_1}D^s_{V_3-V_1}f)(V_1)$$

$$- \sum_{t=0}^{i_2}\binom{i_2}{t}\sum_{s=0}^{i_3}\binom{i_3}{s}\frac{(n-s-t)!}{(n-1)!}(D^t_{V_2-V_1}D^s_{V_3-V_1}f)(V_1)$$

$$= \sum_{s=0}^{i_3}\binom{i_3}{s}\frac{(n-s-i_2-1)!}{(n-1)!}(D^{i_2+1}_{V_2-V_1}D^s_{V_3-V_1}f)(V_1)$$

$$+ \sum_{t=1}^{i_2}\frac{i_2!}{(t-1)!(i_2-t+1)!}\sum_{s=0}^{i_3}\binom{i_3}{s}\frac{(n-s-t)!}{(n-1)!}(D^t_{V_2-V_1}D^s_{V_3-V_1}f)(V_1)$$

$$= \sum_{t=0}^{i_2}\binom{i_2}{t}\sum_{s=0}^{i_3}\binom{i_3}{s}\frac{((n-1)-s-t)!}{(n-1)!}(D^t_{V_2-V_1}D^s_{V_3-V_1}(D_{V_2-V_1}f))(V_1)\ .$$

That is, $(D_{V_2-V_1}R_n)(x,y) = Q_{n-1}(x,y)$ by the induction hypothesis. Since $Q_{n-1}(x,y)$ is the (n-1)st degree Taylor polynomial of $(D_{V_2-V_1}f)(x,y)$ at V_1, we have

$$(D^i_{V_2-V_1} D^j_{V_3-V_1} Q_{n-1})(V_1)$$

$$= \left(D^i_{V_2-V_1} D^j_{V_3-V_1} D_{V_2-V_1} f\right)(V_1) = \left(D^{i+1}_{V_2-V_1} D^j_{V_3-V_1} f\right)(V_1) .$$

Hence, it follows that

$$\left(D^{i+1}_{V_2-V_1} D^j_{V_3-V_1} R_n\right)(V_1) = \left(D^{i+1}_{V_2-V_1} D^j_{V_3-V_1} f\right)(V_1)$$

for all i and j with $0 \leq i,j \leq n-1$ and $0 \leq i+j \leq n-1$. Similarly, we also have

$$\left(D^i_{V_2-V_1} D^{j+1}_{V_3-V_1} R_n\right)(V_1) = \left(D^i_{V_2-V_1} D^{j+1}_{V_3-V_1} f\right)(V_1)$$

for the same values of i and j. That is, the right-hand side expression $R_n(x,y)$ in (8) is the nth degree Taylor polynomial of $f(x,y)$ at V_1. This completes the proof of the theorem.

Now, let $T_1 = T_1(V_1,V_2,V_3)$ and $T_2 = T_2(V_1,V_4,V_2)$ be two closed triangular regions with common edge V_1V_2 (cf. Fig. 2). Consider a function F in $C^r(T_1 \cup T_2)$, $r \geq 0$, such that

$$F\big|_{T_1} = P_n \quad \text{and} \quad F\big|_{T_2} = \hat{P}_n$$

where P_n and $\hat{P}_n$ are polynomials of total degree at most n, and denote their Bézier polynomials by (2) and

$$\text{(10)} \qquad \hat{P}_n(v_1,v_2,v_3) = \sum_{i_1+i_2+i_3=n} b_{i_1i_2i_3} \phi^n_{i_1i_2i_3}(v_1,v_2,v_3)$$

respectively, with Bézier coefficients listed in triangular arrays as shown in Fig. 2.

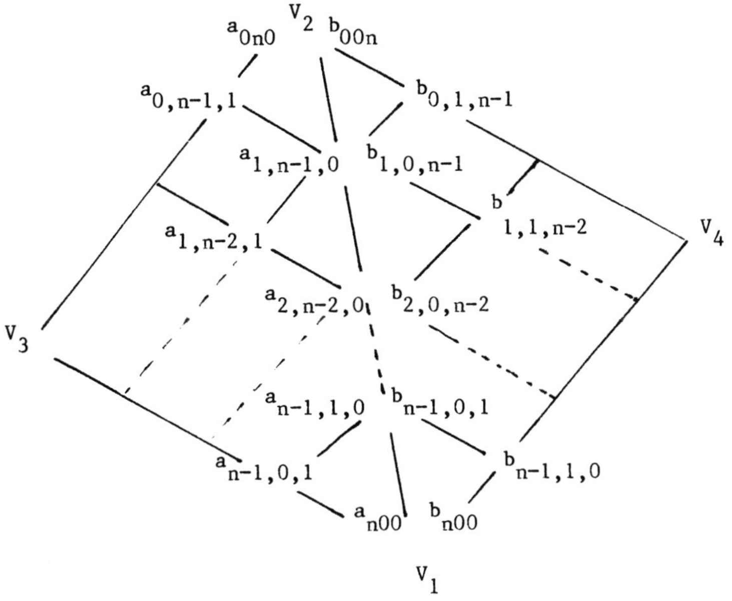

Fig. 2

Let (u_1^0, u_2^0, u_3^0) be the barycentric coordinate representation of V_4 with respect to T_1; that is, $V_4 = u_1^0 V_1 + u_2^0 V_2 + u_3^0 V_3$. Then it follows from (6) that

$$(11) \qquad (D_{V_4 - V_1} \hat{P}_n)(v_1, v_2, v_3) = \left(\frac{\partial}{\partial v_2} \hat{P}_n - \frac{\partial}{\partial v_1} \hat{P}_n\right)(v_1, v_2, v_3) .$$

Since $V_4 - V_1 = u_2^0(V_2 - V_1) + u_3^0(V_3 - V_1)$ and F is in $C^r(T_1 \cup T_2)$, we have

$$(D^{\ell}_{V_4 - V_1} \hat{P}_n)\big|_{V_1 V_2} = (u_2^0 D_{V_2 - V_1} + u_3^0 D_{V_3 - V_1})^{\ell} \, P_n\big|_{V_1 V_2} ,$$

so that by (7) and (11),

$$\frac{n!}{(n-\ell)!} \sum_{i_1+i_2+i_3=n-\ell} \Delta_{21}^{\ell}\, b_{i_1i_2i_3}\phi^{n-\ell}_{i_1i_2i_3}(v_1,v_2,v_3)\Big|_{V_1V_2}$$

$$= \sum_{j=0}^{\ell} \binom{\ell}{j}(u_2^0)^j(u_3^0)^{\ell-j} D^j_{V_2-V_1} D^{\ell-j}_{V_3-V_1} P_n\Big|_{V_1V_2}$$

$$= \sum_{j=0}^{\ell} \binom{\ell}{j}(u_2^0)^j(u_3^0)^{\ell-j} \frac{n!}{(n-j)!}\ \frac{(n-j)!}{(n-j-\ell+j)!}$$

$$\cdot \sum_{i_1+i_2+i_3=n-j-\ell+j} \Delta_{31}^{\ell-j}\ \Delta_{21}^{j}\ a_{i_1i_2i_3}\ \phi^{n-j-\ell+j}_{i_1i_2i_3}(u_1,u_2,u_3)\Big|_{V_1V_2}$$

$$= \frac{n!}{(n-\ell)!} \sum_{j=0}^{\ell} \binom{\ell}{j}(u_2^0)^j(u_3^0)^{\ell-j}$$

$$\cdot \sum_{i_1+i_2+i_3=n-\ell} \Delta_{31}^{\ell-j}\Delta_{21}^{j} a_{i_1i_2i_3}\phi^{n-\ell}_{i_1i_2i_3}(u\ ,u\ ,u\ )\Big|_{V_1V_2}\ ;$$

or equivalently, using $u_1 = v_1$, $u_2 = v_3$, and $u_3 = v_2 = 0$ on V_1V_2, we obtain

$$\sum_{i_1+i_2+i_3=n-\ell} \Delta_{21}^{\ell}\ b_{i_1i_2i_3}\phi^{n-\ell}_{i_1i_2i_3}(u_1,0,u_2)$$

$$= \sum_{i_1+i_2+i_3=n-\ell}\ \sum_{j=0}^{\ell} \binom{\ell}{j}(u_2^0)^j(u_3^0)^{\ell-j}\Delta_{31}^{\ell-j}\Delta_{21}^{j} a_{i_1i_2i_3}\phi^{n-\ell}_{i_1i_2i_3}(u_1,u_2,0).$$

From the linear independence of $\phi^{n-\ell}_{i_1i_2i_3}$, it follows that, for $i = 0,\dots,n-\ell$ and $\ell = 0,\dots,r$,

$$\text{(12)}\qquad \Delta_{21}^{\ell} b_{i,0,n-\ell-i}$$

$$= \sum_{j=0}^{\ell} \binom{\ell}{j}(u_2^0)^j(u_3^0)^{\ell-j}\Delta_{31}^{\ell-j}\Delta_{21}^{j}\ a_{i,n-\ell-i,0}$$

$$= (u_2^0\Delta_{21} + u_3^0\Delta_{31})^{\ell}\ a_{i,n-\ell-i,0}\ .$$

For instance,

(13a)
$$b_{i,0,n-i} = a_{i,n-i,0}$$

(13b)
$$b_{i,1,n-i-1} - b_{i+1,0,n-i-1} = u_2^0(a_{i,n-i,0} - a_{i+1,n-i-1,0}) + u_3^0(a_{i,n-i-1,1} - a_{i+1,n-i-1,0})$$

by setting $\ell = 0$ and 1 respectively. We summarize the above result in the following

LEMMA. Let F be defined on $T_1 \cup T_2$ by $F|_{T_1} = P_n$, $F|_{T_2} = \hat{P}_n$ where P_n and $\hat{P}_n$ are as given in (2) and (10) respectively. Then $F \in C^r(T_1 \cup T_2)$ if and only if the conditions in (12) hold for $i = 0,\ldots,n-\ell$ and $\ell = 0,\ldots,r$.

REMARK 2. The above procedure to arrive at the necessary conditions (12) also shows that the conditions are sufficient. The formulation of these smoothing conditions is somewhat different from that of Farin [4].

REMARK 3. Let P_n and $\hat{P}_n$ be two nth degree Bézier polynomials on T_1 and T_2 given by (2) and (10) respectively, such that

$$(D^i_{V_2-V_1} D^j_{V_3-V_1} P_n)(V_1) = (D^i_{V_2-V_1} D^j_{V_3-V_1} f)(V_1)$$

and

$$(D^i_{V_2-V_1} D^j_{V_4-V_1} \hat{P}_n)(V_1) = (D^i_{V_2-V_1} D^j_{V_4-V_1} f)(V_1)$$

for $i+j \leq r \leq n$ and some function f which has continuous partial derivatives up to order r around V_1. Then the smoothing conditions (12) for $n-r \leq i \leq n-\ell$ and $\ell = 0,\ldots,r$ automatically hold. Hence, in constructing Hermite interpolants of class $C^r(T_1 \cup T_2)$ at V_1, the only remaining smoothing conditions in (12) for the Bézier coefficients of P_n and $\hat{P}_n$ to satisfy are those with $0 \leq i \leq n-r-1$.

REMARK 4. The results in both Theorem 1 and the above lemma can be easily generalized to the m-dimensional setting for any $m \geq 2$. More precisely, if $P_n(u_1,\ldots,u_{m+1})$ and $\hat{P}_n(v_1,\ldots,v_{m+1})$ are Bézier polynomials on the simplices $T(V_1,\ldots,V_{m+1})$ and $T(V_1,V_{m+2},V_2,\ldots,V_m)$ with common plane $V_1\ldots V_m$, then a generalization of (8) to R^m is

$$P_n(u_1,\ldots,u_{m+1})$$

$$= \sum_{i_1+\ldots+i_{m+1}=n} \sum_{t_2=0}^{i_2} \binom{i_2}{t_2} \cdots \sum_{t_{m+1}=0}^{i_{m+1}} \binom{i_{m+1}}{t_{m+1}} \frac{(n-i_2-\ldots-i_{m+1})!}{n!}$$

$$\cdot \left(D^{t_2}_{V_2-V_1} \cdots D^{t_{m+1}}_{V_{m+1}-V_1} f\right)(V_1)\phi^n_{i_1\ldots i_{m+1}}(u_1,\ldots,u_{m+1})$$

and a generalization of (12) is

$$\Delta^{\ell}_{21} b_{i_1,0,i_3,\ldots,i_{m+1}} = \left(\sum_{j=2}^{m+1} u^0_j \Delta_{j1}\right)^{\ell} a_{i_1,i_3,\ldots,i_{m+1},0}$$

where $V_{m+2} = u^0_1 V_1 + \ldots + u^0_{m+1} V_{m+1}$.

3. V-splines

Let Δ be a triangulation of a region D in R^2, r and n nonnegative integers, and $S^r_n = S^r_n(\Delta) = S^r_n(\Delta,D)$ be the space of all functions f in $C^r(D)$ whose restrictions to each cell of the triangulation Δ of D are polynomials of total degree at most n. We may assume, without loss of generality, that the interior vertices of Δ lie in D and that the triangulation Δ itself has been extended so that the closure of the union of all triangular regons contains D. We introduce the following

DEFINITION 1. An S_n^r <u>vertex spline</u> (or simply, a V-<u>spline</u>) is a function in S_n^r whose support contains exactly one vertex of Δ in its interior.

To facilitate our argument and description, we need the following notation. Let V be an interior vertex of Δ surrounded by the vertices $V_1,\ldots,V_m$, in the counterclockwise direction, in the sense that the closed triangular regions $T_1 = T_1(V,V_1,V_2)$, $T_2 = T_2(V,V_2,V_3),\ldots,$ $T_m = T_m(V\ ,V_m,V_1)$ are cells of the triangulation Δ and share the common vertex V. On each triangular region T_j, $j = 1,\ldots,m$, the Bézier polynomial of degree n defined there will always be denoted by

$$P_n^j = P_n^j(u_1^j,u_2^j,u_3^j) = \sum_{i_1+i_2+i_3=n} a^j_{i_1i_2i_3}\,\phi^n_{i_1i_2i_3}(u_1^j,u_2^j,u_3^j),$$

where $(1,0,0)$, $(0,1,0)$, and $(0,0,1)$ are the barycentric coordinates of the vertices V, V_j, and V_{j+1}, respectively (with $V_{m+1} := V_1$), of the triangle T_j. We have the following result.

THEOREM 2. <u>There exist</u> S_n^1 V-<u>splines if and only if</u> $n \geq 4$.

<u>Proof</u>. There are certainly no S_0^1 and S_1^1 V-splines. For $n = 2$, if $s \in S_2^1$ is supported by $T_1 \cup \ldots \cup T_m$ and $s|_{T_j} = P_2^j$, $j = 1,\ldots,m$, then since s vanishes outside $T_1 \cup \ldots \cup T_m$, we have $a^j_{i_1i_2i_3} = 0$ for all $j = 1,\ldots,m$ $i_1 = 0,1$ and all i_2, i_3 with $i_1 + i_2 + i_3 = 2$ by using (13a) and (13b). Choose j so that V_{j-1}, V_j, and V_{j+1} are noncollinear. Then by comparing P_2^j with P_2^{j+1} $(P_n^{n+1} := P_n^1)$ and using the same smoothing conditions, we also have $a^j_{200} = a^{j+1}_{200} = 0$, so that $a^1_{200} = \ldots = a^m_{200}$. That is, s is identically zero. For $n = 3$, the same argument yields $a^j_{i_1i_2i_3} = 0$ for all $j = 1,\ldots,m$ and $i_1 = 0,1$. By comparing P_2^j with P_2^{j+1} using (13a) and (13b), where

V_{j-1}, V_j, V_{j+1} are noncollinear, we also have $a^j_{201} = a^{j+1}_{210}$, $j = 1,\ldots,m$, $(a^{m+1}_{i_1 i_2 i_3} := a^1_{i_1 i_2 i_3})$. The same argument again gives $a^j_{300} = 0$, $j = 1,\ldots,m$. That is, s is again identically zero.

The existence of S^1_n V-splines for $n \geq 4$ is quite wasy to see since the number of restrictions governed by the smoothing conditions (13a) and (13b) is less than the number of parameters; namely, the Bézier coefficients. In fact, for $n = 4$ the difference is exactly one, and it is even larger for $n > 4$. This completes the proof of the theorem.

We remark, however, that it is quite possible that the only S^1_4 V-splines are those which vanish at their own (interior) vertices. This is certainly the case for nonuniform (or irregular) unidiagonal (or type-1) triangulation, as can be seen as a consequence of Theorem 3 that we will establish below. When this occurs, V-splines are then not very useful in applications, especially in interpolation at the vertices, since any linear combination of such V-splines has to vanish at all the vertices. For this reason, we introduce the following

DEFINITION 2. An S^r_n vertex spline s is called a V_ℓ-spline if s does not vanish at its (interior) vertex, and a V_ℓ-spline is called a $V_{\ell h}$-spline if, in addition, both its first x and y partial derivatives vanish at its vertex.

Here, we have used the subscript ℓ and the second subscript h to remind ourselves that these vertex splines are useful in Lagrange and Hermite interpolations, respectively.

To describe the existence result of S^1_4 V_ℓ-splines, we need the following notation. Let $V = (a,b)$, $V_j = (a_j,b_j)$ (with $V_{m+\ell} := V_\ell$, $a_{m+\ell} := a_\ell$, and $b_{m+\ell} := b_\ell$) denote vertices of Δ as described previously, and consider the determinants

$$\eta_{jk} = \begin{vmatrix} 1 & a & b \\ 1 & a_j & b_j \\ 1 & a_k & b_k \end{vmatrix}$$

and

$$\mu_j = \begin{vmatrix} 1 & a_j & b_j \\ 1 & a_{j+1} & b_{j+1} \\ 1 & a_{j+2} & b_{j+2} \end{vmatrix} .$$

Observe that halves of the above quantities are the "directed" areas of the triangular regions $T(V, V_j, V_k)$ and $T(V_j, V_{j+1}, V_{j+2})$ respectively. Now, consider an $s \in S_4^1$ supported by $T_1 \cup \ldots \cup T_m$, and let $s|_{T_j} = P_4^j$ as described earlier. Of course, in order to satisfy (13a) and (13b) across the exterior edges V_jV_{j+1}, we must have

$$a_{004}^j = \ldots = a_{040}^j = 0,$$

$$a_{103}^j = \ldots = a_{130}^j = 0,$$

and

$$a_{220}^j = a_{202}^j = 0 ,$$

for $j = 1, \ldots, m$. The remaining Bézier coefficients which still have to satisfy (13b) across the interior edges VV_j, $j = 1, \ldots, m$, are

$$\alpha := a_{400}^1 = \ldots = a_{400}^m ,$$

$$\beta_{j+1} := a_{310}^{j+1} = a_{301}^j$$

and

$$\gamma_j := a_{211}^j ,$$

$j = 1, \ldots, m$, with $\beta_1 := \beta_{m+1}$. There are two smoothing conditions across each VV_j that they have to satisfy, namely:

$$\beta_j - \alpha = \frac{\eta_{j,j+2}}{\eta_{j+1}} (\beta_{j+1} - \alpha) - \frac{\eta_j}{\eta_{j+1}} (\beta_{j+2} - \alpha) \tag{14}$$

and

$$\gamma_j - \beta_{j+1} = - \frac{\eta_{j,j+2}}{\eta_{j+1}} \beta_{j+1} - \frac{\eta_j}{\eta_{j+1}} (\gamma_{j+1} - \beta_{j+1}), \tag{15}$$

where $\eta_{j,\ell} := \eta_{j,m+\ell}$ and $\eta_j := \eta_{j,j+1}$, $\eta_1 := \eta_{m+1}$.

REMARK 5. Since $s(V) = \alpha$, s is a V_ℓ-spline if and only if $\alpha \neq 0$. In addition, from Theorem 1 it follows that a V_ℓ-spline s is a $V_{\ell h}$-spline if and only if $\beta_j = \alpha$ for all $j = 1,\ldots,m$. Hence an S_4^1 $V_{\ell h}$-spline s satisfying $s(V) = 1$ exists if and only if the linear system

$$(16) \qquad \gamma_j' + \frac{\eta_j}{\eta_{j+1}} \gamma_{j+1}' = -\eta_{j,j+2}/\eta_{j+1}$$

has a solution in $\gamma_j' := \gamma_j - 1$, $j = 1,\ldots,m$.

We have the following result.

THEOREM 3. _For odd_ m, _there exists exactly one_ S_4^1 $V_{\ell h}$_-spline_ s _satisfying_ $s(V) = 1$. _For even_ m, S_4^1 $V_{\ell h}$_-splines exist if and only if the condition_

$$(17) \qquad \sum_{j=1}^{m} (-1)^{j+1} \frac{\eta_{j,j+2}}{\eta_j \eta_{j+1}} = 0$$

is satisfied. Again for even m, S_4^1 V_ℓ_-splines exist if and only if the condition_

$$(18) \qquad \sum_{j=1}^{m} (-1)^{j+1} \frac{\mu_j}{\eta_j \eta_{j+1}} \beta_{j+1} = 0$$

is satisfied for some solution $\beta_1,\ldots,\beta_m$ _of the linear system_ (14) _with_ $\alpha \neq 0$.

REMARK 6. Although the above result is an existence theorem, the V_ℓ and $V_{\ell h}$-splines can actually be computed by solving (14) and (15) with $\alpha = 1$, say.

We consider the following three examples.

Example (a). For $m = 3$, there are exactly 3 linearly independent S_4^1 V-splines s_1, s_2, and s_3 satisfying

$$(19)\qquad \begin{aligned} s_1(V) &= 1\,, & \frac{\partial}{\partial x} s_1(V) &= 0, & \frac{\partial}{\partial y} s_1(V) &= 0 \\ s_2(V) &= 0\,, & \frac{\partial}{\partial x} s_2(V) &= 1, & \frac{\partial}{\partial y} s_2(V) &= 0 \\ s_3(V) &= 0\,, & \frac{\partial}{\partial x} s_3(V) &= 0, & \frac{\partial}{\partial y} s_3(V) &= 1\,. \end{aligned}$$

Hence, there are exactly 3 V_ℓ-splines s_1, s_1+s_2, and s_1+s_3, where s_1 is a $V_{\ell h}$-spline.

Example (b). For $m = 4$, S_4^1 $V_{\ell h}$-splines exist if and only if the areas of the appropriate triangles satisfy:

$$(20)\qquad \eta_{13}(\eta_1\eta_2 - \eta_3\eta_4) - \eta_{24}(\eta_2\eta_3 - \eta_1\eta_4) = 0\,.$$

If (20) is satisfied but

$$(21)\qquad \eta_2\eta_4 - \eta_1\eta_3 + \eta_{13}\eta_{24} = 0$$

is not, then every V_ℓ-spline is a $V_{\ell h}$-spline. If all of (20), (21), and

$$(22)\qquad \mu_1\beta_2\eta_3\eta_4 - \mu_2\beta_3\eta_4\eta_1 + \mu_3\beta_4\eta_1\eta_2 - \mu_4\beta_1\eta_2\eta_3 = 0$$

are satisfied, then there are exactly 3 linearly independent S_4^1 V-splines s_1, s_2, s_3 satisfying (19). Hence, under these 3 assumptions, there are 3 linearly independent V_ℓ-splines s_1, s_1+s_2, and s_1+s_3. In the particular case when V, V_1, V_3 are collinear but V, V_2, V_4 are not, then a $V_{\ell h}$-spline does not exist whenever $\eta_2\eta_3 \neq \eta_1\eta_4$.

Example (c). Consider the type-1 triangulations as shown in Fig. 3 below. From (17) and (18) it can be shown that an S_4^1

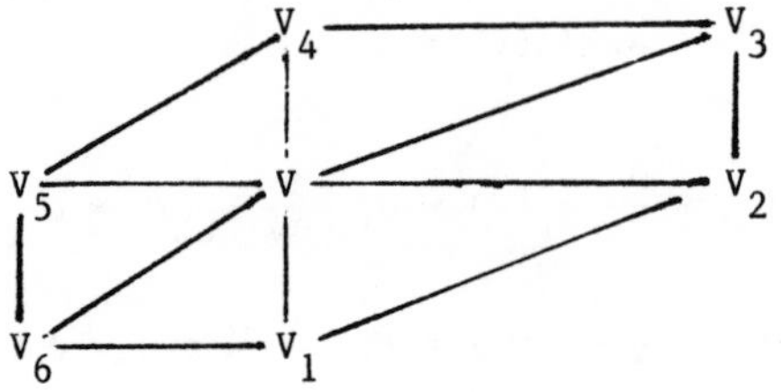

Fig. 3

V_ℓ-spline exists if and only if the two lines V_1V_2 and V_5V_4 are parallel. If V_1V_2 and V_5V_4 are parallel, then there are exactly 3 linearly independent S_4^1 V-splines s_1, s_2, and s_3 satisfying (19). If, however, V_1V_2 and V_5V_4 are not parallel, then there are 2 linearly independent S_4^1 V-splines both of which vanish at the vertex V.

Proof of Theorem 3. By Remark 5, we note that the existence of $V_{\ell h}$-splines is determined by the nonhomogeneous linear equations in (16). The coefficient matrix in (16) can be reduced by Gauss elimination to an upper-triangular matrix with all diagonal elements equal to 1 except one which is

$$1 - \prod_{i=1}^{m} (-\eta_i/\eta_{i+1}) = 1 - (-1)^m .$$

Hence, (16) has a unique solution when m is odd. For even m, the same row-reduction process of the augmented matrix yields (17) in order to preserve consistency.

To study the existence of V_ℓ-splines, we rewrite (15) into the form

$$\gamma_j + \frac{\eta_j}{\eta_{j+1}} \gamma_{j+1} = (\eta_{j+1} - \eta_{j,j+2} + \eta_j)\beta_{j+1}/\eta_{j+1}$$

$$= \frac{\mu_j}{\eta_{j+1}} \beta_{j+1} .$$

Hence, the same row-reduction procedure above yields (18) to preserve consistency. This completes the proof of the theorem.

REMARK 7. It is important to observe that the subspace generated by all S_4^1 V-splines does not contain the constant function. Indeed, if $P_4(u_1,u_2,u_3)$ with Bézier coefficients a_{i_1,i_2,i_3} is the restriction of any V-spline on any triangular region, it is necessary that $a_{220} = a_{202} = 0$. For this reason, it is sometimes essential to use higher degree V-splines.

Let r be any nonnegative integer. We now study V-splines in the space S_{4r+1}^r. We will use the convention:

$$D^\beta = \left(\frac{\partial}{\partial x}\right)^{\beta_1}\left(\frac{\partial}{\partial y}\right)^{\beta_2}, \quad \beta = (\beta_1,\beta_2),$$

and $|\beta| = \beta_1 + \beta_2$. Also, let $s^\alpha = s_V^\alpha$, $\alpha = (\alpha_1,\alpha_2)$, denote an S_{4r+1}^r V-spline satisfying

$$D^\beta s^\alpha(V) = \begin{cases} 0 & \text{if} \quad \beta \neq \alpha \\ 1 & \text{if} \quad \beta = \alpha \end{cases} . \tag{23}$$

We have the following existence result.

THEOREM 4. <u>For each ordered pair</u> α <u>with</u> $0 \leq |\alpha| \leq 2r$, <u>there exists an</u> S_{4r+1}^r <u>V-spline</u> $s^\alpha = s_V^\alpha$ <u>satisfying</u> (23).

<u>Proof</u>. Let $s \in S_{4r+1}^r$ be supported by the polygonal region $T_1 \cup \ldots \cup T_m$ with interior vertex V as described previously, and let $s|_{T_j} = P_{4r+1}^j := P^j$, with Bézier coefficients $a_{i_1 i_2 i_3}^j$, $i_1+i_2+i_3 = 4r+1$,

$j = 1,\ldots,m$. By Theorem 1, the coefficients $a^j_{i_1 i_2 i_3}$ with

(i) $0 \le i_2 + i_3 \le 2r$,

(ii) $0 \le i_1 + i_3 \le 2r$,

and

(iii) $0 \le i_1 + i_2 \le 2r$,

are uniquely determined by the Hermite data (23), $D^\beta s^\alpha(V_j) = 0$, and $D^\beta s^\alpha(V_{j+1}) = 0$, for $0 \le |\beta| \le 2r$, respectively. Applying the previous lemma to the edge $V_j V_{j+1}$, we also have

(iv) $a^j_{k,4r-k-i+1,i} = 0$

for $0 \le i \le 4r - k + 1$ and $k = 0, \ldots, r$. Furthermore, the coefficients $a^j_{k,\ell,i}$ where

(v) $r+1 \le k \le 2r \le \ell \le 3r$, $k+\ell+i = 4r+1$, $i = 1,\ldots,r$

and

(vi) $r+1 \le k \le 2r \le i \le 3r$, $k+\ell+i = 4r+1$, $\ell = 1,\ldots,r$

are governed by the smoothing conditions across the interior edges VV_j and VV_{j+1}, respectively, using the lemma. The remaining coefficients $a^j_{i_1 i_2 i_3}$ with

(vii) $r+1 \le i_1, i_2, i_3 \le 2r+1$, $i_1+i_2+i_3 = 4r+1$

are free parameters. Since the seven groups of coefficients in (i) - (vii) are pairwise disjoint, the existence of s^α_V is guaranteed.

REMARK 8. Let $\{f_{\alpha,V}$: V an interior vertex of Δ and $\alpha \in \Lambda\}$, where Λ is a subset of the set of ordered pairs β with $0 \le |\beta| \le 2r$ be given. Then the bivariate spline

$$s = \sum_V \sum_{\alpha\in\Lambda} f_{\alpha,V} s^\alpha_V \tag{24}$$

interpolates the given date in the sense that

$$D^{\alpha}s(V) = f_{\alpha,V}$$

for all $\alpha \varepsilon \Lambda$ and all interior vertices V.

We will study the order of approximation of these interpolants for some specific settings in the next section.

4. Applications

Let D be a rectangular region $[a,b] \times [c,d]$ in R^2, and let $a = x_0 < \ldots < x_{p+1} = b$, $c = y_0 < y_1 < \ldots < y_{q+1} = d$, and Δ_{pq} be a so-called unidiagonal (or type-1) triangulation of D, which is the triangulation of the $(p+1)(q+1)$ rectangular cells with edges defined by $x = x_i$ and $y = y_j$, $i = 1,\ldots,p$ and $j = 1,\ldots,q$, by drawing in all $(p+1)(q+1)$ diagonals with positive slopes. If we have $x_{i+1} - x_i = x_i - x_{i-1} = h$ and $y_{j+1} - y_j = y_j - y_{j-1} = k$, $i = 1,\ldots,p$ and $j = 1,\ldots,q$, the triangulation is said to be uniform or regular. Note that Δ_{pq} is also assumed to have been extended, by adding, say, $x = x_{-1} < a$, $x = x_{p+2} > b$, $y = y_{-1} < c$, $y = y_{q+2} > d$, and the appropriate diagonals, so that Δ_{pq} has $(p+2)(q+2)$ interior vertices. Note also that the support of each vertex spline in $S_n^r(\Delta_{pq})$ consists of $m = 6$ triangles.

In Example (c) of the previous section, we see that if the triangulation Δ_{pq} is uniform, then there are three V-splines in S_4^1 associated with each vertex. Since they satisfy (19), they can be applied to interpolating Hermite data that are sampled at the vertices. We give their Bézier coefficients (on each triangle) in Figures 4 (a), (b), (c) below.

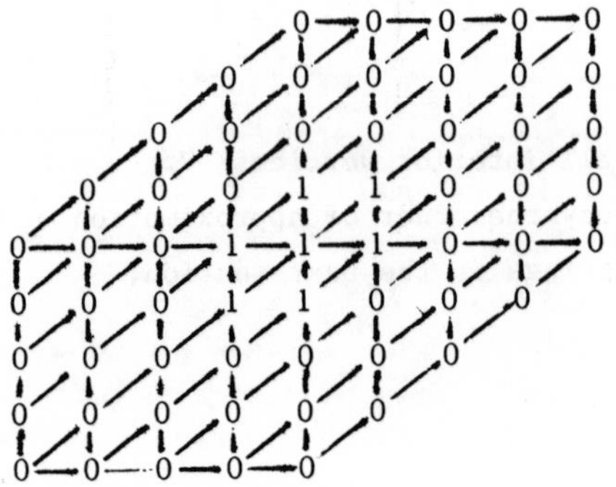

Fig 4 (a)

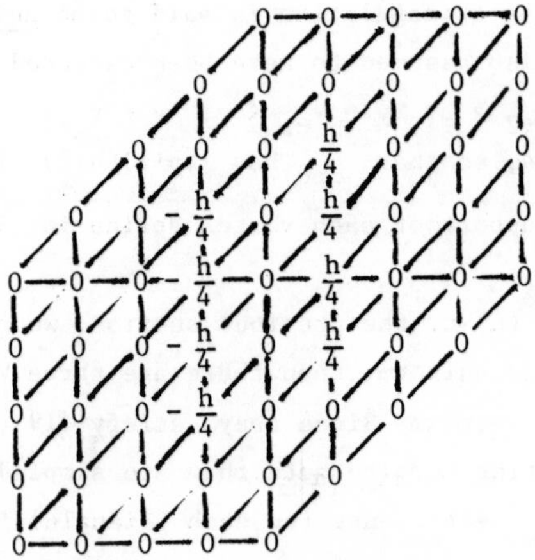

Fig 4(b)

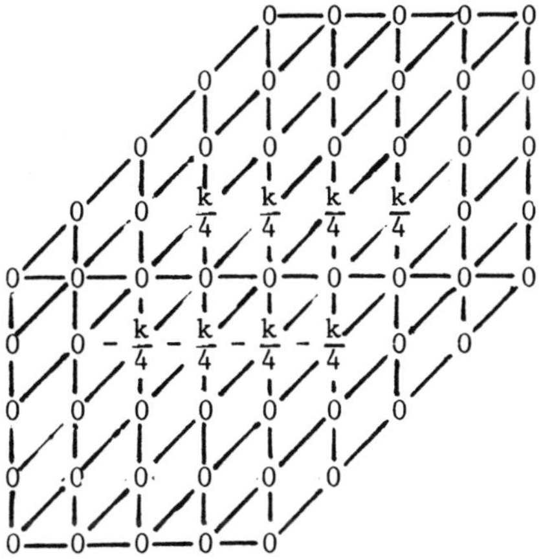

Fig 4(c)

For nonuniform triangulations Δ_{pq}, we need S_5^1 vertex splines (the lowest degree being 5). In this case, it is possible to handle Hermite data up to order two. Note that in the proof of Theorem 4, with $r = 1$, although the coefficient set in (vii) is empty, there are two Bézier coefficients in each of the six triangles, one from (v) and the other from (vi), that are governed by six smoothing conditions across the interior edges. Hence, there are still six free parameters, one for each triangle, corresponding to each V-spline $s_{ij}^{\alpha} := s^{\alpha}(V_{ij})$, $|\alpha| \leq 2$, satisfying (23) at its vertex where $V_{ij} := (x_i, y_j)$. Since each triangular cell is the intersection of the supports of 18 V-splines, 3 for each $\alpha = (\alpha_1, \alpha_2)$, it is possible to choose these 18 parameters on each triangle so that the approximation order of the Hermite interpolants

$$s_f(x,y) = \sum_{i,j} \sum_{|\alpha| \leq 2} (D^{\alpha} f(x_i, y_j)) s_{ij}^{\alpha}(x,y) \tag{25}$$

to a sufficiently smooth function f on D is maximized. We determine 15 of these parameters by requiring $s_g \equiv g$ for all polynomials g with total degree ≤ 4 and the other 3 parameters using some natural conditions on symmetry. The six vertex splines s_{ij}^{α}, where $\alpha = (0,0)$,

(1,0), (0,1), (2,0), (1,1), (0,2), at each vertex $V_{ij} = (x_i, y_j)$ are listed in Figures 5 (a) - (f), and their corresponding 3-dimensional pictures with $x_{i-1} = -1$, $x_i = 0$, $x_{i+1} = 1.2$, $y_{j-1} = -1$, $y_j = 0$, $y_{j+1} = .9$ are shown in Figures 6(a) - (f) below. Here, we have again given the Bézier coefficients of each polynomial piece and used the notation

(26) $$h_i = x_{i+1} - x_i, \quad k_j = y_{j+1} - y_j$$

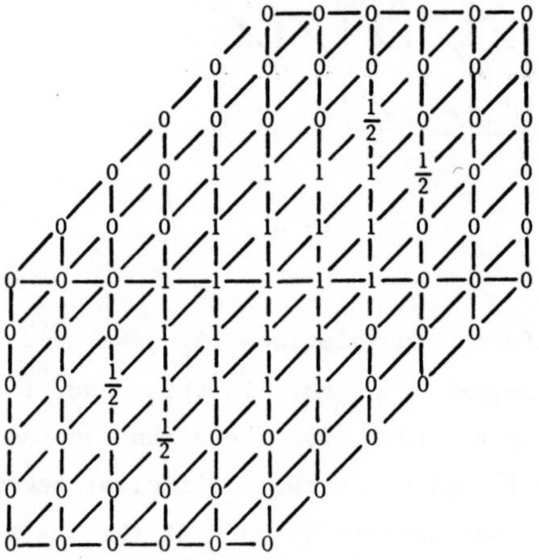

Fig 5(a): $s_{ij}^{(0,0)}$

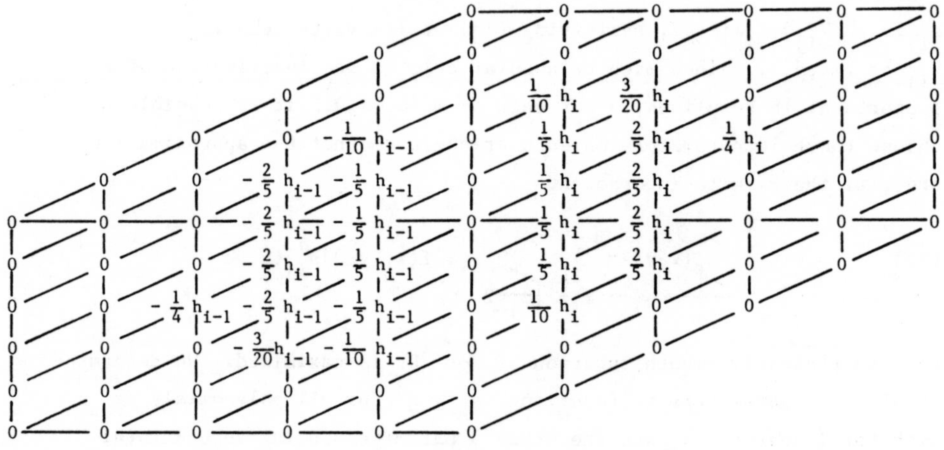

Fig 5(b): $s_{ij}^{(1,0)}$

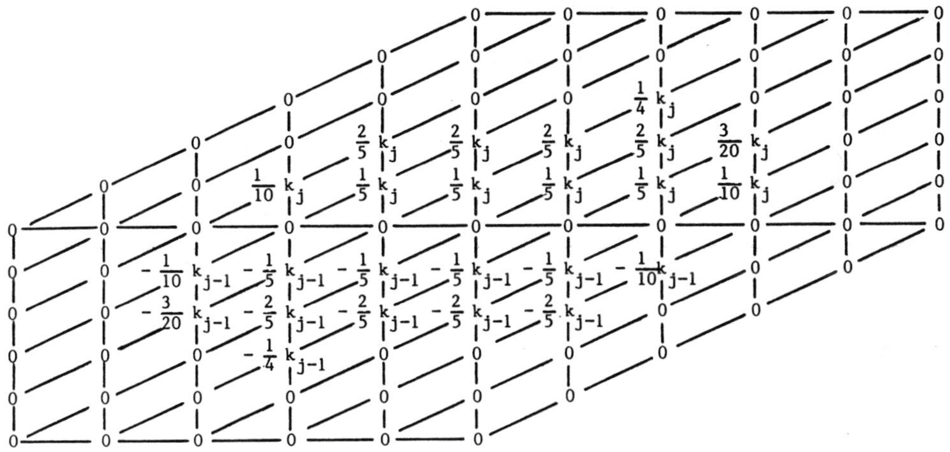

Fig 5(c): $s_{ij}^{(0,1)}$

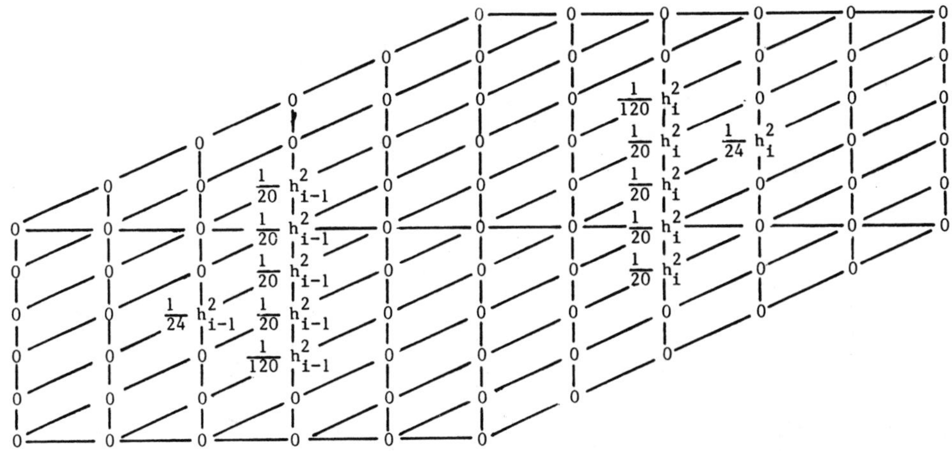

Fig. 5(d): $s_{ij}^{(2,0)}$

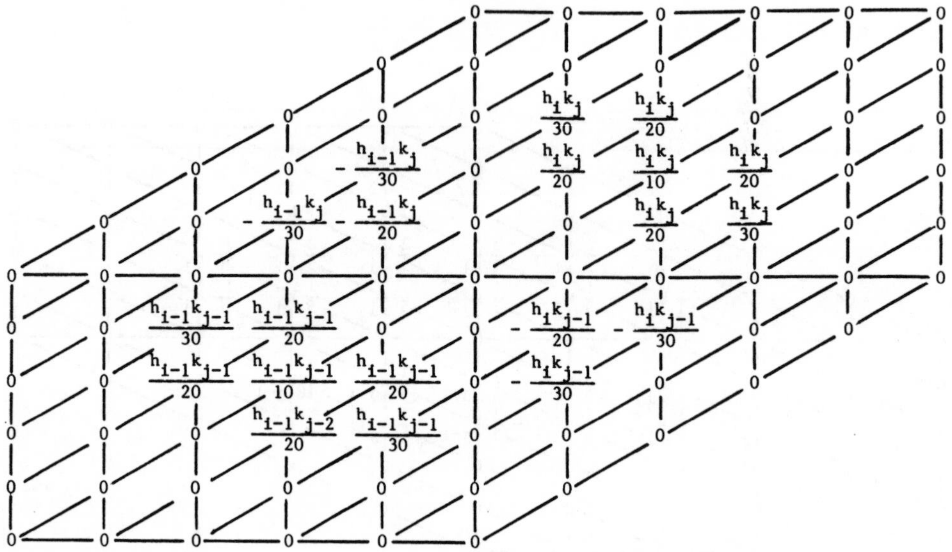

Fig 5(e): $s_{ij}^{(1,1)}$

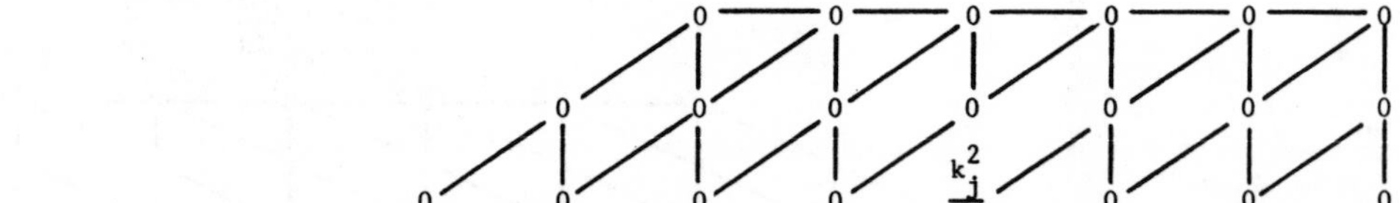

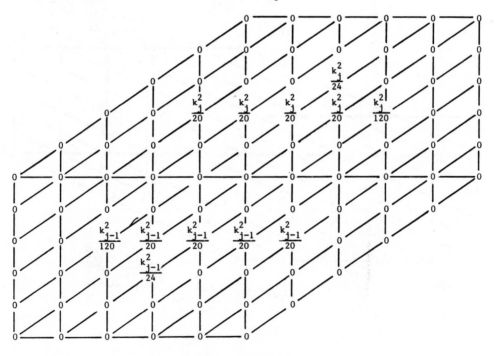

Fig 5(f): $s_{ij}^{(0,2)}$

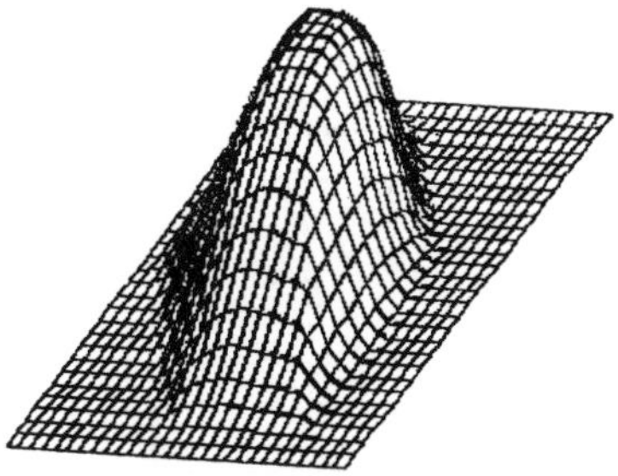

Fig 6(a): $s_{00}^{(0,0)}$

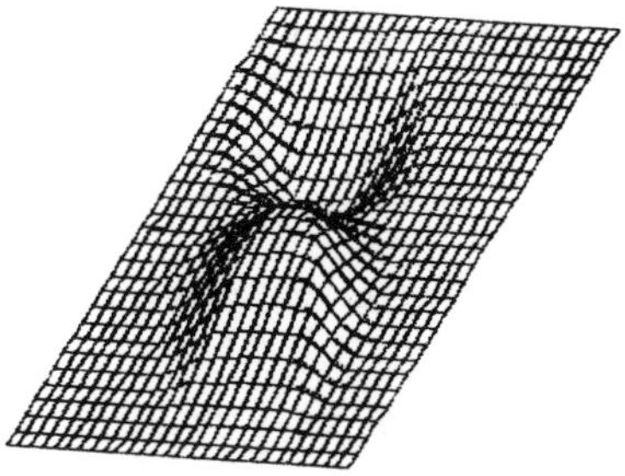

Fig 6(b): $s_{00}^{(1,0)}$

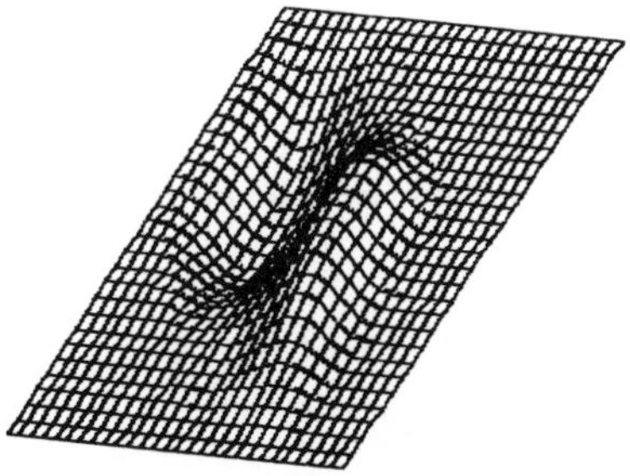

Fig 6(c): $s_{00}^{(0,1)}$

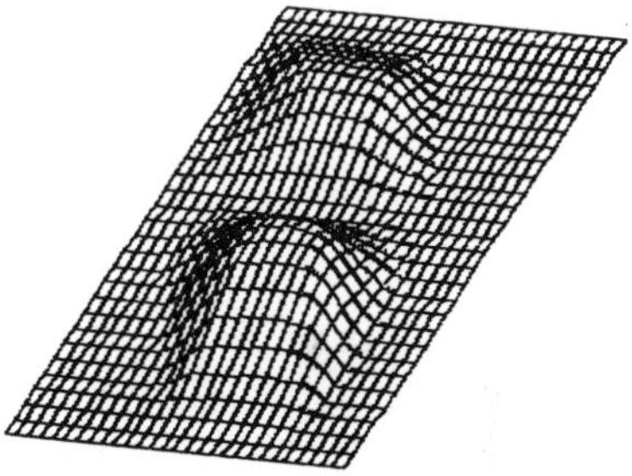

Fig 6(d): $s_{00}^{(2,0)}$

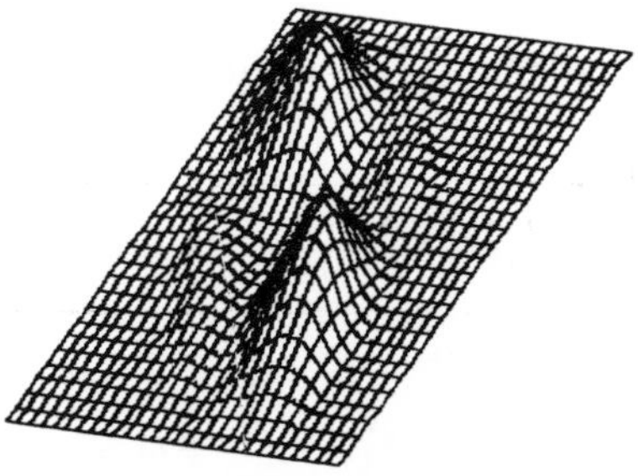

Fig 6(e): $s_{00}^{(1,1)}$

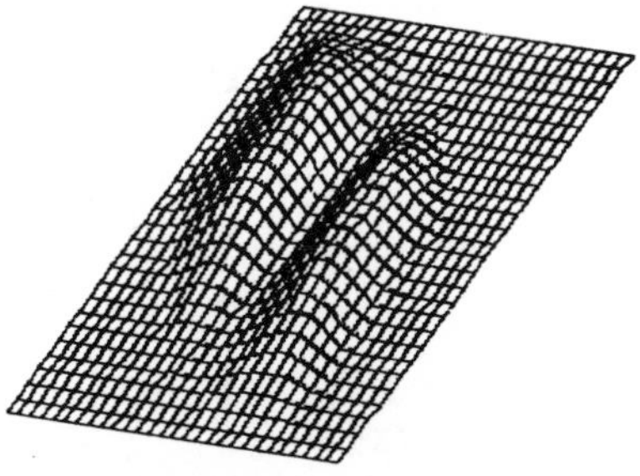

Fig 6(f): $s_{00}^{(0,2)}$

To study the order of approximation of the Hermite interpolation scheme given by (25), we use the notation

$$\|D^k f\|_D = \max\{|D^\alpha f(x,y)| : |\alpha| = k, \quad (x,y) \in D\}$$

and obtain the following result.

THEOREM 5. *Let* $f \in C^5(D)$ *and* s_f *be the bivariate Hermite spline interpolant of* f *defined by* (25). *Then*

(27) $$|s_f(x,y) - f(x,y)| \leq 21\|D^5 f\|_D \, \eta^5$$

for all $(x,y) \in D$ *where*

(28) $$\eta = \max_{i,j}\{h_i, k_j\} .$$

Proof. Since $s_g = g$ where g is the constant function we have

$$s_f(x,y) - f(x,y) = \sum_{i,j} \sum_{|\alpha| \leq 2} [D^\alpha f(x_i,y_j) - D^\alpha f(x,y)] s_{ij}^\alpha(x,y)$$

$$+ \sum_{i,j} \sum_{1 \leq |\alpha| \leq 2} D^\alpha f(x,y) s_{ij}^\alpha(x,y) .$$

By using Taylor's formula at $X = (x,y) \in D$, this expression can be written as

(29) $$s_f(X) - f(X) = \sum_{i,j} \sum_{|\alpha| \leq 2} \sum_{1 \leq |\beta| \leq 4-|\alpha|} D^{\alpha+\beta} f(X)(X_{ij} - X)^\beta s_{ij}^\alpha(X)/\beta!$$

$$+ \sum_{i,j} \sum_{1 \leq |\alpha| \leq 2} D^\alpha f(X) s_{ij}^\alpha(X) + R(X) ,$$

with

(30) $$R(X) = \sum_{i,j} \sum_{|\alpha| \leq 2} \sum_{\substack{|\beta| = 5 \\ \beta \geq \alpha}} D^\beta f(Z_{ij\beta})(X_{ij} - X)^{\beta-\alpha} s_{ij}^\alpha(X)/(\beta-\alpha)! ,$$

for some $Z_{ij\beta}$ that lies on the line segment joining X and X_{ij}. Here and throughout, we use the usual multivariate notation: $X^\beta = x^{\beta_1}y^{\beta_2}$, $\beta! = \beta_1!\beta_2!$, $\alpha \geq \beta$ if and only if $\alpha_1 \geq \beta_1$ and $\alpha_2 \geq \beta_2$. Also, we have set $X = (x,y)$, $X_{ij} = (x_i,y_j)$, $\alpha = (\alpha_1,\alpha_2)$, and $\beta = (\beta_1,\beta_2)$. The expression (29) can be simplified by a change of index and interchanging orders of summation to be

$$\begin{aligned}
s_f(X) - f(X) - R(X) &= \sum_{i,j} \sum_{\alpha \leq 2} \sum_{\substack{1 \leq \beta \leq 4 \\ \beta \geq \alpha}} D^\beta f(X)(X_{ij} - X)^{\beta-\alpha} s_{ij}^\alpha(X)/(\beta-\alpha)! \\
&= \sum_{1 \leq \beta \leq 4} D^\beta f(X)\Big[\sum_{i,j} \sum_{\substack{\alpha \leq \beta \\ \alpha \leq 2}} (X_{ij} - X)^{\beta-\alpha} s_{ij}^\alpha(X)/(\beta-\alpha)!\Big] \\
&= \sum_{1 \leq \beta \leq 4} D^\beta f(X)\Big[\sum_{i,j} \sum_{\substack{\alpha \leq \beta \\ \alpha \leq 2}} \{D^\alpha(X_{ij} - X)^\beta\} s_{ij}^\alpha(X)/\beta!\Big] \\
&= 0 ,
\end{aligned}$$

since $s_g = g$ for all polynomials of total degrees ≤ 4. That is, $s_f(X) - f(X) = R(X)$ for all X. Let X be fixed. Then there are only 3 terms in the summation $\sum_{i,j}$ in (30). Since

$$\sum_{i,j} |s_{ij}^\alpha(X)| \leq \eta^{\alpha} \tag{31}$$

for each α, we have

$$|R(X)| \leq 21 \|D^5 f\|_D \, \eta^5.$$

This completes the proof of the theorem.

We note that the identity $s_f - f = R$ in the above proof does not depend on the grid partition and the basis $\{s_{ij}^\alpha\}$ with the exception that the operator s_f preserves polynomials of degree ≤ 4. Hence, the same proof yields the following more general result.

THEOREM 6. *Let* L *be a linear operator on* $C^k(\Omega)$, Ω *being any convex region in* R^m, $m \geq 1$, *defined by*

$$(Lf)(X) = \sum_{i=1}^{N} \sum_{\alpha \leq k} D^{\alpha} f(X_i) b_i^{\alpha}(X),$$

where α *is an* m-*tuple of nonnegative integers and* $X_1, \ldots, X_N$ *are distinct points in* Ω, *such that* $Lg = g$ *for all polynomials* g *of total degree* $\leq M$, $M \geq k$. *Then for any* $f \in C^{M+1}(\Omega)$ *and* $X \in \Omega$,

$$(Lf)(X) - f(X) = \sum_{i=1}^{N} \sum_{|\alpha| \leq k} \sum_{\substack{|\beta| = M+1 \\ \beta \geq \alpha}} D^{\beta} f(Z_{i\alpha\beta})(X_i - X)^{\beta-\alpha} \, b_i^{\alpha}(X) ,$$

where $Z_{i\alpha\beta}$ *lies in the line segment joining* X_i *and* X.

In most applications, Hermite data are not available. For this reason, we give the following so-called quasi-interpolation scheme that preserves the same polynomials, as s_f in (25) does, using only function values.

THEOREM 7. *There exist constants* $\{a_{ijuv}^{\alpha}\}$ *such that the linear operator* Q *defined by*

$$(Qf)(x,y) = \sum_{i,j} \sum_{\alpha \leq 2} \sum_{u+v \leq 4} a_{ijuv}^{\alpha} f(x_{i+u}, y_{j+v}) s_{ij}^{\alpha}(x,y), \tag{32}$$

where $u, v \geq 0$, *preserves all polynomials of total degree* ≤ 4.

Proof. Let $\phi_{\mu\nu}(x,y) = x^{\mu}y^{\nu}$, and consider the equations

$$(Q\phi_{\mu\nu})(x,y) = s_{\phi_{\mu\nu}}(x,y)$$

where $\mu,\nu \geq 0$ and $\mu+\nu \leq 4$. Since $\{s_{ij}^{\alpha}\}$ is a linearly independent set, we have the linear system

(33) $$\sum_{u+v\leq 4} a^{\alpha}_{ijuv}\phi_{\mu\nu}(x_{i+u},y_{j+v}) = D^{\alpha}\phi_{\mu\nu}(x_i,y_j), \quad \mu+\nu \leq 4 ,$$

where $i = 0, \ldots, p+1$, $j = 0, \ldots, q+1$, and $|\alpha| \leq 2$. Since the coefficient matrix has determinant

$$\det[\phi_{\mu\nu}(x_{i+u},y_{j+v})] = \prod_{0\leq t<s\leq 4} (x_{i+s} - x_{i+t})^{5-s} \prod_{0\leq t<s\leq 4} (y_{j+s} - y_{j+t})^{5-s}$$

which is different from zero, the coefficients a^{α}_{ijuv} in (33) can be uniquely determined using $s_g = g$ for all polynomials of degree ≤ 4, we have completed the proof of the theorem.

REMARK 9. In the above theorem, a forward-sampled scheme was used to determine the quasi-interpolant Q. This can be generalized to other choices of (x_{i+u}, y_{j+v}) as long as the corresponding matrix in (33) is non-singular. For instance, the criterion given in [5] can be applied. More detail in this direction will be considered in a later paper.

When the triangulation Δ_{pq} is uniform we have the following order of approximation.

PROPOSITION. *Let* Q *be the quasi-interpolation operator defined by* (32) *where* Δ_{pq} *is a uniform unidiagonal triangulation of* D *with* $x_{i+1} - x_i = y_{j+1} - y_j = \eta$ *for all* i *and* j. *Then*

$$\max_{(x,y)\in D} \left|(Qf - f)(x,y)\right| = O(\eta^5)$$

as $\eta \to 0$ *for every* $f \in C^5(D)$.

Proof. Fix (i,j). We borrow a notation from [2, p. 737], setting

(34) $$\phi_{st}(x,y) = \frac{\pi_{st}(x,y)}{\pi_{st}(x_s,y_t)}$$

as the quartic polynomials satisfying

$$\psi_{st}(x_{i+u},\ y_{j+v}) = \delta_{su}\delta_{tv}\ ,$$

where δ_{jk} is the kronecker delta, and π_{st} is the appropriate product of four of the linear polynomials $y - y_j, \ldots, y - y_{j+3}$, $x - x_i, \ldots, x_{i+3}, (x+y) - (x_i+y_j) - \eta, \ldots, \quad (x+y) - (x_i+y_j) - 4\eta$. Since each ψ_{st} is a linear combination of the $\phi_{\mu\nu}$'s, (33) becomes

$$\sum_{u+v\leq 4} a^{\alpha}_{ijuv}\psi_{st}(x_{i+u},y_{j+v}) = D^{\alpha}\psi_{st}(x_i,y_j)\ ,$$

or

$$a^{\alpha}_{ijst} = D^{\alpha}\psi_{st}(x_i,y_j)\ .$$

Using (34), we arrive at the estimate

$$a^{\alpha}_{ijst} = O(\eta^{-\alpha})\ .$$

Let $(x,y) \in D$. Suppose that (x,y) lies in the triangle T_0 with (x_{i_0},y_{j_0}) as a vertex. By using Taylor's expansion at (x_{i_0},y_{j_0}), we may write $f = P_4 + R_f$ where P_4 is a polynomial of degree ≤ 4 and $R_f(x,y) = O(\eta^5)$. Hence, we have, using (31),

$$\begin{aligned}(Qf - f)(x,y) &= (QR_f - R_f)(x,y)\\ &= \sum{}' \sum_{|\alpha|\leq 2} a^{\alpha}_{ijst}R_f(x_{i+s},y_{j+t})s^{\alpha}_{ij}(x,y) + O(\eta^5)\\ &= O\Big(\sum_{|\alpha|\leq 2} \eta^{-|\alpha|}\eta^5\eta^{|\alpha|}\Big) + O(\eta^5) = O(\eta^5)\end{aligned}$$

where Σ' indicates the sum over (i,j) where each (x_i,y_j) is a vertex of the triangle T_0. This completes the proof of the proposition.

REMARK 10. The assumption on the uniformity of Δ_{pq} can be weakened by using a more careful estimate.

REMARK 11. Results in this section can also be formulated in the criss-cross (or type-2) triangulation. In fact, computational algorithms and some analogous formulas on Hermite interpolation and quasi-interpolation, as well as their order of approximation, can be obtained. These results will appear in a later paper. When $r = 1$ and all Hermite data are given, (that is, Λ is the set of all β with $0 \leq |\beta| \leq 2$), an application of (24) also yields an S_5^1 interpolation scheme similar to those considered in [1].

We would like to acknowledge Mr. G. Chen who checked the S_5^1 V-splines in Figures 5(a) - (f) and Mr. Herman Chui who provided Figures 6(a) - (f).

References

1. R. E. Barnhill and G. Farin, C^1 quintic interpolation over triangles: Two explicit representations, International J. for Num. Methods in Engineering, Vol. 17 (1981), 1763-1778.

2. K. C. Chung and T. H. Yao, On lattices admitting unique Lagrange interpolations, SIAM J. Num. Anal., Vol. 14 (1977), 735-743.

3. R. Courant, Variational methods for the solution of problems of equilibrium and vibration, Bull. Amer. Math. Soc., Vol. 49 (1943), 1-23.

4. G. Farin, Bézier polynomials over triangles and the construction of piecewise C^r polynomials, TR/91, Dept. of Math., Brunel Univ., Uxbridge, Middlesex, U.K., 1980.

5. M. Gasca and J. I. Macztu, On Lagrange and Hermite interpolation in R^k, Num. Math., Vol. 39 (1982), 1-14.

6. G. Strang, Piecewise polynomials and the finite element method, Bull. Amer. Math. Soc., Vol. 79 (1973), 1128-1137.

C. K. Chui and M. J. Lai, Department of Mathematics, Texas A&M University, College Station, TX 77843, USA

International Series of
Numerical Mathematics, Vol. 75

BIORTHOGONAL SYSTEM OF POLYNOMIALS ON THE STANDARD SIMPLEX

Zbigniew Ciesielski

Mathematical Institute

Polish Academy of Sciences

Sopot

The aim of this note is to announce a construction of "Legendre" type polynomials and a result on approximation in Sobolev spaces on the standard simplex. The results needed in the proofs were announced in |3|. All the proofs will be published elswhere.

The following notation will be used: $R=(-\infty,\infty)$, $N=(1,2,\ldots)$, $N_o=N\cup(0)$, $k\in N$, $e_i\in R^k$, $e_o=(0,\ldots,0)\in R^k$, $e_i=(\delta_{i,j}, j=1,\ldots,k)$, $i=1,\ldots,k$, $n\in N_o$. For $\alpha=(\alpha_1,\ldots,\alpha_k)\in N_o^k$, $\beta\in N_o^k$, $|\alpha| = \alpha_1+\ldots+\alpha_k$, $\alpha! = \alpha_1!\ldots\alpha_k!$, $\alpha_o=n-|\alpha|$ and $\alpha\leq\beta$ iff $\alpha_i\leq\beta_i$ for $i=1,\ldots,k$. For $x=(x_1,\ldots,x_k)\in R^k$, $\alpha\in N_o^k$ we write $x_o= 1-(x_1+\ldots+x_k)$ and $x^\alpha=x_1^{\alpha_1}\ldots x_k^{\alpha_k}$. In what follows the dimension k is fixed. Define $\Pi_n=\text{span}[\,x^\alpha,\ |\alpha|\leq n\,]$. In R^k we consider the standard simplex $Q=(x\in R^k\colon\ x_1+\ldots+x_k\leq 1,\ x_i\geq 0,\ i=1,\ldots,k)$ and in the real space $L^2(Q)$ the scalar product

$$(f,g) = \int_Q f(x)g(x)dx,$$

where dx is the Lebesgue measure in R^k. For $\alpha\in N_o^k$, $|\alpha|\leq n$, define

$$N_{\alpha,n}(x) = \frac{n!}{\alpha_o!\,\alpha!}\, x_o^{\alpha_o}\, x^\alpha .$$

These polynomials are the most degenerate multivariate B-splines with support in Q. They have the following properties:

$N_{\alpha,n}(x)\geq 0$ on Q,

$$\sum_{|\alpha|\leq n} N_{\alpha,n}(x) = 1,$$

$\Pi_n = \mathrm{span}[N_{\alpha,n}: |\alpha|\leq n]$ i.e. $(N_{\alpha,n}, |\alpha|\leq n)$ is a basis in Π_n. There is unique dual basis $(N^*_{\alpha,n}, |\alpha|\leq n)$ i.e. $N^*_{\alpha,n}\in\Pi_n$ and

$$(N_{\alpha,n}, N^*_{\beta,n}) = \delta_{\alpha,\beta} \quad \text{for } |\alpha|\leq n,\ |\beta|\leq n.$$

For convenience introduce $M_{\alpha,n}=(n+k)_k N_{\alpha,n}$ where $(m)_j= m(m-1)\ldots(m-j+1)$. For the functions $N_{\alpha,n}$ we have the following recurrence relation known as "the formula for artificial raising of degree of the Berstein polynomials":

$$(*) \qquad N_{\alpha,n} = \sum_{j=0}^{k} \frac{\alpha_j+1}{n+1} N_{\alpha+e_j,n+1}, \quad |\alpha|\leq n.$$

Finally, for $|\beta|\leq n$ we introduce the kernels

$$R_{\beta,n}(y,x) = m_{|\beta|,n} \sum_{|\alpha|\leq n-|\beta|} M_{\alpha+\beta,n+|\beta|}(y) N_{\alpha,n-|\beta|}(x),$$

where $m_{j,n}=(n)_j/(n+k+j)_j$ for $j=0,\ldots,n$. We define also $m_{\beta,n}=m_{|\beta|,n}$ for $|\beta|\leq n$. The kernel $R_n=R_{0,n}$ is treated in |3|. We know (cf. |3|) that $(m_{\beta,n}, |\beta|\leq n)$ are the eigenvalues for the symmetric Gram matrix $[(N_{\alpha,n}, M_{\beta,n})]_{|\alpha|,|\beta|\leq n}$. Now, $\{\Pi_n, n\in N_0\}$ is an increasing sequence of finite dimensional spaces in $L^2(Q)$ and therefore we have the following orthogonal decomposition

$$L^2(Q) = \bigoplus_0^\infty \Lambda_n,\ \Lambda_0 = \mathrm{span}[1],\ \Lambda_n=\Pi_n\ominus\Pi_{n-1},\ n\in N.$$

Each Λ_n as a finite dimensional subspace of $L^2(Q)$ has unique reproducing kernel say $L_n(x,y)$. Defining

$$P_n f(x) = \int_Q L_n(x,y) f(y) dy, \quad f \in L^2(Q)$$

we find that P_n is the orthogonal projection of $L^2(Q)$ onto Λ_n. Thus, for $f \in L^2(Q)$ we have

$$f = \sum_0^{\infty} P_n f .$$

It is also known that (cf. |3|)

$$R_n f = \sum_{j=0}^{n} m_{j,n} P_n f ,$$

where R_n denotes the operator corresponding to the kernel R_n introduced above.

To state the first result we introduce

$$N_\alpha(x) = \frac{1}{\alpha!} D^\alpha (x_0^{|\alpha|} x^\alpha)$$

with $D=(D_1,\dots,D_k)$, $D_i = \frac{\partial}{\partial x_i}$, and for $\alpha \in N_0^k$

$$N_\alpha^* = N_{\alpha,|\alpha|}^* - \frac{1}{|\alpha|} \sum_{j=1}^{k} \alpha_j N_{\alpha-e_j,|\alpha|-1}^* .$$

THEOREM A. <u>The system</u> $(N_\alpha, N_\beta^*, \alpha,\beta \in N_0^k)$ <u>is biorthogonal i.e.</u> $(N_\alpha, N_\beta^*) = \delta_{\alpha,\beta}$ <u>and</u>

$$L_n(x,y) = \sum_{|\alpha|=n} N_\alpha(x) N_\alpha^*(y) .$$

<u>Clearly</u>, L_n <u>is symmetric.</u>

The proof depends on the dual relation to (*) and on the explicite formulas for the moments $(x^\beta, N_{\alpha,n})$, $(x^\beta, N_{\alpha,n}^*)$, $|\alpha| \le n$, $|\beta| \le n$, as given in |3|. In case k=1 the polynomials $N_\alpha = N_\alpha^*$ are the Legendre polynomials.

LEMMA. *For* $f\in C^n(Q)$ *and* $|\alpha|+|\beta|\leq n$ *we have*

$$(f, D^{\beta}M_{\alpha+\beta,n+|\beta|}) = (-1)^{|\beta|}(D^{\beta}f, M_{\alpha+\beta,n+|\beta|}).$$

In particular we get

$$D^{\beta}R_n f = R_{\beta,n}D^{\beta}f \quad \text{for } |\beta|\leq n.$$

THEOREM B. *Let* $1\leq p\leq\infty$, $j\in N_0$ *and let* $f\in W_p^j(Q)$ *for finite* p *and* $f\in C^j(Q)$ *for* $p=\infty$. *Then*

$$\| f - R_n f \|_{W_p^j(Q)} \longrightarrow 0 \quad \text{as } n \longrightarrow \infty ,$$

where W_p^j *is the Sobolev space with the smootheness index* j *and the exponent of integration* p.

The proof of Theorem B depends again very much on the explicite formulas for the moments.

References

|1| Ciesielski, Z. - Domsta, J., *The degenerate B-splines as basis in the space of algebraic polynomials*. Ann. Polonici Mathematici. (to appear).

|2| Ciesielski, Z., *Approximation by polynomials and extension of Parseval's identity for Legendre polynomial to the* L^p *case*. Acta Scientiarum Mathematicarum Szeged. (to appear).

|3| Ciesielski, Z., *Approximation by algebraic polynomials on simplices*. Proc. of the 50-th Anniversary Conference of The Steklov Institute in Moscow.(to appear).

International Series of
Numerical Mathematics, Vol. 75

ANWENDUNG DER APPROXIMATIONSTHEORIE AUF GEWISSE SINGULÄRE RANDWERTAUFGABEN

Lothar Collatz

Abstract: Approximation and optimization methods have been used for different types of boundary value problems with ordinary or partial differential equations, even for singular and nonlinear problems. These methods are often the only ones which are practicable for getting inclusion intervals for the wanted solution u. One is approximationg u by functions w of a certain set W of functions depending on parameters. Inclusion theorems for the minimal distance show which degree of accuracy one can reach with this approximation from u by W. A numerical example of a singular boundary value problem is given for illustration.

Abstrakt: Bei verschiedenen Klassen von Randwertaufgaben bei gewöhnlichen und partiellen Differentialgleichungen, insbesondere bei singulären und nichtlinearen Aufgaben, bieten Approximations- und Optimierungsmethoden die einzige praktikable Methode zur Einschließung der gesuchten Funktion u in garantierbare Intervalle. Dabei wird u durch Funktionen w einer von p Parametern abhängenden Funktionenklasse W approximiert. Welche Güte der Annäherung von u durch Funktionen w dieser Klasse überhaupt möglich ist, kann in nicht zu komplizierten Fällen mit Hilfe von Einschließungssätzen für die Minimalabweichung abgeschätzt werden. Das wird numerisch am Beispiel einer singulären Randwertaufgabe vorgeführt.

1. Approximations- und Optimierungsaufgaben

Es werden Operatorgleichungen in halbgeordneten Banachräumen R^1, R^2 betrachtet von der Form

(1.1) $$Tu = r$$

Der gegebene lineare oder nichtlineare Operator T bilde einen Definitionsbereich D [in R_1] in einen Wertebereich W [in R_2] ab. r ist gegebenes Element aus R_2 und u gesuchtes Element aus D. Oft liegen auch Gleichungen der Form

(1.2) $$Tu = u$$

vor, dann ist $R_1 = R_2$ und es wird nach einem Fixpunkt u gefragt. Diese Art ist sehr häufig mit großem Erfolg zur numerischen Behandlung, insbesondere nichtlinearer Probleme, unter Verwendung von Iterationsverfahren und Fixpunktsätzen benutzt worden; hier soll aber die Form (1.1) zugrunde gelegt werden.

Die Anwendung monotoner Operatoren wird hier nur kurz skizziert; ausführlichere Darstellungen z.B. bei Collatz [52],[68],[81], Bohl [74], Schröder [80] u.a.

Als Ordnung wird eingeführt: Für in einem Bereich B des n-dimensionalen Punktraumes R^n definierte reellwertige Funktionen f(x), g(x) bedeutet

$$f < g, \text{ daß } f(x) \leq g(x) \quad \text{für alle } x \in B$$

gilt (das Zeichen $\leq$ bedeutet die klassisches Ordnung reeller Zahlen, und x steht für $x_1,\ldots,x_n$. Es wird D in den Anwendungen oft die Menge $C^o(B)$ der in B stetigen Funktionen sein.

Der Operator T heißt "von monotoner Art" falls

$$\text{(1.3)} \qquad \text{aus } Tf < Tg \text{ folgt } f < g \text{ für alle } f,g \in D.$$

Hierfür ist auch die Bezeichnung gebräuchlich: T ist "inversmonoton" (Schröder [56]). Falls dann (1.1) überhaupt eine Lösung u besitzt, ergibt sich eine sehr einfache und viel verwendete Art der Aufstellung von unteren Schranken v und oberen Schranken w für u. Hat man nämlich Funktionen v,w mit

$$\text{(1.4)} \qquad Tv < r < Tw$$

ermittelt, so gilt die Einschließung

$$\text{(1.5)} \qquad v < u < w$$

Zur Aufstellung "guter" Schranken (1.5) läßt man v und w noch von Parametern a_ν, b_μ abhängen:

$$\text{(1.6)} \quad v = v(x,a) = v(x,a_1,\ldots,a_p), \; w = w(x,b) = w(x,b_1,\ldots,b_q)$$

Die Parameter a_ν, b_μ sind aus der semi-infiniten Optimierungsaufgabe zu ermitteln:

$$\text{(1.7)} \begin{cases} \delta_1 \leq w(x,b) - v(x,a) \leq \delta_2 \\ \delta_1 \geq 0, \; \delta_2 \geq 0, \; \delta_1 + \delta_2 = \text{Min} & \text{für alle } x \in B. \\ Tv(x,a) \leq r(x) \leq Tw(x,b) \end{cases}$$

Die monotone Art wurde bei sehr allgemeinen Randwertaufgaben mit linearen und nichtlinearen, gewöhnlichen und partiellen Differentialgleichungen 2. Ordnung von elliptischen und parabolischen Typ und vielen anderen Typen von Funktionalgleichungen bewiesen, vgl. z.B. Nickel [58], Redheffer [67], Walter [70] u.a. Zur Gewinnung eines Einschließungsintervalles ist es nicht nötig, die Optimierungsaufgabe (1.7) streng zu lösen; hat man anstelle der optimalen Parameter a_ν, b_μ Näherungswerte $\tilde{a}_\nu, \tilde{b}_\mu$, die jedoch so gut sein müssen, daß die Ungleichungen (1.7) erfüllt sind. so gilt die Einschließung (1.5); im allgemeinen wird man $u^* = \frac{1}{2}(v+w)$ bilden und hat dann die Fehlerabschätzung

(1.8) $$|u^*-u| \leq \frac{1}{2}(\delta_1+\delta_2) \quad \text{in } B$$

2. Beurteilung erreichbarer Genauigkeit mit Hilfe der H-Mengen

Es sei $\tilde{B}$ ein kompakter metrischer Raum, z.B. etwa ein abgeschlossener beschränkter zusammenhängender Bereich des R^n; wir beschränken uns hier darauf, alle Betrachtungen im Reellen durchzuführen. Als Norm einer Funktion $g \in C^o(\tilde{B})$ werde die Maximumnorm benutzt

$$||g|| = \max_{x \in \tilde{B}} |g(x)|$$

$\tilde{W}$ sei eine gegebene nichtleere Teilmenge von $C(\tilde{B})$ und f eine feste Funktion aus $C(\tilde{B})$; dann existiert die sogenannte "Minimalabweichung" (vgl. z.B. Collatz-Krabs [73] S.38 ff, S. 101 ff, Meinardus [67])

(2.1) $$\varrho(f,\tilde{W}) = \inf_{\varphi \in \tilde{W}} ||\varphi - f||$$

Definition der H-Menge /Haar-Menge): Eine Teilmenge M von $\tilde{B}$ heißt eine H-Menge bezüglich der Funktionenmenge $\tilde{W}$, wenn M die Vereinigung zweier nichtleerer Teilmengen M_1, M_2 ist mit der Eigenschaft: Es gibt kein Paar $\varphi, \mathring{\varphi} \in W$ mit

(2.2) $$\varphi(x) - \mathring{\varphi}(x) \begin{cases} > 0 & \text{für alle } x \in M_1 \\ < 0 & \text{für alle } x \in M_2 \end{cases}$$

Ist $\tilde{W}$ eine lineare Mannigfaltigkeit

$$\tilde{W} = \{ \sum_{\nu=1}^{q} a_\nu \varphi_\nu (x) \},$$

so gehört $\varphi - \mathring{\varphi}$ auch zu W und man hat anstelle des Systems (2.2) nur zu prüfen, ob

$$(2.3)\quad \begin{cases} \sum\limits_{\nu} \alpha_\nu \varphi_\nu(x) > 0 & \text{auf } M_1 \\ -\sum\limits_{\nu} \alpha_\nu \varphi_\nu(x) > 0 & \text{auf } M_2 \end{cases}$$

für reelle α_ν lösbar ist oder zu einem Widerspruch führt. Im Falle eines Widerspruches ist M eine H-Menge; tritt jedoch kein Widerspruch auf, so ist im allgemeinen noch nicht entschieden, ob M eine H-Menge ist oder nicht. Dann gilt der

Einschließungssatz: Es seien f,g gegebene Funktionen, $f \in C(\tilde{B})$, $g \in \tilde{W}$; Es gebe eine H-Menge M mit der Eigenschaft:

1. Der Fehler $\varepsilon = g - f$ ist $\neq 0$ auf M;
2. Es gibt keine Funktion φ aus W mit

$$\varepsilon \cdot (g - \varphi) > 0 \text{ auf } M;$$

dann besteht die Einschließung (Meinardus[67], CollatzKrabs[73])

$$(2.4)\qquad \inf_M |\varepsilon| \le \rho(f, \tilde{w}) \le \|\varepsilon\|$$

3. Eine singuläre Randwertaufgabe

Bei dem Torsionsproblem für einen Träger mit dem Querschnitt B

$B = \{(x,y),\ r^2 = r^2 + y^2 < 1$, ohne den Quadranten $x \le 0$, $y \le 0$, Fig.1

ist die Funktion u(x,y) aus

$$(3.1)\quad \begin{cases} \Delta u = \dfrac{\partial^2 u}{\partial x^2} + \dfrac{\partial^2 u}{\partial y^2} = 0 \text{ in } B \\ u = \frac{1}{4} r^2 \text{ auf dem Rande } \partial B \end{cases}$$

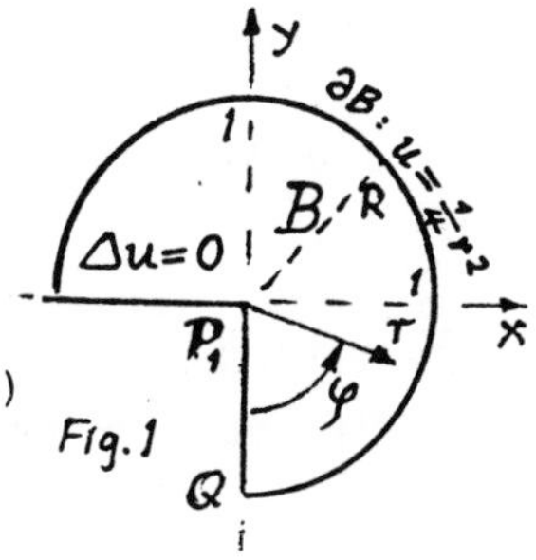

Fig.1

zu ermitteln. Hier liegt im Nullpunkt $P_1 = (0,0)$ eine Singularität vor, welcher durch den Ansatz für eine Näherungsfunktion $\tilde{v}$

$$(3.2)\quad u(x,y) \approx h(x,y) = \sum_{\nu=1}^{p} c_\nu \zeta_\nu(x,y) + \sum_{\mu=1}^{m} d_\mu \psi_\mu(x,y)$$

$$\text{mit Polynomen } \psi_\mu \text{ und } \zeta_\nu = r^{\gamma_\nu} \sin(\gamma_\nu \varphi)$$

Rechnung getragen wird. Dabei seien r, φ von der Ecke P_1 aus gezählte Polarkoordinaten, Fig. 1. Die ζ_ν, ψ_ν mögen der Symmetrie der Aufgabe und $\Delta\zeta_\nu = \Delta\psi_\mu = 0$ genügen,

$$\psi_1 = 1, \ \psi_2 = x+y, \ \psi_3 = xy, \ \psi_4 = x^3 - 3x^2y - 3xy^2 + y^3, \ldots .$$

Die ξ_ν genügen als Imaginärteile der holomorphen Funktion

$$z^\nu = r^\nu e^{i\nu\varphi} = r^\nu(\cos\nu\varphi + i\sin\nu\varphi) \quad \left(\text{für} \qquad z = re^{i\varphi}\right)$$

der Potentialgleichung; Wegen der Symmetrie werden

$$\gamma_1 = \frac{2}{3}, \ \gamma_2 = \frac{10}{3}, \ \gamma_3 = \frac{14}{3}, \ldots$$

gewählt. Über den Typ der Singularität vergleiche man die Arbeiten von Tolksdorf [83], Dobrowolski [83], Schnack [84], Collatz [85] u.a.

Nun mögen die Werte der Funktionen $\zeta_\nu, \psi_\mu, u, h$ auf dem Rande mit $\hat{\zeta}_\nu, \hat{\psi}_\mu, \hat{u}, \hat{h}$ bezeichnet werden, und die reellen Parameter c_ν, d_μ sind so zu bestimmen, daß auf dem Rande ∂B

$$(3.3) \qquad |\hat{h} - \hat{u}| \le \delta, \qquad \delta = \text{Min}$$

wird. Man wählt Parameter $\underline{c_\nu}, \underline{d_\mu}$ für eine untere Schranke $\underline{h} = v$ für u und andere Werte der Parameter $\overline{c_\nu}, \overline{d_\mu}$ für eine obere Schranke $\overline{h} = w$ für u. Die Durchführung der Optimierungsaufgabe (1.7) ergibt für die "garantierbare" Fehlerschranke in Abhängigkeit von der Anzahl der Polynomterme und der Anzahl der regulären Terme die Tabelle:

Werte von δ

	m = 1	m = 2	m = 3	m = 4	m = 6
n = 1			0.5		
n = 2 und 3			0.125		
n = 4	0.107	0.0526	0.0303	0.0279	
n = 7	0.0377	0.00662	0.00542	0.00499	
n = 10	0.0215	0.00527	0.00249	0.00118	0.00108
n = 11				0.00114	0.000904

Zur Illustration ist hier die Fehlerkurve bei n = 10 Polynomtermen und m = 4 singulären Termen wiedergegeben ; daß bei kleinen φ-Werten das Maximum etwas zu groß ausfällt, liegt an der längs des Randes vorgenommenen Diskretisierung.

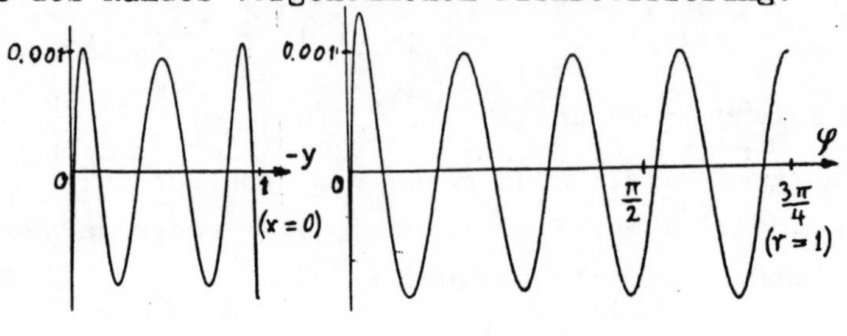

Die zugehörigen Werte der Koeffizienten der Näherungsfunktion lauten :

c_1	1.476061659	d_4	-4.110750101
c_2	-8.557372030	d_5	-7.367654393
c_3	10.255544619	d_6	-5.281362892
c_4	1.667170921	d_7	1.720820592
d_1	-0.001182202	d_8	1.436406473
d_2	-0.087899171	d_9	0.305036823
d_3	-2.220821447	d_{10}	-0.019067048

Ich danke Herrn Zheng Tsinghua aus Schanghai für numerische Rechnung auf dem Computer.

4. H-Mengen für die singuläre Randwertaufgabe

Nun soll wenigstens in den einfachsten Fällen gezeigt werden, wie man mit Hilfe der H-Mengen-Theorie von Nr. 2 die Güte der erreichten Näherungen beurteilen kann. $\tilde{B}$ ist hier der Rand $\partial\tilde{B}$ (wegen der Symmetrie mit $0 \le \varphi \le \frac{3\pi}{4}$ und W die Menge der stetigen Funktionen h auf $\tilde{B}$. Zur Erläuterung werde als einfacher Fall p=1, m=2 herausgegriffen, also

$$(4.1) \quad h = \{d_1 + d_2(x+y) + c_1 r^{2/3} \sin \frac{2\varphi}{3}\}$$

oder in der Bezeichnung von (2.3)

$$\varphi_1 = \psi_1 = 1, \ \varphi_2 = \psi_2 = x+y,$$
$$\varphi_3 = \zeta_1 = r^{2/3} \sin \frac{2\varphi}{3} .$$

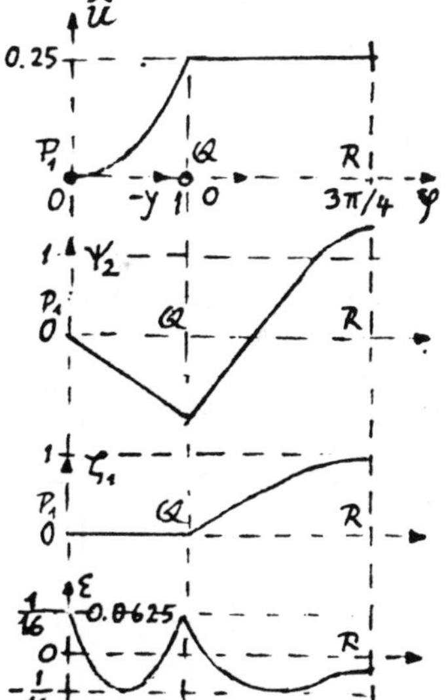

Fig.2

In Fig. 2 ist der Randteil $\tilde{B}$ von P_1 über Q bis R abgewickelt und der Verlauf von $\hat{u}, \hat{\psi}_1, \hat{\psi}_2, \hat{\zeta}_1$, graphisch dargestellt. Nun soll für verschiedene Anordnungen von Punkten P_1, P_2, P_3, P_4 geprüft werden, ob H-Mengen vorliegen.

I.) Als M werden die Punkte P_1, P_2, P_3, P_4 ausgewählt, vergl. Fig 3; dabei ist P_3 ein Punkt des Kreisbogens $x = \sin\varphi$, $y = -\cos\varphi$ mit $0 < \varphi < \frac{3\pi}{4}$. In Fig.3 bis 7 sind die Punkte von M_1 durch einen ausgefüllten Kreis und die von M_2 durch einen leeren Kreis gekennzeichnet. Die Ungleichungen (2.3) werden hier schematisch durch ihre Matrix wiedergegeben.

Operation	Ungleichung Nr.	Punkte P	Koordinaten von P x	y	P gehört zu	Faktoren von d_1	d_2	c_1
	(1)	P_1	0	0	M_1	1	0	0
	(2)	P_2	0	-1	M_2	-1	1	0
	(3)	P_3	$\sin\varphi$	$-\cos\varphi$	M_1	1	$\sigma=\sin\varphi-\cos\varphi$	1
	(4)	P_4	$\alpha=\sqrt{\frac{1}{2}}$	α	M_2	-1	-2α	-1
(3)+(4)	(5)					0	$-\tau=-(2\alpha-\sigma)$	0
$\frac{1}{\tau}(5)+(2)$	(6)					-1	0	0

Die erste Ungleichung ist zu lesen als:

$$1 \cdot d_1 + 0 \cdot d_2 + 0 \cdot c_1 > 0.$$

Aus den Ungleichungen (1) bis (4) werden wie beim Gauß'schen Eliminationsverfahren d_2, c_1 eliminiert, wobei die Ungleichungen nur mit positiven Faktoren multipliziert und addiert werden, wie es in der Spalte "Operation" angegeben ist. Dann stellen (1) und (6) mit $d_1>0$, $-d_1>0$ einen Widerspruch dar; die Punkte P_1 bis P_4 bilden eine H-Menge.

II. Wahl der Punkte P_1, P_2, P_3, P_4 wie in Fig. 4; die Koordinaten sind wieder im Schema angegeben, der Rechnungsgang ist wie bei I.

Operation	Ungleichung Nr.	Punkt P	Koordinaten von P x	y	P gehört zu	Faktoren von d_1	d_2	c_1
	(1)	P_1	0	0	M_1	1	0	0
	(2)	P_2	0	$-\eta$	M_2	-1	$\eta<1$	0
	(3)	P_3	0	-1	M_1	1	-1	0
	(4)	P_4	$\sin\varphi$	$-\cos\varphi$	M_2	-1	$\rho=\sin\varphi-\cos\varphi$	$-\frac{\sin 2\varphi}{3}$
$\frac{\eta(3)+(2)}{1-\eta}$	(5)					-1	0	0
	Widerspruch mit (1)(5)							

auch hier liegt eine H-Menge vor.

Die numerische Rechnung zeigt, daß für die Minimallösung die Extremalpunkte die Anordnung wie bei II.) haben (was bei diesem einfachen Beispiel auch daraus folgt, daß $\zeta_1 \equiv 0$ auf der Strecke $x=0$,

$-1 \leq y \leq 0$ ist).

Wählt man den Winkel φ so, daß eine "Alternante" für den Fehler ε (wie in Fig. 2) und Extrema vom Betrage $\frac{1}{16}$ auftreten, so hat man $\rho = \frac{1}{16}$; es gilt $\inf\limits_{M} |\varepsilon| = \|\varepsilon\| = \frac{1}{16}$ und h ist nach (2.4) eine Minimallösung; man kann mit dem Ansatz (4.1) keine bessere Annäherung erreichen; eine genauere Näherungslösung ist nur durch Erweiterung des Ansatzes (4.1) (oder durch andere Ansätze) erreichbar.

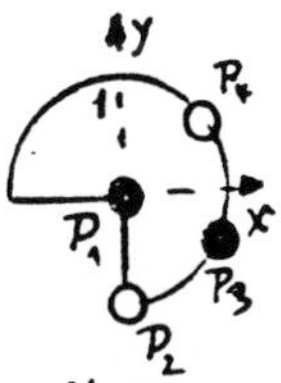

H-Menge
Fig.3

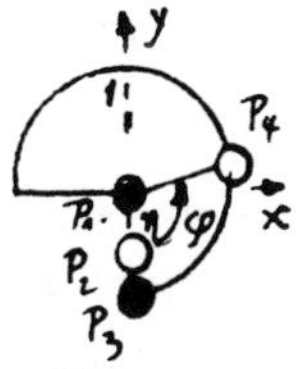

H-Menge
Fig.4

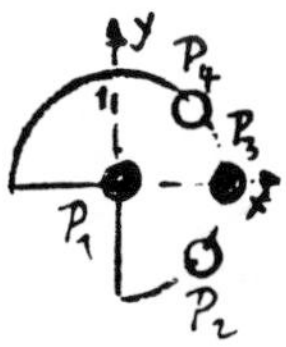

H-Menge
Fig.5

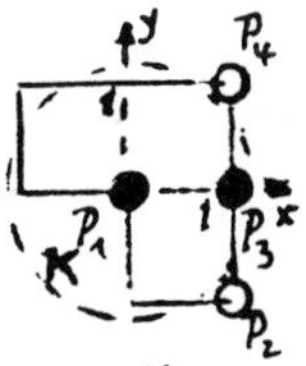

keine H-Menge
Fig.6

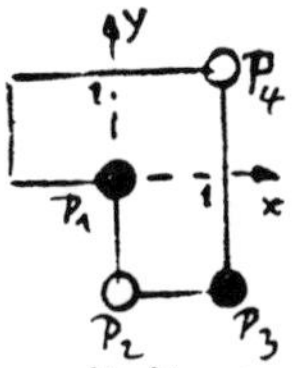

H-Menge
Fig.7

Übrigens geht in obige Algorithmen nur die Lage der genannten 4 Punkte ein und nicht die Gestalt des Randes zwischen diesen Punkten.

III. Wahl der Punkte wie in Fig. 5; das ganz entsprechend wie bei I und II angelegte Schema lautet jetzt etwas verkürzt:

	x	y		(d_1)	(d_2)	(c_1)
P_1	0	0	M_1	1	0	0
P_2	β	$-\beta$	M_2	-1	0	$-1/2$
P_3	1	0	M_1	1	1	$\sqrt{3}/2$
P_4	β	β	M_2	-1	-2β	-1
				$2\beta-1$	0	$\sqrt{3/2}-1$
				τ	0	0

mit $\beta = \sqrt{1/2}$

$\tau = 1+\sqrt{2}-\sqrt{6} < 0$

Mit $d_1 > 0$ und $\tau d_1 > 0$ liegt wegen $\tau < 0$ ein Widerspruch und mit den Punkten P_ν eine H-Menge vor.

IV. Nun werde der Bereich B abgeändert zu dem L-Bereich: $(0<y<1,\ |x|<1\quad (-1<y\leq 0,\ 0<x<1)$, Fig. 6; mit der Lage der Punkte P_ν analog zu Fig. 5 lautet das verkürzte Schema

	x	y	(d_1)	(d_2)	(c_1)
P_1	0	0	1	0	0
P_2	1	-1	-1	0	$-\gamma/2$
P_3	1	0	1	1	$\sqrt{3}/2$
P_4	1	1	-1	-2	$-\gamma$
			1	0	$\sqrt{3}-\gamma$
			τ	0	0

mit $\gamma = \sqrt[3]{2}$

$\tau = 3 - \frac{2\sqrt{3}}{\gamma} > 0$

Hier ergibt sich mit $d_1>0$, $\tau d_1>0$ kein Widerspruch. Es liegt auch tatsächlich keine H-Menge vor, da es einen Kreis K um P_1 gibt, der P_1, P_3 aber nicht P_2, P_4 enthält. Es gibt daher Zahlen d_1, c_1 sodaß $d_1+c_1\zeta_1$ positiv auf M_1 und negativ auf M_2 ist.

V. Bei demselben Bereich wie in IV (und stets denselben Funktionen ψ_1, ψ_2, ζ_1) und einer Anordnung der Punkte P_ν ähnlich wie in Fig. 3 hat man bei Fig. 7 das Schema

	x	y	(d_1)	(d_2)	(c_1)
P_1	0	0	1	0	0
P_2	0	-1	-1	1	0
P_3	1	-1	1	0	$\gamma/2$
P_4	1	1	-1	-2	$-\gamma$
			-3	0	$-\gamma$
			-1	0	0

mit $\gamma = \sqrt[3]{2}$

Auch hier hat man eine H-Menge, da $d_1>0$, $-d_1>0$ widersprüchlich sind.

Bei größerer Anzahl von Parametern wird man die entsprechenden Algorithmen numerisch durchrechnen.

Literatur

Bohl, E. [74] Monotonie, Lösbarkeit und Numerik bei Operatorgleichungen. Springer, 1974, 255 S.

Collatz, L. [52] Aufgaben monotoner Art, Arch.Math.Anal.Mech.3 (1952) 366-376.

Collatz, L. [68] Funktional Analysis und Numerische Mathematik, Springer 1968, 371 S.

Collatz, L. [81] Anwendung von Monotoniesätzen zur Einschließung der Lösungen von Gleichungen; Jahrbuch Überblicke der Mathematik 1981, 189-225.

Collatz, L. [85] Inclusion of regular and singular solutions of certains types of integral equations, Intern.Ser.Num.Math. 73 (1985) 93-102

Collatz, L. - W. Krabs [73], Approximationstheorie, Teubner, Stuttgart 1973, 208 S.

Dobrowolski, M. [83] Vortrag Tagung: Singularities and Constructive Methods for their treatment. Proc. Oberwolfach 21.-26. November 1983.

Meinardus, G. [67] Approximation of functions, Theory and numerical methods, Springer 1967, 198p.

Redheffer, R. [67] Differentialungleichungen unter schwachen Voraussetzungen, Abhandl.Math.Sem.Univ.Hamburg, 31 (1967) 33-50.

Schnack, E., [84] Vortrag MAFELAP 1.-4. May 1984, Proc. ed. J.R. Whiteman.

Schröder, J., [80] Operator inequalities, Acs.Press, (1980)367p.

Tolksdorf, P. [83] Vortrag Tagung: Singularities and Constructive Methods for their treatment. Proc.Oberwolfach 21.-26. November 1983.

Walter, W. [70] Differential and Integral Inequatilies, Springer (1970), 352 p.

Lothar Collatz
Institut für Angewandte Mathematik
der Universität Hamburg
Bundesstraße 55
D-2000 Hamburg 13

International Series of
Numerical Mathematics, Vol. 75

COMBINATORIAL ASPECTS OF MULTIVARIATE SPLINES

Wolfgang Dahmen
Universität Bielefeld
Fakultät für Mathematik
Bielefeld, West Germany

Charles A. Micchelli
IBM T.J. Watson Research Center,
Yorktown Heights, NY

1. Introduction.

Let X denote an $s \times n$ integer matrix with columns $x^1,\dots,x^n \in Z^s \setminus \{0\}$. (Sometimes we will also denote the set of vectors $\{x^1,\dots,x^n\}$ by X too.) We will assume throughout the following discussion that

$$(1.1) \qquad 0 \notin [X],$$

where [A] will mean the convex hull of the set A. The main object of our study is the function

$$(1.2) \qquad t(\alpha \mid X) = |\{\beta \in Z_+^n : X\beta = \alpha\}|,$$

where $\alpha \in Z^s$ and $|A|$ denotes the cardinality of the set A. This function which we have referred to earlier as the "discrete truncated power", $[DM_1]$, counts the number of nonnegative integer solutions $\beta = (\beta_1,\dots,\beta_n)$ to the linear diophantine equations

$$\sum_{j=1}^{n} x_i^j \beta_j = \alpha_i, \quad \alpha_i \in Z, \ i = 1,\dots,s,$$

whose coefficient matrix is X.

Our purpose here is to announce some results concerning the structure of $t(\alpha \mid X)$ as a function on Z^s. For the case $s = 1$, $t(\bullet \mid X)$ was introduced by Sylvester. He referred to it a "denumerant". E.T. Bell proved that when $x_i \in \mathbf{N}$, $i = 1,\dots,n$, and $a \in \mathbf{N}$ is a common multiple of $x_1,\dots,x_n$, that is, $a/x_i \in \mathbf{N}$, $i = 1,\dots,n$, and $0 \le b < a$ then $t(ja + b \mid x_1,\dots,x_r)$ as a function of j is a polynomial of degree n-1, [B]. In general, $t(\bullet \mid X)$ is relevant for the theory of partitions of nonnegative integers (see [M] for some special two dimensional examples). More recently this problem arose in the context of counting (semi) magic squares, [ADG]. To explain this connection, we let $\mathscr{H}_m(r)$ denote the set of $m \times m$ matrices with nonnegative integer entries such that their row and column sums are all equal to r. The quantity $H_m(r) = |\mathscr{H}_m(r)|$ has attracted some interest in the literature [ADG], [S]. In our notation $H_m(r)$ equals $t(re \mid M_m)$ where $e = (1,\ldots,1) \in Z^{(2m-1)}$ and M_m is the $(2m-1) \times m^2$ matrix

(1.3)
$$\begin{array}{c} m-1 \\ \\ \\ \\ m \end{array} \quad \begin{array}{cccc} 0\,0 \cdots 0 & 1\,1 \cdots 1 & \cdots & 0\,0 \cdots 0 \\ 0\,0 \cdots 0 & 0\,0 \cdots 0 & \cdots & 0\,0 \cdots 0 \\ \vdots & \vdots & \vdots & \vdots \\ 0\,0 \cdots 0 & 0\,0 \cdots 0 & \cdots & 1\,1 \cdots 1 \\ \\ 1\,0 \cdots 0 & 1\,0 \cdots 0 & \cdots & 1\,0 \cdots 0 \\ 0\,1 \cdots 0 & 0\,1 \cdots 0 & \cdots & 0\,1 \cdots 0 \\ \vdots & \vdots & \vdots & \vdots \\ 0\,0 \cdots 1 & 0\,0 \cdots 1 & \cdots & 0\,0 \cdots 1 \end{array}$$

The explanation for this is clear; a matrix $A = (a_{i,j})_{i,j=1}^{m}$ is in $\mathscr{H}_m(r)$ if and only if the vector $a = (a_{11},\ldots,a_{1m},\ldots,a_{m1},\ldots,a_{mm})$ satisfies the equation $M_m a = re$.

Our interest in the discrete truncated power came from the study of linear combinations of translates of the box spline $B(\bullet \mid X)$ which is defined by requiring that the equation

(1.4)
$$\int_{R^s} f(x)B(x \mid X)dx = \int_{[0,1]^n} f(Xu)du$$

holds for all $f \in C(R^s)$. The somewhat unexpected relationship between these subjects has the following explanation. Observe first that $t(\alpha \mid X)$ can alternatively be defined by the equation

(1.5)
$$\sum_{\alpha \in Z^s} t(\alpha \mid X)f(\alpha) = \sum_{\beta \in Z_+^n} f(X\beta)$$

for any $f:Z^s \to R$ which vanishes on all but a finite number of lattice points, $\alpha \in Z^s$. In analogy with this equation is the defining relation for the truncated power function $T(x|X)$,

$$(1.6) \qquad \int_{R^s} f(x)T(x|X)dx = \int_{R^n_+} f(Xu)du, \quad f \in C_0(R^s).$$

c.f. [DM_1]. From these two definitions the proof of the following identity taken from [DM_1]

$$(1.7) \qquad T(x|X) = \sum_{\alpha \in Z^s} t(\alpha|X)B(x-\alpha|X),$$

is easily given. We might also mention here that the discrete truncated power was useful in the analysis of a subdivision algorithms for the computation of box spline surfaces, [DM_4].

In order to use (1.7), for the purpose of studying $t(\bullet|X)$, we introduce the following terminology. We call any cone Ω contained in $<X>_+ = \{Xu : u \in R^n_+\}$ which is bounded by but not intersected by the hyperplanes $<U>$ = span U, dim $<U> = s-1$, $U \subset X$ a fundamental X-cone. From the relation

$$(1.8) \qquad D_V T(\bullet|X) = T(\bullet|X\backslash V),$$

$D_v = v \bullet \text{grad}$, and $D_V = \prod_{v \in V} D_v$ it follows that $T(\bullet|X)|_\Omega$ is in the set

$$D(X) = \{f \in \mathscr{D}'(R^s) : D_V f = 0, \ V \in \mathscr{Y}(X)\}$$

where

$$\mathscr{Y}(X) = \{V \subset X : <X\backslash V> \neq R^s\}.$$

It is known that [DM_3]

$$(1.9) \qquad D(X) \subseteq \Pi_{n-s}$$

and if we let

$$\mathscr{B}(X) = \{Y \subset X : |Y| = s, \ <Y> = R^s\}$$

then

$$\text{(1.10)} \qquad \dim \; D(X) = |\mathscr{B}(X)|.$$

Thus we can interpret $(X,\mathscr{B}(X))$ as a represented matroid whose cocircuits are the minimal elements (relative to set inclusion) in $\mathscr{Y}(X)$, [W].

Furthermore, the linear operator

$$(Af)(x) = \sum_{\alpha \in Z^s} f(\alpha)B(x - \alpha \mid X)$$

maps $D(X)$ one to one and onto itself, [BH,DM$_1$] and the translates of the box spline, $B(\bullet - \alpha \mid X)$, $\alpha \in Z^s$ are locally linearly independent if and only if

$$\text{(1.11)} \qquad |\det Y| = 1, \; Y \in \mathscr{B}(X),$$

[DM$_1$]. We say that a matrix X is unimodular when this condition holds. For the importance of the related (and nearly equivalent) notion of total unimodularity of X in integer programming, see [HK]. Applying these results to equation (1.7) we conclude for unimodular matrices X, that for any X-cone Ω, $t(\bullet \mid X)$ agrees on the set

$$b(\Omega \mid X) = \{\alpha \in Z^s : (\text{supp}B(\bullet - \alpha \mid X)) \cap \Omega \neq \phi\},$$

with some polynomial $f_\Omega \in D(X)$. Moreover, with some effort, Poisson's summation formula can be used to show that the leading homogeneous terms of f_Ω and $T(\bullet \mid X)|_\Omega$ agree.

The general description of the discrete truncated power when X is not necessarily unimodular is much more difficult. As a first step for the solution of this problem we observe (in analogy with (1.8)) that for any $V \subset X$ we have the equation

$$\text{(1.12)} \qquad \nabla_V t(\bullet \mid X) = t(\bullet \mid X \backslash V)$$

where $\nabla_y f(\bullet) = f(\bullet) - f(\bullet - y)$, $\nabla_V f = \prod_{y \in V} \nabla_y f$. Since

$$\text{supp } t(\bullet \mid X) = \mathscr{L}_+(X) = \{X\beta : \beta \in Z_+^n\}$$

we can assert that whenever $\langle X \backslash V \rangle \neq R^s$, $t(\bullet \mid X \backslash V)$ vanishes on "almost all" lattice points of Z^s. This leads us to consider the following set

$$\Delta(X) = \{f: \nabla_V f = 0, \quad V \in \mathscr{Y}(X)\}$$

(the discrete analog of D(X)). This space is also important in the study of linear dependence among translates of box splines and a complete characterization of it may be found in [DM_2]. We recall the following facts about $\Delta(X)$: let

$$b(x \mid X) = \{\alpha \in Z^s : B(x - \alpha \mid X) \neq 0\}$$

then

$$(1.13) \qquad \dim \Delta(X) = \mathrm{vol}_s(\mathrm{supp}\, B(\bullet \mid X)) = \sum_{Y \in \mathscr{B}(X)} |\det Y| = |b(x \mid X)|$$

for any $x \in R^s$ not on the cut regions of the translates of the box spline $B(\bullet - \alpha \mid X)$, $\alpha \in Z^s$ which we denote by c(X). Moreover, given any finite sequence $\{d_\alpha\}_{\alpha \in b(x \mid X)}$ for any $x \notin c(X)$, there exists a unique $f \in \Delta(X)$ such that

$$(1.14) \qquad f(\alpha) = d_\alpha, \ \alpha \in b(x \mid X).$$

In general, any $f \in \Delta(X)$ can be written uniquely as

$$(1.15) \qquad f(\alpha) = p(\alpha) + \sum_{z \in A_o(X)} z^\alpha p(\alpha \mid z), \ \alpha \in Z^s,$$

where $A_o(X) = \{z \in C^s \backslash \{(1,...,1)\} : \exists Y \in \mathscr{B}(X) \ni z^y = 1, \forall\, y \in Y\}$, some $p(\bullet \mid z) \in D(X_z)$, $X_z = \{y \in X : z^y = 1\}$ and $p \in D(X)$. Thus $D(X) \subseteq \Delta(X)$ and

$$(1.16) \qquad D(X) = \Delta(X)$$

iff X is unimodular.

We are now prepared to state

Theorem 1. *Let* Ω *be a fundamental* X-cone *then there exists a unique* $f_\Omega \in \Delta(X)$ *such that*

$$f_\Omega(\alpha) = t(\alpha \mid X), \ \alpha \in b(\Omega \mid X).$$

Moreover f_Ω *has the following properties:*

i)

$$f_\Omega(\alpha) = \delta_{0\alpha}, \quad \alpha \in b(u \mid X), \tag{1.17}$$

where $u \in \Omega$ *is chosen so that*

$$b(u \mid X) \cap \mathscr{L}_+(X) = \{0\}.$$

ii)

$$f_\Omega(\alpha) = (-1)^{n-s} f_\Omega(-\alpha - \sum_{j=1}^{n} x^j), \ \alpha \in Z_S. \tag{1.18}$$

Note that in view of (1.14) condition (1.17) uniquely determines f_Ω.

Corollary 1. *Let* $W \subset Z^s$ *be a basis such that* $\mathscr{L}(W) = \{W\alpha : \alpha \in Z^s\} \subset \mathscr{L}(Y)$, *for all* $Y \in \mathscr{B}(X)$ *and let* $\mu \in \{Wu : u \in [0,1)^s\} \cap Z^s$ *be fixed. Then* $t(\mu + W\beta \mid X)$ *as a function of* β *agrees on* $W^{-1}b(\Omega \mid X)$ *with a polynomial in* $D(W^{-1}X)$.

When Corollary 1 is specialized to $s = 1$ it reduces to Bell's result mentioned earlier.

For any integer diagonal matrix $D = \text{diag}\,(d_1 \ldots, d_n)$ we define the discrete box spline $b_D(\alpha \mid X)$ by

$$\sum_{\alpha \in Z^s} f(\alpha) b_D(\alpha \mid X) = \sum_{\substack{\beta \in Z^n_+ \\ 0 \le \beta_i < d_i}} f(X\beta)$$

i.e.

$$b_D(\alpha \mid X) = \mid \{\beta \in Z^n : X\beta = \alpha,\ 0 \le \beta_i < d_i\} \mid$$

Thus the relation

$$b_D(\alpha \mid X) = \nabla_{XD}\ t(\alpha \mid X)$$

determines, in view of the above results, the structure of $b_D(\bullet \mid X)$ as a function on Z^s. In particular, $b_D(\bullet \mid X)$ is a piecewise polynomial if (1.11) holds, i.e. X is unimodular.

For another application of Theorem 1 we return to the problem of counting magic squares. MacMahon showed that for $m \le 3$, $H_m(r)$ is a polynomial in r of degree $(m-1)^2$,[M]. This was conjectured to be true for all m by Anand, Dumir and Gupta [ADG]. Subsequently, Stanley [S] proved the following facts:

i) $H_m(\bullet)$ is a polynomial of degree $(m-1)^2$;

ii) $H_m(-1) = H_m(-2) = \ldots = H_m(-m+1) = 0$;

iii) $H_m(r) = (-1)^{m-1} H_m(-m-r)$.

These results appear as consequences of the above theorem. In fact recalling that $H_m(r) = t(re \mid M_m)$ (c.f.(1.3)), ii) and iii) follow from (1.17) and (1.18) respectively. Furthermore, it can also be shown that M_m is unimodular so that $\Delta(M_m) = D(M_m)$. Since $n\text{-}s = m^2 - 2m + 1 = (m-1)^2$, i) is an immediate consequence of (1.9) and Corollary 1.

As a final remark we mention that it can be shown that

$$\dim D(M_m) = \mid \mathcal{B}(M_m) \mid = m^{2m-2}.$$

Detailed proofs of these results and related facts will appear elsewhere.

References

[ADG],H. Anand, V.C. Dumir, H. Gupta, A combinatorial distribution problem, Duke Math. J., 33 (1966), 757-769.

[B], E.T Bell, Interpolated denumerants and Lambert series, Amer. J. Math 65 (1943), 382-386.

[BH], C. de Boor, K. Höllig, B-splines from parallelpipeds, J. d'Analyse, Math., 42(1982/83), 99-115.

[DM_1], W.Dahmen, C.A. Micchelli, Recent progress in multivariate splines, in Approximation Theory IV, eds., C.K. Chui, L.L. Schumacher, J.W. Ward, Academic Press, 1983, 27-121.

[DM_2], W. Dahmen, C.A. Micchelli, On the solution of certain systems of partial difference equations and linear dependence of translates of box splines, IBM Research Report RC 46405, 1984, to appear TAMS.

[DM_3], W. Dahmen, C.A. Micchelli, On the local linear dependence of translates of multivariate splines, IBM Research Report RC 10168, 1983 to appear Studia Mathematica.

[DM_4], W. Dahmen, C.A. Micchelli, Subdivision algorithms for the generation of box spline surfaces, Computer Aided Geometric Design 1(1984), 115-129.

[HK], A.J. Hoffman and J.B. Kruskal, Integral boundary points of convex polyhedra in: Ann. Math. Study 38, Princeton University Press, N.J. 1956, 223-241.

[M], P.A. MacMahon, Combinatory Analysis, Vol. I, II, Cambridge University Press, 1916; reprinted by Chelsea, New York 1960.

[S], R.P. Stanley, Combinatorics and Commutative Algebra, Birkhäuser, Boston 1983.

[W], D.J.A. Welsh, Matroid Theory, Academic Press, New York, 1976.

International Series of
Numerical Mathematics, Vol. 75

INTERMEDIATE BLENDING INTERPOLATION

Franz-Jürgen Delvos

0. Introduction

N-variate blending interpolation involves functions of (N-1) independent variables as data functions in contrast to N-variate product interpolation which depends on scalars only. It is the objective of this paper to construct new Boolean interpolation schemes which have functions of (N-m) independent variables as interpolation parameters with $1 \leq m \leq N$.

1. Definitions and basic facts

Let D_n be a normal, K_n th order, ordinary, differential operator in the independent variable x_n with real continuous coefficients $\alpha_{ni}(x_n)$, $i = 0,\ldots,K_n$, over the interval $[a_n,b_n]$, $1 \leq n \leq N$:

$$(1.1) \quad D_n = \sum_{j=0}^{K_n} \alpha_{n,j}(x_n) D_{x_n}^j \quad , \quad D_{x_n} = \frac{d}{dx_n} .$$

Let Φ_n be the kernel of D_n and take P_n to be the projector on $C^{K_n} = C^{K_n}[a_n,b_n]$ with range Φ_n:

$$(1.2) \quad P_n(U) = \sum_{i=1}^{K_n} \lambda_i^n(U)\, \phi_i^n$$

where $\{ \phi_i^n : 1 \leq i \leq K_n \}$ is the cardinal basis for Φ_n with with respect to the set of bounded linear functionals $\{ \lambda_i^n : 1 \leq i \leq K_n \}$:

$$(1.3) \quad \lambda_i^n(\phi_k^n) = \delta_{i,k} \quad , \quad i,k = 1,\ldots,K_n \quad .$$

Let T_n denote the right inverse of D_n with respect to the initial projector P_n [11,12,10,1,2,5]. The identity of C^{K_n} is denoted by I_n and the identity operator of C^0 is denoted by J_n . Then the relations

$$(1.4) \quad I_n = P_n + T_n D_n \quad ,$$

$$(1.5) \quad P_n T_n = 0 \quad .$$

$$(1.6) \quad D_n T_n = J_n$$

hold. The operators D_n, I_n, P_n are parametrically extended to the space of N-variate functions $C^{K_1,\ldots,K_N}$. The operators J_n and T_n are parametrically extended to $C^{0,\ldots,0}$. The extensions are denoted by $\tilde{D}_n$, $\tilde{I}_n$, $\tilde{T}_n$, $\tilde{J}_n$, and

$$(1.7) \quad \tilde{P}_n =: Q_n \quad .$$

Moreover, the parametric extension of λ_i^n is denoted by L_i^n . For any function $F \in C^{K_1,\ldots,K_N}$ the function

$$(1.8) \quad G = Q_n(F) = \sum_{i=1}^{K_n} L_i^n(F)\, \phi_i^n(x_n)$$

satisfies the interpolatory conditions

$$(1.9) \quad L_i^n(G) = L_i^n(F) \quad , \quad i = 1,\ldots,K_n \quad .$$

The data functions $L_i^n(F)$ depend on the variables $x_1,\ldots,x_{n-1}$, $x_{n+1},\ldots,x_N$.

The partial differential operator $\tilde{D}_n$ is right invertible with right inverse $\tilde{T}_n$ and initial projector $\tilde{P}_n = Q_n$:

$$(1.10)\qquad \tilde{I}_n = Q_n + \tilde{T}_n \tilde{D}_n \quad ,$$

$$(1.11)\qquad Q_n \tilde{T}_n = 0 \quad ,$$

$$(1.12)\qquad \tilde{D}_n \tilde{T}_n = \tilde{J}_n \quad .$$

Thus, the kernel of $\tilde{D}_n$ is the range of Q_n :

$$(1.13)\qquad \ker(\tilde{D}_n) = \operatorname{ran}(Q_n) \quad .$$

It follows from (1.13) that $G = Q_n(F)$ is the unique function of class $C^{K_1,\ldots,K_N}$ satisfying the interpolatory conditions (1.9) and the partial differential equation

$$(1.14)\qquad \tilde{D}_n G = 0 \quad .$$

By virtue of their definition as parametric extensions the projectors $Q_1,\ldots,Q_N$ are commutative over $C^{K_1,\ldots,K_N}$:

$$(1.15)\qquad Q_m Q_n = Q_n Q_m \quad , \quad 1 \leq m,n \leq N \quad .$$

Then there is a maximal Boolean algebra $\mathbb{B}$ of commutative projectors over $C^{K_1,\ldots,K_N}$ which contains $Q_1,\ldots,Q_N$ [6,7,4,3]. The Boolean algebra $\mathbb{B}$ is closed with respect to the binary operations of multiplication, Boolean addition , and the unary operation of complementation :

$$(1.16)\quad AB = BA \in \mathbb{B} ,$$

$$(1.17)\quad A \oplus B = A + B - AB \in \mathbb{B} ,$$

$$(1.18)\quad A' = I - A \in \mathbb{B}$$

for $A, B \in \mathbb{B}$. I is the identity operator on $C^{K_1,\dots,K_N}$ and J is the identity operator on $C^{0,\dots,0}$. The Boolean algebra is a partial ordered set [6,7] . $A \geq B$ means $AB = A$. Any finite subset of projectors $A_1,\dots,A_K$ has a unique maximal element M in $\mathbb{B}$ which is given by its Boolean sum :

$$(1.19)\quad M = A_1 \oplus A_2 \oplus \dots \oplus A_K .$$

2. Intermediate blending interpolation

The projector of N-variate blending interpolation [6,7] is the maximal element of the projectors $Q_1,\dots,Q_N$:

$$(2.1)\quad M_1 = Q_1 \oplus Q_2 \oplus \dots \oplus Q_N .$$

M_1 has the sum representation

$$(2.2)\quad M_1 = \sum_{n=1}^{N} \Big(\sum_{i_1 < \dots < i_n} Q_{i_1} \dots Q_{i_n} \Big) (-1)^{n-1}$$

where the product projector $Q_{i_1} \dots Q_{i_n}$ is given by

$$(2.3)\quad Q_{i_1} \dots Q_{i_n}(F) = \sum_{s_1=1}^{K_{i_1}} \dots \sum_{s_n=1}^{K_{i_n}} L_{s_1}^{i_1} \dots L_{s_n}^{i_n}(F)\, \phi_{s_1}^{i_1}(x_{i_1}) \dots \phi_{s_n}^{i_n}(x_{i_n})$$

for $F \in C^{K_1,\dots,K_N}$.

The function $Q_{i_1} \dots Q_{i_n}(F)$ satisfies the interpolatory conditions

$$(2.4) \quad L_{s_1}^{i_1} \dots L_{s_n}^{i_n}(Q_{i_1} \dots Q_{i_n}(F)) = L_{s_1}^{i_1} \dots L_{s_n}^{i_n}(F) ,$$

$$s_1 \le K_{i_1}, \dots\dots, s_n \le K_{i_n} .$$

The data functions $L_{s_1}^{i_1} \dots L_{s_n}^{i_n}(F)$ depend on N-n variables. The N-variate blending interpolant $M_1(F)$ has data functions which depend on N-1 variables. The N-variate product interpolant $M_N(F) := Q_1 \dots Q_N(F)$ depends on constant functions only.

The projector of intermediate blending interpolation is defined as the maximal element of the set of projectors

$$\{ Q_{i_1} \dots Q_{i_r} : 1 \le i_1 < \dots < i_r \le N \}$$

which is given by

$$(2.5) \quad M_r = \bigoplus_{i_1 < \dots < i_r} Q_{i_1} \dots Q_{i_r} .$$

Note that

$$M_1 = Q_1 \oplus \dots \oplus Q_N$$

and

$$M_N = Q_1 \cdot \dots \cdot Q_N .$$

<u>Proposition 1.1</u>

Given $F \in C^{K_1, \dots, K_N}$ the intermediate blending interpolant $M_r(F)$ is the unique function in $\mathrm{ran}(M_r)$ which satisfies the interpolatory conditions

$$(2.6)\qquad L_{s_1}^{i_1}\cdots L_{s_r}^{i_r}(M_r(F)) = L_{s_1}^{i_1}\cdots L_{s_r}^{i_r}(F) \quad ,$$

$$s_1 \leqq K_{i_1},\dots,s_r \leqq K_{i_r} \quad , \quad 1 \leqq i_1 < \dots < i_r \leqq N \quad .$$

Proof: It follows from the construction of M_r that

$$(2.7)\qquad Q_{i_1}\cdots Q_{i_r} M_r = Q_{i_1}\cdots Q_{i_r} \quad , \quad 1 \leqq i_1 < \dots < i_r \leqq N.$$

Using (2.4) and (2.7) we obtain (2.6) . Next assume that $G \in \mathrm{ran}(M_r)$ satisfies

$$L_{s_1}^{i_1}\cdots L_{s_r}^{i_r}(G) = 0 \quad ; \quad s_1 \leqq K_{i_1},\dots,s_r \leqq K_{i_r} \quad ;$$
$$1 \leqq i_1 < \dots < i_r \leqq N \quad .$$

This implies

$$Q_{i_1}\cdots Q_{i_r}(G) = 0 \quad , \quad 1 \leqq i_1 < \dots < i_r \leqq N$$

whence $G = M_r(G) = 0$ follows. This completes the proof of proposition 1.1 .

Proposition 1.2

The intermediate blending interpolant $M_r(F)$ satisfies the system of partial differential equations

$$(2.8)\qquad \tilde{D}_{j_1}\cdots\tilde{D}_{j_{\bar{r}}} M_r(F) = 0 \quad , \quad 1 \leqq j_1 < \dots < j_{\bar{r}} \leqq N \quad ,$$
$$\bar{r} = 1 + N - r \quad .$$

Proof: By virtue of their construction the differential operators $\tilde{D}_1,\dots,\tilde{D}_N$ commute over $C^{K_1,\dots,K_N}$.

Moreover we have

$$(2.9)\quad \tilde{T}_{j_1}\cdots\tilde{T}_{j_{\bar{r}}}\tilde{D}_{j_1}\cdots\tilde{D}_{j_{\bar{r}}} = Q'_{j_1}\cdots Q'_{j_{\bar{r}}} \quad ;$$

and

$$(2.10)\quad \tilde{D}_{j_1}\cdots\tilde{D}_{j_{\bar{r}}} Q'_{j_1}\cdots Q'_{j_{\bar{r}}} = \tilde{D}_{j_1}\cdots\tilde{D}_{j_{\bar{r}}} \quad .$$

Thus we obtain

$$(2.11)\quad \ker(\tilde{D}_{j_1}\cdots\tilde{D}_{j_{\bar{r}}}) = \ker(Q'_{j_1}\cdots Q'_{j_{\bar{r}}}) \quad ,$$

$$1 \leqq j_1 < \ldots < j_{\bar{r}} \leqq N \quad , \quad \bar{r} = 1+N-r \quad .$$

Since

$$(2.12)\quad \{i_1,\ldots,i_r\} \cap \{j_1,\ldots,j_{\bar{r}}\} \neq \emptyset \quad ,$$

$$1 \leqq i_1 < \ldots < i_r \leqq N \; , \; 1 \leqq j_1 < \ldots < j_{\bar{r}} \leqq N$$

we can conclude

$$Q'_{j_1}\cdots Q'_{j_{\bar{r}}} M_r = \bigoplus_{i_1 < \ldots < i_r} Q'_{j_1}\cdots Q'_{j_{\bar{r}}} Q_{i_1}\cdots Q_{i_r} = 0$$

whence (2.8) follows in view of (2.10) .

3. A sum representation of intermediate blending

It is the objective of this section to extend the representation formula (2.2) for the projector M_1 of blending interpolation to the projector M_r of intermediate blending interpolation.

Proposition 3.1

The projector M_r of intermediate blending interpolation possesses the sum representation

$$(3.1)\quad M_r = \sum_{k=r}^{N} \Big(\sum_{i_1 < .. < i_k} Q_{i_1} \cdots Q_{i_k} \Big) \binom{k-1}{r-1} (-1)^{k-r} \quad .$$

Proof: We apply induction over N . For this purpose we introduce the projectors

$$(3.2)\quad A_{s,K} = \bigoplus_{1 \leqq i_1 < .. < i_s \leqq K} Q_{i_1} \cdots Q_{i_s} \quad , \quad 1 \leqq s \leqq K \quad .$$

These projectors are elements of the Boolean algebra $\mathbb{B}$. Using these projectors we obtain the representation

$$(3.3)\quad M_r = A_{r,N-1} \oplus (A_{r-1,N-1} Q_N) \quad .$$

Since

$$(3.4)\quad A_{r,N-1} A_{r-1,N-1} = A_{r,N-1}$$

we get

$$(3.5)\quad M_r = A_{r,N-1} + A_{r-1,N-1} Q_N - A_{r,N-1} Q_N \quad .$$

Applying the induction hypothesis to the projectors $A_{r,N-1}$ and $A_{r-1,N-1}$ we can conclude

$$M_r$$

$$= \sum_{k=r}^{N-1} (-1)^{k-r} \binom{k-1}{r-1} \sum_{1 \leqq i_1 < .. < i_k \leqq N-1} Q_{i_1} \cdots Q_{i_k}$$

$$+ \sum_{k=r-1}^{N-1} (-1)^{k+1-r} \binom{k-1}{r-2} \sum_{1 \leqq i_1 < .. < i_k \leqq N-1} Q_{i_1} \cdots Q_{i_k} Q_N \quad -$$

$$- \sum_{k=r}^{N-1} (-1)^{k-r} \binom{k-1}{r-1} \sum_{1 \leqq i_1 < .. < i_k \leqq N-1} Q_{i_1} \cdots Q_{i_k} Q_N$$

$$= \sum_{k=r}^{N-1} (-1)^{k-r} \binom{k-1}{r-1} \sum_{1 \leqq i_1 < .. < i_k \leqq N-1} Q_{i_1} \cdots Q_{i_k}$$

$$+ \sum_{k=r-1}^{N-1} (-1)^{k+1-r} \binom{k-1}{r-2} \sum_{1 \leqq i_1 < .. < i_k \leqq N-1} Q_{i_1} \cdots Q_{i_k} Q_N$$

$$+ \sum_{k=r}^{N-1} (-1)^{k+1-r} \binom{k-1}{r-1} \sum_{1 \leqq i_1 < .. < i_k \leqq N-1} Q_{i_1} \cdots Q_{i_k} Q_N$$

$$= \sum_{k=r}^{N-1} (-1)^{k-r} \binom{k-1}{r-1} \sum_{1 \leqq i_1 < .. < i_k \leqq N-1} Q_{i_1} \cdots Q_{i_k}$$

$$+ \sum_{k=r}^{N-1} (-1)^{(k+1-r)} \left(\binom{k-1}{r-2} + \binom{k-1}{r-1} \right) \sum_{1 \leqq i_1 < .. < i_k \leqq N-1} Q_{i_1} \cdot\cdot Q_{i_k} Q_N$$

$$+ \sum_{1 \leqq i_1 < .. < i_{r-1} \leqq N-1} Q_{i_1} \cdots Q_{i_{r-1}} Q_N$$

$$= \sum_{k=r}^{N-1} (-1)^{k-r} \binom{k-1}{r-1} \sum_{1 \leqq i_1 < .. < i_k \leqq N-1} Q_{i_1} \cdots Q_{i_k}$$

$$+ \sum_{k=r}^{N-1} (-1)^{k+1-r} \binom{k}{r-1} \sum_{1 \leqq i_1 < .. < i_k \leqq N-1} Q_{i_1} \cdots Q_{i_k} Q_N$$

$$+ \sum_{1 \leqq i_1 < .. < i_{r-1} \leqq N-1} Q_{i_1} \cdots Q_{i_{r-1}} Q_N$$

$$=$$

$$= \sum_{k=r}^{N-1} (-1)^{k-r} \binom{k-1}{r-1} \sum_{1 \leqq i_1 < \ldots < i_k \leqq N-1} Q_{i_1} \cdots Q_{i_k}$$

$$+ \sum_{k=r+1}^{N} (-1)^{k-r} \binom{k-1}{r-1} \sum_{1 \leqq i_1 < \ldots < i_{k-1} \leqq N-1} Q_{i_1} \cdots Q_{i_{k-1}} Q_N$$

$$+ \sum_{1 \leqq i_1 < \ldots < i_{r-1} \leqq N-1} Q_{i_1} \cdots Q_{i_{r-1}} Q_N$$

$$= \sum_{1 \leqq i_1 < \ldots < i_r \leqq N-1} Q_{i_1} \cdots Q_{i_r}$$

$$+ \sum_{k=r+1}^{N-1} (-1)^{k-r} \binom{k-1}{r-1} \Big(\sum_{1 \leqq i_1 < \ldots < i_k \leqq N-1} Q_{i_1} \cdots Q_{i_k}$$

$$+ \sum_{1 \leqq i_1 < \ldots < i_{k-1} \leqq N-1} Q_{i_1} \cdots Q_{i_{k-1}} Q_N \Big)$$

$$+ (-1)^{N-r} \binom{N-1}{r-1} \sum_{1 \leqq i_1 < \ldots < i_{N-1} \leqq N-1} Q_{i_1} \cdots Q_{i_{N-1}} Q_N$$

$$+ \sum_{1 \leqq i_1 < \ldots < i_{r-1} \leqq N-1} Q_{i_1} \cdots Q_{i_{r-1}} Q_N$$

$$= \sum_{i_1 < \ldots < i_r \leqq N-1} Q_{i_1} \cdots Q_{i_r} + (-1)^{N-r} \binom{N-1}{r-1} Q_1 \cdots Q_N$$

$$+ \sum_{k=r+1}^{N-1} \Big(\sum_{i_1 < \ldots < i_k} Q_{i_1} \cdots Q_{i_k} \Big) \binom{k-1}{r-1} (-1)^{k-r}$$

$$= \bigoplus_{1 \leqq i_1 < \ldots < i_r \leqq N} Q_{i_1} \cdots Q_{i_r} = M_r$$

which completes the proof of proposition 3.1 .

The first example of intermediate blending interpolation was constructed by Gordon [7] for $N = 3$ and $r = 2$:

$$M_2 = Q_1Q_2 \oplus Q_1Q_3 \oplus Q_2Q_3$$

$$= Q_1Q_2 + Q_1Q_3 + Q_2Q_3 - 2\,Q_1Q_2Q_3 \quad .$$

We list the intermediate blending interpolation projectors M_r for $N = 4$:

$$M_2 = Q_1Q_2 \oplus Q_1Q_3 \oplus Q_1Q_4 \oplus Q_2Q_3 \oplus Q_2Q_4 \oplus Q_3Q_4$$

$$= Q_1Q_2 + Q_1Q_3 + Q_1Q_4 + Q_2Q_3 + Q_2Q_4 + Q_3Q_4$$

$$- 2\,(Q_1Q_2Q_3 + Q_1Q_2Q_4 + Q_1Q_3Q_4 + Q_2Q_3Q_4)$$

$$+ 3\,Q_1Q_2Q_3Q_4 \quad ,$$

$$M_3 = Q_1Q_2Q_3 \oplus Q_1Q_2Q_4 \oplus Q_1Q_3Q_4 \oplus Q_2Q_3Q_4$$

$$= Q_1Q_2Q_3 + Q_1Q_2Q_4 + Q_1Q_3Q_4 + Q_2Q_3Q_4$$

$$- 3\,Q_1Q_2Q_3Q_4 \quad .$$

Remark: I have to thank Dr. Gerd Neumann , University of Siegen, for helpful discussions in proving proposition 3.1 . He conjectured (3.1) .

4. The remainder operator

It follows from the duality theory of Boolean algebras that the remainder projector of N-variate blending interpolation is obtained by replacing Q_i by Q_i' and multiplication by Boolean addition and vice versa :

$$(4.1) \quad M_1' = (Q_1 \oplus Q_2 \oplus \ldots \oplus Q_N)' = Q_1' Q_2' \ldots Q_N' \quad .$$

Applying the method of duality to the projector M_r of intermediate blending interpolation we obtain the associated remainder projector

$$(4.2) \quad M_r' = \prod_{1 \leq i_1 < \ldots < i_r \leq N} Q_{i_1}' \oplus \ldots \oplus Q_{i_r}' \quad .$$

It is easily seen that

$$(4.3) \quad M_r' = \bigoplus_{j_1 < \ldots < j_{\bar{r}}} Q_{j_1}' \ldots Q_{j_{\bar{r}}}' \quad , \quad \bar{r} = 1 + N - r \quad .$$

Thus, M_r' has the same Boolean structure as M_r . An application of proposition 3.1 yields the following proposition .

<u>Proposition 4.1</u>

The remainder projector M_r' of intermediate blending interpolation possesses the sum representation

$$(4.4) \quad M_r' = I - \bigoplus_{i_1 < \ldots < i_r} Q_{i_1} \ldots Q_{i_r}$$

$$= \sum_{k=1+N-r}^{N} \Big(\sum_{i_1 < \ldots < i_k} Q_{i_1}' \ldots Q_{i_k}' \Big) \binom{k-1}{N-r} (-1)^{k-1-N+r} \quad .$$

We list some special cases of (4.4). For arbitrary N we get

$$(4.5) \quad M_N' = \sum_{k=1}^{N} \Big(\sum_{i_1 < \ldots < i_k} Q_{i_1}' \ldots Q_{i_k}' \Big) (-1)^{k-1}$$

which is the remainder projector of N-variate product interpolation [6].

Next assume $N = 3$, $r = 2$. Then we have

$$M_2' = Q_1'Q_2' + Q_1'Q_3' + Q_2'Q_3' - 2\,Q_1'Q_2'Q_3'$$

which is given in [7]. Next we consider $N = 4$ and $r = 2,3$:

$$M_2' = Q_1'Q_2'Q_3' + Q_1'Q_2'Q_4' + Q_1'Q_3'Q_4' + Q_2'Q_3'Q_4' - 3\,Q_1'Q_2'Q_3'Q_4' \quad ,$$

$$\begin{aligned} M_3' = {} & Q_1'Q_2' + Q_1'Q_3' + Q_1'Q_4' + Q_2'Q_3' + Q_2'Q_4' + Q_3'Q_4' \\ & - 2(Q_1'Q_2'Q_3' + Q_1'Q_2'Q_4' + Q_1'Q_3'Q_4' + Q_2'Q_3'Q_4') \\ & + 3\,Q_1'Q_2'Q_3'Q_4' \quad . \end{aligned}$$

Finally we apply proposition 4.1 to derive a unique characterization of the intermediate blending interpolant $M_r(F)$ as the solution of a boundary value problem.

<u>Proposition 4.2</u>

For any function $F \in C^{K_1,\ldots,K_N}$ the intermediate blending interpolant is the unique function $G = M_r(F)$ in $C^{K_1,\ldots,K_N}$ satisfying the interpolatory conditions

$$(4.6)\quad L_{s_1}^{i_1}\ldots L_{s_r}^{i_r}(G) = L_{s_1}^{i_1}\ldots L_{s_r}^{i_r}(F) \;,\; s_1 \le K_{i_1},\ldots,s_r \le K_{i_r} \;, \quad 1 \le i_1 < \ldots < i_r \le N$$

and the system of partial differential equations

$$(4.7)\quad \tilde{D}_{j_1}\ldots\tilde{D}_{j_{\bar r}}\,G = 0 \quad , \; 1 \le j_1 < \ldots < j_{\bar r} \le N \quad , \; \bar r = 1+N-r \quad .$$

<u>Proof:</u> Assume that the function G satisfies the system of partial differential equations (4.7). Since we have

$$\ker(\tilde{D}_{j_1}\ldots\tilde{D}_{j_{\bar r}}) = \ker(Q'_{j_1}\ldots Q'_{j_{\bar r}}) \quad , \quad 1 \leq j_1 < \ldots < j_{\bar r} \leq N \; , \quad \bar r = 1+N-r \; ,$$

we obtain $M'_r(G) = 0$ and therefore

$$G = M_r(G) \quad .$$

Now proposition 4.2 follows from proposition 1.1 and formula (4.3) .

Concluding remarks

We have mainly considered algebraic aspects of multivariate Boolean interpolation which are related to the papers [6,7,4,3]. Approximation properties of function spaces constructed via bivariate blending interpolation are studied in the papers [8,9]. It should be of interest to investigate approximation properties of functions spaces defined by blending interpolation methods of arbitrary dimensions.

References

1 G. BASZENSKI: Zur Konvergenzbeschleunigung von Orthogonal-Doppelreihen. Dissertation , Universität Siegen 1983 .

2 G. BASZENSKI and F.-J. DELVOS: Accelerating the rate of convergence of bivariate Fourier expansions. In "Approximation Theory IV" (Eds.: C.K. Chui, L.L Schumaker, J.D. Ward), Academic Press, New York 1983 .

3 F.-J. DELVOS: d-variate Boolean interpolation. Journal of Approximation Theory 34(1982), 99-114 .

4 F.-J. DELVOS and H. POSDORF: Generalized Biermann interpolation. Resultate der Mathematik 5(1982), 6-18 .

5 F.-J. DELVOS and W. SCHEMPP: The method of parametric extensions applied to right invertible operators. Numer. Funct. Anal. and Optimiz., 6(1983), 135-148 .

6 W.J. GORDON: Distributive lattices and the approximation of multivariate functions. In "Approximation Theory with Special Emphasis on Spline Functions" (Ed.: I.J. Schoenberg), pp. 223-277, Academic Press, New York 1969 .

7 W.J. GORDON: Blending function methods of bivariate and multivariate interpolation and approximation. SIAM J. Numer. Anal. 8(1971), 158-177 .

8 W. HAUSSMANN and K. ZELLER: Blending interpolation and best L^1-approximation. Arch. Math. 40(1983), 542-552 .

9 W. HAUSSMANN, K. JETTER and B. STEINHAUS: Degree of best approximation by trigonometric blending functions. Math. Z. 189(1985), 143-150 .

10 D. PRZEWORSKA-ROLEWICZ: Algebraic theory of right invertible operators. Studia Math. 48(1973), 129-144 .

11 M. TASCHE: Eine einheitliche Herleitung verschiedener Interpolationsformeln mittels der Taylorschen Formel der Operatorenrechnung. ZAMM 61(1981), 379-393 .

12 M. TASCHE: A unified approach to interpolation methods. Journal of Integral Equations 4(1982), 55-75 .

apl. Prof. Dr. Franz-Jürgen DELVOS

Universität Siegen, Lehrstuhl für Mathematik I ,

Hölderlin-Str. 3

D-5900 Siegen (W.-Germany)

International Series of
Numerical Mathematics, Vol. 75

Hermite-Interpolation in N Variables and Minimal Cubature Formulae

Dedicated to Prof. Dr. K. Zeller on the occasion of his 60th birthday

by H. Engels

Summary

A Hermitian interpolating polynomial for a function of N real variables and its first derivatives is introduced, which generalizes the Hermitian interpolating polynomial in one dimension. On integration "good cubature formulae" are obtained, that means the cubature formulae have positive weights, and the nodes are inside the domain of integration if this is convex. In addition the cubature formulae are minimal formulae.

1. Introduction

The well-known Gaussian quadrature formulae have a lot of important properties (cf. e. g. [1]), and so many attempts have been made to generalize these Gaussian formulae to the N-dimensional cubature problem.
It seems to be clear now, that every such generalization has to give up some of these properties, while certain other properties are carried over.

In this paper we construct cubature formulae on integration of a Hermitian interpolating polynomial $H_n(f,x)$ as did Markoff 1885 (cf. [1]) to obtain the Gaussian quadrature formulae.
To this end we establish first a Hermitian interpolating polynomial $H_n(f,\underline{x})$ for $f(\underline{x})$ and its first partial derivatives in N dimensions for n distinct nodes $\underline{x}_i$, $i = 1(1)n$. This is a polynomial of degree 2n-1 as in one dimension, however, it does in general not reproduce any given polynomial of

degree $\leq 2n-1$. Nevertheless we obtain a cubature formula with n nodes on integration of $H_n(f,\underline{x})$:

$$C_n f \equiv \int_\Omega W(t)\, H_n(f,\underline{x})\, d\Omega$$

where $W(\underline{x})$ is a weight-function, which is integrable,and has constant sign in Ω such that the moments

$$M_{|\underline{\alpha}|} = \int_\Omega W(\underline{x})\, \underline{x}^{\underline{\alpha}}\, d\Omega < \infty \quad .$$

exist.

As in one dimension, we require that all the weights of the partial derivatives in $C_n f$ vanish to obtain a nonlinear system S of equations for the nN components of the node vectors $\underline{x}_i$, $i = 1(1)n$.

The system S represents the necessary conditions to minimize

$$\int_\Omega W(\underline{x})\, \omega_n^2(\underline{x})\, d\Omega$$

where $\omega_n^2(\underline{x})$ is the nonnegative nodal polynomial, which for $N = 1$ reduces to $\omega_n^2(x) = (x-x_1)^2 \ldots (x-x_n)^2$. Hence $C_n f$ is a minimal cubature formula. If the system S possesses a solution of n real distinct nodes $\underline{x}_i$, $i = 1(1)n$, then the weights A_i of $C_n f$ are positive, as for $N = 1$. If in addition Ω is a convex domain, then the nodes $\underline{x}_i$ are inside Ω , as for $N = 1$.

So it seems, that most of the important properties of Gaussian quadrature formulae are carried over to these minimal cubature formulae $C_n f$. The main difference with respect to usual generalizations is the lack of an algebraic degree of $C_n f$. In general the constants and some further low degree polynomials are not integrated exactly.(However, this occurs already for certain Gaussian type quadrature procedures such as Wilf-type procedures.)

2.1 The Hermitian interpolating polynomial

Assume that we are given n distinct real nodes $\underline{x}_i$, $i = 1(1)n$, situated in the N-dimensional domain Ω , $\underline{x}_i^T = (x_i^1,\dots,x_i^N)$. We define the nodal polynomial

$$\omega_n^2(\underline{x}) = (\underline{x} - \underline{x}_1)^2 \dots (\underline{x} - \underline{x}_n)^2 ,$$

and the n Lagrange-type cardinal polynomials

$$\lambda_i^2(\underline{x}) = \frac{(\underline{x}-\underline{x}_1)^2 \dots (\underline{x}-\underline{x}_{i-1})^2(\underline{x}-\underline{x}_{i+1})^2 \dots (\underline{x}-\underline{x}_n)^2}{(\underline{x}_i-\underline{x}_1)^2 \dots (\underline{x}_i-\underline{x}_{i-1})^2 (\underline{x}_i-\underline{x}_{i+1})^2 \dots (\underline{x}_i-\underline{x}_n)^2} , \quad i = 1(1)n ,$$

with the property $\lambda_i^2(\underline{x}_k) = \delta_{ik}$ (= Kronecker-delta).

As for $N = 1$ the $\lambda_i^2(\underline{x})$ and $\omega_n^2(\underline{x})$ are closely connected

$$\frac{\operatorname{grad} \omega_n^2(\underline{x}_k)}{\omega_n^2(\underline{x}_k)} = \operatorname{grad} \lambda_k^2(\underline{x}_k) = 2 \sum_{\substack{j=1 \\ j \neq k}}^{n} \frac{\underline{x}_k - \underline{x}_j}{(\underline{x}_k - \underline{x}_j)^2} .$$

With these polynomials we obtain the wanted Hermitian interpolating polynomial.

Theorem 1

Let $\underline{x}_1,\dots,\underline{x}_n$ be n distinct given nodes, and $f(\underline{x})$ a function which is defined and differentiable at least in a nonempty ball around each node. Then the polynomial

$$H_n(f,\underline{x}) \equiv \sum_{i=1}^{n} \Big\{ [1 - (\underline{x} - \underline{x}_i) \operatorname{grad} \lambda_i^2(\underline{x}_i)] f(\underline{x}_i) + (\underline{x} - \underline{x}_i) \operatorname{grad} f(\underline{x}_i) \Big\} \lambda_i^2(x) \in \mathbb{P}_{2n-1}$$

interpolates the function $f(\underline{x})$ and its gradient vector $\operatorname{grad} f(\underline{x})$ at the nodes $\underline{x}_1,\dots,\underline{x}_n$.

The proof is nearly the same as in one dimension.

Note that in $N = 1$ dimension $H_n(f,x)$ is the well-known Hermitian interpolating polynomial of degree 2n-1 with $[\lambda_i^2(x_i)]' = 2\lambda_i'(x_i) = \omega_n''(x_i)/\omega_n'(x_i)$.

2.2 Properties of $H_n(f,\underline{x})$

For $N = 1$ dimension $H_n(f,x)$ reproduces every polynomial $p_k(x)$ of degree at most $2n-1$ identically

$$H_n(p_k(x),x) = p_k(x) \quad , \quad p_k(x) \in \mathbb{P}_{2n-1} \quad .$$

For $N > 1$ this is no longer true in general, since there are

$$\binom{N+2n-1}{N} = \frac{(N+2n-1)!}{N!(2n-1)!}$$

monomials of degree at most $2n-1$, while we interpolate for $n(N+1)$ function values and derivatives only, and in general

$$n(N+1) \leq \binom{N+2n-1}{N} \quad .$$

Equality occurs for $N = 1$, n arbitrary, and for $n = 1$, $N > 1$ arbitrary so that we cannot expect that every polynomial $p_k(\underline{x}) \in \mathbb{P}_{2n-1}$ is a fixed element of $H_n(f,\underline{x})$.
Nevertheless there exists a subspace in $\mathbb{P}_{2n-1}$ which is reproduced:

Theorem 2

Assume that $\mathbb{R}_\ell$, $\ell = n(N+1)$, is the convex hull of

$$\left\{\lambda_k^2(\underline{x}) \text{ and } (x^j - x_k^j)\, \lambda_k^2(\underline{x}) \quad , \quad k = 1(1)n \quad , \quad j = 1(1)N\right\} .$$

Then for every $p(\underline{x}) \in \mathbb{R}_\ell \subseteq \mathbb{P}_{2n-1}$ we have that

$$H_n(p(\underline{x}),\underline{x}) = p(\underline{x}) \quad \text{identically.}$$

The proof is essentially as for $N = 1$ (cf. [1]).

2.3 Error-representation and convergence of $H_n(f,\underline{x})$

Concerning the error of interpolation and the convergence of $H_n(f,\underline{x})$ for $n \to \infty$ there is hardly anything to be said until now.
Trivially, the error is to be represented by a function

$$E_n(f,\underline{x}) = \omega_n^2(\underline{x})\, r_n(f,\underline{x}) \quad ,$$

however, $r_n(f,\underline{x})$ is not yet determined. Because of this, we cannot prove convergence using the error of interpolation. However, if the nodes $\underline{x}_i$ become dense in Ω for $n \to \infty$, and if the coefficients

$$1 - (\underline{x} - \underline{x}_i)\ \mathrm{grad}\ \lambda_i^2(\underline{x}_i) \quad , \quad i = 1(1)n \quad ,$$

are not negative in Ω then $H_n(f,\underline{x})$ is a positive operator, and theorems of Korovkin type may be applied.

3.1 Cubature formulae

Assume we are given a weight function $W(\underline{x})$, defined and nonnegative in Ω such that the moments

$$\int_\Omega W(\underline{x})\, \underline{x}^{\underline{\alpha}}\, d\Omega < \infty \quad , \quad |\underline{\alpha}| = 0(1)\ldots$$

exist, and $W(\underline{x})$ is not identically zero.
Then on integration of $W(\underline{x})\, H_n(f,\underline{x})$ we obtain the cubature formula

$$C_n f = \int_\Omega W(\underline{x})\, H_n(f,\underline{x})\, d\Omega = \sum_{i=1}^{n} (A_i\, f(\underline{x}_i) + \underline{B}_i\ \mathrm{grad}\ f(\underline{x}_i)) \quad .$$

In view of Gauß quadrature formulae where the weights of the derivatives vanish, we require that

$$\underline{B}_i = \int_\Omega W(\underline{x})\, (\underline{x} - \underline{x}_i)\, \lambda_i^2(\underline{x})\, d\Omega = \underline{0} \quad , \quad i = 1(1)n \quad .$$

This is a nonlinear system of equations for the nN components x_i^j of the n nodes $\underline{x}_i$, $i = 1(1)n$, $j = 1(1)N$. For $N = 1$ dimension we know the solution of the system $B_i = 0$, $i = 1(1)n$: The nodes x_i then are the uniquely determined nodes of the orthogonal polynomial $\omega_n(x) \perp \mathbb{P}_{n-1}$ with respect to $W(x)$. For $N > 1$, however, this is no longer valid since the polynomials $\lambda_i^2(\underline{x})$ cannot be split into a polynomial $\omega_n(\underline{x})$ of degree n independent of i , and another polynomial $p_i(\underline{x}) \in \mathbb{P}_{n-1}$.
Obviously the nonnegative polynomials $\omega_n^2(\underline{x})$ play the same role here for $N > 1$ dimensions as do the orthogonal polynomials $\omega_n(x)$ for $N = 1$.

3.2 Properties of C_nf

We show now that the cubature formulae C_nf are minimal, positive cubature formulae.

Theorem 3

If the system $\underline{B}_i = \underline{0}$, $i = 1(1)n$, possesses a real solution giving n distinct vectors $\underline{x}_i$, $i = 1(1)n$, then C_nf is a positive cubature formula.

Proof:

We have that

$$A_i = \int_\Omega W(\underline{x}) \, [1 - (\underline{x} - \underline{x}_i) \operatorname{grad} \lambda_i^2(\underline{x}_i)] \, \lambda_i^2(\underline{x}) \, d\Omega \quad .$$

This is transformed to give

$$A_i = \int_\Omega W(\underline{x}) \, \lambda_i^2(\underline{x}) \, d\Omega - \sum_{j=1}^{N} \frac{\partial}{\partial x^j} \lambda_i^2(\underline{x}_i) \int_\Omega W(\underline{x})(x^j - x_i^j) \, \lambda_i^2(\underline{x}) \, d\Omega =$$

$$= \int_\Omega W(\underline{x})\ \lambda_i^2(\underline{x})\ d\Omega - \underline{B}_i \text{ grad } \lambda_i^2(\underline{x}_i)$$

$$> 0 \quad \text{for} \quad \underline{B}_i = \underline{0} \quad , \quad i = 1(1)n \quad ,$$

since $W(\underline{x}) \geq 0$ in Ω . □

In addition $C_n f$ is a minimal cubature formula.

Theorem 4

The system of equation $\underline{B}_i = \underline{0}$, $i = 1(1)n$, is the necessary condition for

$$\int_\Omega W(\underline{x})\ \omega_n^2(\underline{x})\ d\Omega$$

to be minimal among the nonnegative polynomials with n distinct real zeros $\underline{x}_i$, $i = 1(1)n$, and normalized in the same way.

Proof:

The integral

$$I_n := \int_\Omega W(\underline{x})\ (\underline{x} - \underline{x}_1)^2 \ \ldots \ (\underline{x} - \underline{x}_n)^2\ d\Omega$$

is a function of the nN variables x_i^k , $i = 1(1)n$, $k = 1(1)N$. Hence we have the necessary conditions

$$\frac{\partial}{\partial x_i^k} I_n = 0 \quad , \quad i = 1(1)n \quad , \quad k = 1(1)N \quad ,$$

for I_n to be minimal. This is equivalent with

$$2 \int_\Omega W(\underline{x})(\underline{x} - \underline{x}_1)^2 \ldots (\underline{x} - \underline{x}_{i-1})^2 (x^k - x_i^k)(\underline{x} - \underline{x}_{i+1})^2 \ldots (\underline{x} - \underline{x}_n)^2\ d\Omega = 0$$

or

$$\int_\Omega W(\underline{x})(\underline{x} - \underline{x}_i)\ \lambda_i^2(\underline{x})\ d\Omega = \underline{B}_i = \underline{0} \quad , \quad i = 1(1)n \quad .$$

□

In $N = 1$ dimension the nodes of the Gaussian quadrature formulae are always inside the interval of integration. This interval is trivially always assumed to be convex. We prove that for $N > 1$ the convexity of Ω is sufficient for the nodes to be inside Ω .

Theorem 5

Let Ω be a convex area, and suppose that $\underline{B}_i = \underline{0}$, $i = 1(1)n$, possesses a solution of distinct vectors $\underline{x}_i$, $i = 1(1)n$. Then for every real $\underline{x}_i$ we have that $\underline{x}_i \in \mathrm{int}(\Omega)$, $i = 1(1)n$.

Proof:

The nodes $\underline{x}_i$ satisfy the system

$$\underline{B}_i = \int_\Omega W(\underline{x})(\underline{x} - \underline{x}_i)\, \lambda_i^2(\underline{x})\, d\Omega = \underline{0} \quad , \quad i = 1(1)n \quad .$$

Assume there is a node $\underline{x}_i \notin \mathrm{int}(\Omega)$. Since Ω is convex, there exists a hyperplane passing through $\underline{x}_i$ which can be represented by

$$h(\underline{x}) = \alpha_1(x^1 - x_i^1) + \alpha_2(x^2 - x_i^2) + \dots + \alpha_N(x^N - x_i^N)$$

such that its zero-line does not cut $\mathrm{int}(\Omega)$. Hence the linear function $h(\underline{x})$ representing the hyperplane has constant sign in Ω , and therefore

$$\int_\Omega W(\underline{x}) \sum_{j=1}^{N} \alpha_j(x^j - x_i^j)\, \lambda_i^2(\underline{x})\, d\Omega \neq 0$$

which contradicts $\underline{B}_i = 0$, $i = 1(1)n$. If several nodes are assumed to be not in $\mathrm{int}(\Omega)$ the same argument is applicable. □

3.3 Examples

We present two simple examples.

Example 1

n = 1 : We expect that the only node $\underline{x}_1$ is the center of gravity of Ω. In this case $\lambda_1^2(\underline{x}) = 1$ identically, and we have that

$$\int_\Omega W(\underline{x})(x^j - x_1^j)\, d\Omega = 0 \quad , \quad j = 1(1)N \quad .$$

This means that

$$x_i^j = \frac{\int_\Omega W(\underline{x})\, x^j\, d\Omega}{\int_\Omega W(x)\, d\Omega} \quad , \quad j = 1(1)N \quad ,$$

and hence

$$A_1 = \int_\Omega W(\underline{x})\, d\Omega > 0 \quad .$$

Example 2

n = 2 : We consider the following area

$$\Omega = \left\{ \underline{x} \;\middle|\; |\underline{x}_1| \leq 1 \text{ and } |\underline{x}_j| \leq a \ , \ j = 2(1)N \right\} \quad ,$$

and choose $W(\underline{x}) = 1$ identically in Ω. Then the system $\underline{B}_i = 0$, $i = 1,2$, is

$$\frac{2}{3} x_2^1 + \frac{1}{3} x_1^1 \, [(N-1)\, a^2 + 1] + x_1^1 \, |\underline{x}_2|^2 = 0$$

$$\frac{2}{3} x_2^i \, a^2 + \frac{1}{3} x_1^i \, [(N-1)\, a^2 + 1] + x_1^i \, |\underline{x}_2|^2 = 0 \quad , \quad i = 2(1)N$$

$$\frac{2}{3} x_1^2 + \frac{1}{3} x_2^1 \, [(N-1)\, a^2 + 1] + x_2^1 \, |\underline{x}_1|^2 = 0$$

$$\frac{2}{3} x_1^i \, a^2 + \frac{1}{3} x_2^i \, [(N-1)\, a^2 + 1] + x_2^i \, |\underline{x}_1|^2 = 0 \quad , \quad i = 2(1)N \quad .$$

If we choose $x_1^i = x_2^i = 0$, $i = 2(1)N$, then this system reduces to the first and third of these equations. These two reduce to one only if we choose

$$\underline{x}_1^T = (-\alpha, 0, \ldots, 0) \quad , \quad \underline{x}_2^T = (\alpha, 0, \ldots, 0) \quad .$$

Then α is determined by

$$\alpha^2 = \frac{1}{3}[1 - (N-1)\, a^2] \quad ,$$

and we have found a solution of $\underline{B}_i = \underline{0}$. Note that this gives the Gaussian two-point quadrature formula for $N = 1$.
For $N > 1$ we obtain a real solution $\underline{x}_1 \neq \underline{x}_2$ for $C_2 f$ if

$$a^2 < \frac{1}{N-1} \quad .$$

If $a^2(N-1) = 1$ then $\alpha = 0$, and hence $\underline{x}_1 = \underline{x}_2$ so that we have no longer distinct nodes.

This example shows, that there may exist a real solution of $\underline{B}_i = \underline{0}$, $i = 1(1)n$, however, the nodes are not necessarily distinct.
For the weights A_1 and A_2 of $C_2 f$ we obtain the value

$$\begin{aligned} A_1 = A_2 &= \int_\Omega \lambda_1^2(\underline{x})\, d\Omega = \frac{1}{4\alpha^2} \int_\Omega (|x|^2 + \alpha^2)\, d\Omega \\ &= \frac{2^{N-2}\, a^{N-1}}{3\alpha^2} \left\{1 + 3\alpha^2 + (N-1)\, a^2\right\} \\ &= \frac{(2a)^{N-1}}{1-(N-1)\, a^2} \quad \text{since} \quad \alpha^2 = \frac{1}{3}[1 - (N-1)\, a^2] \quad . \end{aligned}$$

For $N = 1$ we have $A_1 = A_2 = 1$, the weights of the Gaussian two-point quadrature formula. For $N > 1$ the cubature formula

$$C_2 f = \frac{(2a)^{N-1}}{1-(N-1)\, a^2} [f(\underline{x}_1) + f(-\underline{x}_1)] \quad , \quad \underline{x}_1^T = (-\alpha, 0, \ldots, 0) \quad ,$$

does no longer integrate the constant function $f(\underline{x}) = 1$ exactly since

$$\int_\Omega d\Omega - C_2 f = 2^N a^{N-1} - \frac{2^N a^{N-1}}{1-(N-1)\, a^2} = \frac{2^N a^{N+1}(1-N)}{1-(N-1)\, a^2} = 0 \quad \text{for } N = 1 \text{ only.}$$

Finally we show, that $C_2 f$ is not only a minimal cubature formula but also an optimal one, since the integral

$$\int_\Omega \omega_n^2(\underline{x})\, d\Omega$$

is really minimized. To this end we calculate ($\underline{e}_1^T = (1,0,\dots,0)$ here) for arbitrary perturbation vectors $\underline{t}_1$ and $\underline{t}_2$

$$I := \int_\Omega (\underline{x} - \alpha\underline{e}_1 - \underline{t}_1)^2(\underline{x} + \alpha\underline{e}_1 - \underline{t}_2)^2\, d\Omega - \int_\Omega (\underline{x} - \alpha\underline{e}_1)^2(\underline{x} - \alpha\underline{e}_2)^2\, d\Omega$$

$$= \int_\Omega \left[(\underline{x} - \alpha\underline{e}_1)^2\, \underline{t}_2^2 + (\underline{x} + \alpha\underline{e}_1)^2\, \underline{t}_1^2 + 4(\underline{x} - \alpha\underline{e}_1, \underline{t}_1)(\underline{x} + \alpha\underline{e}_1, \underline{t}_2) + \underline{t}_1^2\, \underline{t}_2^2\right] d\Omega$$

$$= \int_\Omega \left[(\underline{x}^2 + \alpha^2)\underline{t}_2^2 + (\underline{x}^2 + \alpha^2)\underline{t}_1^2 + 4(\underline{x} - \alpha\underline{e}_1, \underline{t}_1)(\underline{x} + \alpha\underline{e}_1, \underline{t}_2) + \underline{t}_1^2\, \underline{t}_2^2\right] d\Omega$$

$$= \frac{1}{3}\, 2^N\, a^{N-1} \Big\{ (\underline{t}_1^2 + \underline{t}_2^2)\, [1 + (N-1)\, a^2] + 3\alpha^2\, (\underline{t}_1^2 + \underline{t}_2^2)$$

$$+ 4\, [(1 - 3\alpha^2 - a^2)\underline{t}_1^1\, \underline{t}_2^1 + a^2(\underline{t}_1, \underline{t}_2)] + 3\underline{t}_1^2\, \underline{t}_2^2 \Big\} .$$

Replacing α we obtain

$$I = \frac{1}{3}\, 2^N a^{N-1} \left\{2(\underline{t}_1^2 + \underline{t}_2^2) + 3\underline{t}_1^2\, \underline{t}_2^2 + 4a^2(\underline{t}_1, \underline{t}_2) + 4(N-2)\, a^2\right\}$$

$$\geq \frac{1}{3}\, 2^N a^{N-1} \left\{2(\underline{t}_1^2 + \underline{t}_2^2) + 3\underline{t}_1^2\, \underline{t}_2^2 - 4(\underline{t}_1, \underline{t}_2) + 4(N-2)\, a^2\right\}$$

since

$$a^2 \leq \frac{1}{N-1} \leq 1$$

for real nodes.

Hence

$$I \geq \frac{1}{3}\, 2^N a^{N-1} \left\{2(\underline{t}_1 - \underline{t}_2)^2 + 3\underline{t}_1^2\, \underline{t}_2^2 + 4(N-2)\, a^2\right\}$$

where the last term is nonnegative for $N > 1$.

So we find that for any real cubature formula $C_2 f$

$$I \geq 0$$

and $I = \min$ iff $\underline{t}_1 = \underline{t}_2 = 0$ so that the minimal value of I is obtained for $\underline{x}_1 = -\alpha\, \underline{e}_1$ and $\underline{x}_2 = \alpha\, \underline{e}_1$.

References

[1] Engels, H.:
Numerical Quadrature and Cubature, Academic Press, 1980

Author's address:
Institut für Geometrie und Praktische
Mathematik der RWTH Aachen
Templergraben 55, D-5100 Aachen
Fed. Rep. Germany

International Series of
Numerical Mathematics, Vol. 75

SOME REFLECTIONS ON MULTIDIMENSIONAL EULER AND POISSON SUMMATION FORMULAS

W. Freeden - P. Hermann, RWTH Aachen

Abstract: The purpose of this paper is to give a brief introduction to some new aspects of the theory of multidimensional summation formulas.

1. Lattices

Let $g_1, \ldots, g_q$ be linearly independent vectors of $\mathbb{R}^q$. The set Λ of all points

$$g = \sum_{i=1}^{q} n_i g_i \qquad (n_i \in \mathbb{Z})$$

is called a lattice in $\mathbb{R}^q$ with basis $g_1,\ldots,g_q$.

Let F be the half-open parallelotope consisting of all points $x \in \mathbb{R}^q$ with

$$x = \sum_{i=1}^{q} t_i g_i \qquad (-1/2 \leq t_1,\ldots,t_q < 1/2).$$

F is called fundamental cell of the lattice Λ. As is well known (cf.e.g. [1]), the volume $\|F\|$ of F is just equal to the quantity

$$\|F\| = |\det(g_1,\ldots,g_q)|.$$

If Λ is a lattice in $\mathbb{R}^q$, then the set of all points $h \in \mathbb{R}^q$ such that the inner product gh is an integer for all $g \in \Lambda$ is again a lattice called the inverse lattice Λ^{-1} of Λ.

2. Lattice Function

The functions ϕ_h, $h \in \Lambda^{-1}$, defined by

$$\phi_h(x) = \frac{1}{\sqrt{\|F\|}} e^{2\pi i(hx)} \quad , \; x \in \mathbb{R}^q \tag{2.1}$$

are periodic with respect to the lattice Λ, i.e. $\phi_h(x) = \phi_h(x+g)$ for all $g \in \Lambda$. The system $\{\phi_h | h \in \Lambda^{-1}\}$ is orthonormal in the sense that

$$\int_F \phi_h(x)\, \overline{\phi_{h'}(x)}\, dx = \begin{cases} 1 \text{ for } h = h' \\ 0 \text{ for } h \neq h' \end{cases}$$

(dx : volume element). For fixed $\lambda \in \mathbb{R}$ and $a \in \mathbb{R}^q$ we set

$$\begin{aligned} D &= \Delta + 4\pi i(a\nabla) + \lambda \\ \overline{D} &= \Delta - 4\pi i(a\nabla) + \lambda \end{aligned} \tag{2.2}$$

(∇ : Nabla operator, $\Delta=\nabla\nabla$:Laplace operator). A simple calculation gives

$$(D-d_h)\phi_h(x) = 0, \; x \in \mathbb{R}^q, \quad d_h = (\lambda-4\pi^2[(h+a)^2-a^2]). \tag{2.3}$$

The functions ϕ_h,$h \in \Lambda^{-1}$, are the only twice continuously differentiable eigenfunctions corresponding to the eigenvalues d_h to the differential operator D and the "boundary condition" of Λ-periodicity.

<u>Definition 1: A function $G : \mathbb{R}^q \backslash \Lambda \to \mathbb{C}$ is called Λ-lattice function with respect to the operator D, if it satisfies the following properties:</u>

(i) <u>For all $x \notin \Lambda$ and $g \in \Lambda$</u>

$$G(x + g) = G(x).$$

(ii) <u>G is twice continuously differentiable for $x \notin \Lambda$ with</u>

$$D\, G(x) = \frac{1}{\sqrt{\|F\|}} \sum_{\substack{h\in\Lambda^{-1} \\ d_h=0}} \phi_h(x).$$

(iii) <u>In the neighbourhood of the origin</u>

$$G(x) - (2\pi)^{-\frac{q}{2}} e^{-2\pi i(ax)} (-\lambda-4\pi^2 a^2)^{\frac{q-2}{4}} |x|^{\frac{2-q}{2}} K_{\frac{q-2}{2}}(\sqrt{-\lambda-4\pi^2 a^2}\,|x|)$$

is continuously differentiable (K_ν : *modified Bessel function of order* ν) .

(iv) *For all* $h \in \Lambda^{-1}$ *with* $d_h = 0$

$$\int_F G(x)\,\overline{\phi_h(x)}\,dx = 0.$$

By the defining properties G is uniquely determined. The Λ-lattice function G defined above is Green's function to the operator D and the "boundary condition" of Λ-periodicity (cf.[9]).

Definition 2: *The function* $G^{(m)} : \mathbb{R}^q \setminus \Lambda \to \mathbb{C}$ *recursively given by*

$$G^{(m)}(x) = \int_F G(x-y)G^{(m-1)}(y)\,dy \quad , \quad m = 2,3,\ldots$$

$$G^{(1)}(x) = G(x)$$

is called Λ-*lattice function with respect to the operator* D^m.

Obviously, for all $x \notin \Lambda$ and $g \in \Lambda$, we have

$$G^{(m)}(x+g) = G^{(m)}(x).$$

In analogy to techniques of potential theory it can be proved that, for $x \in F$,

$$G^{(m)}(x) = \begin{cases} O(|x|^{2m-q}\ln|x|) & \text{for } 2m \geq q,\ q \text{ even} \\ O(|x|^{2m-q}) & \text{otherwise.} \end{cases}$$

Furthermore,

$$D\,G^{(m)}(x) = -G^{(m-1)}(x) \quad , \quad m = 2,3,\ldots \qquad (2.4)$$

for all $x \notin \Lambda$.

$G^{(m)}$ possesses the (formal) Fourier expansion

$$G^{(m)}(x) \sim \frac{1}{\sqrt{\|F\|}} \sum_{\substack{h \in \Lambda^{-1} \\ d_h \neq 0}} \frac{1}{(-d_h)^m}\,\phi_h(x).$$

For $m > q/2$, $G^{(m)}$ is continuous in $\mathbb{R}^q$, and we have for any two $x,y \in \mathbb{R}^q$,

$$G^{(m)}(x-y) = \sum_{\substack{h\in\Lambda^{-1} \\ d_h \neq 0}} \frac{1}{(-d_h)^m} \phi_h(x)\overline{\phi_h(y)} \tag{2.5}$$

in the sense of absolute and uniform convergence.

3. Euler Summation Formula

In the sequel we use the following extended version of Green's formula

$$\int_{G} f(x)\, D^m g(x)\, dx = \int_{G} g(x)\, \overline{D}^m f(x)\, dx + \int_{\partial G} B[f(x),g(x)]\, dS \tag{3.1}$$

with

$$\int_{\partial G} B[f(x),g(x)]\, dS = \sum_{r=0}^{m-1} \int_{\partial G} [\overline{D}^r f(x)][\frac{\partial}{\partial n^*} D^{m-(r+1)} g(x)]\, dS - \sum_{r=0}^{m-1} \int_{\partial G} [\frac{\partial}{\partial n} \overline{D}^r f(x)][D^{m-(r+1)} g(x)]\, dS \tag{3.2}$$

for a regular region $G \subset \mathbb{R}^q$ (i.e. a finite region for which the Gauss theorem is valid, dS: surface element, ∂G : boundary of G). $\partial/\partial n$ denotes the derivative in the direction of the outer normal, while $\partial/\partial n^*$ is defined by $\partial/\partial n^* = \partial/\partial n + 4\pi i(a\nabla)$.

Theorem 1: Let G be a regular region with continuously differentiable boundary ∂G. Suppose that $f : \overline{G} \to \mathbb{R}$ is a function of class $C^{(2m)}(\overline{G})$, $\overline{G} = G \cup \partial G$. Then

$$\sum_{\substack{g\in\Lambda \\ g\in\bar{G}}}{}' f(g) = \frac{1}{\sqrt{\|F\|}} \sum_{\substack{h\in\Lambda^{-1} \\ d_h=0}} \int_G f(x)\phi_h(x)\,dx$$

$$+ (-1)^m \int_G G^{(m)}(x)[\bar{D}^m f(x)]\,dx$$

$$- \sum_{r=0}^{m-1} (-1)^r \int_{\partial G} [\bar{D}^r f(x)] \frac{\partial}{\partial n^*} G^{(r+1)}(x)\,dS$$

$$+ \sum_{r=0}^{m-1} (-1)^r \int_{\partial G} G^{(r+1)}(x) [\frac{\partial}{\partial n} \bar{D}^r f(x)]\,dS ,$$

<u>where</u>

$$\sum_{\substack{g\in\Lambda \\ g\in\bar{G}}}{}' f(g) = \sum_{\substack{g\in\Lambda \\ g\in G}} f(g) + 1/2 \sum_{\substack{g\in\Lambda \\ g\in\partial G}} f(g) .$$

<u>Proof.</u> For sufficiently small $\varepsilon > 0$, Green's formula yields

$$\int_{\substack{x\in\bar{G} \\ |x-g|\geq\varepsilon}} f(x)[D^m G^{(m)}(x)]\,dx = \int_{\substack{x\in\bar{G} \\ |x-g|\geq\varepsilon}} G^{(m)}(x)[\bar{D}^m f(x)]\,dx$$

$$+ \int_{\substack{x\in\partial G \\ |x-g|\geq\varepsilon}} B[f(x), G^{(m)}(x)]\,dS$$

$$- \sum_{\substack{g\in\Lambda \\ g\in\bar{G}}} \int_{\substack{|x-g|=\varepsilon \\ x\in\bar{G}}} B[f(x), G^{(m)}(x)]\,dS.$$

From condition (ii) of Definition 1 in connection with (2.4) we obtain

$$\int_{\substack{x\in\bar{G} \\ |x-g|\geq\varepsilon}} f(x)[D^m G^{(m)}(x)]\,dx = \frac{(-1)^{m-1}}{\sqrt{\|F\|}} \sum_{\substack{h\in\Lambda^{-1} \\ d_h=0}} \int_{\substack{x\in\bar{G} \\ |x-g|\geq\varepsilon}} f(x)\phi_h(x)\,dx .$$

Furthermore, we find

$$\int_{\substack{|x-g|=\varepsilon \\ x\in\overline{G}}} B[f(x), G^{(m)}(x)]\,dS = \sum_{r=0}^{m-1} (-1)^{m-(r+1)} \int_{\substack{|x-g|=\varepsilon \\ x\in\overline{G}}} [\frac{\partial}{\partial n} \overline{D}^r f(x)]\, G^{(r+1)}(x)\,dS$$

$$- \sum_{r=0}^{m-1} (-1)^{m-(r+1)} \int_{\substack{|x-g|=\varepsilon \\ x\in\overline{G}}} [\overline{D}^r f(x)] \frac{\partial}{\partial n^*} G^{(r+1)}(x)\,dS.$$

Hence, by observing the characteristic singularity of $G^{(r+1)}(x)$, $r=0\ldots, m-1$ and using standard arguments of potential theory, Theorem 1 follows by passing to the limit $\varepsilon \to 0_+$. □

Our summation formula has been formulated for iterated operators D^m and arbitrary lattices Λ. Therefore, all summation formulas are included which are based on iterations of arbitrary second order elliptic differential operators with constant coefficients.

4. Poisson Summation Formula in $\mathbb{R}^q$

The Euler summation formula now will be exploited to derive sufficient conditions for the validity of Poisson's summation formula in $\mathbb{R}^q$. For that purpose we start from the following specialization of Theorem 1

$$\sum_{\substack{g\in\Lambda \\ |g+y|\leq N}}{}' f(g+y) = \sum_{\substack{h\in\Lambda^{-1} \\ d_h=0}} \overline{\phi_h(y)} \int_{|x|\leq N} f(x)\,\phi_h(x)\,dx \tag{4.1}$$

$$+ (-1)^m \int_{|x|\leq N} G^{(m)}(x-y)[\overline{D}^m f(x)]\,dx$$

$$+ (-1)^m \int_{|x|=N} B[f(x), G^{(m)}(x-y)]\,dS(x)$$

that holds for every fixed $y \in \mathbb{R}^q$. By observation of the characteristic singularity of the Λ-lattice function with respect to the operator D^m it has been shown (cf.[2],[9]) that the asymptotic relations

$$\int_{|x|=N} |G^{(r)}(x-y)|\,dS(x) = O(N^{q-1})$$
$$\int_{|x|=N} \left|\frac{\partial}{\partial n} G^{(r)}(x-y)\right| dS(x) = O(N^{q-1}) \tag{4.2}$$

are valid for each positive integer r as N tends to infinity.

Theorem 2: Suppose that $f : \mathbb{R}^q \to \mathbb{R}$ is a function of class $C^{(2m)}(\mathbb{R}^q)$ satisfying the following properties:

(i) The asymptotic relations

$$|\overline{D}^r f(x)| = o(|x|^{1-q})$$
$$|\nabla\overline{D}^r f(x)| = o(|x|^{1-q})$$

hold for $r = 0,\ldots, m-1$ and $|x| \to \infty$.

(ii) There exists a positive number $\varepsilon > 0$ such that

$$|\overline{D}^m f(x)| = O(|x|^{-(q+\varepsilon)}).$$

Then the limit

$$\lim_{N\to\infty} \left[\sum_{\substack{g\in\Lambda \\ |g+y|\leq N}} f(g+y) - \sum_{\substack{h\in\Lambda^{-1} \\ d_h=0}} \overline{\phi_h(y)} \int_{|x|\leq N} f(x)\phi_h(x)\,dx \right]$$

exists and is equal to

$$(-1)^m \int_{\mathbb{R}^q} G^{(m)}(x-y)[\overline{D}^m f(x)]\,dx.$$

Proof. From condition (i) and a classical result due to Gauss[5] it follows that

$$\sum_{\substack{g\in\Lambda \\ |g+y|=N}} f(g+y) = o(N^{1-q} \sum_{\substack{g\in\Lambda \\ |g+y|=N}} 1) = o(1).$$

Furthermore, for the surface integrals we obtain from condition (i)

$$\int_{|x|=N} B[f(x), G^{(m)}(x-y)]\,dS(x)$$

$$= o(N^{1-q} \sum_{r=o}^{m-1} \int_{|x|=N} \{|G^{(r)}(x-y)| + |\frac{\partial}{\partial n} G^{(r)}(x-y)|\}dS(x)) .$$

Hence, according to (4.2), for $N \to \infty$, we have

$$\int_{|x|=N} B[\ f(x), G^{(m)}(x-y)]\,dS(x) = o(1) .$$

Finally, we find in connection with condition (ii),

$$\int_{N' \leqslant |x| \leqslant N} |G^{(m)}(x-y)[\bar{D}^m f(x)]|\,dx$$

$$= O(\int_{N'}^{N} \frac{\rho^{q-1}}{(1+\rho)^{q+\varepsilon}} \{ \int_{|x|=\rho} |G^{(m)}(x-y)|dS(x)\}d\rho) .$$

Thus, because of (4.2), the integral

$$(-1)^m \int_{\mathbb{R}^q} G^{(m)}(x-y)[\bar{D}^m f(x)]\,dx$$

is absolutely convergent. This proves Theorem 2. □

In order to ensure the convergence of the series

$$\sum_{g \in \Lambda} f(g+y)$$

in the spherical sense

$$\sum_{g \in \Lambda} f(g+y) = \lim_{N \to \infty} \sum_{|g+y| \leqslant N} f(g+y)$$

we have to require the additional condition

(iii) <u>the integral(s)</u>

$$\sum_{\substack{h \in \Lambda^{-1} \\ d_h = 0}} \overline{\phi_h(y)} \int_{\mathbb{R}^q} f(x)\,\phi_h(x)\,dx$$

exist(s) in the sense

$$\int_{\mathbb{R}^q} \ldots\, dx = \lim_{N\to\infty} \int_{|x|\leq N} \ldots\, dx.$$

Theorem 3: Let $f \in C^{(2m)}(\mathbb{R}^q)$ satisfy the conditions (i),(ii),(iii). Then

$$\sum_{g\in\Lambda} f(g+y) = \sum_{\substack{h\in\Lambda^{-1}\\ d_h=0}} \overline{\phi_h(y)} \int_{\mathbb{R}^q} f(x)\, \phi_h(x)\, dx$$

$$+ (-1)^m \int_{\mathbb{R}^q} G^{(m)}(x-y)[\overline{D}^m f(x)]\, dx.$$

Suppose now that $f \in C^{(2m)}(\mathbb{R}^q)$ satisfies the aforementioned conditions (i),(ii),(iii) and let $m > q/2$, in addition. Then, $G^{(m)}$ has an absolutely and uniformly convergent Fourier expansion. Thus Lebesgue's theorem gives us

$$(-1)^m \int_{\mathbb{R}^q} G^{(m)}(x-y)[\overline{D}^m f(x)]\, dx$$

$$= \sum_{\substack{h\in\Lambda^{-1}\\ d_h\neq 0}} \frac{1}{d_h{}^m}\, \overline{\phi_h(y)} \int_{\mathbb{R}^q} \phi_h(x)[\overline{D}^m f(x)]\, dx.$$

By repeated application of Green's formula in connection with (i) it can be deduced that

$$\int_{\mathbb{R}^q} \phi_h(x)[\overline{D}^m f(x)]\, dx$$

$$= \int_{\mathbb{R}^q} [D^m \phi_h(x)]\, f(x)\, dx$$

$$= d_h{}^m \int_{\mathbb{R}^q} f(x)\, \phi_h(x)\, dx.$$

Thus we finally get from Theorem 3

Theorem 4: Let $f \in C^{(2m)}(\mathbb{R}^q)$, $m > q/2$, satisfy the conditions (i),(ii),(iii). Then, for fixed $y \in \mathbb{R}^q$,

$$\sum_{g\in\Lambda} f(g+y) = \sum_{h\in\Lambda^{-1}} \overline{\phi_h(y)} \int_{\mathbb{R}^q} f(x)\phi_h(x)\,dx$$

and, in particular,

$$\sum_{g\in\Lambda} f(g) = \frac{1}{\sqrt{\|F\|}} \sum_{h\in\Lambda^{-1}} \int_{\mathbb{R}^q} f(x)\phi_h(x)\,dx.$$

The identities of Theorem 4 are referred to as Poisson's Summation Formula. It should be noted that the sufficient conditions stated above do not imply the absolute convergence of the series on the left hand side. Therefore our Poisson Summation Formula is applicable even for alternating sums (e.g. in Analytic Theory of Numbers (cf. [2],[9])).

5. Poisson Summation Formula for Regular Regions

We shall now give an answer to the question in what respect the series

$$\sum_{h\in\Lambda^{-1}} \overline{\phi_h(y)} \int_{G} f(x)\phi_h(x)\,dx$$

can be "summed" to

$$\sum_{\substack{g\in\Lambda \\ g+y\in\overline{G}}}{}' f(g+y)$$

when G is a regular region in $\mathbb{R}^q$.

Theorem 5: Let $G \subset \mathbb{R}^q$ be a regular region with continuously differentiable boundary ∂G. Suppose that $f : \overline{G} \to \mathbb{R}$ is an element of class $C^{(o)}(\overline{G})$. Then, for fixed $y \in \mathbb{R}^q$,

$$\sum_{\substack{g\in\Lambda \\ g+y\in\overline{G}}}{}' f(g+y) = \lim_{\tau\to o_+} \sum_{h\in\Lambda^{-1}} e^{-\tau\pi^2|h|^2}\, \overline{\phi_h(y)} \int_{G} f(x)\phi_h(x)\,dx.$$

<u>Proof.</u> According to Theorem 4 we get via the formula of Weber and Sonine (cf.[6] § 7)

$$(\tau\pi)^{-q/2} \sum_{g\in\Lambda} \int_G e^{-|x-(g+y)|^2/\tau} f(x)\,dx \tag{5.1}$$

$$= \sum_{h\in\Lambda^{-1}} e^{-\tau\pi^2|h|^2} \overline{\phi_h(y)} \int_G f(x)\phi_h(x)\,dx$$

for all $\tau > 0$.

Take a (sufficiently large) positive constant R such that $|x+y| \leq R$ for all $x \in \overline{G}$ and $|x-(g+y)|^2 \geq \frac{1}{2}|g+y|^2$ for all $g \in \Lambda$ with $|g+y| > R$. Then, because of the continuity of f, we are able to see that

$$(\tau\pi)^{-q/2} \sum_{\substack{g\in\Lambda \\ |g+y|\geq R}} \int_G e^{-|x-(g+y)|^2/\tau} f(x)\,dx$$

$$= O\Big((\tau\pi)^{-q/2} \sum_{\substack{g\in\Lambda \\ |g+y|\geq R}} e^{-|g+y|^2/2\tau}\Big)$$

$$= O\Big((\tau\pi)^{-q/2} \int_{|x+y|\geq R} e^{-|x+y|^2/2\tau} dx\Big)$$

for $\tau \to 0_+$. Moreover, there exists a positive constant $T > 0$ such that $\operatorname{dist}(g,\overline{G}) \geq T$ for all $g \notin \overline{G}$.
Thus,

$$\sum_{\substack{g\in\Lambda \\ g+y\notin\overline{G} \\ |g+y|\leq R}} (\tau\pi)^{-q/2} \int_G e^{-|x-(g+y)|^2/\tau} f(x)\,dx$$

$$= O\Big((\tau\pi)^{-q/2} \sum_{\substack{g\in\Lambda \\ g+y\notin\overline{G} \\ |g+y|\leq R}} \int_G e^{-|x-(g+y)|^2/\tau} dx\Big)$$

$$= O((\tau\pi)^{-q/2} (\int_{|x|\geq T} e^{-|x|^2/\tau} dx) \sum_{\substack{g\in\Lambda \\ g+y\notin\overline{G} \\ |g+y|\leq R}} 1)$$

$$= O((\tau\pi)^{-q/2} \int_{|x|\geq T} e^{-|x|^2/\tau} dx)$$

for $\tau \to 0_+$.

Summarizing our results we therefore obtain

$$\sum_{\substack{g\in\Lambda \\ g+y\notin\overline{G}}} (\tau\pi)^{-q/2} \int_G e^{-|x-(g+y)|^2/\tau} f(x)dx \tag{5.2}$$

$$= O\left(\int_{R^2/2\tau}^{\infty} e^{-r} r^{q/2-1} dr + \int_{T^2/\tau}^{\infty} e^{-r} r^{q/2-1} dr\right)$$

$$= o(1) \qquad (\tau \to 0_+).$$

On the other hand it may be proved by methods similar to those e.g. used in [10] that

$$\lim_{\tau\to 0_+} (\tau\pi)^{-q/2} \int_G e^{-|x-(g+y)|^2/\tau} f(x)dx$$

$$= \begin{cases} f(g+y) & \text{for } g+y \in G \\ \frac{1}{2} f(g+y) & \text{for } g+y \in \partial G . \end{cases}$$

Consequently,

$$\lim_{\tau\to 0_+} (\tau\pi)^{-q/2} \sum_{\substack{g\in\Lambda \\ g+y\in\overline{G}}} \int_G e^{-|x-(g+y)|^2/\tau} f(x)dx \tag{5.3}$$

$$= \sum_{\substack{g\in\Lambda \\ g+y\in\overline{G}}}{}' f(g+y) .$$

Combining the relations (5.1),(5.2),(5.3) we get the assertion of Theorem 5. □

We conclude our considerations with the following consequence of Theorem 5.

Theorem 6: Let $G \subset \mathbb{R}^q$ be a regular region with continuously differentiable boundary ∂G. Suppose that $f : \overline{G} \to \mathbb{R}$ is continuous in $\overline{G}$. Furthermore, for fixed $y \in \mathbb{R}^q$, assume that

$$\sum_{h \in \Lambda^{-1}} \overline{\phi_h(y)} \int_G f(x) \phi_h(x) dx \tag{5.4}$$

is convergent. Then

$$\sum_{\substack{g \in \Lambda \\ g+y \in \overline{G}}}{}' f(g+y) = \sum_{h \in \Lambda^{-1}} \overline{\phi_h(y)} \int_G f(x) \phi_h(x) dx.$$

For the case $q = 2$ and every $y \in \mathbb{R}^2$, the convergence of (5.4) can be guaranteed for a twice continuously differentiable function f on a disk G around the origin (see [2]). However, it is well known that, for dimension $q \geq 3$ and $y = 0$, the sum (5.4) is divergent even for a constant function f on a ball G around the origin.

First experiences (cf.[3] ,[4]) give us the hope that the investigations developed in our paper will lead to further new results in numerical computation of multidimensional integrals and series.

References:

[1] Cassels, J.W.S.: An Introduction to the Geometry of Numbers, Springer Verlag, Berlin-Göttingen-Heidelberg (1959)

[2] Freeden, W.: Eine Verallgemeinerung der Hardy-Landauschen Identität, Manuscripta math. 24, 2o5-216 (1978)

[3] Freeden, W.: Multidimensional Euler Summation Formulas and Numerical Cubature, ISNM 57, 77-88 (1982)

[4] Freeden, W. - Fleck, J.: Numerical Integration of Oscillatory Functions by Adapted Euler Summation Formulas, to appear

[5] Gauß, C.F.: De nexu inter multitudinem classicum, in quas formae binariae secundi gradus distribuuntur, ..., Werke, vol.2, 269-291 (1863)

[6] Magnus, W. - Oberhettinger, F.: Formeln und Sätze für die speziellen Funktionen der math. Physik, Springer Verlag, Berlin-Göttingen-Heidelberg (1948)

[7] Mordell, L.J.: Poisson's Summation Formula and the Riemann Zeta Function, J.London Math.Soc., Vol.4, 285-296 (1929)

[8] Mordell, L.J.: Poisson's Summation Formula in Several Variables, Cambr.Phil.Soc. 25, 412-42o (1928/29)

[9] Müller, Cl. - Freeden, W.: Multidimensional Euler and Poisson Summation Formulas, Res.d.Math. 3, 33-63 (198o)

[1o] Stein, E.M. - Weiss, G.: Introduction to Fourier Analysis on Euclidean Spaces, Princeton N.J., University Press (1971)

Prof. Dr. W.Freeden - Prof. Dr. P.Hermann

Rheinisch-Westfälische
Technische Hochschule Aachen
Institut für Reine und
Angewandte Mathematik

Templergraben 55
D-51oo Aachen/West-Germany

International Series of
Numerical Mathematics, Vol. 75

ON THE DIMENSION OF THE SPLINE SPACE $S_2^1(\Delta)$ IN SPECIAL CASES

by

R.H.J. GMELIG MEYLING and P.R. PFLUGER

1. INTRODUCTION

We consider a closed subset $\Omega \subset \mathbb{R}^2$ with a polygonal boundary. Let Δ be a *triangulation* of Ω consisting of open triangles Ω_i, $i = 1, \ldots, T$ satisfying the following standard conditions:

1. $\Omega_i \cap \Omega_j = \Phi$ for $i \neq j$.
2. $\Omega = \bigcup_{i=1}^{T} \bar{\Omega}_i$.
3. No vertex of any Ω_i lies in the interior of an edge of any Ω_j.

Let us denote the space of all *bivariate polynomials* of degree d by

$$\pi_d = \left\{ p \mid p(x_1, x_2) = \sum_{i=o}^{d} \sum_{j=o}^{d-i} a_{ij} x_1^i x_2^j \right\}.$$

We will now consider the space of all *spline functions* s of smoothness r and of degree d (the restriction of s to each Ω_i belongs to π_d) [8]:

$$S_d^r(\Delta) = \{ s \mid s \in C^r(\Omega),\ s|_{\Omega_i} \in \pi_d \}.$$

In particular we are interested in the *dimension* of this space. For $o \leq d \leq r$ we have $S_d^r(\Delta) = \pi_d$ with $\dim \pi_d = \binom{d+2}{2}$. For $o \leq r < d$ Schumaker gave lower and upper bounds for the dimension of $S_d^r(\Delta)$ ([6], [7]). We will state here briefly his result.

Let V_o (resp. V_b) denote the number of interior (resp. boundary) vertices of Δ and let E_o (resp. E_b) denote the number of interior (resp. boundary) edges of Δ. Furthermore, we use the notation $V = V_o + V_b$ and $E = E_o + E_b$. We will number all interior vertices $\underline{x}^1, \ldots, \underline{x}^{V_o}$ in such a way that every vertex $\underline{x}^i$ is connected by an edge to at least one vertex $\underline{x}^j$ having a lower number $(j < i)$. Hence the boundary vertices get the numbers $V_o + 1, V_o + 2, \ldots, V_o + V_b = V$. For every interior vertex $\underline{x}^i$ we define the nonnegative integer values σ_i and $\tilde{\sigma}_i$:

(1.1a) $$\sigma_i = \sum_{j=1}^{d-r} (r+j+1-j\,e_i)_+$$

(1.1b) $$\tilde{\sigma}_i = \sum_{j=1}^{d-r} (r+j+1-j\,\tilde{e}_i)_+ ,$$

where e_i equals the number of edges of different slopes connected to vertex $\underline{x}^i$ and $\tilde{e}_i$ equals the number of edges of different slopes connecting vertex $\underline{x}^i$ to vertices $\underline{x}^j$ with $j > i$. The values e_i depend on the triangulation Δ, the values $\tilde{e}_i$ depend also on the numbering of the vertices. Although e_i is always greater or equal to 2, $\tilde{e}_i$ may become 0. The following inequalities hold trivially for $i = 1, \ldots, V_o$

$$e_i \geqq \tilde{e}_i \quad \text{and hence} \quad \sigma_i \leqq \tilde{\sigma}_i .$$

Now we can state the result of Schumaker[7]:

(1.2) $$\alpha + \beta E_o - \gamma V_o + \sum_{i=1}^{V_o} \sigma_i \leqq \dim S_d^r(\Delta) \leqq \alpha + \beta E_o - \gamma V_o + \sum_{i=1}^{V_o} \tilde{\sigma}_i ,$$

where the parameters α, β, γ depend only on r and d, namely

(1.3) $$\alpha = \binom{d+2}{2}; \quad \beta = \binom{d-r+1}{2}; \quad \gamma = \alpha - \binom{r+2}{2} .$$

In the case of *continuous* splines $(r = 0)$ it is immediate that $\sigma_i = 0$, for $i = 1, \ldots, V_o$. Thus (1.2) gives

(1.4) $$\binom{d+2}{2} + \binom{d+1}{2} E_o - \binom{d+2}{2} V_o + V_o \leqq \dim S_d^o(\Delta) .$$

It can be shown that this lower bound is indeed *equal* to the dimension of $S_d^o(\Delta)$. Furthermore, Chui and Schumaker gave explicitly a basis of local support elements [1].

For the spline space $S_d^1(\Delta)$ the situation is more difficult. For $d \geqq 5$ the dimension of $S_2^1(\Delta)$ is equal to the lower bound given in (1.2) (Morgan and Scott[3]). Schumaker and Alfeld recently announced that the dimension is also equal to the lower bound for $d = 3, 4$ [9]. There remains the case $d = 2$ of C^1-*continuous quadratic* splines. Quadratic polynomials of two variables are well suited for contour plotting and hence the space $S_2^1(\Delta)$ may be of practical importance. It is specially intriguing that the dimension of this space can *not* be determined explicitly. This fact follows from a special triangulation given by Morgan and Scott[4]. (See Fig. 2.1.)

2. THE DIMENSION OF THE SPACE $S_2^1(\Delta)$

For the space $S_2^1(\Delta)$ we have $\alpha = 6$, $\beta = 1$, $\gamma = 3$ and the formulas (1.1) can be written in a simpler form, namely

(2.1) $$\sigma_i = (3 - e_i)_+ ; \quad \tilde{\sigma}_i = (3 - \tilde{e}_i)_+ .$$

If only two edges of different slopes meet in a vertex $\underline{x}^i$, then $e_i = 2$ and hence $\sigma_i = 1$. For all other vertices σ_i is equal to zero. We will denote by σ the number of interior vertices with $e_i = 2$, i.e.

(2.2a) $$\sigma = \sum_{i=1}^{V_o} \sigma_i$$

and similarly

(2.2b) $$\tilde{\sigma} = \sum_{i=1}^{V_o} \tilde{\sigma}_i .$$

Formula (1.2) gives for this special space

(2.3) $$6 + E_o - 3V_o + \sigma \leqq \dim S_2^1(\Delta) \leqq 6 + E_o - 3V_o + \tilde{\sigma} .$$

Using the formula of Euler $(T = E - V + 1)$ and the equality $3T = E + E_o$ one can easily verify

(2.4a) $$6 + E_o - 3V_o = V_b + 3$$

and the following identity which will be used later

(2.4b) $$6 + E_o - 3V_o = 3V - E.$$

Thus (2.3) can be simplified to

(2.5) $$V_b + 3 + \sigma \leqq \dim S_2^1(\Delta) \leqq V_b + 3 + \tilde{\sigma} .$$

As a first example we consider two *topologically equivalent* triangulations Δ^1 and Δ^2 (see Fig. 2.1). For both triangulations the upper bound is equal to the lower bound and thus equal to the dimension:
$\dim S_2^1(\Delta^1) = 4 + 3 + 1 = 8$ $(\sigma_1 = \tilde{\sigma}_1 = 1)$ and $\dim S_2^1(\Delta^2) = 4 + 3 + 0 = 7$ $(\sigma_1 = \tilde{\sigma}_1 = 0)$.

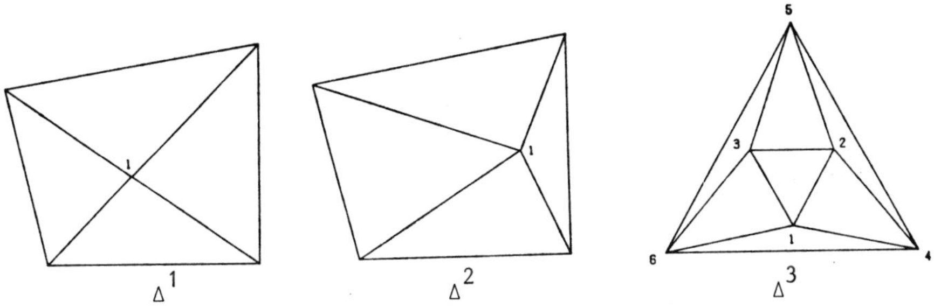

Fig. 2.1.

Hence the dimension depends not only on the topological structure of the triangulation, but also on the precise location of the vertices. For the triangulation Δ^3 (see Fig. 2.1) given by Morgan and Scott[4] (2.5) gives

$$6 \leqq \dim S_2^1(\Delta^3) \leqq 7,$$

since $\sigma_1 = \sigma_2 = \sigma_3 = 0$ and $\tilde{\sigma}_1 = \tilde{\sigma}_2 = 0$, $\tilde{\sigma}_3 = 1$.

If the vertices are chosen in a *symmetric way* then the dimension is indeed 7 (upper bound). No matter how the symmetry is destroyed the dimension of $S_2^1(\Delta^3)$ drops to 6. We were interested for which class of triangulations the dimension of $S_2^1(\Delta)$ is strictly larger than the lower bound given in (2.5). In order to investigate C^1-quadratic spline functions we use a special representation of quadratic polynomials on a triangle Ω_i suggested by Heindl[2].

3. REPRESENTATION OF ELEMENTS IN $S_2^1(\Delta)$

We consider an arbitrary quadratic polynomial $p \in \pi_2$ of two variables on a certain triangle $[\underline{x}^1, \underline{x}^2, \underline{x}^3]$. Instead of using the standard representation

(3.1) $$p(\underline{x}) = a_{11}x_1^2 + 2a_{12}x_1x_2 + a_{22}x_2^2 + b_1x_1 + b_2x_2 + c,$$

we express p in terms of *barycentric coordinates* $\lambda_1, \lambda_2, \lambda_3$ with respect to the vertices $\underline{x}^1, \underline{x}^2, \underline{x}^3$. (See Fig. 3.1).

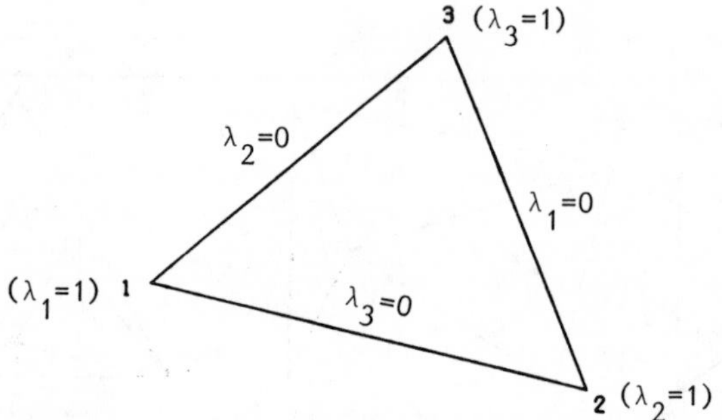

Fig. 3.1.

These barycentric coordinates $\lambda_1, \lambda_2, \lambda_3$ in a certain point $\underline{x} = (x_1, x_2)^T$ are affine functions of $\underline{x}$ defined by the equations

(3.2) $$\underline{x} = \sum_{i=1}^{3} \lambda_i \underline{x}^i \quad \text{and} \quad \sum_{i=1}^{3} \lambda_i = 1.$$

Using (3.2) we transform (3.1) into $p(\underline{x}) = p(\lambda_1, \lambda_2, \lambda_3)$, where

(3.3) $$p(\underline{x}) = p(\underline{x}^1)\lambda_1^2 + p(\underline{x}^2)\lambda_2^2 + p(\underline{x}^3)\lambda_3^2 + d_{12}\,\lambda_1\lambda_2 + d_{23}\,\lambda_2\lambda_3 + d_{31}\,\lambda_3\lambda_1.$$

Instead of using the parameters d_{12}, d_{23}, d_{31} we like to represent p by *function values* and *first-order derivatives* in the vertices, i.e.

(3.4) $$\begin{cases} p_i = p(\underline{x}^i) & , \quad i = 1,2,3, \\ (g_i, h_i) = (p_{x_1}(\underline{x}^i),\, p_{x_2}(\underline{x}^i)) = \nabla p(\underline{x}^i) & , \quad i = 1,2,3. \end{cases}$$

Obviously, these nine parameters cannot be chosen arbitrarily, but have to satisfy certain restrictions, which we will investigate next. The *differential* of p at a point $\underline{x}^i$ with increment $\underline{z} = (z_1, z_2)^T \in \mathbb{R}^2$ is defined by

(3.5) $$\nabla p(\underline{x}^i)\underline{z} = g_i z_1 + h_i z_2.$$

The differential of p at $\underline{x}^1$ with increment $\underline{x}^2 - \underline{x}^1$ can be calculated by differentiating p with respect to the barycentric coordinates, i.e.

(3.6a) $$\nabla p(\underline{x}^1)(\underline{x}^2 - \underline{x}^1) = p_{\lambda_2}(1,0,0) - p_{\lambda_1}(1,0,0) = -2p_1 + d_{12}.$$

For the vertex $\underline{x}^2$ one obtains a similar equation

$$(3.6b)\qquad \nabla p(\underline{x}^2)(\underline{x}^1-\underline{x}^2) = p_{\lambda_1}(0,1,0) - p_{\lambda_2}(0,1,0) = -2p_2 + d_{12}.$$

Eliminating d_{12} from (3.6a) and (3.6b) gives the following restriction on the parameters (See Heindl[2])

$$(3.7)\qquad \nabla p(\underline{x}^1)(\underline{x}^2-\underline{x}^1) + 2p_1 = \nabla p(\underline{x}^2)(\underline{x}^1-\underline{x}^2) + 2p_2.$$

The edges $[\underline{x}^2, \underline{x}^3]$ and $[\underline{x}^3, \underline{x}^1]$ can be treated in a similar way. Replacing the gradient $\nabla p(\underline{x}^i)$ by its components (g_i, h_i) we obtain

$$(3.8)\qquad g_i(x_1^j-x_1^i) + h_i(x_2^j-x_2^i) + 2p_i = g_j(x_1^i-x_1^j) + h_j(x_2^i-x_2^j) + 2p_j$$

for edges $[\underline{x}^i, \underline{x}^j]$, where (i,j) ranges over $\{(1,2), (2,3), (3,1)\}$. For any choice of the parameters (3.4) satisfying the equation (3.8) corresponding to the edges of the triangle, there is precisely one quadratic polynomial p with function values p_i and first derivatives (g_i, h_i) in the vertices.

Let us now consider the complete triangulation Δ. Parameters p_i, g_i, h_i associated with the vertices $\underline{x}^i$, $i = 1, \dots, V$ must satisfy equation (3.8) on each of the E edges $[\underline{x}^i, \underline{x}^j]$ of Δ. Let us denote the *coefficientmatrix* of this linear system of E equations in $3V$ parameters by $A(\Delta)$.

Since function values and first order derivatives of polynomials defined on adjacent triangles agree along common edges the resulting spline function belongs to $C^1(\Omega)$. If we call q the rank of the matrix $A(\Delta)$ and p the number of its singular values equal to zero $(p+q = E)$, then the dimension of $S_2^1(\Delta)$ is given by

$$(3.9)\qquad \dim S_2^1(\Delta) = 3V - q = 3V - E + p = V_b + 3 + p \qquad \text{(See 2.4b)}.$$

In the next section we determine the dimension of $S_2^1(\Delta)$ for several triangulations Δ by computing the *singular value decomposition* of $A(\Delta)$ using the routine F02WBF from the NAG library[5]. The rank of $A(\Delta)$ is equal to q if for the singular values $\sigma_1 \geqslant \sigma_2 \geqslant \dots \geqslant \sigma_E \geqslant 0$ holds

$$(3.10)\qquad \frac{\sigma_q}{\sigma_1} > \varepsilon \quad \text{and} \quad \frac{\sigma_{q+1}}{\sigma_1} \leqslant \varepsilon,$$

where $\varepsilon = 10^{-14}$ is the machine accuracy of the CDC 170/750.

4. SPECIAL TRIANGULATIONS

In this section we consider some triangulations Δ for which the dimension of $S_2^1(\Delta)$ is strictly larger than the lower bound given by Schumaker. Let us first discuss the triangulation Δ^3 of Fig. 2.1. If the vertices are located in a symmetric way on two *concentric* circles with radii r_1 and r_2, $0 < r_2 < 1/2\, r_1$, then the smallest singular value of the matrix $A(\Delta^3)$ is equal to zero and the dimension of $S_2^1(\Delta^3)$ is 7. The basis of $S_2^1(\Delta^3)$ consists of the 6 basis-elements of π_2 and one *non-polynomial element* which can be given explicitly.
We calculate the singular value decomposition of the 12×18-matrix $A(\Delta_\varepsilon^3)$, where Δ_ε^3 is obtained from Δ^3 by replacing $\underline{x}^4$ by $\underline{x}^4 + (\varepsilon,0)^T$, $\varepsilon > 0$. Fig. 4.1 shows in which way the smallest singular value $\sigma_{12}(\varepsilon)$ of $A(\Delta_\varepsilon^3)$ depends on ε in the case $r_1 = 1$, $r_2 = 1/3$ $(\sigma_1 \cong 5.50)$.

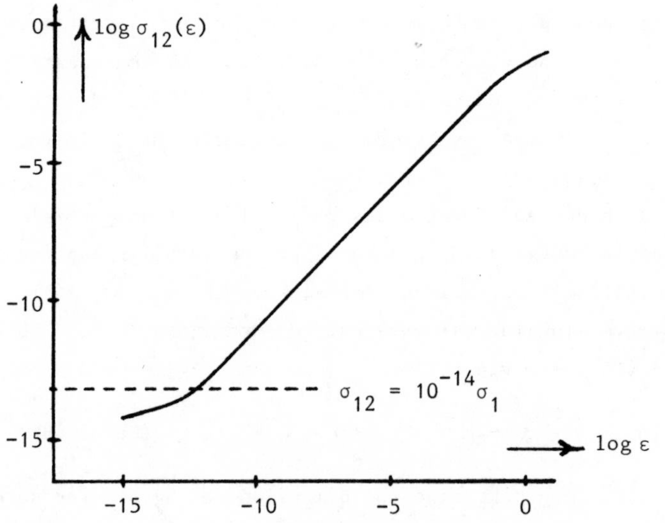

Fig. 4.1.

In Fig. 4.2 we give two symmetric triangulations Δ^4 and Δ^5, with $V = 12$, $E = 30$, $V_b = 3$, $p = 1$ and $\dim S_2^1(\Delta^i) = 7$ for $i = 4,5$.
The vertices are located on three concentric circles with radii $r_1 = 1$, $r_2 = 1/4$, $r_3 = 1/8$. The two smallest singular values of the matrix $A(\Delta^4)$ resp. $A(\Delta^5)$ are

$$\sigma_{29} = 2.5.10^{-2} \quad \text{and} \quad \sigma_{30} = 3.5.10^{-15} \quad (\sigma_1 = 5.96) \quad \text{resp.}$$
$$\sigma_{29} = 2.4.10^{-3} \quad \text{and} \quad \sigma_{30} = 1.0.10^{-15} \quad (\sigma_1 = 5.94).$$

Using the symmetry of the triangulations one can explicitly give a non-polynomial element in $S_2^1(\Delta^i)$, $i = 4,5$.

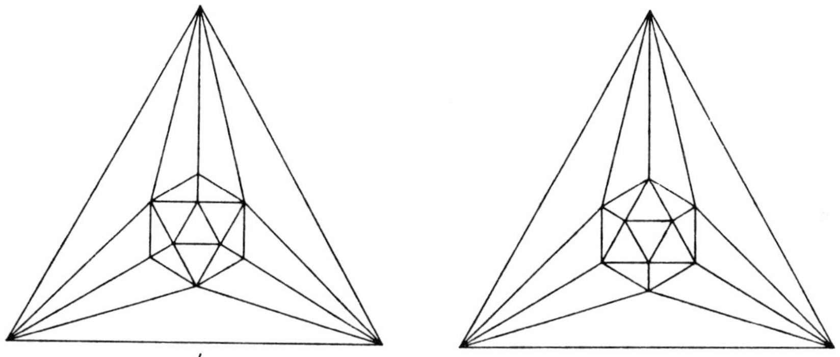

Δ^4 Δ^5

Fig. 4.2.

Let us now consider the two triangulations Δ^6 (with $V_b = 6$, $V = 19$, $E = 48$) and Δ^7 (with $V_b = 6$, $V = 31$, $E = 84$) of Fig. 4.3. In the completely symmetric case we have $\dim S_2^1(\Delta^6) = 11$ and $\dim S_2^1(\Delta^7) = 13$, which agrees with the upper bound in both cases. In Table 4.1 and 4.2 the smallest singular values are given for triangulations Δ^6, Δ_j^6 and Δ^7, Δ_j^7 resp., where Δ_j^i is obtained from Δ^i by distorting a single vertex $\underline{x}^j$ by $\Delta\underline{x} = (10^{-3},0)^T$. (See Fig. 4.3).

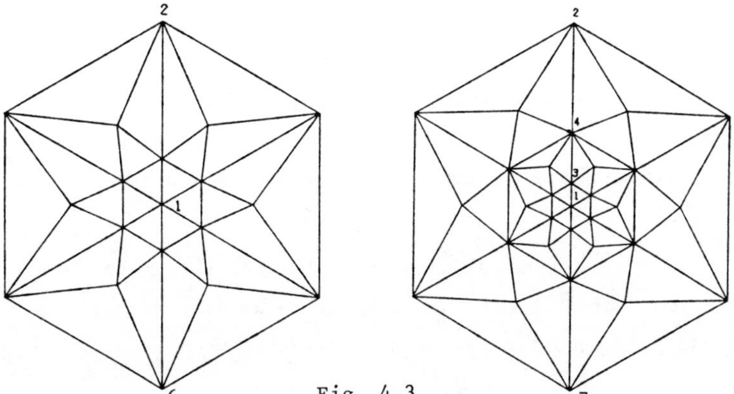

Δ^6 Fig. 4.3. Δ^7

Δ	σ_{46}	σ_{47}	σ_{48}	$\dim S_2^1(\Delta)$
Δ^6	$4.4.10^{-2}$	$3.7.10^{-15}$	$9.4.10^{-16}$	11
Δ_1^6	$4.4.10^{-2}$	$4.8.10^{-7}$	$7.4.10^{-15}$	10
Δ_2^6	$4.4.10^{-2}$	$1.6.10^{-5}$	$1.4.10^{-5}$	9

Table 4.1. *Smallest singular values of* $A(\Delta^6)$ *and* $A(\Delta_j^6)$, $j = 1,2$, *for vertices located on* 3 *concentric circles with radii* $r_1 = 1$, $r_2 = \frac{1}{2}$ *and* $r_3 = \frac{1}{4}$ $(\sigma_1 = 5.96)$.

Δ	σ_{80}	σ_{81}	σ_{82}	σ_{83}	σ_{84}	$\dim S_2^1(\Delta)$
Δ^7	$1.4.10^{-2}$	$6.2.10^{-15}$	$4.2.10^{-15}$	$1.5.10^{-15}$	$8.4.10^{-16}$	13
Δ_1^7	$1.4.10^{-2}$	$4.5.10^{-7}$	$5.9.10^{-15}$	$3.6.10^{-15}$	$3.5.10^{-15}$	12
Δ_2^7	$1.4.10^{-2}$	$3.0.10^{-5}$	$9.3.10^{-6}$	$4.7.10^{-15}$	$1.5.10^{-15}$	11
Δ_3^7	$1.4.10^{-2}$	$9.5.10^{-5}$	$8.8.10^{-5}$	$2.8.10^{-5}$	$2.7.10^{-15}$	10
Δ_4^7	$1.4.10^{-2}$	$9.7.10^{-5}$	$4.8.10^{-5}$	$1.7.10^{-5}$	$1.1.10^{-5}$	9

Table 4.2. *Smallest singular values of* $A(\Delta^7)$ *and* $A(\Delta_j^7)$, $j = 1,2,3,4$, *for vertices located on* 5 *concentric circles with radii* $r_1 = 1$, $r_2 = \frac{3}{5}$, $r_3 = \frac{2}{5}$, $r_4 = \frac{1}{4}$ *and* $r_5 = \frac{1}{8}$ $(\sigma_1 = 6.55)$.

Observe that the difference between the dimension of the spline space and the lower bound can be made *arbitrarily* large by nesting these triangulations Δ^i sufficiently many times. (Compare for instance triangulations Δ^6 and Δ^7).

Finally, we give two general classes of triangulations for which one can actually *prove* that at least one singular value of the matrix A is zero by expressing one equation (3.8) as a linear combination of the others.

A triangulation of *class* $C_1(m)$ consists of $2m$ vertices located in a symmetric way on two concentric circles, namely m vertices on each circle. Similarly, if we have 3 circles with radii r_1, r_2, r_3, $r_1 > r_2 > r_3$ and m_j vertices on circle j ($m_1 = 2m$, $m_2 = m_3 = m$), we call the triangulation of *class* $C_2(m)$. (See Fig. 4.4).

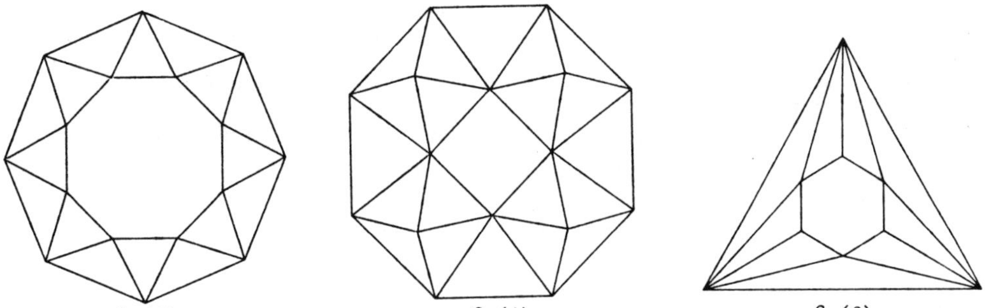

$C_1(8)$ $C_2(4)$ $C_3(2)$

Fig. 4.4.

Suppose that for a special choice of r_1, r_2 and r_3 a triangulation Δ of *class* $C_2(m)$ contains m vertices with $e_i = 2$. In this case, precisely m (and *not* $m+1$) singular values of $A(\Delta)$ will be zero.

As is shown in this section there are many triangulations Δ for which

$$(4.1) \qquad V_b + 3 + \sigma < \dim S_2^1(\Delta).$$

However, the precise classification of these triangulations is not clear. We point out that for some symmetric triangulations the dimension is *equal* to the lower bound. For instance, $A(\Delta)$ will always be of *full* rank for a triangulation of *class* $C_3(m)$, $m \geqslant 2$, consisting of $3m$ vertices located in a symmetric way inside an equilateral triangle (see Fig. 4.4).

Department of Mathematics, University of Amsterdam,
Roetersstraat 15, 1018 WB Amsterdam, The Netherlands.

REFERENCES

[1] CHUI, C.K., SCHUMAKER, L.L., and WANG, R.H., "On spaces of piecewise polynomials with boundary conditions", II and III, in *Second Edmonton Conference on Approximation Theory*, AMS Vol.3, American Math.Soc., Providence(1985), pp. 51-80.

[2] HEINDL, G., "Interpolation and approximation by piecewise quadratic C^1-functions of two variables", in *Multivariate Approximation Theory*, W. Schempp and K. Zeller, eds., Birkhäuser, Basel(1979), pp. 146-161.

[3] MORGAN, J., and SCOTT, R., "A nodal basis for C^1-piecewise polynomials of degree $n \geqslant 5$", Math.Comp. 29(1975), pp. 736-740.

[4] MORGAN, J., and SCOTT, R., "The dimension of piecewise polynomials", manuscript (1977), unpublished.

[5] Numerical Algorithms Group, FORTRAN version, Mark 10, Oxford, England, 1984.

[6] SCHUMAKER, L.L., "On the dimension of spaces of piecewise polynomials in two variables", in *Multivariate Approximation Theory*, W. Schempp and K. Zeller, eds., Birkhäuser, Basel(1979), pp. 396-412.

[7] SCHUMAKER, L.L., "Bounds on the dimension of spaces of multivariate piecewise polynomials", Rocky Mountain J. of Math. Vol.14, No.1, 1984, pp. 251-264.

[8] SCHUMAKER, L.L., "On spaces of piecewise polynomials in two variables", in *Approximation Theory and spline functions*, Proc. NATO Conf., ed. S.P. Singh, Newfoundland, Canada, North-Holland, 1984.

[9] SCHUMAKER, L.L., and ALFELD, P., private communication, 1984.

International Series of
Numerical Mathematics, Vol. 75

DEGREE OF BEST APPROXIMATION BY BLENDING FUNCTIONS

Manfred v. Golitschek
Institut für Angewandte Mathematik und Statistik
der Universität Würzburg
Würzburg

1. Introduction

Practical problems in numerical analysis, especially in representing surfaces or solving integral equations, often require the approximation of bivariate functions by a combination of univariate functions. Of this type are the so-called "blending methods" of Gordon [3 ; 4] of the following framework:
Let S and T be compact intervals of the real line or the circle $\mathbb{T}$ (in the 2π-periodic case). If $U \subset C(S)$ and $V \subset C(T)$ are given finite-dimensional linear subspaces of continuous real-valued functions on S or T, and $f \in C(S\times T)$ is to be approximated, then one chooses two linear projection operators, $P: C(S) \to U$ and $Q: C(T) \to V$. Next, P and Q are extended to operate on $C(S \times T)$ by ignoring t in the case of P and ignoring s in the case of Q. The new operators are denoted by $\bar{P}$ and $\bar{Q}$. Then the Boolean sum of $\bar{P}$ and $\bar{Q}$,

$$B := \bar{P} \oplus \bar{Q} = \bar{P} + \bar{Q} - \bar{P}\bar{Q}$$

will produce approximations $w = Bf$ of f.
The functions w are called blending functions. They are elements of $W := U \otimes C(T) + C(S) \otimes V$, i.e.

$$w(s,t) = \sum_{j=1}^{m} u_j(s)\, x_j(t) \;+\; \sum_{k=1}^{n} y_k(s)\, v_k(t) \quad ,$$

$x_j \in C(T)$, $y_k \in C(S)$. Here the u_j and v_k are base functions of U and V , respectively.
For more background on the theory of blending functions see a recent survey paper of E. W. Cheney [1] .

It is the purpose of this paper to prove a theorem of the Jackson-Favard type for blending functions by modifying Gordon's blending method slightly.

2. Jackson-Favard Theorem for Blending Functions

We suppose that $\|\cdot\|$, $\|\cdot\|_S$, $\|\cdot\|_T$ are norms on $C(S\times T)$, $C(S)$, $C(T)$, respectively, for which the relation

$$\|f\| = \|(\|f(s,\cdot)\|_T)\|_S = \|(\|f(\cdot,t)\|_S)\|_T \tag{1}$$

is valid for any $f \in C(S\times T)$. In particular, this is true for the L_p-norms on $S\times T$, S , T , $1 \le p \le \infty$.
For any non-negative integers r and q we denote

$$W_{r,S} := \left\{ g \in C^r(S) : \|g^{(r)}\|_S \le 1 \right\} ,$$

$$\operatorname{dist}(W_{r,S} , U) := \sup_{g\in W_{r,S}} \left(\inf_{u\in U} \|g - u\|_S \right) ,$$

$$C^{r,q} := \left\{ f \in C(S\times T) \ : \frac{\partial^{i+j} f}{\partial s^i \partial t^j} \in C(S\times T), 0\le i\le r, 0\le j\le q \right\} .$$

We shall need the following lemma.

LEMMA 1. <u>For any</u> $h \in C(S\times T)$ <u>and any</u> $\varepsilon > 0$ <u>there exist functions</u> $a_k \in C(S)$, $k=1,\dots,n$, <u>depending on</u> ε <u>such that</u>

$$\left\| h(s,\cdot) - \sum_{k=1}^{n} a_k(s)\, v_k \right\|_T \leq \varepsilon + \inf_{v\in V} \left\| h(s,\cdot) - v \right\|_T$$

is valid for each $s \in S$.

PROOF. Following the idea of the proof of [2 ; Theorem 2,p.127] we use the Michael Selection Theorem (Holmes [7 ; p.183]) for the set-valued function $F: S \to 2^{R^n}$,

$$F(s) := \left\{ (z_1,\dots,z_n) \in R^n : \left\| h(s,\cdot) - \sum_{k=1}^{n} z_k v_k \right\|_T \leq E(s) \right\},$$

where we put $E(s) := \varepsilon + \inf_{v\in V} \| h(s,\cdot) - v \|_T$.

Let $\mathcal{O} \subset R^n$ be an open set, and $\mathcal{O}^* := \{ s \in S : F(s) \cap \mathcal{O} \neq \emptyset \}$. Let $s_o \in \mathcal{O}^*$. There exists a $z_o = (z_{1o},\dots,z_{no}) \in F(s_o) \cap \mathcal{O}$ such that

$$\left\| h(s_o,\cdot) - \sum_{k=1}^{n} z_{ko} v_k \right\|_T < E(s_o) .$$

If s_o is not an interior point of $\mathcal{O}^*$ then there exists a sequence s_i in $S \setminus \mathcal{O}^*$ which converges to s_o. In particular, $z_o \notin F(s_i)$ for all i and thus

$$\left\| h(s_o,\cdot) - \sum_{k=1}^{n} z_{ko} v_k \right\|_T \geq \underline{\lim}_{i\to\infty} E(s_i) = E(s_o) ,$$

a contradiction. Hence $\mathcal{O}^*$ is an open set, F is lower semicontinuous. Since $F(s)$ is a non-empty closed convex subset of R^n for any $s \in S$, we may apply the Michael Selection Theorem which states that there is a continuous selection $a = (a_1,\dots,a_n): S \to R^n$ for F . ▫

THEOREM 1. *Under the above assumptions, the inequality*

$$\inf_{w\in W} \| f - w \| \leq \operatorname{dist}(W_{r,S}, U)\, \operatorname{dist}(W_{q,T}, V) \left\| \frac{\partial^{r+q} f}{\partial s^r \partial t^q} \right\| \tag{2}$$

is valid for each function $f \in C^{r,q}$.

REMARK. It follows by [6 ; Theorem 2] that the inequality in Theorem 1 is best possible for the function class $C^{r,q}$ if $p \in [1,\infty]$ and $\|\cdot\|$, $\|\cdot\|_S$, $\|\cdot\|_T$ are the L_p-norms.

PROOF OF THEOREM 1. We put $A:=\mathrm{dist}(W_{r,S},U)$, $B:=\mathrm{dist}(W_{q,T},V)$ and choose an $\varepsilon > 0$. Because of Lemma 1 there exist functions $a_k \in C(S)$ for which

$$\left\|\frac{\partial^r f}{\partial s^r}(s,\cdot) - \sum_{k=1}^{n} a_k(s) v_k\right\|_T \leq \varepsilon + B\left\|\frac{\partial^{r+q} f}{\partial s^r \partial t^q}(s,\cdot)\right\|_T ,$$

$s \in S$, is valid. Let a_k^* be an r-th integral of a_k and

$$f^*(s,t) := f(s,t) - \sum_{k=1}^{n} a_k^*(s) v_k(t) \quad , \quad (s,t) \in S \times T \quad .$$

We apply Lemma 1 to f^* and U : There exist functions $b_j \in C(T)$ for which

$$\left\|f^*(\cdot,t) - \sum_{j=1}^{m} b_j(t) u_j\right\|_S \leq \varepsilon + A\left\|\frac{\partial^r f^*}{\partial s^r}(\cdot,t)\right\|_S ,$$

$t \in T$, is valid. Finally we define $w \in W$ by

$$w(s,t) := \sum_{k=1}^{n} a_k^*(s) v_k(t) + \sum_{j=1}^{m} b_j(t) u_j(s) \quad . \tag{3}$$

Applying the relation (1) we then obtain

$$\begin{aligned} \| f - w \| &= \|(\|f(\cdot,t) - w(\cdot,t)\|_S)\|_T \\ &\leq O(\varepsilon) + A \left\|\left(\left\|\frac{\partial^r f^*}{\partial s^r}(\cdot,t)\right\|_S\right)\right\|_T \\ &= O(\varepsilon) + A \left\|\left(\left\|\frac{\partial^r f^*}{\partial s^r}(s,\cdot)\right\|_T\right)\right\|_S \\ &\leq O(\varepsilon) + A\, B \left\|\left(\left\|\frac{\partial^{r+q} f}{\partial s^r \partial t^q}(s,\cdot)\right\|_T\right)\right\|_S \quad . \quad \square \end{aligned}$$

We shall now show that the method of proof of Theorem 1 is closely related to Gordon's blending method described in the introduction. For convenience we suppose that each $g \in C(S)$ and each $h \in C(T)$ have unique best approximations in U and V respectively. By $P: C(S) \to U$ and $Q: C(T) \to V$ we denote the not necessarily linear proximity maps for U and V, i.e.

$$\|g-Pg\|_S = \inf_{u \in U} \|g-u\|_S \quad , \qquad \|h-Qh\|_T = \inf_{v \in V} \|h-v\|_T \quad .$$

Because of the uniqueness properties of U and V the proximity maps P and Q are continuous, hence Lemma 1 holds for $\varepsilon = 0$ and the extensions

$$\bar{P}: C(S \times T) \to U \otimes C(T) \quad , \qquad \bar{Q}: C(S \times T) \to C(S) \otimes V$$

exist. We introduce the differential operator $D^r := \frac{d^r}{ds^r}$ and choose a selection $D^{-r}: C(S) \to C^r(S)$ of the set-valued inverse of D^r. Their extensions are denoted by $\bar{D}^r$ and $\bar{D}^{-r}$. With the above operators and the identity I on $C(S \times T)$ we construct the operator $B: C^{r,q} \to W$,

$$B := \bar{D}^{-r} \bar{Q} \bar{D}^r + \bar{P} (I - \bar{D}^{-r} \bar{Q} \bar{D}^r) \quad .$$

Following the proof of Theorem 1 we realize that the element $w \in W$ in (3) which establishes the inequality (2) is identical with $w = Bf$.

3. Trigonometric Blending Functions

In this section the function f is 2π-periodic in both variables. f is approximated by the blending functions

$$\tilde{W} := T_{m-1}(S) \otimes C(T) + C(S) \otimes T_{n-1}(T)$$

with the domains $S := T := \mathbb{T}$ and the building-stones $U := T_{m-1}$ and $V := T_{n-1}$ of trigonometric polynomials of degree $\leq m-1$ and

$\leq n-1$, respectively. For $1 \leq p \leq \infty$, $\|\cdot\|$ denotes the usual L_p-norm on the square $[0,2\pi) \times [0,2\pi)$.

Recently, Haußmann, Jetter, Steinhaus [5] have investigated the approximation properties of $\widetilde{W}$ in detail. Their main result is the following.

THEOREM 2. _For positive integers_ r, q, m, n _the degree of best approximation of a function_ $f \in C^{r,q}(\mathbb{T}\times\mathbb{T})$ _by the trigonometric blending functions_ $\widetilde{W}$ _can be estimated by_

$$(4) \qquad \inf_{w\in\widetilde{W}} \|f - w\| \leq K_r K_q m^{-r} n^{-q} \left\| \frac{\partial^{r+q} f}{\partial s^r \partial t^q} \right\|$$

where $K_r := \sum_{j=0}^{\infty} \left(\frac{(-1)^j}{2j+1} \right)^{r+1}$.

Haußmann et al. have pointed out that the right hand side of (4) is best possible in the class $C^{r,q}(\mathbb{T}\times\mathbb{T})$ if $p = \infty$.

It is easy to verify that Theorem 2 is a special case of our Theorem 1 because of the Jackson-Favard-Achieser-Krein inequality $\mathrm{dist}(W_{r,S}, T_{m-1}) \leq K_r m^{-r}$ with equality for $p = \infty$. See Timan [8 ; p.292].

REFERENCES

1. Cheney, E.W., _The best approximation of multivariate functions by combinations of univariate functions_. In: Approximation Theory IV (C.K. Chui et al., Eds.),pp.1-26. New York-London: Academic Press 1983.

2. Cheney, E.W. - v.Golitschek, M., _The best approximation of bivariate functions by separable functions_. Contemporary Mathematics, Vol.21, pp.125-136. Providence: Amer. Math. Soc. 1983.

3. Gordon, W.J., _Distributive lattices and the approximation of multivariate functions_. In: Approximation with Special Emphasis on Spline Functions (I.J. Schoenberg, Ed.) , pp. 223-277. New York: Academic Press 1969.

4. Gordon, W.J., Blending-function methods of bivariate and multivariate interpolation and approximation. SIAM J. Numer. Anal. 8, 158-177 (1971).

5. Haußmann, W. - Jetter, K. - Steinhaus, B., Degree of best approximation by trigonometric blending functions. Mathematische Zeitschrift 189, 143-150 (1985).

6. Haußmann, W. - Zeller, K., Mixed norm multivariate approximation with blending functions. In: Constructive Theory of Functions (Bl. Sendov et al., Eds.), pp.403-408. Sofia: Bulgarian Academy of Sciences 1984.

7. Holmes, R.B., Geometric Functional Analysis and its Applications. New York: Springer-Verlag 1975.

8. Timan, A.F., Theory of Approximation of Functions of a Real Variable. New York: MacMillan 1963.

International Series of
Numerical Mathematics, Vol. 75

SHAPE PRESERVING APPROXIMATION BY POLYHEDRAL SPLINES

T.N.T. Goodman

1. Introduction

In applications such as Computer Aided Geometric Design it is useful to have operators which approximate a given bivariate function f by a spline function S which in some sense preserves the shape of f, i.e. the shape of the surface represented by f. It seems reasonable to require that if f is monotone in a given direction or is convex, then so is S. We would also like in general that S is no more 'bumpy' than is f. To see if this is the case we need some measure of the 'bumpiness' of a function f. One possible measure is the total variation of f (over a region A in R^2), which for suitably smooth f can be defined as

$$V(f,A) := \int_A |\text{grad } f| = \int_A (f_x^2 + f_y^2)^{\frac{1}{2}}. \tag{1.1}$$

This has the desirable properties that it is invariant under rotation in R^2 and is additive in the sense that for disjoint sets A and B, $V(f,A\cup B) = V(f,A) + V(f,B)$. The total variation vanishes if and only if the function is constant. It might seem more reasonable, however, to regard a function as having 'no bumps' if and only if it is linear. We thus define

$$V_1(f,A) := \int_A (f_{xx}^2 + 2f_{xy}^2 + f_{yy}^2)^{\frac{1}{2}}, \tag{1.2}$$

since this is invariant under rotation, additive in the above sense, and vanishes if and only if f is linear. In practice, however, we shall want to consider functions which do not have integrable second derivatives because the first derivatives have discontinuity across a given line segment ℓ. In such a case we include in $V_1(f,A)$ the term

$$V_1(f,\ell) := \int_\ell |\mathrm{grad}\, f_1 - \mathrm{grad}\, f_2| \,, \tag{1.3}$$

where f_1 and f_2 denote the restrictions of f to either side of ℓ.

Finally we note that Chang and Hoscheck [4] have considered the expression

$$V_1^*(f,A) := \int_A |f_{xx} + f_{yy}| \tag{1.4}$$

which is also invariant under rotation and additive in the above sense. In the case when the first derivatives of f have a discontinuity across a line segment ℓ, they include in $V_1^*(f,A)$ the same term (1.3).

In §2 we recall some results on the shape preserving properties of Bernstein polynomials on triangles. Some of these results are used in §3 in studying the shape preserving properties of approximation operators formed from box splines on a 3-direction mesh. Finally in §4 we mention some analogous results when box splines are replaced by half-box splines.

2. Bernstein Polynomials

For any function f on a triangle T we define the Bernstein polynomial of degree n by

$$B_n(f)(u,v,w) := \sum_{i+j+k=n} f\left(\frac{i}{n}, \frac{j}{n}, \frac{k}{n}\right) \frac{n!}{i!j!k!} u^i v^j w^k, \tag{2.1}$$

where u, v, w denote barycentric coordinates. We denote by $\hat{f}_n$ the function on T which interpolates f at the points with barycentric coordinates $(\frac{i}{n}, \frac{j}{n}, \frac{k}{n})$ and which is linear on each element of the regular triangulation of T formed by lines parallel to the sides of T through the same points $(\frac{i}{n}, \frac{j}{n}, \frac{k}{n})$. We call $\hat{f}_n$ <u>the nth Bézier net of $B_n(f)$</u>.

<u>Theorem 1</u> a) If $\hat{f}_n$ is increasing in a given direction, then so is $B_n(f)$.

b) If $\hat{f}_n$ is convex, then so is $B_n(f)$.

c) $V(B_n(f),T) \le \frac{2n}{n+1} V(\hat{f}_n,T)$. (2.2)

d) $V_1(B_n(f),T) \le V_1(\hat{f}_n,T)$. (2.3)

e) $V_1^*(B_n(f),T) \le V_1^*(\hat{f}_n,T) = V_1(\hat{f}_n,T)$. (2.4)

Proof We have not seen a proof of a) but it is easy to show that if $\hat{f}_n$ is increasing in a given direction, then the derivative of $B_n(f)$ in that direction is positive. Part b) is proved in [3], parts c) and d) in [10], and part e) in [4].

3. 3. Box Splines

We recall from [1] that for any set $X = \{x^0,\dots,x^{n+1}\}$ of non-zero vectors in R^2, the box spline $B(.|X)$ is defined on R^2 by requiring that for all f in $C(R^2)$,

$$\int_{R^2} f(x)B(x|X)\,dx = \int_{[0,1]^{n+2}} f(u_0x^0+\dots+u_{n+1}x^{n+1})\,du_0\dots du_{n+1} \ . \tag{3.1}$$

For further details on box splines see [1], [7]. We shall consider only the case when X comprises $e^1 = (1,0)$, $e^2 = (0,1)$, $e^3 = (1,1)$ with multiplicities p,q,r respectively, $\min\{p,q,r\} \geq 1$, $p + q + r = n + 2$. In this case we shall denote $B(.|X)$ by B_{pqr}. The support of B_{pqr} is

$$\text{supp } B_{pqr} = \{ue^1 + ve^2 + we^3 : 0 \leq u \leq p,\ 0 \leq v \leq q,\ 0 \leq w \leq r\} \tag{3.2}$$

and B_{pqr} is strictly positive in the interior of supp B_{pqr}. We shall denote by Ω the regular triangulation of R^2 formed by the lines $\{\alpha + te^j : t \in R\}$, $\alpha \in Z^2$, $j = 1,2,3$. Then B_{pqr} is a polynomial of degree n on each element of Ω and for any α in Z^2 it has continuous derivatives of order $n - p$, $n - q$, $n - r$ on the lines $\{\alpha + te^j : t \in R\}$ for $j = 1,2,3$ respectively.

We now define, for any function f on Z^2,

$$T_{pqr}(f)(x) = \sum_{\alpha \in Z^2} f(\alpha)B_{pqr}(x-\alpha) \ . \tag{3.3}$$

We denote by $\hat{f}$ the function which is linear on each element of Ω and satisfies $\hat{f}(\alpha) = f(\alpha)$ for all α in Z^2. Then we have

$$T_{111}(f)(x) = \hat{f}(x-e^3) \ . \tag{3.4}$$

Theorem 2

a) If $\hat{f}$ is increasing in a given direction, then so is $T_{pqr}(f)$.

b) If $\hat{f}$ is convex, then so is $T_{pqr}(f)$.

c) $V(T_{pqr}(f)) \le V(\hat{f})$. (3.5)

d) $V_1(T_{pqr}(f)) \le V_1(\hat{f})$. (3.6)

e) $V_1^*(T_{pqr}(f)) \le V_1^*(\hat{f}) = V_1(\hat{f})$. (3.7)

Remarks Here $V(\hat{f})$ denotes $V(\hat{f},R^2)$ and similarly for the other expressions. The only case of interest is when these expressions are finite but this will certainly be the case if $f(\alpha)$ is non-zero for only a finite number of α, which will be the case in any practical application.

Proof We shall prove a), b) and c) by using the subdivision algorithm for box splines derived independently by a number of authors [5], [8], [11]. This tells us that for any integer $m \ge 1$ we have

$$T_{pqr}(f)(x) = \sum_{\alpha\in m^{-1}Z^2} C^m_{pqr}(\alpha)B_{pqr}(m(x-\alpha)) \tag{3.8}$$

where $$C^m_{pqr}(\alpha) = A_1^{p-1}A_2^{q-1}A_3^{r-1}\hat{f}(\alpha + (m^{-1}-1)e^3) \tag{3.9}$$

and for $j = 1,2,3$, A_j is the averaging operator

$$A_j g(\alpha) = \frac{1}{m}\sum_{i=0}^{m-1} g(\alpha - \frac{ie^j}{m}). \tag{3.10}$$

It is shown in [6] that if σ_{pqr} is the centre of supp B_{pqr}, i.e. $\sigma_{pqr} = \frac{1}{2}(pe^1 + qe^2 + re^3)$, then for α in $m^{-1}Z^2$,

$$\begin{aligned}&|C^m_{pqr}(\alpha) - T_{pqr}(f)(\alpha + m^{-1}\sigma_{pqr})|\\ &\le Km^{-2}\max_{|\beta|=2} \| D^\beta T_{pqr}(f)\|_\infty (\alpha+m^{-1}\mathrm{supp}B_{pqr})\end{aligned} \tag{3.11}$$

where the constant K depends only on p,q and r. We denote by $\hat{C}^m_{pqr}$ the function which is linear on each element of $m^{-1}\Omega$ and satisfies $\hat{C}^m_{pqr}(\alpha) = C^m_{pqr}(\alpha)$ for all α in $m^{-1}Z^2$.

To prove a) we suppose $\hat{f}$ is increasing in a given direction. Then by (3.9) we see that $\hat{C}^m_{pqr}$ is increasing in this direction. But by (3.11), $\hat{C}^m_{pqr}$ converges to $T_{pqr}(f)$ as $m \to \infty$ uniformly on compact sets, and so $T_{pqr}(f)$ is increasing in this direction.

To prove b) we note that $\hat{f}$ is convex if and only if for all α in Z^2 we have $\hat{f}(\alpha) + \hat{f}(\alpha + e^1) \le \hat{f}(\alpha - e^2) + \hat{f}(\alpha + e^3)$, $\hat{f}(\alpha) + \hat{f}(\alpha + e^2) \le \hat{f}(\alpha - e^1) + \hat{f}(\alpha + e^3)$, $\hat{f}(\alpha) + \hat{f}(\alpha + e^3) \le \hat{f}(\alpha + e^1) + \hat{f}(\alpha + e^2)$. Thus if $\hat{f}$ is convex, it follows from (3.9) that $\hat{C}^m_{pqr}$ is convex. Since $\hat{C}^m_{pqr}$ converges to $T_{pqr}(f)$, as above, it follows that $T_{pqr}(f)$ is convex.

We remark that we have been informed by W. Dahmen and C. Micchelli that they have also proved a) and b).

We next prove c). For α in Z^2 let L_α and U_α denote the triangles with vertices $\alpha, \alpha + e^1, \alpha + e^3$, and vertices $\alpha, \alpha + e^2, \alpha + e^3$, respectively. Then

$$V(\hat{f}, L_\alpha) = \tfrac{1}{2}|(\hat{f}(\alpha+e^1) - \hat{f}(\alpha),\ \hat{f}(\alpha+e^3) - \hat{f}(\alpha+e^1))| ,$$
$$V(\hat{f}, U_\alpha) = \tfrac{1}{2}|(\hat{f}(\alpha+e^3) - \hat{f}(\alpha+e^2),\ \hat{f}(\alpha+e^2) - \hat{f}(\alpha))| .$$

Then from (3.9) we see that $V(\hat{C}^m_{pqr}) \le V(\hat{f})$. But by the quadratic convergence in (3.11), $V(\hat{C}^m_{pqr}) \to V(T_{pqr}(f))$ as $m \to \infty$ and so $V(T_{pqr}(f)) \le V(\hat{f})$.

We shall derive d) and e) from (2.3) and (2.4). We denote by $\hat{a}_{pqr}$ the function on R^2 whose restriction to L_α and to U_α for any α in Z^2 is the nth Bézier net of the restriction of $T_{pqr}(f)$ to L_α and to U_α respectively. This is consistent on the sides of the triangles in Ω because $T_{pqr}(f)$ is continuous. Now for α in Z^2 let ℓ^j_α denote the line segment from α to $\alpha + e^j$, $j = 1,2,3$. Also for β in $n^{-1}Z^2$ we write

$$b^1_{pqr}(\beta) = \hat{a}_{pqr}(\beta) + \hat{a}_{pqr}(\beta+n^{-1}e^1) - \hat{a}_{pqr}(\beta+n^{-1}e^3) - \hat{a}_{pqr}(\beta-n^{-1}e^2),$$
$$b^2_{pqr}(\beta) = \hat{a}_{pqr}(\beta) + \hat{a}_{pqr}(\beta+n^{-1}e^2) - \hat{a}_{pqr}(\beta+n^{-1}e^3) - \hat{a}_{pqr}(\beta-n^{-1}e^1),$$
$$b^3_{pqr}(\beta) = \hat{a}_{pqr}(\beta) + \hat{a}_{pqr}(\beta+n^{-1}e^3) - \hat{a}_{pqr}(\beta+n^{-1}e^1) - \hat{a}_{pqr}(\beta+n^{-1}e^2).$$

Then direct calculation shows that for α in Z^2, $j = 1,2,3$,

$$V_1(T_{pqr}(f), \ell^j_\alpha) = \int_0^1 |n \sum_{i=0}^{n-1} b^j_{pqr}(\alpha+in^{-1}e^j)\binom{n-1}{i} t^i(1-t)^{n-1-i}|\,dt$$
$$\le \sum_{i=0}^{n-1} |b^j_{pqr}(\alpha+in^{-1}e^j)| = V_1(\hat{a}_{pqr}, \ell^j_\alpha) .$$

Combining this with (2.3) and (2.4) gives respectively

$$V_1(T_{pqr}(f)) \le V_1(\hat{a}_{pqr}),\ V_1^*(T_{pqr}(f)) \le V_1^*(\hat{a}_{pqr}) = V_1(\hat{a}_{pqr}) .$$

Thus to prove d) and e) it remains only to show that $V_1(\hat{a}_{pqr}) \le V_1(\hat{f})$. From (3.4), $\hat{a}_{111} = \hat{f}(.-e^3)$ and so it is sufficient to prove that for any $i, j, k \geq 1$, $\max\{V_1(\hat{a}_{i+1,j,k}), V_1(\hat{a}_{i,j+1,k}), V_1(\hat{a}_{i,j,k+1})\} \leq V_1(\hat{a}_{ijk})$. We shall prove

$$V_1(\hat{a}_{i+1,j,k}) \leq V_1(\hat{a}_{ijk}) \tag{3.12}$$

the other two inequalities following similarly. We shall use the following algorithm [2]. Letting $i + j + k = m$, define $\bar{a}_{ijk}(\beta)$ for β in $(m+1)^{-1}Z^2$ by

$$\bar{a}_{ijk}(\alpha - \frac{s}{m+1}e^1 + \frac{t}{m+1}e^2) = \hat{a}_{ijk}(\alpha - \frac{s}{m}e^1 + \frac{t}{m}e^2), \ \alpha \in Z^2,$$
$$0 \leq s \leq m, \ -s \leq t \leq m - s.$$

Then for any β in $(m+1)^{-1}Z^2$,

$$\hat{a}_{i+1,j,k}(\beta) = \sum_{\nu=0}^{m} \bar{a}_{ijk}(\beta - \frac{\nu}{m+1}e^1).$$

Inequality (3.12) follows on noting that $V_1(\hat{a}_{ijk}) = \sum\{|b^{\ell}_{ijk}(\beta)|: \beta \in m^{-1}Z^2, \ \ell = 1,2,3\}$.

4. Half-Box Splines

Some of the techniques of §3 may be applicable to other approximation operators involving polyhedral splines. We shall consider analogues of (3.6) and (3.7) for operators involving half-box splines [9], [11], [12], which we proceed to define. For $X = \{x^0,\ldots,x^{n+1}\} \subset R^2$ we define $H(.|X)$ on R^2 by

$$\int_{R^2} f(x)H(x|X)\,dx = \int_{[0,1]^{n+1}} \int_0^{u_1} f(u_0x^0 + \ldots + u_{n+1}x^{n+1})\,du_0\ldots du_{n+1}$$

for f in $C(R^2)$. We suppose $\{x^2,\ldots,x^{n+1}\}$ comprises e^1, e^2, e^3 with multiplicities p, q, r respectively, $\min\{p,q,r\} \geq 1$, $p + q + r = n$. If $x^0 = e^1$, $x^1 = e^2$, we write $H(.|X) = U_{pqr}$, the 'upper half-box spline'. If $x^0 = e^2$, $x^1 = e^1$, we write $H(.|X) = L_{pqr}$, the 'lower half-box spline'. U_{pqr} and L_{pqr} are polynomials of degree n on each element of Ω and for any α in Z^2 they have continuous derivatives of order $n - p - 1$, $n - q - 1$, $n - r - 1$ on the lines $\{\alpha+te^j : t\in R\}$ for $j = 1,2,3$ respectively. We shall consider only U_{pqr}, corresponding results for L_{pqr} following similarly. We define, for any function f on Z^2,

$$S_{pqr}(f)(x) = \sum_{\alpha\in Z^2} f(\alpha)U_{pqr}(x-\alpha) \tag{4.1}$$

We let $\hat{d}_{pqr}$ denote the nth Bézier net of $S_{pqr}(f)$, defined in the same manner as the nth Bézier net $\hat{a}_{pqr}$ of $T_{pqr}(f)$. Since $S_{pqr}(f)$ is C^1 we can apply (2.3) and (2.4) to give

$$V_1(S_{pqr}(f)) \le V_1(\hat{d}_{pqr}),\ V_1^*(S_{pqr}(f)) \le V_1^*(\hat{d}_{pqr}) = V_1(\hat{d}_{pqr}) \ . \tag{4.2}$$

Now $\hat{d}_{111}$ can be found explicitly in terms of $\hat{f}$ and direct calculation shows that

$$V_1(\hat{d}_{111}) \le V_1(\hat{f}) \ . \tag{4.3}$$

We can express $\hat{d}_{i+1,j,k}$ in terms of $\hat{d}_{ijk}$ by exactly the same algorithm as for $\hat{a}_{i+1,j,k}$ in terms of $\hat{a}_{ijk}$ and it follows that $V_1(\hat{d}_{i+1,j,k}) \le V_1(\hat{d}_{ijk})$. Similarly $V_1(\hat{d}_{i,j+1,k}), V_1(\hat{d}_{i,j,k+1}) \le V_1(\hat{d}_{ijk})$ and so $V_1(\hat{d}_{pqr}) \le V_1(\hat{d}_{111})$. Combining this with (4.2) and (4.3) gives

$$V_1(S_{pqr}(f)) \le V_1(\hat{f}),\ V_1^*(S_{pqr}(f)) \le V_1(\hat{f}) = V_1^*(\hat{f}) \ .$$

References

1. C. De Boor, K. Höllig, B-splines from parallelipipeds, J. d'Analyse Math. 42 (1982/3), 99-115.

2. W. Boehm, Triangular spline algorithms, to appear in Computer Aided Geometric Design.

3. G. Chang, P.J. Davis, The convexity of Bernstein polynomials over triangles, J. Approx. Theory 40 (1984), 11-28.

4. G. Chang, J. Hoscheck, these proceedings.

5. E. Cohen, T. Lyche, R. Riesenfeld, Discrete box splines and refinement algorithms, Computer Aided Geometric Design 1 (1984), 131-148.

6. W. Dahmen, N. Dyn, D. Levin, On the convergence rates of subdivision algorithms for box spline surfaces, to appear in Constructive Approximation.

7. W. Dahmen, C.A. Micchelli, Recent progress in multivariate splines, in: Approximation Theory IV, ed. C.K. Chui, L.L. Schumaker, J. Ward, Academic Press, New York (1983), 27-121.

8. W. Dahmen, C.A. Micchelli, Subdivision algorithms for the generation of box spline surfaces, to appear in Computer Aided Geometric Design.

9. P.O. Frederickson, Generalised triangular splines, Mathematics Report # 7-71, Lakehead University (1971).

10. T.N.T. Goodman, Variation diminishing properties of Bernstein polynomials on triangles, to appear in J. Approximation Theory.

11. H. Prautzsch, Unterteilungsalgorithmen fur multivariate Splines - ein geometrischer Zugang, Ph.D. Thesis, Technische Universitat Braunschweig, 1984.

12. M.A. Sabin, The use of piecewise forms for the numerical representation of shape, Ph.D. Dissertation, Hungar. Acad. of Science, Budapest (1977).

International Series of
Numerical Mathematics, Vol. 75

NUMERICAL REALIZATION OF BOUNDARY COLLOCATION METHODS

K. Gürlebeck[1], W. Sprößig[1], M. Tasche[2]

[1] Technische Hochschule Karl-Marx-Stadt

[2] Wilhelm-Pieck-Universität Rostock

During the last 50 years several methods for the solution of fundamental problems of equations of mathematical physics (difference methods, finite element methods, Galerkin method, boundary element methods) have been developed and successfully applied. In this paper, special techniques in approximation theory and in numerical collocation are studied. Using the theory of quaternionic-valued functions and the operational calculus we construct an effective numerical algorithm. Numerical experiments for 2-dimensional boundary value problems of elliptic partial differential equations are presented. This algorithm can successfully be used for domains with complicated boundary.

1. Prelimaries

Using the operational calculus for a linear right-invertible operator D acting in a linear space X, a linear right inverse T of D and the corresponding initial value operator F (see [1], [6], [9]), we obtain following relationships:

(i) $DT = I$ on X,

(ii) $I - TD = F$ on $\mathrm{Dom}\, D$,

(iii) $TX \subset \mathrm{Dom}\, D$, $\mathrm{Dom}\, D \subseteq X$, $\mathrm{Dom}\, T = X$.

Here Dom D and Dom T denote the domain of D and T, respectively. Further, I signifies the identity. This general principle is very useful in the following for the numerical treatment of special systems of partial differential equations.

We characterize vectors of R^4 by $u = (u_0,\hat{u})$, $\hat{u} = (u_1,u_2,u_3)$ and $v = (v_0,\hat{v})$, $\hat{v} = (v_1,v_2,v_3)$. By introducing the (non-commutative) product

$$u \circ v = (u_0 v_0 - (\hat{u},\hat{v}), \hat{u} \times \hat{v} + u_0\hat{v} + \hat{u}v_0), \tag{1.1}$$

R^4 gets the structure of the quaternion algebra Q, where $(\hat{u},\hat{v})$ and $\hat{u} \times \hat{v}$ denote the scalar product and cross-product, respectively. The vector $\overline{u} = (u_0, - \hat{u})$ denotes the conjugated quaternion of u.

Let $x = (x^1,x^2,x^3) \in R^3$ be the vector of independent variables. Let $G \subset R^3$ be a bounded domain with sufficiently smooth boundary $\Gamma = \partial G$. The Banach spaces C_Q^k, L_Q^p and H_Q^s of Q-valued functions are explained by their components in the sense of the spaces C^k, L^p and H^s, respectively. For instance, we recall the definition of the inner product for $u,v \in L_Q^2(G)$:

$$(u,v)_{L_Q^2(G)} = \int_G \overline{u(x)} \circ v(x)\, dx.$$

By the help of the so-called <u>generalized Cauchy-Riemann operator</u>

$$D = (0,\frac{\partial}{\partial x^1},\frac{\partial}{\partial x^2},\frac{\partial}{\partial x^3}),$$

we obtain for $u \in C_Q^1(G)$

$$D \circ u = (- \operatorname{div} \hat{u}, \operatorname{rot} \hat{u} + \operatorname{grad} u_0). \tag{1.2}$$

The functions $u \in \operatorname{Ker} D(G) \cap C_Q^1(G)$ that means $(Du)(x) = 0$ for all $x \in G$ are called <u>Q-analytic</u>. In the case of componentwise application of the Laplacian Δ to $u \in C_Q^2(G)$, we receive

$$D \circ D \circ u = - \Delta u. \tag{1.3}$$

The weak singular integral operator T

$$(Tu)(x) = \frac{1}{4\pi} \int_G \frac{\theta \circ u(y)}{|x-y|^2}\, dy, \quad x \in R^3, \tag{1.4}$$

where $\theta = (0, (x-y)/|x-y|)$, is a right inverse of D in the following sense:

$$(DTu)(x) = \begin{cases} u(x), & x \in G \\ 0, & x \in R^3 \setminus \overline{G}. \end{cases}$$

<u>Theorem 1</u> ([7]): Let $f \in L^2_Q(G)$ be given. Then any solution of $D \circ u = f$ can be represented by the formula $u = v + Tf$ with $v \in \operatorname{Ker} D(G) \cap L^2_Q(G)$.

As corresponding initial value operator F in the sense of the above-mentioned operational calculus, we obtain the 3-dimensional analogue of the Cauchy-integral of the complex function theory

$$(Fu)(x) = \frac{1}{4\pi} \int_\Gamma \frac{\theta \circ n \circ u(y)}{|x-y|^2}\, d\Gamma_y, \quad x \notin \Gamma \tag{1.5}$$

with $n = (0, \hat{n})$, where $\hat{n}$ is the unit vector of the outer normal on Γ in the point $y \in \Gamma$. The above-mentioned relation (ii) reads now as follows:

$$(Fu)(x) + (TDu)(x) = \begin{cases} u(x), & x \in G, \\ 0, & x \in R^3 \setminus \overline{G}. \end{cases} \tag{1.6}$$

The integral

$$(Su)(x) = \frac{1}{2\pi} \int_\Gamma \frac{\theta \circ n \circ u(y)}{|x-y|^2}\, d\Gamma_y, \quad x \in \Gamma \tag{1.7}$$

is defined in the sense of Cauchy's principal value and exhibits an analogue of the singular Cauchy integral of the complex function theory. Using S, we can verify generalized formulas of Plemelj-Sochozki type: If $u \in C^{0,\alpha}_Q(\Gamma)$ $(0 < \alpha \leq 1)$, then for $x \to x' \in \Gamma$ and $x \in G$

$$\lim_{x \to x'} (Fu)(x) = \frac{1}{2} (u + Su)(x') = (Pu)(x'), \tag{1.8}$$

and for $x \to x' \in \Gamma$ and $x \in R^3 \setminus \overline{G}$

$$\lim_{x \to x'} (Fu)(x) = \frac{1}{2} (u - Su)(x') = (Qu)(x'). \tag{1.9}$$

For the operators P, Q and S, the following identities are true

$$S^2 = I, \ P^2 = P, \ Q^2 = Q, \ PQ = QP = 0, \ P + Q = I.$$

Let A be a linear elliptic partial differential operator of second order and R a linear boundary operator. For approximative solution of the well-posed boundary value problem

$$Au = 0 \quad \text{in } G, \quad Ru = g \quad \text{on } \Gamma \tag{1.10}$$

with the exact solution u, the following problems are treated:

a) Construction of complete systems of basis functions φ_i

b) Discussion of the properties of the constructed system of basis functions

c) Calculation of an approximative solution u_n of the problem (1.10) by

$$u_n(x) = \sum_{i=1}^{n} \varphi_i(x) \circ a_{in} \tag{1.11}$$

where the coefficients $a_{in} \in Q$ are determined by the collocation conditions

$$(Ru_n)(x_j) = g(x_j), \quad j=1,\dots,n. \tag{1.12}$$

The points $x_j \in \Gamma$ are termed as collocation points.

d) Proof of convergence $u_n \to u$ for $n \to \infty$ in an adequate space

Since the collocation method is very simple to implement, we choose to use this approach.

Using the above-mentioned operators we can construct global decompositions for some classes of elliptic boundary value problems. We sketch this decomposition only in an important special case. Let us consider the Dirichlet-problem

$$\Delta u = 0 \quad \text{in } G, \quad \gamma_o u = g \quad \text{on} \tag{1.13}$$

with given $g \in H_Q^s(\Gamma)$, $s > \frac{3}{2}$, where γ_o signifies the trace-operator.

<u>Theorem 2</u> ([7]): The solution u of the Dirichlet-problem (1.13) can be represented by $u = v + Tw$, where v and w are uniquely defined solutions of the boundary value problems

$$Dv = 0 \quad \text{in } G, \quad \gamma_o v = Pg \quad \text{on } \Gamma, \tag{1.14}$$

$$Dw = 0 \quad \text{in } G, \quad \gamma_o Tw = Qg \quad \text{on } \Gamma. \tag{1.15}$$

<u>Remark:</u> An analogous result for boundary value problems of the linear static theory of elasticity is verified in [8]. Assertions for Neumann-problems are contained in [2], see [3] for the Helmholtz equation. Connections between the boundary integral equations in (1.14) - (1.15) and the integral equations of potential theory are given in [4].

2. Complete Systems of Basis Functions

The decomposition given in Theorem 2 has the consequence that the foundation and the numerical implementation of the collocation method are to be carried out only for boundary value problems of Q-analytic functions. First it is necessary to find complete systems of basis functions in appropriate spaces. In regard of a simple numerical implementation we seek such systems all elements of which can be described by simple analytic expressions of elementary functions. The basis functions given in Theorem 3 are calculated by using of fundamental solutions of D the singularities of which have to be chosen in appropriate sense.

A system $\{\varphi_i\}_{i=1}^{\infty} \subset X = \text{Ker } D(G) \cap H_Q^s(G)$ $(s > 0)$ is called <u>Q-complete</u> in X, if for every $f \in X$ there exists a sequence of functions

$$f_n \in \mathrm{span}_Q\langle \varphi_1, \dots, \varphi_n \rangle = \{\sum_{i=1}^{n} \varphi_i \circ a_i : a_i \in Q\},$$

such that

$$\lim_{n \to \infty} \|f - f_n\|_{H_Q^s(G)} = 0.$$

Theorem 3 ([2]): Let G_I, G and G_A be bounded star-shaped domains with sufficiently smooth boundaries $\Gamma_I = \partial G_I$, $\Gamma = \partial G$ and $\Gamma_A = \partial G_A$, such that $\overline{G}_I \subset G$ and $\overline{G} \subset G_A$. Furthermore, let

$$\{x_i\}_{i=1}^{\infty} \subset \Gamma_A, \quad \{y_i\}_{i=1}^{\infty} \subset \Gamma_I$$

be dense subsets of Γ_A and Γ_I, respectively. The functions φ_i and ψ_i, i=1,2,... are defined by

$$\varphi_i(x) = (0, (x-x_i)/|x-x_i|^3), \quad x \neq x_i,$$
$$\psi_i(x) = (0, (x-y_i)/|x-y_i|^3), \quad x \neq y_i.$$

Then follows for $s > 0$:

(i) $\{\varphi_i\}_{i=1}^{\infty}$ is Q-complete in $H_Q^s(G) \cap \mathrm{Ker}\, D(G)$.

(ii) $\{\gamma_o \varphi_i\}_{i=1}^{\infty}$ is Q-complete in $H_Q^s(\Gamma) \cap \{f : Sf = f\}$.

(iii) $\{\gamma_o \psi_i\}_{i=1}^{\infty}$ is Q-complete in $H_Q^s(\Gamma) \cap \{f : Sf = -f\}$.

(iv) $\{\gamma_o \varphi_i, \gamma_o \psi_i\}_{i=1}^{\infty}$ is Q-complete in $H_Q^s(\Gamma)$.

3. Systems with Special Properties

The minimal property in Michlin's sense [5] is an essential characteristic for the numerical implementation of interpolation or approximation procedures with a given system of basis functions. The systems defined in Theorem 3 do not possess this minimal property. The problem of transfer given systems into minimal ones is solved by the following algorithm, whose implementation does not require the calculation of inner products. In the following we denote $\operatorname{Ker} D(G) \cap L^2_Q(G)$ briefly by X.

<u>Theorem 4</u> ([2]): Let $\{h_i\}_{i=1}^{\infty}$ be a Q-complete system in X. Further let $\{x_i\}_{i=1}^{\infty} \subset G$ be given, such that $\{h_i\}_{i=1}^{n}$ is unisolvent on $\{x_i\}_{i=1}^{n}$ for all n=1,2,... . Moreover, let

$$g_1 = h_1, \quad g_j = h_j - \sum_{i=1}^{j-1} g_i \circ a_{ij} \qquad j=2,3,\dots \tag{3.1}$$

where the coefficients $a_{ij} \in Q$ are solutions of the following system of linear equations

$$\sum_{i=1}^{j} g_i(x_j) \circ a_{i,n+1} = h_{n+1}(x_j) \tag{3.2}$$

with j=1,...,n and n=1,2,... .
Then the system $\{g_i\}_{i=1}^{\infty}$ is Q-complete and satisfies the minimal property in X. Furthermore, the following conditions are fulfilled:

$$\begin{aligned} g_i(x_j) &= 0 \qquad \text{for all } j<i,\ i=2,3,\dots, \\ g_i(x_i) &\neq 0 \qquad \text{for all } i=1,2,\dots . \end{aligned} \tag{3.3}$$

If $\{g_i\}_{i=1}^{\infty}$ is a set of basis functions and $\{x_i\}_{i=1}^{\infty}$ is a set of collocation points, then the properties (3.3) ensure that the system (3.2) is triangle-shaped.

If we study connections between the solutions of the collocation problem using a system $\{g_i\}_{i=1}^{\infty}$ which satisfies the minimal property with (3.3), and the best approximations in $\operatorname{span}_Q\langle g_1,\dots,g_n\rangle$ [2], then we attain to the concept of the optimal basis of interpolation:

Let $\{g_i\}_{i=1}^{\infty}$ be a Q-complete system in X. Further, let $\{x_j\}_{j=1}^{\infty} \subset G$ and $X_n = \operatorname{span}_Q\langle g_1,\dots,g_n\rangle$. If for all $f \in X$ and every n=1,2,... the generalized interpolation function

$$P_n f = \sum_{i=1}^{n} g_i \circ a_{in}, \quad a_{in} \in Q \tag{3.4}$$

with $(P_n f)(x_j) = f(x_j)$, $j=1,\dots,n$ and the best $L^2_Q(G)$-approximation of f in X_n coincide, then $\{g_i\}_{i=1}^{\infty}$ is called an optimal basis of interpolation with respect to $\{x_j\}_{j=1}^{\infty}$. Further, a set $\{x_j\}_{j=1}^{\infty} \subset G$ of collocation points is called total, if for arbitrary $u \in \mathrm{Ker}\, D(G)$ the condition $u(x_j) = 0$ for all $j=1,2,\dots$ implies $u = 0$.

Theorem 5 ([2]): For all $\{x_j\}_{j=1}^{\infty} \subset G$ there exists an orthonormal system $\{g_i\}_{i=1}^{\infty} \subset X$ with (3.3). If $\{x_j\}_{j=1}^{\infty}$ is chosen total in G, then the system $\{g_i\}_{i=1}^{\infty}$ is Q-complete in X.

Theorem 6 ([2]): Let $\{g_i\}_{i=1}^{\infty}$ be a Q-complete orthonormal system in X, let $\{x_j\}_{j=1}^{\infty}$ G be a total set and let P_n be defined by (3.4). Then holds for all $f \in X$

$$\lim_{n \to \infty} \| P_n f - f \|_{L^2_Q(G)} = 0.$$

The convergence is monotonous.

Several possibilities for the construction of optimal systems and the connection with the optimal interpolation in the sense of Sard are discussed in [2] and [10].

5. Numerical Examples

Now we demonstrate the favourable numerical properties of the collocation method by means of some examples of 2-dimensional Dirichlet problems. Using the maximum principle for the Laplace equation (1.13), the C(G)-error in the approximation u_n (see (1.11)) to the solution u is bounded by $\|u_n - g\|_{C(\Gamma)}$. In the following, the norm of $C(\Gamma)$ is approximated by a discrete $C(\Gamma)$-seminorm with respect to 5000 nodes on Γ. The disk $\{(x,y) \in R^2 : x^2 + y^2 < 1\}$ is denoted by K.

Examples 1 - 3: $\Delta u = 0$ in K, $u = g_i$ on $\Gamma = \partial K$, i=1,2,3 with $g_1(x,y) = e^x \cos y - x^2 + y^2$, $g_2(x,y) = 2x^2 - 5y^2 + 3$ and $g_3(x,y) = |x|$. The singularities of the basis functions are located on $\{(x,y) : x^2 + y^2 = 2\}$ in each case, n denotes the number of used basis functions, δ_i is the relative error of the approximative solution in $C(\Gamma)$ for the i-th example and def_i is the absolute error of the approximative solution in the collocation points.

n	δ_1	δ_2	δ_3	def_1	def_2	def_3
20	9.5e-6	2.5e-6	5.8e-2	e-15	e-15	e-15
40	7.6e-12	9.3e-8	3.0e-2	e-15	e-15	e-12
60	7.5e-15	5.3e-8	2.0e-2	e-15	e-14	e-9
80	5.8e-15	8.2e-8	1.5e-2	e-15	e-12	e-6

The examples show that the rate of convergence and the stability depend upon the smoothness of g.

If the distance between the singularities and Γ is changed in dependence of n, then we can obtain some corrections.

Example 4: $\Delta u = 0$ in K, $u = g_3$ on $\Gamma = \partial K$.

Let h be the minimal distance of adjoining collocation points on Γ. The singularities are chosen on $\{(x,y) : x^2 + y^2 = 1 + d,\ d > 0\}$.

n	d/h	δ	def
20	0.639	3.6e-2	e-15
40	0.637	1.7e-2	e-15
60	0.762	1.3e-2	e-15
80	0.769	1.0e-2	e-14
100	0.793	7.7e-3	e-14

Improvements of the rate of convergence and the stability can be seen in comparison with example 3. However, the quality of the approximative solution can depend upon d/h only a little. For this reason, we consider the same example 4 in the case n = 80.

d/h	δ	def
0.256	2.1e-1	e-14
0.513	2.1e-2	e-14
0.769	1.0e-2	e-14
1.282	1.3e-2	e-15
2.564	1.4e-2	e-14
6.410	1.4e-2	e-11
12.82	1.5e-2	e-6

Example 5: $\Delta u = 0$ in $K \setminus (K_1 \cup K_2 \cup K_3)$,

$u = 2$ on Γ, $u = 1$ on $\Gamma_1 \cup \Gamma_2 \cup \Gamma_3$,

where $K_1 = \{(x,y) : 16x^2 + (4y - 2)^2 < 1\}$, $K_2 = \{(x,y) : (4x + 2)^2 + (4y + 2)^2 < 1\}$, $K_3 = \{(x,y) : (4x - 2)^2 + (4y + 2)^2 < 1\}$ and $\Gamma_i = \partial K_i$, i=1,2,3. Now n/4 collocation points are located on every circle Γ, Γ_1, Γ_2 and Γ_3. The singularities are arranged on $\{(x,y) : x^2 + y^2 = 2\}$ and on circles within K_1, K_2 and K_3, respectively.

n	δ	def
40	8.1e-2	e-15
60	4.3e-2	e-15
80	2.5e-2	e-15
100	1.6e-2	e-14
120	9.4e-3	e-14

This example demonstrates the practical applicability of this collocation method for non-convex domains.

Example 6: $\Delta u = 0$ in K, $u = 2$ on $\Gamma = \partial K$

The last example shows a comparison between the collocation method (CM) and the Galerkin method (GM) with respect to exactness, stability, computing-time (T) and main store requirement (MSR). The integrals necessary in using the Galerkin method are calculated by means of the central-point rule.

n	δ_{CM}	δ_{GM}	def_{CM}	def_{GM}	MSR_{CM}	MSR_{GM}	T_{GM}/T_{CM}
20	1.4e-7	1.4e-7	e-15	e-13	88 K	82 K	1.5
40	5.8e-13	9.8e-10	e-15	e-9	94	82	3.3
60	4.7e-15	2.6e+10	e-15	e+10	110	98	5.6
80	6.1e-15	4.0e+10	e-14	e+10	132	108	7.8
100	7.3e-15	6.5e+15	e-14	e+10	160	124	11.5

References

1. Berg, L.: Operatorenrechnung, I. Algebraische Methoden, Berlin 1972.

2. Gürlebeck, K.: Über die optimale Interpolation verallgemeinert analytischer quaternionenwertiger Funktionen und ihre Anwendung zur näherungsweisen Lösung wichtiger räumlicher Randwertaufgaben der Mathematischen Physik, Dissertation (A), Tech. Hochsch. Karl-Marx-Stadt 1984.

3. Gürlebeck, K.: Hypercomplex factorization of the Helmholtz-equation, Z. Anal. Anwendungen (in print).

4. Gürlebeck, K.: Faktorisierung elliptischer Randwertprobleme und klassische Ansätze, Wiss. Z. Tech. Hochsch. Karl-Marx-Stadt 27 (1985), 48 - 52.

5. Michlin, S.G.: Numerische Realisierung von Variationsmethoden, Berlin 1969.

6. Przeworska-Rolewicz, D.: Algebraic theory of right invertible operators, Studia Math. 48 (1973), 129 - 144.

7. Sprößig, W.: Über eine mehrdimensionale Operatorrechnung mit Operatoren über beschränkten Gebieten des Euklidischen Raumes und deren Anwendung zur Lösung partieller Differentialgleichungen, Dissertation (B), Tech. Hochsch. Karl-Marx-Stadt 1979.

8. Sprößig, W., Gürlebeck, K.: A hypercomplex method of calculating stresses in three-dimensional bodies, Rend. Circ. Mat. Palermo (2) 6 (1984), 271 - 284.

9. Tasche, M.: Funktionalanalytische Methoden in der Operatorenrechnung, Nova Acta Leopoldina (N.F.) 231 (Nr. 49), 1978

10. Tasche, M.: A unified approach to interpolation methods, J. Integral Equations 4 (1982), 55 - 75.

Dr. Klaus Gürlebeck
Doz. Dr. Wolfgang Sprößig
Technische Hochschule Karl-Marx-Stadt
Sektion Mathematik
Postschließfach 964
DDR - 9010 Karl-Marx-Stadt, German Democratic Republic

Doz. Dr. Manfred Tasche
Wilhelm-Pieck-Universität Rostock
Sektion Mathematik
Universitätsplatz 1
DDR - 2500 Rostock, German Democratic Republic

International Series of
Numerical Mathematics, Vol. 75

INTERPOLATION BY POLYNOMIALS AND NATURAL SPLINES ON NORMAL LATTICES

H.Hakopian

In this paper we extend the polynomial interpolation on normal lattices, given in [2], to tensor product natural spline interpolation of minimum semi-norm.

Let us begin with some notation and few definitions.

As usual, for $x=(x_1,\dots,x_k)\in R^k$ and multiindex $\alpha=(\alpha_1,\dots,\alpha_k)\in Z_+^k$ we denote $x^\alpha=x_1^{\alpha_1}\dots x_k^{\alpha_k}$, $D^\alpha=(\partial/\partial x_1)^{\alpha_1}\dots(\partial/\partial x_k)^{\alpha_k}$.

A finite set of multiindices $J\subset Z_+^k$ is said to be normal (or lower) iff $\alpha\in J$ and $\beta\leq\alpha$ (i.e. $\beta_i\leq\alpha_i$, $i=1,\dots,k$) imply $\beta\in J$.

The linear space of the k-variate polynomials with degree-multiindices in J we denote by $P_J:=P_J(R^k)$,

$$P_J=\mathrm{span}\{x^\alpha:\alpha\in J\}.$$

It is convenient to fix the following sequences

$$T^{(i)}=(t_{i,j})_{j=0}^{\infty}\ ,\quad i=1,\dots,k\ ,$$

of distinct knots on the i-th axis of R^k, although we shall use their finite subsequences, only.

The lattice T_J is determined by the set $J\subset Z_+^k$ and sequences $T^{(i)}$, $i=1,\dots,k$:

$$T_J:=\{t_\alpha:\alpha\in J\},$$

where $t_\alpha=(t_{1,\alpha_1},\dots,t_{k,\alpha_k})\in R^k$. Moreover, for $\alpha,\beta\in Z_+^k$, $\alpha\leq\beta$ we denote

$$T_{\alpha,\beta}=\{t_\gamma:\alpha\leq\gamma\leq\beta\}\quad ,\quad T_{\alpha,\beta}^{(i)}=\{t_{i,\gamma_i}:\alpha_i\leq\gamma_i\leq\beta_i\}\ .$$

In the case $\alpha=\bar{0}=(0,\dots,0)$ we shall briefly write

$$T_\beta:=T_{\bar{0},\beta}\quad ,\quad T_\beta^{(i)}:=T_{\bar{0},\beta}^{(i)}\ .$$

Definition. The divided difference of the function f with respect to the lattice $T_{\alpha,\beta}$ is

$$[T_{\alpha,\beta}]f:=[T_{\alpha,\beta}^{(1)}]\dots[T_{\alpha,\beta}^{(k)}]f\ ,$$

where $[T_{\alpha,\beta}^{(i)}]f=[t_{i,\alpha_i},\dots,t_{i,\beta_i}]f$ is the usual univariate divided difference with respect to the i-th variable of f.

Using the well-known pointwise and integral (through B-splines) representations of univariate divided differences, we readily obtain respectively

(1) $$[T_{\alpha,\beta}]f=\sum_{\alpha\le\gamma\le\beta} c_\gamma f(t_\alpha),$$

where c_γ is independent of f,

(2) $$[T_{\alpha,\beta}]f=\int_A D^{\beta-\alpha}f(x)\ M(x|T_{\alpha,\beta})\,dx,$$

where A contains the convex hull of $T_{\alpha,\beta}$, and

$$M(x|T_{\alpha,\beta})=\prod_{i=1}^{k} M(x_i|T^{(i)}_{\alpha,\beta}),$$

with $M(x_i|T^{(i)}_{\alpha,\beta})=M(x_i|t_{i,\alpha_i},\dots,t_{i,\beta_i})$ being the univariate B-spline.

The following theorem (see Th. 1 of [2]) gives the normal polynomial interpolation.

Theorem 1. For every normal set $J\subset Z^k_+$ and every k-variate function $f:A\to R$, $T_J\subset A\subset R^k$, there is a unique polynomial $p_f\in P_J$, which interpolates f with respect to the lattice T_J, i.e.

$$p_f(t_\alpha)=f(t_\alpha),\ \alpha\in J.$$

Moreover the following equality holds

$$p_f(x)=\sum_{\alpha\in J}[T_\alpha]f\prod_{i=1}^{k}\prod_{j=0}^{\alpha_i-1}(x_i-t_{i,j}).$$

Now we are going to present an extension of this interpolation which minimizes the semi-norm $\int_\Omega|D^\gamma g|^2$ over all functions $g\in H^\gamma(\Omega)$ -interpolants of f. Here $\gamma\in Z^k_+$, $\gamma_i>0$, $i=1,\dots,k$, Ω is a region containing the convex hull of T_J (more precisely it may contain the convex hulls of $T_{\alpha,\alpha+\gamma}\subset T_J$, only) and $H^\gamma(\Omega)$ is the class of functions g with $D^\gamma g\in L^2(\Omega)$ and $D^{\gamma-e^i}f(x)$ ($e^i\in Z^k_+$, $(e^i)_j=\delta^i_j$, $j=1,\dots,k$) being continuous according to the variable x_i, $i=1,\dots,k$.

For this end we define

i) space of k-variate polynomials P_I with $I=J/G$, $G=\{\alpha\in Z^k_+,\alpha\ge\gamma\}$,

ii) space of natural tensor product splines

$$S^{nat}_{J,\gamma}=\mathrm{span}\{\sigma(x|T_{\alpha,\alpha+\gamma}),\alpha,\alpha+\gamma\in J\}\ \text{with}\ \sigma\in H^\gamma(\Omega),\ D^\gamma\sigma(x|T_{\alpha,\alpha+\gamma})=M(x|T_{\alpha,\alpha+\gamma}).$$

Then we can formulate the following (the general setting is due to Goodman [1]).

Theorem 2. For every normal set $J\subset Z^k_+$ and every k-variate function $f:A\to R$, $T_J\subset A\subset R^k$, there is a unique function $\sigma_f\in P_I+S^{nat}_{J,\gamma}$, which interpolates f with respect to the lattice T_J.

Moreover

(3) $$\int_\Omega|D^\gamma\sigma_f|^2\le\int_\Omega|D^\gamma g|^2,$$

for all g in $H^\gamma(\Omega)$ which interpolate f.

Proof. Making use of the relations (1),(2) we obtain

that for functions g which vanish on T_J, $D^\gamma g$ is orthogonal to the space $S_{J,\gamma}$ of tensor product splines,

$$S_{J,\gamma} = \text{span}\,\{M(x|T_{\alpha,\alpha+\gamma}) : \alpha, \alpha+\gamma \in J\}$$

i.e.

(4) $\int_\Omega D^\gamma g \cdot s = 0$, for all $s \in S_{J,\gamma}$

with $g(t_\alpha)=0, \alpha \in J$.

Since $\dim(P_I \cap S^{nat}_{J,\gamma})=0$ and $\dim P_I + \dim S^{nat}_{J,\gamma} = \# J$, where $\#$ denotes the cardinality, for the existence and uniqness of σ_f it is sufficient to prove that $\sigma \in P_I + S^{nat}_{J,\gamma}$ and $\sigma(t_\alpha)=0, \alpha \in J$ imply $\sigma \equiv 0$.

Thus suppose that $\sigma(x) = p(x) + \sum_{\alpha,\alpha+\gamma \in J} a_\alpha \sigma(x|T_{\alpha,\alpha+\gamma})$ and $p \in P_I$, $\sigma(t_\alpha)=0, \alpha \in J$.

We have $D^\gamma \sigma(x) = \sum_{\alpha,\alpha+\gamma \in J} a_\alpha M(x|T_{\alpha,\alpha+\gamma})$ and according to (4) it is orthogonal to the space $S_{J,\gamma}$, hence $a_\alpha = 0$, $\alpha, \alpha+\gamma \in J$. Then the Theorem 1 implies $\sigma \equiv 0$.

Let us prove the inequality (3). Assume that the function $g \in H^\gamma(\Omega)$ interpolates f. Then the function $g-\sigma_f$ vanishes on T_J and according to relation (4) $D^\gamma(g-\sigma_f)$ is orthogonal to $D^\gamma \sigma_f \in S_{J,\gamma}$.

Hence we have

$$\int_\Omega |D^\gamma g|^2 = \int_\Omega |D^\gamma \sigma_f|^2 + \int_\Omega |D^\gamma (g-\sigma_f)|^2.$$

It is clear that this equality implies (3).

References

I. T.N.T.Goodman, Interpolation in minimum semi-norm and multivariate B-splines, J. Approximation Theory 37 (I983) 2I2-223.

2. H.Hakopian, Integral reminder formula of the tensor product interpolation, Bull. Ac. Pol.: Math., 3I (I983), 267-272.

Department of Mathematics, University of Yerevan, Yerevan, Armenian SSR, USSR

International Series of
Numerical Mathematics, Vol. 75

BIVARIATE APPROXIMATION PROCEDURES

Werner Haußmann and Karl Zeller

Department of Mathematics
University of Duisburg
D-4100 Duisburg

Department of Mathematics
University of Tübingen
D-7400 Tübingen

1. Introduction

While univariate approximations can often be achieved by "brute force", in many cases "fine craft" is required for dealing with bivariate approximation. One reason is that in the bivariate (or multivariate) case rather complicated functions and domains occur such that suitable decompositions and transformations are advisable. Another reason is that an approximation procedure can be quite time-consuming and costly; therefore fast methods yielding good approximations for the practitioner are desirable.

We describe several procedures of the latter type. Thereby we mainly treat the square $[-1,1]^2$. Other domains can be covered by transformations. The methods employ Fourier coefficients, thus fast transforms and the Carathéodory-Fejér method can be used. We outline a simple but useful case of the latter method (in which good error estimates are available). Finally we consider certain decomposable functions.

2. Approximation Methods

We consider bivariate real-valued functions h defined and continuous in a compact non-empty set $B \subset \mathbb{R}^2$. For approximation purposes we use the norm

$$\|h\|_\infty := \sup_{(x,y)\in B} |h(x,y)|$$

and polynomials taken from the space

$$\mathbb{P}_{mn} := \{ \sum_{\mu=0}^{m} \sum_{\nu=0}^{n} a_{\mu\nu} x^\mu y^\nu, \quad a_{\mu\nu} \in \mathbb{R}, \ 0\le\mu\le m, \ 0\le\nu\le n \}.$$

We mention several methods for obtaining good or best approximations (from $\mathbb{P}_{mn}$ or other spaces) and distinguish (in a rough way) bivariate and univariate procedures. The former use the Remez principle, grids, linear optimization (cf. Watson [17]). The latter are connected with the idea of the Cartesian or tensor product (compare with two-dimensional and iterated integration).

For example a univariate method can proceed in the following way (to approximate h on a square B): For every y we determine an (almost) best approximation $p(.,y)$; then we obtain a polynomial q by a smoothing process. Of course there are many modifications possible. We mention some pertinent publications: Weinstein [18], Angelos-Schmidt [1], Henry [11], Jetter-Locher [12] as well as [7-9] and [16].

In the present paper we describe two procedures of the univariate type. They are connected with Fourier coefficients and the Carathéodory-Fejér principle (the latter is described in Gutknecht-Trefethen [6]). The first procedure employs columnwise reduction of a Fourier expansion (Section 4), the second one the line approximation mentioned above (Section 5). Again several modifications and auxiliary tools can be introduced, for instance different interpolation and attenuation processes.

In addition, we present the Carathéodory-Fejér method in the Zolotarev case (Section 7) and the bivariate approximation of certain decomposable functions using grids and dependent points (Section 8).

3. Fourier Chebyshev Expansions

We assume that after a preliminary approximation (e.g. done by a fast/discrete Fourier transform) the function h to be approximated is given by

$$h(x,y) = \sum_{k=o}^{m'} \sum_{l=o}^{n} c_{kl} T_k(x) T_l(y) ,$$

where T_j denotes the Chebyshev polynomial of the first kind. The coefficients are given by $c_{kl} = L_{kl}(h)$, where for $k,l = 0, 1,2,3,\ldots$ the linear functional L_{kl} is defined by

$$L_{kl}(h) := \frac{2^{\varepsilon}}{\pi^2} \int_{-1}^{1} \int_{-1}^{1} h(x,y) T_k(x) T_l(y) w(x) w(y) dxdy$$

with $\varepsilon := \varepsilon_{kl} := 2 - \delta_{ko} - \delta_{ol}$ (Kronecker δ), $w(z) := (1-z^2)^{-\frac{1}{2}}$ the familiar weight function. The integral may be written as a double sum plus remainder (discretization). For the coefficients we have the estimate

$$(1) \qquad |c_{kl}| \leq \left(\frac{4}{\pi}\right)^{\varepsilon} E'_{kl}(h) \qquad (\varepsilon := \varepsilon_{kl} \text{ as above}) ,$$

where for $0 \leq k \leq m'$, $0 \leq l \leq n$ we define

$$E'_{kl} := \inf \{ \|h-t\|_{\infty} \mid t(x,y) = \sum_{i=o}^{M} \sum_{j=o}^{N} \gamma_{ij} T_i(x) T_j(y) ,$$

$$M, N \text{ arbitrary in } \mathbb{N} \cup \{0\}, \text{ but } \gamma_{kl} = 0 \} .$$

In order to prove (1), we observe that for any t of this form we have

$$|c_{kl}| = |L_{kl}(h)| = |L_{kl}(h-t)| \leq \|L_{kl}\|_{\infty} \|h-t\|_{\infty} ,$$

hence $|c_{kl}| \leq \left(\frac{4}{\pi}\right)^{\varepsilon} E'_{kl}(h)$. □

In fact, in (1) even equality holds; the proof is based on Fourier series of certain step functions. Furthermore, we have (introducing univariate coefficients)

$$c_{kl} = a_k b_l \qquad \text{for } h(x,y) = f(x) g(y) ,$$

and this can be extended to finite sums, hence to the case of the tensor product.

4. Column Approximation

We write

$$h(x,y) = \sum_{l=0}^{n} f_l(x) T_l(y) ,$$

where

$$f_l(x) := \sum_{k=0}^{m'} c_{kl} T_k(x) .$$

This leads to the idea of columnwise approximation: We replace each f_l by a (good) approximation p_l and obtain

$$r(x,y) := \sum_{l=0}^{n} p_l(x) T_l(y) .$$

If all p_l are in $\mathbb{P}_m$ (:= univariate polynomials of degree $\leq m$), then r is in $\mathbb{P}_{mn}$. We get the following estimate of the remainder (using the sup-norm over $[-1,1]^2$ resp. $[-1,1]$):

PROPOSITION 1. For r as given above, the inequality

$$\| h - r \|_\infty \leq \sum_{l=0}^{n} \| f_l - p_l \|_\infty$$

holds.

The decomposition described in Section 3 shows that in many cases the coefficients c_{kl} are quite small if $k+l$ is fairly large (e.g. for $k+l > m'$). Hence in our context one can often expect the following state of affairs. For larger l the degree of approximation $E_m(f_l)$ is small and a good approximation p_l can easily be obtained (for instance by truncation). In the main we have to deal only with few values of l (here the Carathéodory-Fejér method might be useful, see Section 7). Altogether the column approximation is especially efficient under these circumstances. Furthermore the estimate in Proposition 1 is then rather sharp.

We have reduced the degree with respect to x (namely m' to m). Of course this can be done also with respect to y, and we can employ several steps (e.g. alternatingly).

5. Line Approximation

The basic idea is to approximate h on horizontal or vertical lines (i.e. to approximate the partial functions $h(.,y)$ or $h(x,.)$) and to combine the results. Here we do this in the following way. We consider (notation as in Section 4)

$$h(x_k,y) = \sum_{l=o}^{n} f_l(x_k)T_l(y) ,$$

where

$$x_k = \cos\frac{k\pi}{m}, \quad \text{hence} \quad |T_m(x_k)| = 1 \quad \text{for} \quad k = 0,1,\dots,m .$$

Then we proceed by interpolation and define

$$q(x,y) := \sum_{k=o}^{m'} \sum_{l=o}^{n} a_{kl}T_k(x)T_l(y) ;$$

here we have (cf. Fox-Parker [5, p. 67] and Rivlin [15, p. 151])

$$a_{kl} := f_l(x_k) + f_l(x_{2m-k}) \quad \text{for} \quad k = 0,1,\dots,m-1 ,$$

$$a_{ml} := f_l(x_m) ,$$

provided that $m' \le 2m$; otherwise more terms enter.

PROPOSITION 2. For the q defined above this estimate holds:

$$\|h - q\|_\infty \le (L_m+1) \sup_{-1\le y\le 1} E_m(h(.,y)) .$$

In order to prove this we insert the proximum p (for given y):

$$\|h(.,y) - p(.,y)\|_\infty =: E_m(h(.,y)) .$$

The Lebesgue constant L_m satisfies $L_m \le \frac{2}{\pi}\log(m+1) + 1$ (see Rivlin [15, p. 18] and Ehlich-Zeller [4]). For suitable classes of functions one has smaller bounds.

Several modifications are possible: We can use the zeros of T_{m+1}. And we could interpolate in $\mathbb{P}_{m+2}$ and then apply the Carathéodory-Fejér method (see Section 7). The method described here seems to be preferable over the method in Section 4 if the regular behaviour mentioned there is not assured.

6. Lower Bounds

We are interested in lower bounds for the degree of approximation. Such bounds indicate how good a given approximation is. We write

$$h(x,y) \quad = \quad \sum_{k=o}^{m'} g_k(y) T_k(x) \, ,$$

where

$$g_k(y) \quad := \quad \sum_{l=o}^{n} c_{kl} T_l(y) \, .$$

The bivariate degree of approximation is defined by

$$E_{mn}(h) \quad := \quad \| h - p^*_{mn} \|_\infty \, ,$$

where p^*_{mn} is a proximum to h in $\mathbb{P}_{mn}$.

PROPOSITION 3. The following estimates are valid:

$$E_{mn}(h) \quad \geq \quad \sup_{-1 \leq y \leq 1} |g_k(y)| \quad \text{for} \quad \max(m, \tfrac{m'}{3}) < k \leq m' \, .$$

For the proof we use the linear functionals (cf. Meinardus [13])

$$L_k(f) \quad := \quad \frac{1}{k+2} \sum_{j=o}^{k+1}{}'' \; (-1)^j f(\cos \frac{j\pi}{k+2})$$

for $\max(m, \frac{m'}{3}) < k \leq m'$ and $f \in C[-1,1]$. Σ'' indicates that we have to insert the factor 1/2 for $j=o$ and $j=k+1$. The L_k's have norm 1 and vanish for $f \in \mathbb{P}_m$. Hence the functionals

$$L_{ky}(h) \quad := \quad L_k(h(.,y)) \qquad \text{for} \quad -1 \leq y \leq 1$$

have norm 1, too, and vanish on $\mathbb{P}_{mn}$. Thus

$$E_{mn}(h) = \| h - p^*_{mn} \|_\infty \geq |L_{ky}(h)| = |g_k(y)| . \quad \square$$

If, in general, $\max(m, \frac{m'}{3}) < k \leq m'$ is not satisfied, then one can use functionals given by an integral (like those in Section 3) and has to multiply the right hand side by $\pi/4$.

Finer estimates employ $g_k(y)$ for $k=m+1$, $m+2$ or for more values and introduce sums of absolute values or squares (see also [9]).

7. Carathéodory-Fejér Approximation

This method (CF approximation) has recently found much attention, see e.g. Gutknecht-Trefethen [6]. We describe it in the Zolotarev case (which was treated in detail in [10]), starting from the expansion

$$\frac{1-bz}{1-b/z} = -bz + (1-b^2)(1 + bz^{-1} + b^2z^{-2} + \ldots)$$

with $-1 < b < 1$, $|z| = 1$. We multiply by $z^{m+1}(1-b^2)^{-1}$, take the real part, then pass to Chebyshev polynomials and obtain the series

$$aT_{m+2} + T_{m+1} + bT_m + b^2T_{m-1} + \ldots ,$$

where

$$a := \frac{-b}{1-b^2}, \qquad T_{-k} := T_k .$$

In $[-1,1]$, this series has modulus $(1-b^2)^{-1}$. We truncate it in a modified way putting

$$p := \sum_{k=1}^{2m+1} b^k T_{m+1-k} - ab^{2m+2}T_{-m} .$$

Estimating via our identity we obtain

PROPOSITION 4. For a, b, p as above the estimate

$$\| aT_{m+2} + T_{m+1} + p \|_\infty \le \frac{1 + |b^{2m+2}|}{1 - b^2}$$

holds true. Further we have

$$E_m(aT_{m+2} + T_{m+1}) \ge \frac{1 - |b^{2m+2}|}{1 - b^2} .$$

Thus for a not too large $-p$ is an almost best approximation and the function in Proposition 4 is a good replacement for a Zolotarev polynomial. For large a one can take $p = 0$ or use a stretched T_{m+2} which is then the exact Zolotarev polynomial (see Reddy [14] resp. Carlson-Todd [2]). For small a there are simplified approximations available (see Section 9 and also [10]).

8. Dependent Points and Decomposable Functions

We consider decomposable functions of the type

$$h(x,y) = f(x) + g(y) \qquad \text{with} \quad f,\ g \in C[-1,1]$$

and ask for a proximum from $\mathbb{P}_{mn}$ to h. Using the univariate proxima p^* and q^* in $\mathbb{P}_m$ resp. $\mathbb{P}_n$ satisfying

$$\|f - p^*\|_\infty = E_m(f), \qquad \|g - q^*\|_\infty = E_n(g),$$

we get

PROPOSITION 5. For h, p^*, q^* as above a proximum in $\mathbb{P}_{mn}$ to h is given by

$$r^*(x,y) := p^*(x) + q^*(y).$$

The proof employs the notion of dependent points and Lemma 6 below. In general, a proximum will not be uniquely determined. If we approximate $h(x,y) := |x| - |y|$ on $[-1,1]^2$ with respect to $\mathbb{P}_{11}$ then all functions $r^*_\varepsilon(x,y) = \varepsilon xy$ $(|\varepsilon| \le 1)$ are proxima.

Let $B \subset \mathbb{R}^d$ be a compact set, $d \in \mathbb{N}$. We say that a system of points in B is dependent with respect to a subspace $V \subset C(B)$ if the corresponding system of point functionals is linearly dependent in the dual space of V.

In the univariate case, given $f \in C[-1,1]$ and its proximum $p^* \in \mathbb{P}_m$, then the error $f - p^*$ has an extremal alternation of length $m+2$: $x_o < x_1 < \ldots < x_{m+1}$. These points are dependent, and we have (with suitable $a_i \in \mathbb{R}$ which alternate in sign)

$$\sum_{i=o}^{m+1} a_i u(x_i) = 0 \qquad (u \in \mathbb{P}_m). \tag{2}$$

Similarly, for $g \in C[-1,1]$ and its proximum $q^* \in \mathbb{P}_n$ we obtain

$$\sum_{j=o}^{n+1} b_j v(y_j) = 0 \qquad (v \in \mathbb{P}_n), \tag{3}$$

where $y_o < y_1 < \ldots < y_{n+1}$ constitute an extremal alternation, and the b_j alternate.

These considerations lead to

LEMMA 6. Given x_i, y_j, a_i, b_j as above, then the systems

$$(x_i, y_j) \qquad \text{for } i+j \text{ even resp. } i+j \text{ odd}$$

are dependent. The dependency relation of the point functionals is given by

$$\sum_{i+j \text{ even}} c_{ij} w(x_i, y_j) = 0 \quad \text{resp.} \quad \sum_{i+j \text{ odd}} d_{ij} w(x_i, y_j) = 0$$

for $w \in \mathbb{P}_{mn}$ with

$$c_{ij} := (-1)^{\frac{i+j}{2}} \cdot a_i b_j \quad \text{resp.} \quad d_{ij} := (-1)^{\frac{i+j+1}{2}} \cdot a_i b_j .$$

Proof. It is sufficient to consider polynomials of the form $w(x,y) = u(x)v(y)$ with $u \in \mathbb{P}_m$ and $v \in \mathbb{P}_n$. This leads to (in the case $i+j$ even)

$$\sum_{i+j \text{ even}} (-1)^{\frac{i+j}{2}} a_i b_j w(x_i, y_j) =$$

$$= \Big(\sum_{i \text{ even}} a_i u(x_i)\Big)\Big(\sum_{j \text{ even}} b_j v(y_j)\Big) - \Big(\sum_{i \text{ odd}} a_i u(x_i)\Big)\Big(\sum_{j \text{ odd}} b_j v(y_j)\Big)$$

$$= \Big(\sum_{i=o}^{m+1} a_i u(x_i)\Big)\Big(\sum_{j \text{ even}} b_j v(y_j)\Big) -$$

$$\Big(\sum_{i \text{ odd}} a_i u(x_i)\Big) \cdot \Big(\sum_{j \text{ even}} b_j v(y_j) + \sum_{j \text{ odd}} b_j v(y_j)\Big) = 0$$

by (2) and (3). The case $i+j$ odd is proved similarly. □

We apply this result in order to prove Proposition 5. $h - r^*$ has alternating error (of modulus $\|f-p^*\|_\infty + \|g-q^*\|_\infty$) at the points

$$(x_i, y_j) \qquad \text{for } i+j \text{ even resp. } i+j \text{ odd} .$$

Now Lemma 6 shows that we cannot improve this error. □

Our definition of dependent points is of course related to the notion of an H-set which is used quite often in multivariate approximation problems; see for instance the book by Collatz-Krabs [3].

9. Remarks

It is quite natural to utilize univariate methods for multivariate problems - as done in many branches of mathematics. In the realm of approximation there are many ways to implement this principle. We have considered "columns", "lines", and "decompositions".

For general problems ordinary Fourier coefficients are a good starting point. Then one can apply the Carathéodory-Fejér idea, modified interpolation, attenuation, homotopy and others. In the case of Zolotarev polynomials (Section 7) we get for small values of a the good approximations $p := -aT_m$ or $p := -\frac{a}{2}T_m$ by modified interpolation resp. attenuation. But one should not forget that there are other orthogonal or biorthogonal systems available.

In more specific problems there may be natural decompositions of a given function. We believe that it is worth-wile to consider corresponding approximations (as we have done in the case of functions of the form $h(x,y) = f(x) + g(y)$ in Section 8) and to develop a theory suitable also for practical purposes. Decomposable functions of product type $h(x,y) = f(x)g(y)$ are more intricate to handle than sums. In the product case one can give easily upper and lower bounds for the degree of approximation. These show that suitable weighted norm approximations of the components will in general give better results. Similar considerations apply to the case where one approximates functions of functions. Further one is lead to the question how to decompose a given bivariate function such that one can easily achieve good or near-best approximations.

Finally we give some hints concerning contiguous generalizations and problems: One could consider domains different from squares or rectangles, other approximators, various norms. Also one would like to introduce constraints as well as take into account questions of evaluation and complexity.

References

1. Angelos, J., Schmidt, D.: Some remarks on product approximation. Internat. Ser. Numer. Math. 61, 27-35 (1982).

2. Carlson, B. C., Todd, J.: Zolotarev's first problem - the best approximation by polynomials of degree $\leq n-2$ to $x^n - n\sigma x^{n-1}$ in $[-1,1]$. Aequationes Math. 26, 1-33 (1983).

3. Collatz, L., Krabs, W.: Approximationstheorie. Stuttgart: Teubner 1973.

4. Ehlich, H., Zeller, K.: Auswertung der Normen von Interpolationsoperatoren. Math. Ann. 164, 105-112 (1966).

5. Fox, L., Parker, I. B.: Chebyshev polynomials in numerical analysis. London: Oxford University Press 1968.

6. Gutknecht, M. H., Trefethen, L. N.: Real polynomial approximation by the Carathéodory-Fejér method. SIAM J. Numer. Anal. 19, 358-371 (1982).

7. Haußmann, W., Luik, E., Zeller, K.: Biorthogonality in approximation. Internat. Ser. Numer. Math. 61, 185-189 (1982).

8. Haußmann, W., Luik, E., Zeller, K.: Bequeme Verfahren zur Approximation. Z. Angew. Math. Mech. 63, T 349-350 (1983).

9. Haußmann, W., Luik, E., Zeller, K.: Interpolation and instant approximation. Internat. Ser. Numer. Math. 67, 109-117 (1984).

10. Haußmann, W., Zeller, K.: Approximate Zolotarev polynomials. Comput. Math. Appl., to appear.

11. Henry, M. S.: Product approximation: Error estimates. Internat. Ser. Numer. Math. 61, 201-209 (1982).

12. Jetter, K., Locher, F.: A note on numerical Fourier analysis and uniform approximation on cubes. Lecture Notes Math. 571, 109-118. Berlin-Heidelberg-New York: Springer 1977.

13. Meinardus, G.: Approximation von Funktionen und ihre numerische Behandlung. Berlin-Göttingen-Heidelberg-New York: Springer 1964.

14. Reddy, A. R.: A note on a result of Zolotarev and Bernstein. Manuscripta Math. 20, 95-97 (1977).

15. Rivlin, T. J.: The Chebyshev polynomials. New York-London: Wiley 1974.

16. Scherer, R., Zeller, K.: Gestufte Approximation in zwei Variablen. Internat. Ser. Numer. Math. 52, 281-288 (1980).

17. Watson, G. A.: Approximation theory and numerical methods. Chichester-New York: Wiley 1980.

18. Weinstein, S. E.: Approximation of functions of several variables: Product Chebyshev approximations I. J. Approx. Theory 2, 433-447 (1969).

International Series of
Numerical Mathematics, Vol. 75

CONSTRUCTION AND APPLICATIONS OF HERMITE INTERPOLATING QUADRATIC SPLINE FUNCTIONS OF TWO AND THREE VARIABLES

Gerhard Heindl
Bergische Universität-Gesamthochschule Wuppertal

Summary

The aim of this paper is to present some basic constructions which can be used to derive solutions of certain Hermite interpolation problems in the class of simplicial quadratic spline functions and the class of homogeneous quadratic spline functions with respect to a simplicial cone complex.

The results are applied to construct some new C^1-finite elements and to solve a Hermite interpolation problem on the sphere, occuring in Geodesy.

Simplical quadratic spline functions

A finite set K of simplexes $s \subset R^n$ is called a (homogeneous n-dimensional simplicial) <u>complex</u> iff it has the following properties:

(1) If s is in K, and s' is a face of s, then s' is in K.

(2) If s and t are in K, then $s \cap t$ either is empty, or is a common face of s and t.

(3) If s is in K, then s is a face of a n-dimensional t in K.

The o-dimensional simplexes of a complex are its <u>vertices</u>, the 1-dimensional simplexes its <u>edges.</u>

$$|K| := \bigcup_{s \in K} s$$

is called the <u>polyhedron of K</u>.

A complex K' is a <u>refinement</u> of a complex K iff

(1) $|K'| = |K|$.

(2) If s' is in K', then s' is a subset of some $s \in K$.

Given a complex K, a function $\phi : |K| \to R$ is called a <u>quadratic spline function with respect to K</u> ($\phi \in \mathbb{P}_2(K)$) iff

(1) $\phi \in C^1(|K|)$

(2) For every $s \in K$ there is a polynomial $p : R^n \to R$ of degree ≤ 2 ($p \in P_2(R^n)$) such that

$$\phi|s = p|s \quad .$$

<u>A simplicial quadratic spline function</u> is a quadratic spline function with respect to some K.

A Hermite interpolation problem

The central question considered in this paper is the

following: Given a finite subset V of R^n, how can we construct a complex K such that $\{\{x\} : x \in V\}$ is a subset of the set of vertices of K and such that for any given

$$w_x \in R\ ,\ \beta_x \in R^n\ ,\ x \in V$$

there is a $\phi \in \mathbb{P}_2(K)$ satisfying the Hermite interpolation conditions

$$\text{(i)} \qquad \begin{aligned} \phi(x) &= w_x \\ \operatorname{grad}\phi(x) &= \beta_x \end{aligned} \qquad \text{for all } x \in V\ ?$$

It is natural to study the problem first for complexes K having $\{\{x\} : x \in V\}$ as their set of vertices*). For those complexes there is an elementary uniqueness and existence result:

Lemma 1

(1) If $\phi \in \mathbb{P}_2(K)$ satisfies (i), $\langle x_o,\dots,x_n\rangle \in K$ is a n-dimensional simplex with vertices $x_o,\dots,x_n$, and

$$x = \sum_{i=o}^{n} \lambda_i x_i\ ,\ \text{where } \lambda_i \geq 0\ ,\ i = 0,\dots,n,\ \text{and } \sum_{i=o}^{n} \lambda_i = 1\ ,$$

then

$$\phi(x) = \sum_{i=o}^{n} w_{x_i}\lambda_i^2 + \sum_{\substack{i,j=o\\ i<j}}^{n} (2w_{x_i} + \beta_{x_i}^T (x_j - x_i)\lambda_i\lambda_j$$

$$= \sum_{i=o}^{n} w_{x_i}\lambda_i^2 + \sum_{\substack{i,j=o\\ i<j}}^{n} (2w_{x_j} + \beta_{x_j}^T (x_i - x_j))\lambda_i\lambda_j\ .$$

(2) There is a $\phi \in \mathbb{P}_2(K)$ having the desired interpolation property (i) iff for every edge $\langle x,y\rangle \in K$ with vertices x,y the edge condition

$$\text{(EC)} \qquad 2w_x + \beta_x^T (y-x) = 2w_y + \beta_y^T (x-y)$$

*) We assume, that such a complex exists.

is satisfied.

Proof. Essentially the same as the proof given in [2] for the two dimensional case.

The second part of Lemma 1 shows that in order to solve the interpolation problem it is necessary to introduce complexes having more vertices than the $\{x\}$, $x \in V$. Therefore the following construction procedure is suggested:

Step 1: Construct a complex K such that $\{\{x\} : x \in V\}$ is the set of vertices of K .

Step 2: Try to introduce additional vertices z together with new edges such that, given any $w_x \in R$, $\beta_x \in R^n$, $x \in V$, it is possible to satisfy (EC) for the new edges by computing uniquely defined artificial interpolation data $w_z \in R$, $\beta_z \in R^n$ for the new vertices z .

Step 3: Repeat Step 2 until a refinement K' of K is obtained such that (EC) can be satisfied for all edges of K' .

Step 4: Given any $w_x \in R$, $\beta_x \in R^n$, $x \in V$, compute $\phi \in \mathbb{P}_2(K')$ uniquely defined by the interpolation property (i).

The proposed procedure was used in the examples given in [2].

In the next two sections there are given additional examples for the cases $n=2$ and $n=3$.

Solutions of the interpolation problem in the case n=2

The results given in this section mainly are derived from some basic constructions which shall be presented first. All assertions made in this section can be verified by elementary algebraic calculations.

1. Let $\langle x,y,z\rangle \subset R^2$ denote a triangle and assume that for the data $w_x, w_y, w_z \in R$, $\beta_x, \beta_y, \beta_z \in R^2$ (EC) holds for the line segments $\langle z,x\rangle$ and $\langle z,y\rangle$.

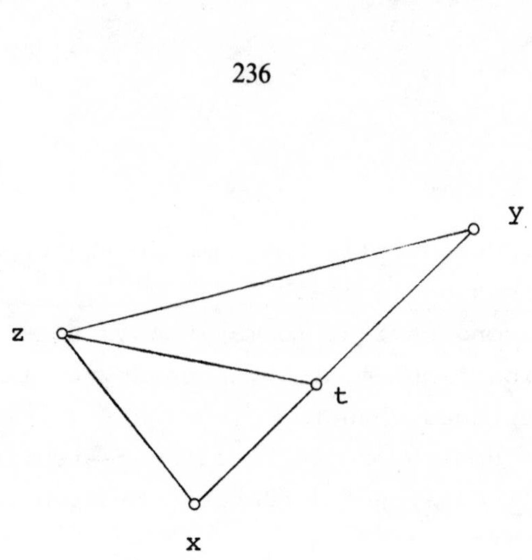

Fig. 1

Then given

$t = \lambda x + (1-\lambda)y$ where $0 < \lambda < 1$, there is an unique $w_t \in R$ and an unique $\beta_t \in R^2$ such that (EC) holds for $\langle t,x\rangle$, $\langle t,y\rangle$, $\langle t,z\rangle$.

w_t and β_t can be computed from

$$w_t = \lambda w_x + (1-\lambda)w_y + \frac{1}{2}\lambda(1-\lambda)(\beta_x-\beta_y)^T(y-x) \ ,$$

$$\beta_t^T(y-x) = 2(w_y-w_x) - (\lambda\beta_y + (1-\lambda)\beta_x)^T(y-x) \ ,$$

$$\beta_t^T(z-t) = (\lambda\beta_x + (1-\lambda)\beta_y)^T(z-t) \ .$$

As an important fact we mention that w_t and β_t are independent of w_z and β_z .

2.

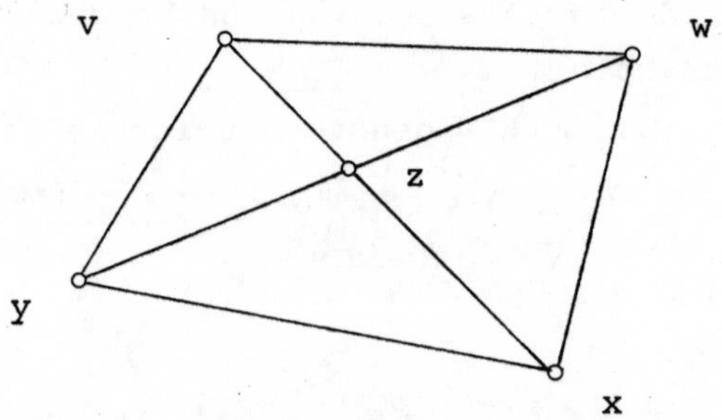

Fig. 2

Let $\langle v,w,x,y\rangle \subset R^2$ denote a convex quadrangle, z the intersection point of its diagonals. Assume that for the data $w_v,w_w,w_x,w_y \in R$, $\beta_v,\beta_w,\beta_x,\beta_y \in R^2$ (EC) holds for $\langle v,w\rangle$, $\langle w,x\rangle$, $\langle x,y\rangle$, $\langle y,v\rangle$. Then there is an unique $w_z \in R$ and an unique $\beta_z \in R^2$ such that (EC) holds also for

$$\langle z,v\rangle \, , \, \langle z,w\rangle \, , \, \langle z,x\rangle \, , \, \langle z,y\rangle \, .$$

Since 2. was already used in [2], readers interested in formulas for the computation of w_z and β_z are referred to that paper. But it is also an easy task to derive these formulas from the basic construction 1.

3.

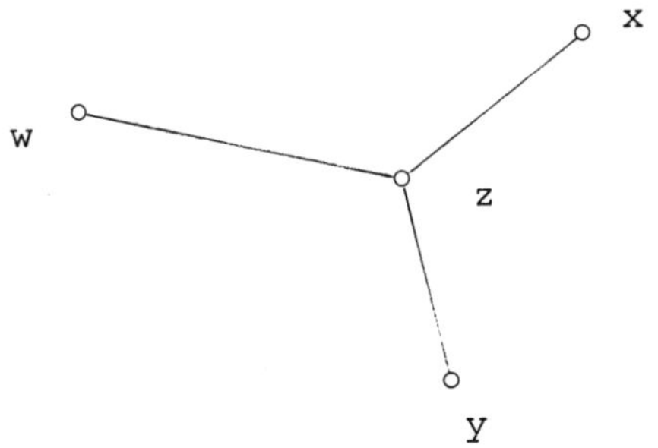

Fig. 3

Let $\langle w,x,y\rangle \subset R^2$ denote a triangle and

$$z = \lambda_1 w + \lambda_2 x + \lambda_3 y$$

a point such that

$$\lambda_1 + \lambda_2 + \lambda_3 = 1 \quad \text{and} \quad \lambda_i \neq 0 \, , \; i = 1,2,3 \, .$$

Then for any data $w_w,w_x,w_y \in R$, $\beta_w,\beta_x,\beta_y \in R^2$ there is an unique $w_z \in R$ and an unique $\beta_z \in R^2$ such that (EC) holds for the segments

$$\langle z,w\rangle \, , \, \langle z,x\rangle \, , \, \langle z,y\rangle \, .$$

$$w_z = \frac{1}{2}[\ \lambda_1(2\ w_w + \beta_w^T(z-w))$$
$$+\lambda_2(2\ w_x + \beta_x^T(z-x))$$
$$+\lambda_3(2\ w_y + \beta_y^T(z-y))]\ ,$$

and β_z can be computed from any two of the three linear equations:

$$\beta_z^T(w-z) = (1-\lambda_1)(2\ w_w + \beta_w^T(z-w))$$
$$-\lambda_2\ (2\ w_x + \beta_x^T(z-x))$$
$$-\lambda_3\ (2\ w_y + \beta_y^T(z-y))$$

$$\beta_z^T(x-z) = -\lambda_1\ (2\ w_w + \beta_w^T(z-w))$$
$$+(1-\lambda_2)(2\ w_x + \beta_x^T(z-x))$$
$$-\lambda_3\ (2\ w_y + \beta_y^T(z-y))$$

$$\beta_z^T(y-z) = -\lambda_1\ (2\ w_w + \beta_w^T(z-w))$$
$$-\lambda_2\ (2\ w_x + \beta_x^T(z-x))$$
$$+(1-\lambda_3)(2\ w_y + \beta_y^T(z-y))\ .$$

Let us show now in a typical example how to use the basic constructions in the proposed procedure. The steps are illustrated in the next figures. Figure 4 shows a set V of interpolation points.

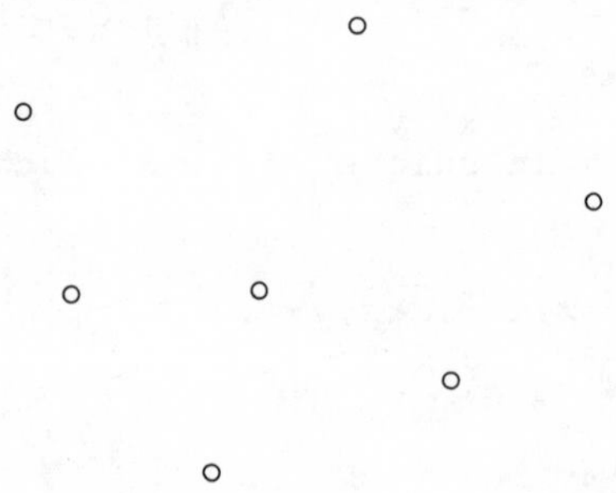

Fig. 4

Fig. 5 shows a complex K with $\{\{x\} : x \in V\}$ as its set of vertices.

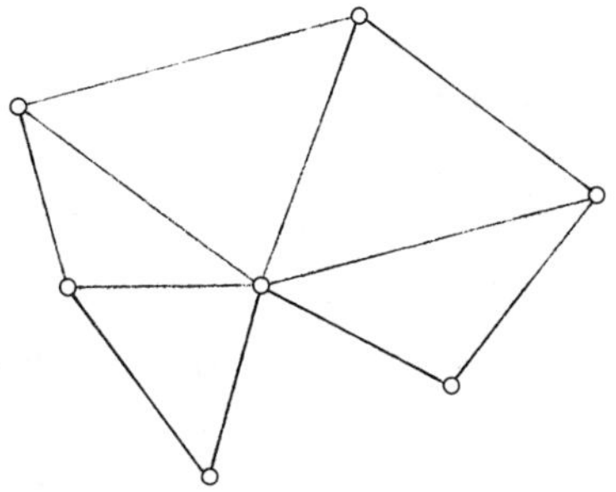

Fig. 5

Fig. 6 is obtained from Fig. 5 by performing basic constructions of type 3.

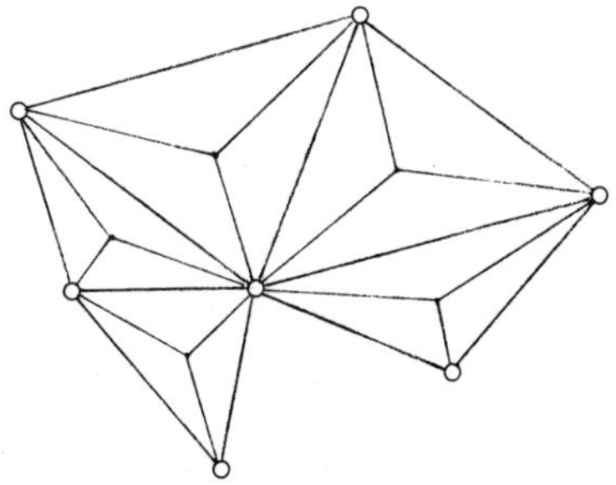

Fig. 6

Fig. 7 is obtained from Fig. 6 by performing basic constructions of type 1 and 2.

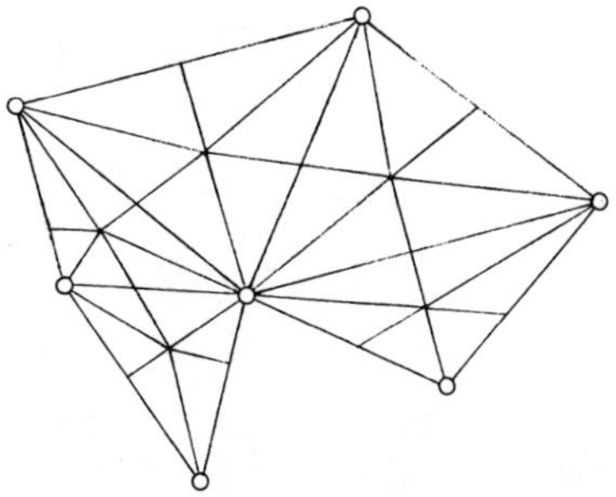

Fig. 7

Now a complex K' is constructed such that for any given $w_x \in R$, $\beta_x \in R^2$, $x \in V$, there is exactly one $\varphi \in \mathbb{P}_2(K')$ satisfying (i). φ can be computed from the formulas derived in the basic constructions and from Lemma 1 (1).

The constructions performed in the example can also be used to derive some new C^1- macro elements suitable for an application in the Finite Element Method. Given a complex K as indicated in Fig. 8 then for any parameters $w_i \in R$, $\beta_i \in R^2$, $i = 1,2,3$, there is exactly one $\varphi \in \mathbb{P}_2(K)$ such that

$$\varphi(x_i) = w_i \;,\; \text{grad}\, \varphi(x_i) = \beta_i \;,\; i = 1,2,3.$$

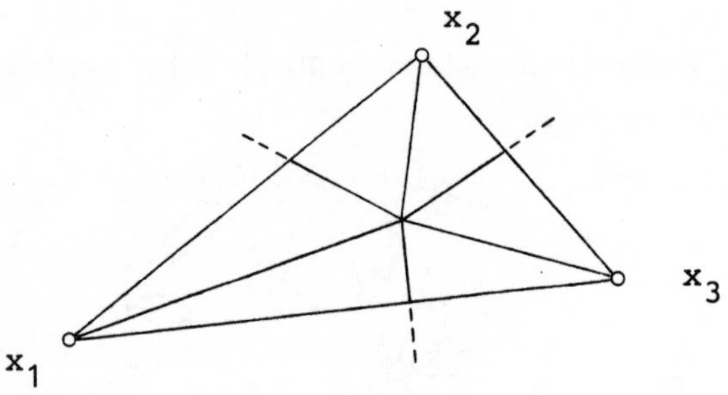

Fig. 8

Composing two of such triangular macro elements results in a quadrangular macro element. Fig. 9 shows the corresponding complex K for a square.

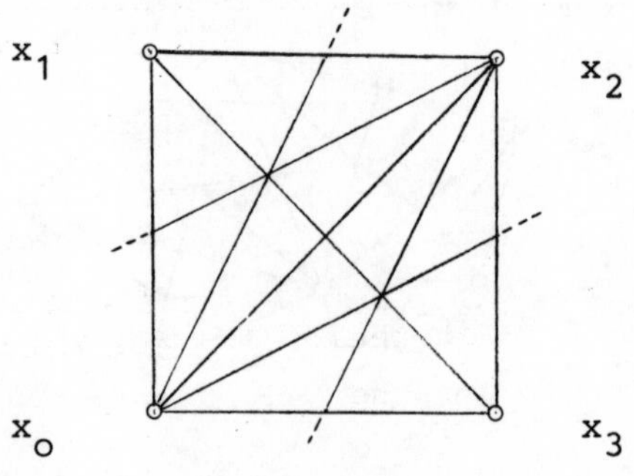

Fig. 9

For any parameters $w_i \in R$, $\beta_i \in R^2$, $i=0,\dots,3$, there is exactly one $\varphi \in \mathbb{P}_2(K)$ such that

$$\varphi(x_i) = w_i \ , \ \text{grad}\ \varphi(x_i) = \beta_i \ , \ i=0,\dots,3 \ .$$

The complex K corresponding to an other square shaped macro element considered already in [2] is shown in Fig. 10 .

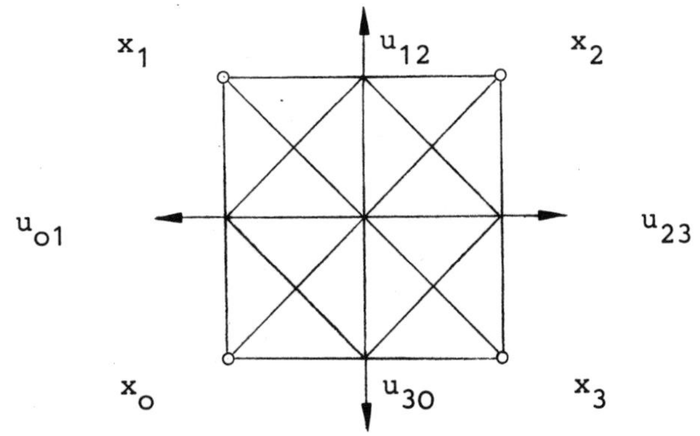

Fig. 10

For any parameters $w_i \in R$, $\beta_i \in R^2$, $i=0,\dots,3$, there is a $\varphi \in \mathbb{P}_2(K)$ such that

$$\varphi(x_i) = w_i \ , \ \text{grad}\ \varphi(x_i) = \beta_i \ , \ i=0,\dots,3,$$

and there is exactly one with the additional property:

$$\text{grad}\ \varphi((x_{i-1} + x_i)/2)^T u_{i-1,i} = \tfrac{1}{2}(\beta_{i-1} + \beta_i)^T u_{i-1,i} \ ,$$

for all $i \in Z_4$.

As a consequence the assertions made in [2] about Example 2 are not completely correct (Beatson).

Solutions of the interpolation problem in the case n=3

In the case n=3 basic constructions play an important role too. We will describe three of them.

1.

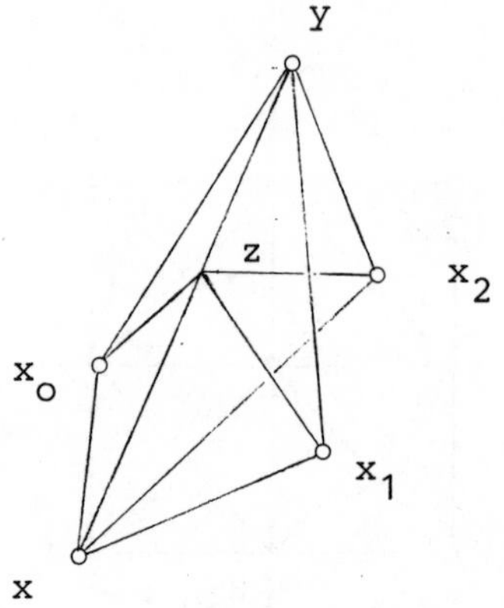

Fig.11

Let us consider points $x_o, x_1, x_2, x, y \in R^3$ where x_o, x_1, x_2 span a plane intersecting the linie segment $\langle x,y \rangle$ in exactly one point $z = \mu x + \varepsilon y = \lambda_o x_o + \lambda_1 x_1 + \lambda_2 x_2$, $\mu, \varepsilon > 0$, $\mu + \varepsilon = 1$, $\lambda_o + \lambda_1 + \lambda_2 = 1$.
We assume that $x_j \notin \langle z, x_i \rangle$ whenever $j \neq i$. Given $w_{x_i} \in R$, $\beta_{x_i} \in R^3$, $i=0,1,2$, $w_x, w_y \in R$, $\beta_x, \beta_y \in R^3$ such that (EC) holds for $\langle x, x_i \rangle$, $\langle y, x_i \rangle$, $i=0,1,2$, then there is an unique $w_z \in R$ and an unique $\beta_z \in R^3$ such that (EC) holds for $\langle z,x \rangle$, $\langle z,y \rangle$, $\langle z, x_i \rangle$, $i=0,1,2$, too. β_z can be computed from the equations

$$\beta_z^T(x-y) = 2(w_x - w_y) - \varepsilon\beta_x^T(x-y) - \mu\beta_y^T(x-y),$$

$$\beta_z^T(x_1-x_o) = 2(w_{x_1} - w_{x_o}) - \beta_{x_1}^T(x_1-z) + \beta_{x_o}^T(x_o-z),$$

$$\beta_z^T(x_2-x_o) = 2(w_{x_2}-w_{x_o}) - \beta_{x_2}^T(x_2-z) + \beta_{x_o}^T(x_o-z) ,$$

w_z from one of the equations

$$w_z = \mu(w_x - \frac{1}{2}\varepsilon\beta_x^T(x-y)) + \varepsilon(w_y + \frac{1}{2}\mu\beta_y^T(x-y)) ,$$

$$w_z = \sum_{i=o}^{2}\lambda_i(w_{x_i} - \frac{1}{2}\beta_{x_i}^T(x_i-z)) .$$

These formulas are easily verified.

2.

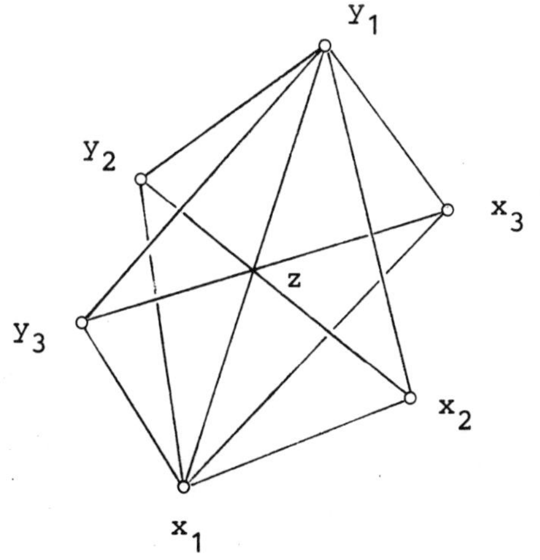

Fig. 12

In the second basic construction we consider points $z, x_i = z + u_i, y_i = z - \alpha_i u_i \in R^3$, $i=1,2,3$, where u_1, u_2, u_3 are linearly independent and $\alpha_i > 0$, $i=1,2,3$. Given w_{x_i}, $w_{y_i} \in R$, $\beta_{x_i}, \beta_{y_i} \in R^3$, $i=1,2,3$, such that (EC) holds for $<x_1,x_i>$, $<x_1,y_i>$, $<y_1,x_i>$, $<y_1,y_i>$, $i=2,3$, then there is an unique $w_z \in R$ and an unique $\beta_z \in R^3$ such that (EC) holds for $<z,x_i>$, $<z,y_i>$, $i=1,2,3$, too. It is easily seen that β_z can be computed from the equations

$$\beta_z^T(y_i-x_i) = 2(w_{y_i}-w_{x_i}) - \beta_{y_i}^T(y_i-z) + \beta_{x_i}^T(x_i-z), i=1,2,3,$$

w_z from one of the equations

$$w_z = \frac{\alpha_i}{1+\alpha_i} w_{x_i} + \frac{1}{1+\alpha_i} w_{y_i} + \frac{1}{2} \frac{\alpha_i}{(1+\alpha_i)^2} (\beta_{x_i} - \beta_{y_i})^T (y_i - x_i), i=1,2,3.$$

3. The third basic construction is similar to the third basic construction in the case $n=2$.

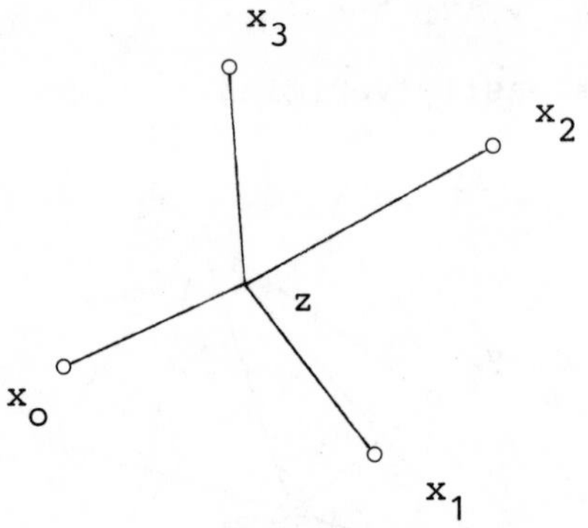

Fig. 13

Let $x_i \in R^3$, $i=0,..,3$ denote four affinely independent points and

$$z = \sum_{i=0}^{3} \lambda_i x_i$$

a point such that

$$\lambda_0+\lambda_1+\lambda_2+\lambda_3 = 1 \quad \text{and} \quad x_j \notin \langle z,x_i \rangle \quad \text{whenever} \quad j \neq i .$$

Then for any data $w_{x_i} \in R$, $\beta_{x_i} \in R^3$, $i=0,\ldots,3$ there is an unique $w_z \in R$ and an unique $\beta_z \in R^3$ such that (EC) holds for the segments

$$\langle z,x_i \rangle , i=0,\ldots,3 .$$

$$w_z = \frac{1}{2} \sum_{i=0}^{3} \lambda_i (2 w_{x_i} + \beta_{x_i}^T (z-x_i)) ,$$

and β_z can be computed from the equations

$$\beta_z^T(x_i-x_o) = 2(w_{x_i}-w_{x_o}) - \beta_{x_i}^T(x_i-z) + \beta_{x_o}^T(x_o-z),\ i=1,2,3.$$

As an example it is shown how two of the described basic constructions can be used to solve our interpolation problem for a $V \subset R^3$ consisting of four affinely independent points x_i, $i=0,\ldots,3$. The essential steps of the construction are illustrated in Fig. 14 - 16.

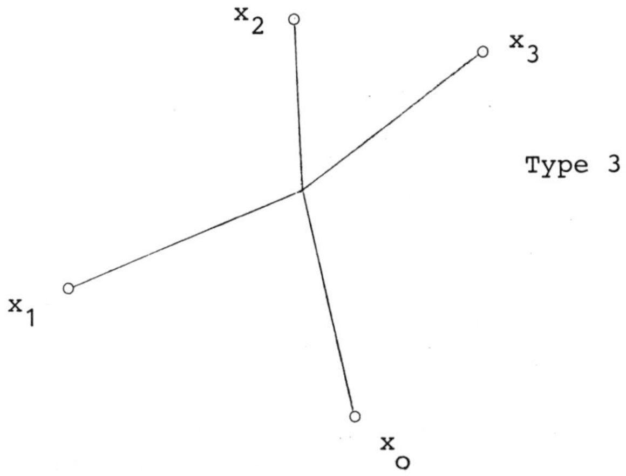

Fig. 14

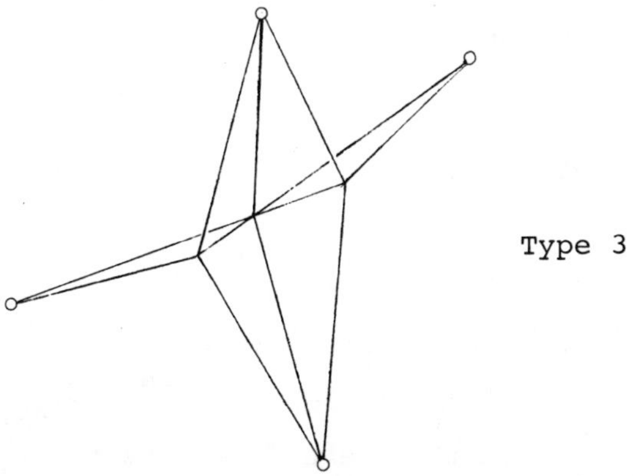

Fig. 15

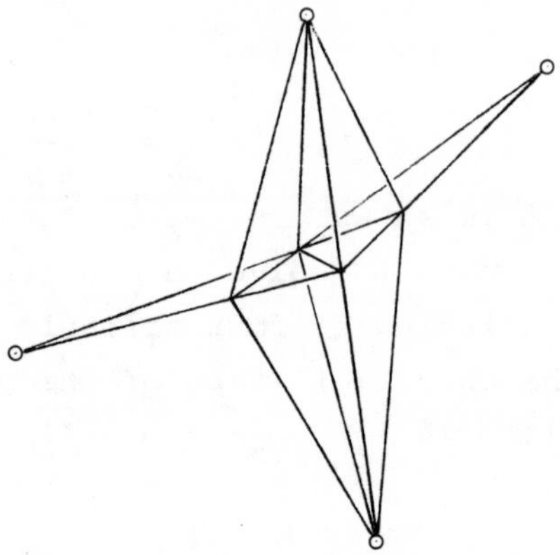

Type 1

Fig. 16

There results a complex K with $|K| = \langle x_o, x_1, x_2, x_3 \rangle$ and the property that for any $w_{x_i} \in R$, $\beta_{x_i} \in R^3$, $i=0,\ldots,3$, there is exactly one $\varphi \in \mathbb{P}^2(K)$ satisfying the interpolation conditions (i).

Homogeneous quadratic spline functions

Certain geodetic problems like the interpolation problem of geoidal hights (see [1]) suggest the definition of some kind of simplicial spline functions on a sphere. The aim of the rest of the paper is to derive such functions as restrictions of certain homogeneous quadratic spline functions $\varphi : R^3 \to R$.

Definitions:

A set
$$c_{\{x_o,\ldots,x_k\}} := \{\sum_{i=o}^{k} \lambda_i x_i : \lambda_i \geq 0\} ,$$

where $x_o,\ldots,x_k \in R^n$ are linearly independent, is called a (k+1)-dimensional (simplicial) cone (in R^n). $c_{\{x'_o,\ldots,x'_j\}}$ is a face of $c_{\{x_o,\ldots,x_k\}}$ iff there is a subset $\{x_{i_o},\ldots,x_{i_j}\}$

of $\{x_o,\ldots,x_k\}$ such that

$$c_{\{x'_o,\ldots,x'_j\}} = c_{\{x_{i_o},\ldots,x_{i_j}\}} .$$

A finite set C of cones is called a (homogeneous n-dimensional) <u>cone complex</u> iff it has properties similar to that of a complex K.

$$|C| := \bigcup_{c \in C} c$$

is the <u>polyhedral cone of</u> $\underline{C}$.

A cone complex C' is called a <u>refinement</u> of a cone complex C, iff it has similar properties as the refinements of complexes.

Given a cone complex C, a function $\varphi : |C| \to R$ is called a (homogeneous) <u>quadratic spline function with respect to</u> $\underline{C}$ ($\varphi \in \mathbb{P}_2^h(C)$) iff

(1) $\varphi \in C^1(|C|)$

(2) For every $c \in C$ there is a homogeneous polynomial $p : R^n \to R$ of degree ≤ 2 ($p \in P_2^h(R^n)$) such that

$$\varphi|c = p|c .$$

A Hermite interpolation problem

Let us consider now a Hermite interpolation problem similar to that described in section 2. Given a finite subset V of $R^n \setminus \{o\}$ with the property

$\{\lambda x : \lambda \geq 0\} \neq \{\lambda y : \lambda \geq 0\}$ whenever $x,y \in V$ and $x \neq y$, how can we construct a cone complex

$$C \supset \bigcup_{x \in V} \{\{\lambda x : \lambda \geq 0\}\}$$

such that for any given data

$$w_x \in R,\ \beta_x \in R^n,\ x \in V,$$

for which the Eulerian relation

(E) $\quad \beta_x^T x = 2\, w_x$

holds, there is a $\varphi \in \mathbb{P}_2^h(C)$ satisfying the interpolation conditions

$$(i_h) \qquad \begin{aligned} \varphi(x) &= w_x \\ \operatorname{grad} \varphi(x) &= \beta_x \end{aligned} \qquad \text{for all } x \in V \ ?$$

The following Lemma shows that a procedure similar to that in the nonhomogeneous case can help to solve this problem.

Lemma 1'

Given

(a) a cone complex C ,

(b) $x_c \in c\backslash\{o\}$ for every one dimensional $c \in C$,

(c) $w_x \in R$, $\beta_x \in R^n$ satisfying (E) for every

$$x \in V := \{x_c : c \in C \text{ and } \dim c = 1\} ,$$

then we can conclude:

1) If there is a $\varphi \in \mathbb{P}_2^h(C)$ having the interpolation property (i_h) , then

$$\varphi(x) = \sum_{i=o}^{n-1} w_{x_i} \lambda_i^2 + \sum_{\substack{i,j=o \\ i<j}}^{n-1} \beta_{x_i}^T x_j \lambda_i \lambda_j$$

$$= \sum_{i=o}^{n-1} \frac{1}{2} \beta_{x_i}^T x_i \lambda_i^2 + \sum_{\substack{i,j=o \\ i<j}}^{n-1} \beta_{x_j}^T x_i \lambda_i \lambda_j$$

whenever

$$x = \sum_{i=o}^{n-1} \lambda_i x_i \quad , \quad \lambda_i \geq 0 \ , \ i=0,\ldots,n-1 \ ,$$

$\{x_o,\ldots,x_{n-1}\} \subset V$ and $c_{\{x_o,\ldots,x_{n-1}\}} \in C$.

Hence φ is uniquely determined by (i_h) .

2) There is a $\varphi \in \mathbb{P}_2^h(C)$ satisfying (i_h) iff for all $x,y \in V$ for which $c_{\{x,y\}} \in C$, the following <u>symmetry - condition</u>

(SC) $\beta_x^T y = \beta_y^T x$

holds.

Proof. Observing that (SC) is equivalent to (EC) when (E) holds, it is an easy task to develop a proof of Lemma 1' from that of Lemma 1. In order to illustrate the construction procedure in the case $n = 3$ we introduce two basic constructions first.

2'

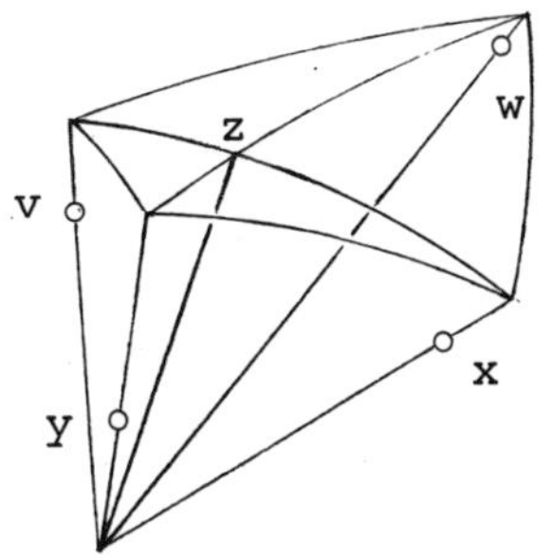

Fig. 17

Assumptions: (i) The cone spanned by $v,w,x,y \in R^3\backslash\{o\}$ is convex and nondegenerated. (ii) The data $w_v,w_w,w_x,w_y \in R$ and $\beta_v,\beta_w,\beta_x,\beta_y \in R^3$ satisfy (E), and (SC) for v,w; w,x; x,y; y,v.

(iii)

$$z \in \text{relint } c_{\{v,x\}} \cap \text{relint } c_{\{w,y\}} .$$

Then there is an unique $w_z \in R$ and an unique $\beta_z \in R^3$ such that

$$\beta_z^T z = 2\, w_z$$

and (SC) holds for

$$z,v;\ z,w;\ z,x;\ z,y .$$

One of four linear systems which can be used to compute β_z and w_z is

$$\beta_z^T v = \beta_v^T z$$
$$\beta_z^T w = \beta_w^T z$$
$$\beta_z^T x = \beta_x^T z$$
$$\beta_z^T z - 2\, w_z = 0 \quad .$$

3'

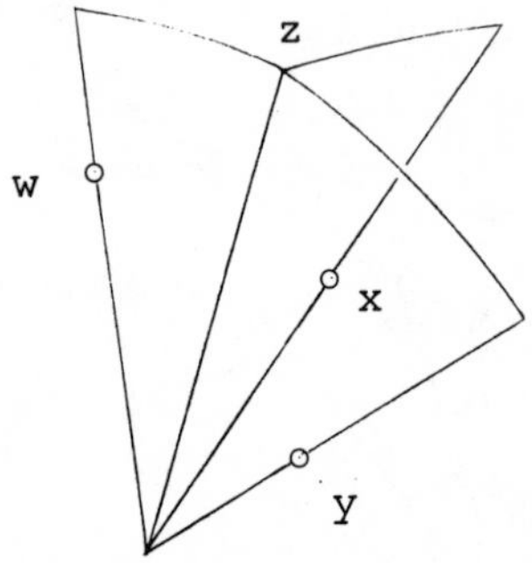

Fig. 18

Assumptions: (i) $w,x,y \in R^3$ are linearly independent.
(ii) $z = \lambda_1 w + \lambda_2 x + \lambda_3 y \notin \{o,w,x,y\}$, $\lambda_i \geq 0$, $i=1,2,3$.
(iii) The data $w_w, w_x, w_y \in R$, $\beta_w, \beta_x, \beta_y \in R^3$ satisfy (E) .
Then there is an unique $w_z \in R$ and an unique $\beta_z \in R^3$ such that

$$\beta_z^T z = 2\, w_z$$

and (SC) holds for z,w; z,x; z,y . β_z and w_z can be computed by solving the linear system

$$\beta_z^T w = \beta_w^T z$$
$$\beta_z^T x = \beta_x^T z$$
$$\beta_z^T y = \beta_y^T z$$
$$\beta_z^T z - 2 w_z = 0 \quad .$$

Using these basic constructions it is possible to solve the Hermite interpolation problem in the homogeneous case $n = 3$ in the same way as it was shown for the nonhomogeneous case $n = 2$ (figures 4 - 7).

An application to a Hermite interpolation problem for functions on the sphere

In Geodesy a solution of the following problem is of interest: Given a finite

$$X \subset S_2 = \{x \in R^3 : |x| = 1\} ,$$

$w_x \in R$ and $u_x \in R^3$ such that

$$u_x \perp x \quad \text{for all} \quad x \in X ,$$

find a cone complex C (in R^3) and a $\varphi \in \mathbb{P}_2^h(C)$ such that $\psi := \varphi|S_2$ has the interpolation property

(i') $\psi(x) = w_x$, grad $\psi(x) = u_x$ for all $x \in X$. The problem can be solved in the following way:

(1) Set

$$\beta_x := u_x + 2\, w_x x \quad \text{for all} \quad x \in X$$

(then (E) is valid for all $x \in X$).

(2) Construct a cone complex C with the property

$$\{\lambda x : \lambda \geq o\} \in C \quad \text{for all} \quad x \in X$$

and a $\varphi \in \mathbb{P}_2^h(C)$ satisfying

$$\varphi(x) = w_x \text{ and } \operatorname{grad} \varphi(x) = \beta_x \quad \text{for all} \quad x \in X .$$

Then $\psi := \varphi|S_2$ has property (i').

φ is a C^1 extension of ψ which is homogeneous of degree 2.

A C^1 extension of ψ which is homogeneous of degree K is given by

$$\varphi_K : R^3\backslash\{o\} \ni x \longmapsto \varphi(|x|^{\frac{K}{2}-1} x) .$$

References

1. Gerstl, M., Heindl,G., Reinhart, E.: Interpolation and Approximation by Piecewise Smooth Functions of two Variables XVII IUGG General Assembly International Association of Geodesy December 2 - 15, 1979 Canberra.

2. Heindl, G.: Interpolation and Approximation by Piecewise Quadratic C^1-Functions of Two Variables. Multivariate Approximation Theory, ed. by W. Schempp and K. Zeller, ISNM Vol. 51, Birkhäuser, Basel 1979.

International Series of
Numerical Mathematics, Vol. 75

HERMITE-FEJER AND HIGHER HERMITE-FEJER INTERPOLATION WITH BOUNDARY CONDITIONS

Hans-Bernd Knoop

Department of Mathematics
University of Duisburg
D-4100 Duisburg

1. Introduction

In this paper we investigate the question of positivity and convergence for Hermite-Fejêr and higher Hermite-Fejêr interpolation with boundary conditions. To state the problem, let the integers $m \geq 1$, $r,s \geq 0$ and m nodes x_{km} with

(1) $$-1 < x_{mm} < x_{m-1,m} < \dots < x_{1m} < 1$$

be given. We denote by $C(I)$ the Banach space of all continuous real valued functions on $I:=[-1,1]$ with the sup-norm $\|.\|$. For any $f \in C(I)$ there is an uniquely determined polynomial $F_{r,s;m}f$ of degree at most $2m+r+s-1$ satisfying the conditions

(2) $$F_{r,s;m}f(x_{km}) = f(x_{km}) \ , \quad 1 \leq k \leq m,$$

(3) $$(F_{r,s;m}f)'(x_{km}) = 0 \ , \quad 1 \leq k \leq m,$$

(4) $$F_{r,s;m}f(1) = f(1) \ , \quad (F_{r,s;m}f)^{(\rho)}(1) = 0$$
$$\text{for } r \geq 1 \text{ and } 1 \leq \rho \leq r-1 \ ,$$

(5) $$F_{r,s;m}f(-1) = f(-1) \ , \quad (F_{r,s;m}f)^{(\sigma)}(-1) = 0$$
$$\text{for } s \geq 1 \text{ and } 1 \leq \sigma \leq s-1.$$

This polynomial can be represented in the following form

$$F_{r,s;m}f(x) = L_{om}(x)\cdot f(1) + L_{m+1,m}(x)\cdot f(-1) + \sum_{k=1}^{m} v_{km}(x)\cdot L_{km}(x)\cdot f(x_{km})$$

with

$$L_{km}(x) = \left(\frac{1-x}{1-x_{km}}\right)^r \cdot \left(\frac{1+x}{1+x_{km}}\right)^s \cdot (l_{km}(x))^2$$

and polynomials L_{Om} and $L_{m+1,m}$ of degree at most $2m+r+s-1$. l_{km} is the k-th Lagrange polynomial of degree $m-1$ determined by the nodes (1). v_{km} is a polynomial of degree 1 with

(6) $$v_{km}(x) = 1 - \left(\frac{\omega_m''(x_{km})}{\omega_m'(x_{km})} - \frac{r}{1-x_{km}} + \frac{s}{1+x_{km}}\right)(x - x_{km}).$$

Here ω_m is the polynomial with

$$\omega_m(x) = \prod_{k=1}^{m} (x - x_{km}) .$$

If the nodes x_{km} are the roots of the Jacobi polynomial $P_m^{(\alpha,\beta)}$ of degree m (with regard to the weight function $x \mapsto (1-x)^{\alpha}(1+x)^{\beta}$), we use the notation

$$x_{km}^{(\alpha,\beta)}, \; l_{km}^{(\alpha,\beta)}, \; \omega_m^{(\alpha,\beta)}, \; v_{km}^{(\alpha,\beta)} \text{ and } F_{r,s;m}^{(\alpha,\beta)} .$$

If $r = s = 0$ then $F_{0,0;m}^{(\alpha,\beta)}f$ is the (classical) Hermite-Fejér interpolation polynomial of degree at most $2m-1$ corresponding to the nodes $x_{km}^{(\alpha,\beta)}$. It is well known that the operators $F_{0,0;m}^{(\alpha,\beta)}$ are positive for $(\alpha,\beta) \in]-1,0[^2$ and that we have for these (α,β) :

$$\lim_{m\to\infty} \| f - F_{0,0;m}^{(\alpha,\beta)}f \| = 0 \qquad \text{for each } f \in C(I)$$

(see Szegö [14], Locher [10]).
For (α,β) outside of the square $]-1,0]^2$ there exists a constant $K = K(\alpha,\beta) > 0$ with

$$\| F_{0,0;m}^{(\alpha,\beta)} \| \geq K\, m^{\max(\alpha,\beta)}$$

for all $m \geq m_o$. (Here $\|.\|$ denotes the operator-norm induced by the sup-norm on $C(I)$.) With the uniform boundedness principle we obtain the existence of a function $f_o \in C(I)$ with

(7) $$\limsup_{m \to \infty} \| f_o - F^{(\alpha,\beta)}_{0,0;m} f_o \| \neq 0 \quad .$$

For $\max(\alpha,\beta) = 0$ a function f_o with (7) can be constructed (see Szegö [14]). These results arise two questions:

I) Does there exist a subspace $U = U^{(\alpha,\beta)} \subset C(I)$ such that

$$\lim_{m \to \infty} \| f - F^{(\alpha,\beta)}_{0,0;m} f \| = 0 \qquad \text{for any} \quad f \in U \; ,$$

if $(\alpha,\beta) \in]-1,\infty[^2 \setminus]-1,0[^2$. Answers to this question were given by Szabados [13] and Vertési [16]. Especially in the case $\alpha = \beta = 0$ we obtain:

$$\lim_{m \to \infty} \| f - F^{(0,0)}_{0,0;m} f \| = 0 \quad \text{if and only if}$$

$$f(1) = f(-1) = \frac{1}{2} \int_{-1}^{1} f(x)\, dx$$

(see Fejér [3], Egerváry-Turán [2], Schönhage [12]).

II) Does there hold uniform convergence for all $f \in C(I)$, if we prescribe additional interpolation conditions at the endpoints -1 and $+1$? Answers to this question can be found in the papers of Vertési [15] for $(\alpha,\beta) \in]-1,2[^2$.

In this paper we consider the second question: Let $(\alpha,\beta) \in]-1,\infty[^2$ be given; does there exist $(r,s) \in \mathbb{N}_0^2$ such that

$$\lim_{m \to \infty} \| f - F^{(\alpha,\beta)}_{r,s;m} f \| = 0 \qquad \text{for each} \quad f \in C(I) \; ?$$

2. Positivity of the operators $F^{(\alpha,\beta)}_{r,s;m}$

Choosing the nodes x_{km} arbitrary in the interior of I we obtain by Rolle's theorem that

$$L_{0m}(x) \geq 0 \; , \; L_{m+1,m}(x) \geq 0 \qquad \text{for all} \quad x \in I$$

(independent of r and s). Thereby the operator $F_{r,s;m}$ is positive if and only if $v_{km}(\pm 1) \geq 0$ for each $k \in \{1,\dots,m\}$.

From the differential equation for the Jacobi polynomials (see Szegö [14]) we conclude from (6)

$$v_{km}^{(\alpha,\beta)}(x) = 1 - \frac{\gamma - \delta + (\gamma+\delta+2)x_{km}^{(\alpha,\beta)}}{1-(x_{km}^{(\alpha,\beta)})^2}\,(x - x_{km}^{(\alpha,\beta)})$$

where $\alpha = \gamma + r$, $\beta = \delta + s$. Thus we obtain

Lemma. Let $(r,s) \in \mathbb{N}_0^2$ and $(\gamma,\delta) \in [-1,0]^2$ be given with $\alpha := \gamma + r > -1$ and $\beta := \delta + s > -1$. Then $F_{r,s;m}^{(\alpha,\beta)}$ is a positive operator from $C(I)$ into itself.

3. Generalized Lobatto formulae

For $r = s = 0$ there is a strong connection to Gauß-Jacobi quadrature. In general there is a connection to Lobatto formulae (see Scherer-Zeller [11]). We consider formulae of the form ($\gamma,\delta > -1$)

$$\int_{-1}^{1} f(t)(1-t)^{\gamma}(1+t)^{\delta}dt = \sum_{k=1}^{m} \lambda_{km}^{(r,s)} f(x_{km})$$

$$+ \sum_{\rho=0}^{r-1} \bar{\lambda}_{\rho m}^{(r,s)} f^{(\rho)}(1) + \sum_{\sigma=0}^{s-1} \tilde{\lambda}_{\sigma m}^{(r,s)} f^{(\sigma)}(-1) + R_m^{(r,s)}(f)$$

with $R_m^{(r,s)}(p) = 0$ for all polynomials p of degree at most $2m+r+s-1$. Let x_{km} be the roots of the Jacobi polynomial $P_m^{(\gamma+r,\delta+s)}$ and let $\lambda_{km}^{(r,s)}$, $\bar{\lambda}_{\rho m}^{(r,s)}$ and $\tilde{\lambda}_{\sigma m}^{(r,s)}$ be the integrals of the fundamental functions of the corresponding Hermite interpolation polynomial, for example

$$\lambda_{km}^{(r,s)} = \int_{-1}^{1} v_{km}^{(\alpha,\beta)}(t)\; L_{km}^{(\alpha,\beta)}(t)\; (1-t)^{\gamma}(1+t)^{\delta}dt$$

with $\alpha = \gamma + r$, $\beta = \delta + s$, then we get a solution of the problem stated above. We obtain

$$\lambda_{km}^{(r,s)} = 2^{\alpha+\beta+1}\cdot\frac{\Gamma(m+\alpha+1)\;\Gamma(m+\beta+1)}{m!\;\Gamma(m+\alpha+\beta+1)}\cdot$$

$$\cdot(1-x_{km}^{(\alpha,\beta)})^{-r}(1+x_{km}^{(\alpha,\beta)})^{-s}(1-(x_{km}^{(\alpha,\beta)})^2)^{-1}(P_m^{(\alpha,\beta)\prime}(x_{km}))^{-2}.$$

The following estimation holds true

$$(8) \qquad \sum_{k=1}^{m} \lambda_{km}^{(r,s)} = O(1) \qquad \text{for} \quad m \to \infty .$$

In certain cases these formulae are well known quadrature formulae:

for $r = s = 0$: Gauß-Jacobi formulae ,

for $r = 1$, $s = 0$ or $r = 0$, $s = 1$: Bouzitat-formulae of first kind

especially for $\alpha = \beta = 0$: Radau formulae

for $r = s = 1$: Bouzitat-formulae of second kind

especially for $\alpha = \beta = 0$: Lobatto formulae.

4. Convergence of the operators $F_{r,s;m}^{(\alpha,\beta)}$

Now let $(\alpha,\beta) \in]-1,\infty[^2$ be given. Then there exist one and only one $(r,s) \in \mathbb{N}_0^2$ and one and only one $(\alpha,\beta) \in [-1,0[^2$ with $\alpha = r + \gamma$, $\beta = s + \delta$.

According to the lemma we obtain that $F_{r,s;m}^{(\alpha,\beta)}$ is a positive operator from $C(I)$ into itself. If e is a constant function we have $F_{r,s;m}^{(\alpha,\beta)}e = e$; therefore the theorem of Bohman-Korovkin (see DeVore [1]) yields for any $x \in I$

$$|f(x) - F_{r,s;m}^{(\alpha,\beta)}f(x)| \le 2\, \omega(f,|\varepsilon_m(x)|)$$

with

$$\varepsilon_m^2(x) = (F_{r,s;m}^{(\alpha,\beta)} g_x)(x)$$

and

$$g_x(t) = (x-t)^2 \qquad \text{for} \quad t \in I.$$

Here ω denotes the usual modulus of continuity. The function ε_m^2 can be estimated from above. We have

$$\varepsilon_m^2(x) = L_{Om}^{(\alpha,\beta)}(x)\cdot(x-1)^2 + L_{m+1,m}^{(\alpha,\beta)}(x)\cdot(x+1)^2$$
$$+ (1-x)^r(1+x)^s(P_m^{(\alpha,\beta)}(x))^2\, c_m^{(\alpha,\beta)}\cdot$$
$$\cdot \sum_{k=1}^{m} \lambda_{km}^{(r,s)}\, v_{km}^{(\alpha,\beta)}(x)\, (1-(x_{km}^{(\alpha,\beta)})^2) .$$

Because of (cf. Szegö [14, Theorem 7.32.2] and [5])

$$L_{Om}^{(\alpha,\beta)}(x)\cdot(x-1)^2 = O(m^{-2(\gamma+1)})\cdot m^{2\max(\gamma,\delta,-1/2)},$$

$$L_{m+1,m}^{(\alpha,\beta)}(x)\cdot(x+1)^2 = O(m^{-2(\delta+1)})\cdot m^{2\max(\gamma,\delta,-1/2)},$$

$$c_m^{(\alpha,\beta)} = O(1),$$

$$v_{km}^{(\alpha,\beta)}(x)\cdot(1-(x_{km}^{(\alpha,\beta)})^2) = O(1),$$

$$(1-x)^r(1+x)^s(P_m^{(\alpha,\beta)}(x))^2 = O(m^{2\max(\gamma,\delta,-1/2)})$$

uniformly for $x\in I$ and $m\to\infty$, and because of (8) we obtain

Proposition 1. Let (α,β), (r,s) and (γ,δ) be given as above. For each $f\in C(I)$ follows

$$\|f - F_{r,s;m}^{(\alpha,\beta)}f\| = O(\omega(f,m^{\max(\gamma,\delta,-1/2)}))$$

as $m\to\infty$.

If $(r,s)\in\mathbb{N}_0^2$ is given then for each $(\alpha,\beta)\in[r-1,r[\times[s-1,s[\,\cap\,]-1,\infty[^2$ we have

$$(9)\qquad \lim_{m\to\infty}\|f - F_{r,s;m}^{(\alpha,\beta)}f\| = 0 \qquad \text{for every } f\in C(I).$$

In [5] a wider field $K_{r,s}$ of pairs $(\alpha,\beta)\in]-1,\infty[^2$, for which (9) holds, is given.

5. The operators $K_{r,s;m}^{(\alpha,\beta)}$

Now we investigate the question of convergence for Hermite-Fejér interpolation of higher order, introduced by Kryloff-Stayermann [7]. For $f\in C(I)$ the uniquely determined polynomial $K_{r,s;m}f$ of degree at most $4m+r+s-1$ is defined by (2), (4), (5) and

$$(K_{r,s;m}f)^{(i)}(x_{km}) = 0 \qquad \text{for } 1\le k\le m,\ 1\le i\le 3,$$

instead of (3).

In [6] is shown that the operator $K_{0,0;m}^{(\alpha,\beta)}$ (i.e. the nodes (1) are the roots of $P_m^{(\alpha,\beta)}$) is positive for all $m \in \mathbb{N}$, if $(\alpha,\beta) \in [-3/4,-1/4]^2$. Further there is given an estimation with the modulus of continuity, which implies

$$\lim_{m\to\infty} \|f - K_{0,0;m}^{(\alpha,\beta)} f\| = 0 \qquad \text{for arbitrary} \quad f \in C(I)$$

and $(\alpha,\beta) \in [-3/4,-1/4[^2$.

If $\alpha = \beta = -1/4$ there exists a function f_0 with

$$\limsup_{m\to\infty} \|f_0 - K_{0,0;m}^{(\alpha,\beta)} f_0\| \neq 0$$

(cf. Laden [8]). Locher [9] has shown that for $(\alpha,\beta) \in]-1,\infty[^2$ with $\min(\alpha,\beta) \geq -3/4$ we have pointwise convergence for all x with $|x| < 1$, that means

$$\lim_{m\to\infty} |f(x) - K_{0,0;m}^{(\alpha,\beta)} f(x)| = 0 \quad .$$

Therefore the question arises how to get uniform convergence for each $f \in C(I)$, if (α,β) is outside of $[-3/4,-1/4[^2$.

One of my students, Mr. Kook, has shown, that for given $(r,s) \in \mathbb{N}_0^2$

$$\lim_{m\to\infty} \|f - K_{r,s;m}^{(\alpha,\beta)} f\| = 0$$

holds for each $f \in C(I)$, if (α,β) is an element of a certain region of $]-3/4,\infty[^2$, which contains the square

$$[-\tfrac{3}{4} + \tfrac{r}{2}, -\tfrac{1}{4} + \tfrac{r}{2}[\times [-\tfrac{3}{4} + \tfrac{s}{2}, -\tfrac{1}{4} + \tfrac{s}{2}[\ .$$

6. The multidimensional case

Let $F_{r,s;m}^{(\alpha,\beta)} \otimes F_{p,q;n}^{(\zeta,\xi)}$ be the tensor product of two one-dimensional Hermite-Fejér operators, then we have interpolation conditions on a rectangular grid. For $r,s,p,q \in \mathbb{N}$ the values of the function $f \in C(I^2)$ are prescribed in some points of the boundary of I^2. Since the operators $F_{r,s;m}^{(\alpha,\beta)}$ resp. $F_{p,q;m}^{(\zeta,\xi)}$ are uniform bounded for $(\alpha,\beta) \in K_{r,s}$ resp. $(\zeta,\xi) \in K_{p,q}$ we obtain (see Haußmann-Pottinger [4])

Proposition 2. Let (α,β) and (ζ,ξ) be given as above. Then we can state

$$\| f - (F_{r,s;m}^{(\alpha,\beta)} \otimes F_{p,q;n}^{(\zeta,\xi)})(f)\| = o(1)$$

for each $f \in C(I^2)$ as $m,n \to \infty$.

For example let $r = s = 1 = p = q$. Then we can choose

$$\alpha = \beta = \zeta = \xi = \frac{1}{2}$$

or

$$\alpha = \beta = \zeta = \xi = -\frac{1}{2} .$$

In the first case we get a tensor product of two univariate positive operators, in the second case the univariate operators are not positive.

Similarly we can consider the tensor product of two univariate operators $K_{r,s;m}^{(\alpha,\beta)}$ and $K_{p,q;n}^{(\zeta,\xi)}$.

References

1. DeVore, R.A.: The approximation of continuous functions by positive linear operators. Lecture Notes Math. 293. Berlin-Heidelberg-New York: Springer 1972.
2. Egerváry, E., Turán, P.: Notes on Interpolation. V (On the Stability of Interpolation). Acta Math. Acad. Sci. Hungar. 9, 259-267 (1958).
3. Fejér, L.: Über Interpolation. Göttinger Nachrichten 66-91 (1916) resp. Gesammelte Arbeiten, Bd. II (ed. by P. Turán), 25-48, Basel-Stuttgart: Birkhäuser 1970.
4. Haußmann, W., Pottinger, P.: On the Construction and Convergence of Multivariate Interpolation Operators. J. Approx. Theory 19, 205-221 (1977).
5. Knoop, H.-B.: Hermite-Fejér-Interpolation mit Randbedingungen. Habilitationsschrift. Universität Duisburg 1981.
6. Knoop, H.-B., Stockenberg, B.: On Hermite-Fejér Type Interpolation. Bull. Austral. Math. Soc. 28, 39-51 (1983).
7. Kryloff, N.M., Stayermann, E.: sur quelques formules d'interpolation convergentes pour toute fonction continue. Bull.

Acad. de l'Oucraine 1, 13-16 (1923).

8. Laden, H.N.: An application of the classical orthogonal polynomials to the theory of interpolation. Duke Math. J. 8, 591-610 (1941).
9. Locher, F.: On Hermite-Fejér Interpolation at Jacobi zeros. J. Approx. Theory, to appear 1985.
10. Locher, F.: Convergence of Hermite-Fejér-interpolation via Korovkin's theorem. These proceedings.
11. Scherer, R., Zeller, K.: Lobatto-Quadratur und Fixpunkte. Internat. Ser. Numer. Math. 45, 245-251 (1979).
12. Schönhage, A.: Zur Konvergenz der Stufenpolynome über den Nullstellen der Legendre-Polynome. Internat. Ser. Numer. Math. 20, 448-451 (1972).
13. Szabados, J.: On Hermite-Fejér Interpolation for the Jacobi Abscissas. Acta Math. Acad. Sci. Hungar. 23, 449-464 (1972).
14. Szegö, G.: Orthogonal Polynomials. Amer. Math. Soc. Coll. Publ. 23. Providence, R.I.: Amer. Math. Soc. 1975.
15. Vertési, P.: Hermite-Fejér Type Interpolations. I-III. Acta Math. Acad. Sci. Hungar. 32, 349-369 (1978), 33, 333-343 (1979), 34, 67-84 (1979).
16. Vertési, P.: Hermite-Fejér Type Interpolations. IV (Convergence Criteria for Jacobi Abscissas). Acta Math. Acad. Sci. Hungar. 39, 83-93 (1982).

International Series of
Numerical Mathematics, Vol. 75

Some uniqueness problems in best Chebyshev and mean multivariate approximation

András Kroó
Mathematical Institute of the
Hungarian Academy of Sciences
Budapest, Reáltanoda u. 13-15.
H-1364, Hungary

/Dedicated to my daughter Anita, born January 19, 1985./

The purpose of this note is to give a survey of some recent results on uniqueness of best multivariate approximation in C and L_1 -norms.

Let C(K) denote the space of real or complex continuous functions endowed with the supremum norm on the compact Hansdorff space K. The classical Haar-Kolmogorov theorem states that each $f \in C(K)$ has a unique best approximant out of an n-dimensional linear subspace U_n of C(K) if and only if U_n satisfies the so--called Haar property, i.e. each $q \in U_n \setminus \{o\}$ has at most n-1 zeros at K. In real case the Haar property imposes a strict restriction on the compact set K. Namely, by the wellknown result of Mairhuber real C(K) possesses Haar subspaces of dim>1 only if K is homeomorphic to a subset of the circle. Thus we can not ensure uniqueness of best Chebyshev approximation for all real multivariate continuous functions. The only way to get some uniqueness results in this situation is to restrict our considerations to certain classes of functions in C(K). This approach was applied by Collatz [2] who showed that real differentiable functions have unique linear polynomials of least uniform deviation on convex compact subsets of $\mathbb{R}^2$. We shall consider now the question of uniform approximation of differentiable functions.

1. Uniform approximation of differentiable functions, semi-Haar spaces. Let U_n be an n-dimensional subspace of C(K). Then the set of m distinct points $\{x_k\}_{k=1}^m \subset K$ ($1 \le m \le n+1$ in the real case and $1 \le m \le 2n+1$ in the complex case) is called an extremal

set of U_n at K if there exist nonzero numbers a_k, $1 \le k \le m$ (coefficients of the extremal set) such that $\sum_{k=1}^{m} a_k g(x_k) = 0$ for all $g \in U_n$. It is known that $U_n \subset C(K)$ statisfies the Haar property at K if and only if no nontrivial element of U_n vanishes at an extremal set of U_n. Let K be a convex compact subset of $\mathbb{R}^2$ and denote by $C^1(K)$ the set of (real or complex) continuously differentiable functions at K endowed with the supremum norm. Let us say that $U_n \subset C^1(K)$ is a <u>semi-Haar space</u> if each function in $C^1(K)$ has a unique best approximant out of U_n. The next theorem gives a characterization of semi-Haar spaces in the case $K = S^2 = \{(x, y) \in \mathbb{R}^2 : x^2+y^2 \le 1\}$. (The considerations can be extended to more general regions but for simplicity we present only this case.)

<u>Theorem 1</u> ([8]). $U_n \subset C^1(S^2)$ is a semi-Haar space if and only if there does not exist an extremal set $\{(x_k, y_k)\}_{k=1}^{m} \subset S^2$ of U_n with coefficients $\{a_k\}_{k=1}^{m}$ such that for some $p \in U_n \setminus \{0\}$ (i) $p(x_k, y_k) = 0$, $1 \le k \le m$; (ii) $\text{Re}\, a_k p'_y(x_k, y_k) = \text{Re}\, a_k p'_x(x_k, y_k) = 0$ if $x_k^2+y_k^2 < 1$; (iii) $x_k \,\text{Re}\, a_k p'_y(x_k, y_k) = y_k \text{Re}\, a_k p'_x(x_k, y_k)$ if $x_k^2+y_k^2 = 1$.

In case of real univariate functions a similar statement was verified earlier by Garkavi [5]. Independently from the author Brosowski and Guerreiro [1] proved the real version of Theorem 1 (in somewhat more general context).

Naturally, the most interesting problem is the question of existance of semi-Haar spaces. Let us consider this problem at first in the real case. As it was mentioned above Collatz [2] proved that the set of real linear polynomials $L_3 = \{a_1x+a_2y+a_3 : a_i \in \mathbb{R}\}$ is a semi-Haar space at S^2. In [8] we showed that $L_4 = \{a_1xy+a_2x+a_3y+a_4 : a_i \in \mathbb{R}\}$ also satisfies the semi-Haar property at S^2. Moreover, in [1] it is pointed out that

$L_5=\{a_1(x^2-y^2)+a_2xy+a_3x+a_4y+a_5 : a_i\in \mathbb{R}\}$ is a semi-Haar space at an ellipsoid. Thus we have examples of real semi-Haar spaces of dim≤5. But on the other hand Rivlin and Shapiro [13] verified that the set of quadratic polynomials $L_6=\{\sum_{i+j\leq 2} a_{ij}x^iy^j : a_{ij}\in \mathbb{R}\}$ in general does not satisfy the semi-Haar property. Therefore it is very unlikely that real semi-Haar spaces can have dim>5. This leads to the following

Conjecture 1. There do not exist real semi-Haar spaces of dim>5 on regions in $\mathbb{R}^2$ with nonempty interior.

The above considerations indicate that we can not achieve global unicity for real multivariate functions even assuming their smoothness. Nevertheless, we can ensure uniqueness for some special polynomial functions. Let $p_n(x)$ and $p_m(y)$ be real univariate algebraic polynomials of degree n and m, respectively. Denote by $\tilde{p}_k(x)$ and $\tilde{p}_s(y)$ their best uniform approximants at $I=[-1,1]$ by polynomials of degree at most k and s, respectively ($0\leq k<n$, $o\leq s<m$). By a result of Shapiro [14] polynomial $p^*(x,y)=p_n(x)\tilde{p}_s(y)+\tilde{p}_k(x)p_m(y)-\tilde{p}_k(x)\tilde{p}_s(y)$ is a best Chebyshev approximant of $p_n(x)p_m(y)$ on $I^2=[-1,1]\times[-1,1]$ out of the set

$$P(n,m,k,s)=\{\sum_{j=o}^{s}\sum_{i=o}^{n} a_{ij}x^iy^j+\sum_{j=o}^{m}\sum_{i=o}^{k} b_{ij}x^iy^j : a_{ij},b_{ij}\in \mathbb{R}\}.$$

Furthermore, it is shown in [8] that under the condition $\min\{2k+2-n, 2s+2-m\}>0$ $p^*(x,y)$ is the unique best approximant of $p_n(x)p_m(y)$ in $P(n,m,k,s)$, and in general this condition is necessary for uniqueness. In particular, this immediately implies that certain Chebyshev and Zolotarjov type extremal problems for real polynomials of two variables have unique solutions. This extends an earlier result by Erlich-Zeller [3].

Thus we feelthat real multivariate semi-Haar spaces are very rare, in fact we expect that a Mairhuber type negative result holds with respect to them. Naturally, the situation is different in the complex case. In [8] we considered spaces of lacunary complex polynomials satisfying semi-Haar property. It is shown in [8] that polynomial spaces of the form

$$\tilde{P}_n = \{ \sum_{j=0}^{r} c_j z^j + \sum_{j=r+1}^{n} c_j z^{q_j} : c_j \in \mathbb{C} \}$$

are semi-Haar spaces at $\{|z|\le 1\}$ if $r \ge [\frac{3q_n - 2}{4}]$ ($r<q_{r+1}<\dots<q_n$ are fixed integers). Evidently, any lacunary polynomial space is not a Haar space at $\{|z|\le 1\}$, i.e. in the complex multivariate case the family of semi-Haar spaces is essentially wider than the family of Haar spaces, and we have nontrivial examples of semi-Haar spaces of arbitrary dimension. It would be of some interest to give a description of those sets of lacunary complex polynomials which satisfy the semi-Haar property (for the solution of this problem in real case see [9]).

2. L_1-approximation, A-spaces. Let us turn to the question of uniqueness of best L_1-approximation of continuous functions. The problem of characterizing those subspaces which provide unicity of best L_1-approximation for all continuous functions has been considered by many authors but nothing as elegant and simple as the Haar-Kolmogorov theorem has been obtained. The main reason for this is that the Haar property is weight independent, i.e. if we alter the supremum norm at K to any norm of the form $\|f\|_{C,\omega} = \max_{x\in K} \omega(x)|f(x)|$ where ω is a positive continuous function at K, then Haar-Kolmogorov theorem remains true. On the other hand it can be shown by simple examples that uniqueness of best L_1-approximation is weight dependent, that is we may have uniqueness of best L_1-approximation for all continuous functions with respect to some weights and nonuniqueness with respect to others.

This indicates that we may hope to get a nice characterization only of those spaces which provide unicity of best L_1-approximation to all continuous functions with respect to all positive weights.

Let $C_\omega(K)$ denote the space of (real or complex) functions continuous at the compact convex set $K \subset \mathbb{R}^m$ ($m\ge 1$, $\mathrm{Int}\, K \ne \emptyset$), and endowed with the norm $\|f\|_\omega = \int_K \omega(x)|f(x)|dx$. Here $\omega \in W = \{\omega : \omega$ is measurable and $0 < \inf_{x\in K} \omega(x) \le \sup_{x\in K} \omega(x) < \infty\}$.

Consider an arbitrary n-dimensional subspace U_n in $C(K)$. Set $U_n^* = \{q_n^* \in C(K):$ there exists $q_n \in U_n$ such that $q_n^*(x) = \pm q_n(x)$ for each $x \in K\}$.

Definition. We say that U_n is an A-space at K if for any $q_n^* \in U_n^* \setminus \{0\}$ there exists a $q_n \in U_n$ such that (i) $q_n = 0$ a.e. on the set of zeros of q_n^*; (ii) $\mathrm{Re}\, q_n \bar{q}_n^* \geq 0$ at K and this inequality is strict on a subset of K of positive measure.

Theorem 2 ([11]). In order that for any $\omega \in W$ and $f \in C_\omega(K)$ its best L_1-approximant in U_n be unique it is necessary and sufficient that U_n is an A-space.

The sufficiency of the A-property in the real univariate case was varified by Strauss [15]. The necessity of the A-property in the real univariate case was verified by the author [10] and, independently, by Pinkus [12].

A-spaces are well-studied in case of real univariate functions. In this situation they essentially consist of Haar spaces and certain families of spline functions (for complete characterization of real A-spaces on intervals see [12]).

Let us consider real multivariate case. Evidently, the set of real linear polynomials is an A-space in multivariate setting, too. But it can be easily seen that quadratic polynomials fail to satisfy the A-property. A simple example of A-spaces of arbitrary dimension can be given by considering spaces spanned by functions with disjoint support. Namely, let K_j, $1 \leq j \leq p$, be convex open disjoint subsets of K and let $U_n = \mathrm{span}\{\psi_1, \ldots, \psi_p\}$, where $\psi_j \in C(K)$, $\psi_j > 0$ at K_j and $\mathrm{supp}\psi_j = K_j$ $(1 \leq j \leq p)$. Then it can be easily verified that U_n is an A-space at K. Another example of trivial A-spaces is given by spaces which can be transformed by a diffeomorphic transformation of the region to univariate A-spaces. For instance the set $P_n^* = \{\sum_{i+j=n} a_{ij} x^i y^j : a_{ij} \in \mathbb{R}\}$ of homogenous polynomials is an A-space at the halfdisc $\{(x,y) \in \mathbb{R}^2 : x^2+y^2 \leq 1;\ 0 \leq x \leq 1\}$. But again we feel that apart from the above degenerate cases there do not exist real multivariate A-spaces of $\dim > 3$.

Conjecture 2. Let $K \subset \mathbb{R}^m$ $(m>1,\ \mathrm{Int}\, K \neq \emptyset)$. Then any real A-space at K of dim > 3 either has a basis of functions with disjoint support or can be transformed by a diffeomorphic transformation of the region to a univariate A-space.

Thus we again expect a Mairhuber type negative result. Of course the situation is different for complex A-spaces, since for instance any finite dimensional subspace consisting of analytic functions is an A-space at $K \subset \mathbb{R}^2$.

We may conclude that study of weight independent uniqueness of best L_1-approximation is very useful in case of real univariate functions or complex functions of two variables but is not very helpful for real multivariate functions. Nevertheless, some interesting results can be obtained even in this situation if we consider uniqueness only with respect to the weitht $\omega \equiv 1$, that is space $C_1(K)$. For example, it is shown in [6] that if K is a rectangular region in $\mathbb{R}^2$ then each real continuous function at K possesses unique best L_1-approximant by elements of the tensor product of a two-dimensional and k-dimensional $(k \in \mathbb{N})$ real univariate Haar spaces. This gives a nontrivial example of a subspace of arbitrary dimension providing unicity in $C_1(K)$. In particular, real algebraic polynomials of two variables which are linear with respect to only one variable have this uniqueness property. (Evidently, spaces of this type are not A-spaces.) We believe that the above result can be extended to arbitrary polynomial spaces.

Conjecture 3. Let K be a rectangular region in $\mathbb{R}^2$. Then every real continuous function f at K has a unique best L_1-approximant in $P_n = \{ \sum_{i+j \leq n} a_{ij} x^i y^j : a_{ij} \in \mathbb{R} \}$.

In [7] we were able to verify this conjecture only for $f \in P = \cup_n P_n$, but even this result is stronger than what can be obtained in case of Chebyshev approximation by polynomials of two variables. It was also shown in [7] that a great variety of Chebyshev and Zolotarjov type extremal L_1-problems for real multivariate polynomials have unique solutions (see [4] for an earlier result in this direction).

References

[1] B. Brosowski, C.Guerreiro, Conditions for the Uniqueness of best Generalized Rational Chebyshev Approximation to Differentiable and Analytic Functions, J. Approx. Th. 42 (1984) 149-173.

[2] L. Collatz, Approximation von Funktionen bei einer und bei mehreren Veranderlichen, Zeit. Angew. Math. Mech., 36 (1956), 198-211.

[3] H. Ehrlich, K.Zeller, Cebysev-Polynome in mehreren Veranderlichen, Math. Zeit. 93 (1966), 142-143.

[4] Fromm, L_1-approximation to Zero, Math. Zeit. 151 (1976), 31-33.

[5] A.L.Garkavi, Dimensionality of polyhedra of best approximation for differentiable functions, Izv. Akad.Nauk SSSR, ser. math., 23 (1959), 93-114.

[6] A.Kroó, Some theorems on unicity of multivariate L_1-approximation, Acta Math. Acad. Sci. Hungar., 40 (1982), 179-189.

[7] A.Kroó, On the unicity of best L_1-approximation by polynomials of several variables, Acta Math. Hung. 42 (1983), 309-318.

[8] A.Kroó, On Chebyshev subspaces in the space of multivariate differentiable functions, Trans. Amer. Math.Soc., to appear.

[9] A.Kroó, On the unicity of best Chebyshev approximation of differentiable functions, Acta Sci. Math. Szeged, 47 (1984), to appear

[10] A.Kroó, On an L_1-approximation problem, Proc, Amer. Math. Soc., to appear.

[11] A.Kroó, A genaral approach to the study of Chebyshev subspaces in L_1-approximation of continuous functions, to appear.

[12] A.Pinkus, Unicity subspaces in L^1-approximation, J. Approx. Th., to appear.

[13] T. J. Rivlin, H.S. Shapiro, Some uniqueness problems in approximation theory, Comm. Pure Appl. Math., 13 (1960), 35-47.

[14] H.S. Shapiro, Topics in Approximation Theory, Lecture Notes in Math. 187, Springer Verlag (Berlin-Heidelberg-New York, 1971).

[15] H. Strauss, Best L_1-approximation, J. Approx. Th. 41 (1984) 297-308.

International Series of
Numerical Mathematics, Vol. 75

MINIMAL PROJECTIONS IN TENSOR PRODUCT SPACES

W.A. Light

University of Lancaster, Lancaster, LA1 4YL, U.K.

1. Introduction

In this paper we present a condensed survey of recent results on minimal projections in tensor product spaces. The idea of a minimal projection is an old one. We have a Banach space Z and a complemented subspace W. Then the projection constant $\delta(W,Z)$ is defined by

$$\delta(W,Z) = \inf\{\|P\| \ : \ P \text{ is a projection from } Z \text{ onto } W\}.$$

Any projection P from Z onto W for which $\|P\| = \delta(W,Z)$ is called a minimal projection. The general theory about minimal projections is not very satisfactory - they are hard to discover and indeed, it is difficult to be sure, even in quite elementary circumstances, that they exist. The most satisfactory condition for the existence of minimal projections is that W be finite-dimensional. The best-known example of a minimal projection is probably the Fourier projection

$$(S_n x)(t) = \frac{1}{2} a_0 + \sum_{k=1}^{n} (a_k \cos kt + b_k \sin kt).$$

Here the a_k, b_k are the usual Fourier coefficients of x and S_n is a minimal projection from Z to M_n where M_n is the subspace of trigonometric polynomials of degree n and Z can be any one of the spaces $L^p_{2\pi}$, $1 \le p \le \infty$ or $C_{2\pi}$.

The difficulties of this subject are such that one would not normally expect to obtain satisfactory results in a more complex setting. However, this is our intention. We shall always consider Z as a tensor product of two Banach spaces X and Y with respect to a suitable crossnorm α. Of course, our chief interest lies in the choices of the triple (X,Y,α) which give the familiar bivariate function spaces. For example, the so called least reasonable crossnorm λ given by

$$\lambda\left(\sum_{i=1}^{n} x_i \otimes y_i\right) = \sup\left\{ \left\|\sum_{i=1}^{n} \phi(x_i) y_i\right\| \ : \ \phi \in X^*, \ \|\phi\| = 1\right\}$$

has the property that $C(S)\otimes_\lambda C(T)$ is isometrically isomorphic with $C(S\times T)$ where S and T are compact Hausdorff spaces. Similarly, the so-called greatest crossnorm γ, given by

$$\gamma(z) = \sup\{ \sum_{i=1}^{n} \|x_i\| \, \|y_i\| \quad : z = \sum_{i=1}^{n} x_i \otimes y_i \}$$

has the property that $L_1(S) \otimes_\gamma L_1(T)$ is isometrically isomorphic with $L_1(S\times T)$. Here S and T must be σ-finite measure spaces. The notation $X\otimes_\alpha Y$ represents the completion of the tensor product of X and Y with respect to the α-norm, while $(X\otimes Y,\alpha)$ refers to the incompleted space. A less well-known isomorphism is that under the "p-nuclear norm",

$$\alpha_p(z) = \inf\{ \left(\sum_{i=1}^{n} \|x_i\|^p\right)^{1/p} \sup\{ \left(\sum_{i=1}^{n} |\psi(y_i)|^q\right)^{1/q} : \psi \in Y^*, \|\psi\|=1\} : z = \sum_{i=1}^{n} x_i \otimes y_i \},$$

we have $L_p(S)\otimes_{\alpha_p} L_p(T)$ is isometrically isomorphic to $L_p(S\times T)$.

The sort of question which may be posed about tensor product spaces is the one of "inheritance". An easy example is the following. Suppose G is a complemented subspace of X. Then do we have $\delta(G,X)=\delta(G\otimes_\alpha Y, X\otimes_\alpha Y)$ for all Y? Furthermore, if P is a minimal projection from X onto G, is $P\otimes I$ a minimal projection from $X\otimes_\alpha Y$ onto $G\otimes_\alpha Y$? It turns out that these questions are fairly easy to answer. Of more interest are the subspaces of $X\otimes_\alpha Y$ of the form $X\otimes_\alpha H + G\otimes_\alpha Y$. Now if P is minimal from X onto G and Q is minimal from Y onto H then we might expect the "Boolean sum"

$$(P\otimes I)\oplus(I\otimes Q) = P\otimes I + I\otimes Q - P\otimes Q$$

to be minimal from $X\otimes_\alpha Y$ onto $X\otimes_\alpha H + G\otimes_\alpha Y$. There is one technicality that arises with all questions of this type. If G is a subspace of X, the process of forming $G\otimes_\alpha Y$ from $(G\otimes Y,\alpha)$ by taking the completion may not produce a closed subspace of $X\otimes_\alpha Y$. Indeed the following theorem shows such an occurrence to be rather rare for the γ-norm.

<u>1.1 THEOREM</u> : Suppose Y has the property that wherever G is a closed subspace of a Banach space X then $G\otimes_\gamma Y$ is a closed subspace of $X\otimes_\gamma Y$. Then Y^* is an injective Banach space.

However, if G is finite-dimensional then $(G\otimes Y,\alpha)$ and $G\otimes_\alpha Y$ are synonymous and the problem of subspace formation does not arise. In this case, we shall often write $G\otimes Y$ for $G\otimes_\alpha Y$. Our notation and terminology for tensor products is more or less consistent with Diestel and Uhl [2]. Other good sources are

Schatten [11] and Gilbert and Leih [4].

2. The subspace $G\otimes_\alpha Y$

In this section we shall present briefly the elementary situation. We shall need to assume that α is a reasonable uniform crossnorm. That is, if S and T are bounded linear operators from X to X and Y to Y respectively then $S\otimes T$ (defined in the usual way) is a bounded linear operator from $X\otimes_\alpha Y$ to $X\otimes_\alpha Y$ with $\|S\otimes T\| = \|S\|\ \|T\|$. We define mappings

$$e_y : X \to X\otimes Y, \quad r_\psi : X\otimes Y \to X \quad \text{by}$$

$$e_y(x) = x\otimes y \quad \text{and} \quad r_\psi(x\otimes y) = x\psi(y)\ .$$

Here y is a fixed member of Y, ψ is a fixed member of Y^* and the mapping r_ψ is extended by linearity to $X\otimes Y$. It is then easy to see that $\|e_y\| = \|y\|$. Using the fact that α is a reasonable crossnorm it follows that $\|r_\psi\| = \|\psi\|$.

Now suppose $G\otimes_\alpha Y$ is a complemented subspace of $(X\otimes Y,\alpha)$. Take $R : X\otimes Y \to G\otimes_\alpha Y$ where R is a projection. Then it is easily seen that $P = r_\psi R\, e_y$ is a projection from X onto G. Furthermore, if $\|y\| = \|\psi\| = \psi(y) = 1$ then $\|P\otimes I\| \leq \|R\|$. This gives us a result of Franchetti and Cheney [3].

2.1 THEOREM : Let $G\otimes_\alpha Y$ be a complemented subspace of $X\otimes_\alpha Y$ where α is a uniform reasonable crossnorm. Then $\delta(G\otimes_\alpha Y, X\otimes_\alpha Y) = \delta(G,X)$. Furthermore, if P is a minimal projection from X onto Y, then $P\otimes I$ is a minimal projection from $X\otimes_\alpha Y$ onto $G\otimes_\alpha Y$.

3. The Subspace $X\otimes_\alpha H + G\otimes_\alpha Y$

In 1983 Jameson and Pinkus [9] showed that $\delta(C(S)+C(T),C(S\times T)) = 3$ and exhibited a minimal projection, viz

$$(Pz)(s,t) = z(s,t_0) + z(s_0,t) - z(s_0,t_0)$$

where (s_0,t_0) is a fixed point in $S\times T$, and S,T are compact Hausdorff spaces. This result falls within the scope of this section, since if we write π_n for the subspace of $C(S)$ or $C(T)$ consisting of polynomials of degree n, then $C(S) + C(T)$ is better written as $C(S)\otimes\pi_0 + \pi_0\otimes C(T)$. By the isomorphism mentioned in section 1 we have $C(S\times T) = C(S)\otimes_\lambda C(T)$ and so the above result may be written

$$\delta(C(S)\otimes\pi_0 + \pi_0\otimes C(T),\ C(S\times T)) = 3\ .$$

In [6], Halton and Light showed the analogous result in L_1 : $\delta(L_1(S)\otimes\pi_0 + \pi_0\otimes L_1(T),\ L_1(S\times T)) = 3$. Here, and throughout this section S and T will denote either compact Hausdorff spaces or finite non-atomic measure spaces - the choice being obvious from the context.

Franchetti and Cheney [3], improved the result of Jameson and Pinkus by showing that if G and H were finite-dimensional subspaces of $C(S)$ and $C(T)$ respectively and if each contained the constant functions then $\delta(C(S)\otimes H + G\otimes C(T),\ C(S\times T)) \geqq 3$. In particular, this shows that $\delta(C(S)\otimes\pi_1 + \pi_1\otimes C(T),\ C(S\times T)) = 3$. Again Halton and Light [8] derived the corresponding L_1 result. The proof in the L_1-case turns out to be surprisingly easy compared with that of Franchetti and Cheney. It is also known, [1], that the same result holds in $L_\infty(S\times T)$. From the limited experience in $C(S\times T)$ it seems natural to conjecture that if G and H are finite-dimensional subspaces in $C(S)$ and $C(T)$ respectively, then

$$\begin{aligned}\delta(C(S)\otimes H + G\otimes C(T),\ C(S\times T)) &= \delta(G,C(S)) + \delta(H,C(T))\\ &\quad + \delta(G,C(S))\delta(H,C(T))\ .\end{aligned}$$

This is, in fact, conjecture 1 of [3]. However, Shektman (unpublished, but see [1] for details) showed that this is not the case. His example consisted of taking $S=T=[0,\frac{1}{3}] \cup \{1\}$ and $G=[g]$, $H=[h]$ where $g(s)=s$ and $h(t)=t$. Then

$$\delta(C(S)\otimes H + G\otimes C(T),\ C(S\times T)) = 1\ ,$$

and a minimal projection is given by

$$(Pz)(s,t)=z(1,t)g(s) + z(s,1)h(t)-z(1,1)g(s)h(t)\ .$$

All these results except Shektman's have their roots in the theorems about projections on spaces of $n\times n$ matrices although it is sometimes difficult to see the connection immediately. The typical subproblem about matrices is to discover the minimal projection from the set of all $n\times n$ matrices to the subspace consisting of matrices of the form $G+H$ where G is an $n\times n$ matrix constant along its rows and H is an $n\times n$ matrix constant down its columns. The choice of norm is to be one of the ℓ_p-norms, where

$$\|A\|_p = \Big(\sum_{i,j} |a_{ij}|^p\Big)^{1/p}\ , \qquad 1 \leqq p < \infty$$

or $\|A\|_\infty = \max_{i,j}|a_{ij}|$.

The papers [9] and [6] made it clear that for $p=1,2$ or ∞ the same projection is minimal. This projection can be described as the Boolean sum of two projections P_G and P_H. If $A = (a_{ij})$ then

$$(P_G A)_{ij} = \sum_{k=1}^{n} a_{ik}, \quad (P_H A)_{ij} = \sum_{k=1}^{n} a_{kj} .$$

Then we write $P = P_G \oplus P_H$ where $\oplus$ denotes the Boolean sum so that $P_G \oplus P_H = P_G + P_H - P_G P_H$.
Hence

$$(PA)_{ij} = \sum_{\ell=1}^{n} a_{i\ell} + \sum_{k=1}^{n} a_{kj} - \sum_{k,\ell=1}^{n} a_{k\ell} .$$

For $p=2$, we have the usual result that $||P|| = 1$ while for $p = 1,\infty$ the curious formula $||P|| = 3 - n^{-2}(4n-2)$ holds. The preponderance of the number 3 in so many of the previous results is due to an appropriate identification between those settings and the limiting value of $||P||$ as $n \to \infty$. One might suppose, from the fact that P is minimal for $p=1,2$ and ∞, that P is minimal for all values of p such that $1 \leqq p \leqq \infty$. This was shown in [7] to be true. Also, if the correct limiting arguments are employed, this matrix situation can be closely allied with the consideration of $L_p(S) + L_p(T)$ as a subspace of $L_p(S\times T)$. The projection P given above is associated via these same limiting arguments with the projection

$$(Qz)(s,t) = \frac{1}{\mu(S)} \int_S z(a,t)da + \frac{1}{\nu(T)} \int_T z(s,b)db - \frac{1}{\mu(S)\nu(T)} \iint_{S\times T} z(a,b)dadb ,$$

and Q is a minimal projection from $L_p(S\times T)$ onto $L_p(S)+L_p(T)$ for $1 \leqq p \leqq \infty$.

The above result was obtained more or less by direct computation. However, it is possible to utilise an "averaging theorem" due to Rudin [10]. This enables one to derive the result for $L_p(S\times T)$ directly without reference to the matrix case. A description of many of these averaging theorems, including the one by Rudin, can be found in [12]. These techniques can be employed in a rather more general setting and give, for example, that

$$\delta(C_{2\pi}\otimes M_n + M_m\otimes C_{2\pi}, C_{2\pi}\otimes_\lambda C_{2\pi}) = \delta(M_n,C_{2\pi}) + \delta(M_m,C_{2\pi}) + \delta(M_n,C_{2\pi})\delta(M_m,C_{2\pi}) .$$

Here $C_{2\pi}$ is the space of functions which are continuous on $[0,2\pi]$ and 2π-periodic. The subspace of $C_{2\pi}$ denoted by M_n is the subspace of trigonometric polynomials of degree n. In the introduction, S_n denoted the Fourier projection from $C_{2\pi}$ onto M_n. The projection

$$P = (I\otimes S_n)\oplus(S_m\otimes I) = I\otimes S_n + S_m\otimes I - S_m\otimes S_n$$

is a minimal projection from $C_{2\pi}\otimes_\lambda C_{2\pi}$ onto $C_{2\pi}\otimes M_n + M_m\otimes C_{2\pi}$. Similar results can be obtained when $C_{2\pi}$ is replaced by $L_p^{2\pi}$.

From [3] one knows that $\delta(C(S)\otimes\pi_n+\pi_m\otimes C(T),C(S\times T))$ is at least 3. However, from the known value of $\delta(\pi_n,C(S))$ one would expect this value to behave like (logn)(logm). If $S = T = [-1,1]$ then the mapping which takes $\bar{z} \in C(S\times T)$ into $\bar{z} \in C_{2\pi}\otimes_\lambda C_{2\pi}$, where $\bar{z}(\theta,\phi) = z(\cos\theta, \cos\phi)$ can be used in the usual way to show that a lower bound is

$$\delta(C(S)\otimes\pi_n + \pi_m\otimes C(T),C(S\times T)) \geqq \pi^{-4}(\pi^2(\log n+\log m)+4\log n \log m).$$

4. Open Problems

In this section we conclude by citing a few open problems. The first two are restatements of problems from [3].

4.1 PROBLEM : If G and H are finite-dimensional subspaces of X and Y respectively, when does

$$\delta(X\otimes H + G\otimes Y, X\otimes_\alpha Y) = \delta(G,X)+\delta(H,Y) + \delta(G,X)\ \delta(H,Y) ?$$

Perhaps in 4.1 we need to take $\alpha=\lambda$ or $\alpha=\gamma$. Even with $\alpha=\lambda$, Shektmann's example shows that something further is needed.

4.2 PROBLEM : With the same set-up as in 4.1 does there always exist a minimal projection from $X\otimes Y$ onto $X\otimes H + G\otimes Y$?

Some results pertaining to 4.2 are known - see Halton [5] for details. Note that when G and H are finite-dimensional then $X\otimes H + G\otimes Y$ is always complemented in $X\otimes Y$.

4.3 PROBLEM : What is the form of minimal projections from $X\otimes Y$ onto $X\otimes H + G\otimes Y$? In particular, with the setting of 4.1, is there a minimal projection of the form $(P\otimes I) \oplus (I\otimes Q)$?

Again from [5], every projection can be written in the form $P\oplus Q$ where P is a projection of $X\otimes Y$ onto $X\otimes H$ and Q is a projection of $X\otimes Y$ onto $G\otimes Y$. In the case $X\otimes_\alpha Y = C(S)\otimes_\lambda C(T) = C(S\times T)$ an affirmative answer to 4.3 would provide an affirmative answer to 4.1 for many choices S and T.

4.4 PROBLEM : If G and H are finite-dimensional subspaces of $L_p(S)$ and $L_p(T)$ respectively, and each contain the constants then is

$$\delta(L_p(S)\otimes H+G\otimes L_p(T),L_p(S\times T)) \geq \delta(L_p(S)+L_p(T),L_p(S\times T)) \ ?$$

From section 3, the answer is affirmative when $p=1,\infty$.

5. Bibliography

We do not cite an exhaustive list, although most of the important references are given. A more complete list can be found in [1].

1. Cheney, E.W. and Light, W.A. "Approximation Theory in Tensor Product Spaces", Springer Lecture Notes, Heidelberg, 1985.

2. Diestel, J. and Uhl, J.J. "Vector Measures". Math. Surveys, Vol. 15, American Math. Soc., 1977.

3. Franchetti, C. and Cheney, E.W. "Minimal projections in tensor-product spaces", J. Approx. Th. 41 (4), 1984, 367-381.

4. Gilbert, J.E. and Leih, T.J. "Factorization, tensor products and bilinear forms in Banach space theory" in "Notes in Banach Spaces", H.E. Lacey, ed., The University of Texas Press, Austin, 1980.

5. Halton, E.J. "Projections in Tensor-product spaces", Thesis, University of Lancaster, 1985.

6. Halton, E.J. and Light, W.A. "Minimal Projections in Bivariate Function Spaces", J. Approx. Th. (to appear).

7. Halton, E.J. and Light, W.A. "Minimal Projections in L_p-spaces", Proc. Camb. Phil. Soc. (1985) 97, 127-136.

8. Halton, E.J. and Light, W.A. "Projections in Tensor product spaces", Trans. Amer. Math. Soc. 287 (1) 1985, 161-165.

9. Jameson, G.J.O. and Pinkus, A. "Positive and minimal projections in function spaces", J. Approx. Th. 37 (1983), 182-195.

10. Rudin, W. "Projections on invariant subspaces", Proc. Amer. Math. Soc. 13 (1962), 429-432.

11. Schatten, R. "A Theory of cross-spaces", Princeton University Press, Princeton 1950.

12. Schempp, W. "Identities and Inequalities via Symmetrization", in "General Inequalities 3", eds: E.F. Beckenbach and W. Walter, International Series for Numerical Mathematics 64, Birkhäuser Verlag, Basel.

International Series of
Numerical Mathematics, Vol. 75

CONVERGENCE OF HERMITE-FEJÉR INTERPOLATION VIA KOROVKIN'S THEOREM

F. Locher

FB Mathematik und Informatik

Fernuniversität Hagen

1. Introduction

From the concept of Hermite-Fejér interpolation there result interpolatory proofs of the Weierstraß approximation theorem for continuous functions of one or several real variables. The one-dimensional problem was posed and solved by L. Fejér [1] in 1916 in case of Chebyshev nodes. Later on in 1930 G. Szegö [11,12] treated the case of arbitrary Jacobian nodes. About 1960 new ideas came in by the Korovkin theorems, but only for Jacobian nodes i.e. for zeros of the Jacobi polynomials $P_m^{(\alpha,\beta)}$ with $\max(\alpha,\beta) \leq 0$ where the Hermite-Fejér operator is a positive one. Shisha-Mond [9] considered in 1965 the problem of multidimensional Hermite-Fejér interpolation using Chebyshev nodes and tensor product methods. The multidimensional case was also treated in detail by Haußmann [3] and Haußmann-Pottinger [4]. Knoop [5,6] introduced a smoothing concept to enlarge the possible parameter area (α,β) of the Jacobi polynomials $P_m^{(\alpha,\beta)}$ for which one gets uniform convergence.

We show in this article that the Hermite-Fejér interpolation problem may be treated by Korovkin's theorem in all Jacobi cases with $\alpha,\beta > -1$ i.e. also for operators which are not positive in the usual sense. This is possible by introducing the concept of *asymptotic positivity*. Moreover it is shown that the convergence of the Hermite-Fejér process $F_m^{(\alpha,\beta)}$ for the test function $g_x : t \to (x-t)^2$ may be easily proved as $(F_m^{(\alpha,\beta)} g_x)(x)$ is a constant multiple of $\{P_m^{(\alpha,\beta)}(x)\}^2$. In this way we get an elementary proof for the convergence of the Hermite-Fejér interpolation process in one or several variables.

2. The Hermite-Fejér interpolation process

We start with the Jacobi polynomials $P_{m_i}^{(\alpha_i,\beta_i)}$, $i=1,\dots,k$, of degree $m_i \geq 1$ and parameters $\alpha_i,\beta_i > -1$. Let $\xi_\nu = \xi_\nu^{(m_i)}$, $\nu=1,\dots,m_i$, be the zeros of $P_{m_i}^{(\alpha_i,\beta_i)}$ in ascending order

$$-1 < \xi_1 < \dots < \xi_{m_i} < 1 \quad .$$

Then the k-dimensional Hermite-Fejér process is defined by the tensor product of the k one-dimensional Hermite-Fejér processes (cf. Sisha-Mond [10]).
We get these processes by considering functions

$$f : C([-1,1]^k) \to \mathbb{R}$$

and

$$F_{m_1,\dots,m_k} : f \to F_{m_1,\dots,m_k} f \quad ,$$

where

$$(F_{m_1,\dots,m_k} f)(x_1,\dots,x_k)$$

$$:= \sum_{\mu_1=1}^{m_1} \dots \sum_{\mu_k=1}^{m_k} f(\xi_{\mu_1}^{(m_1)},\dots,\xi_{\mu_k}^{(m_k)})\, l_{\mu_1}^{(m_k)}(x_1)\cdots l_{\mu_k}^{(m_k)}(x_k).$$

Here $l_{\mu_i}^{(m_i)}$, $\mu_i = 1,\dots, m_i$, $i=1,\dots,k$, are the one-dimensional basis polynomials of degree $2m_i-1$ to the nodes $\xi_{\mu_i}^{(m_i)}$, i.e.

$$l_{\mu_i}^{(m_i)}(x_i) := \{1- \frac{\omega''_{m_i}\left(\xi_{\mu_i}^{(m_i)}\right)}{\omega'_{m_i}\left(\xi_{\mu_i}^{(m_i)}\right)}(x_i-\xi_{\mu_i}^{(m_i)})\}\{L_{\mu_i}(x_i)\}^2 ,$$

$$\omega_{m_i}(x_i) := \prod_{\lambda=o}^{m_i} (x_i-\xi_{\mu_\lambda}^{(m_i)}) ,$$

$$L_{\mu_i}(x_i) := \frac{\omega_{m_i}(x_i)}{\omega'_{m_i}(\xi_{\mu_i}^{(m_i)})(x_i-\xi_{\mu_i}^{(m_i)})} .$$

Obviously $F_{m_1,\dots,m_k} f$ is a polynomial of k variables with degree $m_1,\dots,m_k$ respectively. The question is whether the sequence of the Hermite-Fejér polynomials $F_{m_1,\dots,m_k} f$ converges for all $f \in C([-1,1]^k)$ pointwise or uniform in the k-dimensional unit cube $[-1,1]^k$ if $m_i \to \infty$, $i=1,\dots,k$. We get these convergence results from the one dimensional case treated in the next chapter. As a consequence from one-dimensional convergence (cf. Theorem 2) there results

Theorem 1. The sequence of the Hermite-Fejér polynomials $F_{m_i,\dots,m_k} f$ converges for every $f \in C([-1,1]^k)$ to f

(1) pointwise for $|x_i|<1$, if $\alpha_i, \beta_i > -1$,

(2) uniform for $|x_i| \leq 1-\delta$, $\delta > o$, if $\alpha_i, \beta_i > -1$,

(3) uniform for $|x_i| \leq 1$, if $\alpha_i, \beta_i > -1$ and

$\max(\alpha_i, \beta_i) < o$, $i=1,\dots,k$.

We point to the fact that only the result (3) may be proved directly via the Korovkin theorem as in this case one has positive functionals resp. operators from $C([-1,1]^k)$ to the k-dimensional polynomials of degree $\sum_{\mu=1}^{k} m_\mu$.

3. Application of Korovkin's theorem

In the following we consider the one dimensional case and omit the subscript i used in the section before. To prove that the sequence $F_m \varphi$ of the one-dimensional Hermite-Fejér polynomials

$$(F_m \varphi)(x) := \sum_{\mu=1}^{m} \varphi(\xi_\mu^{(m)})\, l_{\mu o}^{(m)}(x) \quad ,$$

$$l_{\mu o}^{(m)}(x) := \left\{ 1 - \frac{\omega_m''(\xi_\mu^{(m)})}{\omega_m'(\xi_\mu^{(m)})} (x - \xi_\mu^{(m)}) \right\} \left\{ l_\mu^{(m)}(x) \right\}^2 ,$$

$$l_\mu^{(m)}(x) := \frac{\omega_m(x)}{(x-\xi_\mu^{(m)})\, \omega_m'(\xi_\mu^{(m)})} \quad ,$$

$$\omega_m(x) := \binom{m+\alpha}{m}^{-1} P_m^{(\alpha,\beta)}(x) , \quad \alpha, \beta > -1 ,$$

converges to $\varphi \in C[-1,1]$ we will apply Korovkin's theorem (cf. [13]. So we have to show that

(1) $(F_m g_x)(x) \longrightarrow g_x$ if $m \longrightarrow \infty$ for the test function

$$g_x : t \longmapsto (x-t)^2 \quad ,$$

(2) F_m is a positive operator on $C[-1,1]$,

resp.

(2') F_{mx} defined by $F_{mx}\varphi := (F_m\varphi)(x)$ are

positive funcionals on $C[-1,1]$ for all $x \in [-1,1]$.

We start with the Hermite-Fejér operator

$$H_m\varphi := F_m\varphi + \sum_{\mu=1}^{m} \varphi'(\xi_\mu^{(m)})\, l_{\mu 1}^{(m)} \quad ,$$

where

$$l_{\mu 1}^{(m)}(x) := (x-\xi_\mu^{(m)})\,\{l_\mu^{(m)}(x)\}^2 \quad .$$

Then $\quad (\dot{} := \frac{d}{dt})$

$$F_m g_x = H_m g_x - \sum_{\mu=1}^{m} \dot{g}_x\,(\xi_\mu^{(m)})\, l_{\mu 1}^{(m)}$$

and as

$$H_m g_x = g_x \;,\; (H_m g_x)(x) = g_x(x) = 0 \;,\; m \geqq 2 \;,$$

we get

$$(F_m g_x)(x) = 2\cdot\{P_m^{(\alpha,\beta)}(x)\}^2 \sum_{\mu=1}^{m} [P_m^{(\alpha,\beta)\,'}(\xi_\mu^{(m)})]^{-2} .$$

By considering the weights of Gauß-Jacobi quadrature it is seen that this sum is bounded with respect to m. So we get

$$(3.1)\quad (F_m g_x)(x) = O(1)\ \{P_m^{(\alpha,\beta)}(x)\}^2 \quad \text{as} \quad m \to \infty .$$

By a result of Szegö [11] we know that F_{mx} is a positive functional for all $x \in [-1,1]$ iff $\max(\alpha,\beta) \leq 0$. But one may show that F_{mx} can be splitted in the form

$$F_{mx} = \tilde{F}_{mx} - N_{mx} ,$$

where $\tilde{F}_{mx}$ and N_{mx} are both positive functionals on $C[-1,1]$ and

$$(3.2)\quad \|N_{mx}\| = O(1)\ \{P_m^{(\alpha,\beta)}(x)\}^2 \quad \text{as} \quad m \to \infty$$

($\|\ldots\|$: usual operator norm induced by the sup-norm of $C[-1,1]$). If $\|N_{mx}\|$ tends to zero as $m \to \infty$ we say that F_{mx} is an *asymptotically positive* functional. The estimates (3.1) and (3.2) are of the same type. By known bounds of the Jacobi polynomials (cf. Szegö [12]) we get

$$(3.3)\quad \left\{P_m^{(\alpha,\beta)}(x)\right\}^2 = o(1) \begin{cases} \text{pointwise for } |x|<1, \text{if } \alpha,\beta>-1, \\ \text{uniform for } |x|\leq 1-\delta, \delta>0, \text{if } \alpha,\beta>-1, \\ \text{uniform for } |x|\leq 1, \text{if } \alpha,\beta>-1 \\ \qquad \text{and } \max(\alpha,\beta)<0. \end{cases}$$

Now we apply (3.3) to (3.1) and (3.2). Then we may see that the Korovkin theorem may be applied in a slightly modified form to the positive functional $\tilde{F}_{mx}$. Altogether we have the following

Theorem 2. The sequence of Hermite-Fejér polynomials $F_m\varphi$ converges for every $\varphi \in C[-1,1]$ to φ

- pointwise for $|x| < 1$, if $\alpha,\beta > -1$,
- uniform for $|x| \leqq 1-\delta$, $\delta > o$, if $\alpha,\beta > -1$,
- uniform for $|x| \leqq 1$, if $\alpha,\beta > -1$ and $\max(\alpha,\beta) < o$.

4. Concluding remarks

The concept of Hermite-Fejér interpolation was generalized in several directions: It is possible to allow nodes with multiplicity four (cf. Goodenough-Mills [2], Knoop-Stockenberg [7])or to smooth the Hermite-Fejér process at the ends of the interval $[-1,1]$ in a manner which is related to the construction of generalized Gauß-Radau und Gauß-Lobatto quadrature formulae (Bouzitat formulae of the first and second kind). This was done by Knoop [5,6]. It may be shown that in the case of nodes of multiplicity four one can get an analogous representation of $\bar{F}^{(\alpha,\beta)}_{mx} g_x$ where $\bar{F}^{(\alpha,\beta)}_{mx}$ is the generalized Hermite-Fejér functional; moreover it may be shown that the functionals are asymptotically positive as $m \to \infty$

- for $|x| < 1$ if $\min(\alpha,\beta) \geqq -\frac{3}{4}$,

- for $|x| \leqq 1$ if $(\alpha,\beta) \in [-\frac{3}{4}, \frac{1}{4})^2$.

In this way there results the pointwise resp. uniform convergence of the generalized Hermite-Fejér process with nodes of multiplicity four [8].

References

[1] Fejér, L.: Über Interpolation, Nachr. Ges. Wiss. Göttingen, 66-91 (1916).

[2] Goodenough, S.J., Mills, T.M.: The asymptotic behaviour of certain interpolation polynomials. J. Approx. Theory 28, 309-316 (1980).

[3] Haußmann, W.: Tensorproduktmethoden bei mehrdimensionaler Interpolation. Math. Z. 124, 191-198 (1972).

[4] Haußmann, W., Pottinger, P.: On the construction and convergence of multivariate interpolation operators. J. Approx. Theory 19, 205-221 (1977).

[5] Knoop, H.B.: Hermite-Fejér-Interpolation mit Randbedingungen. Habilitationsschrift Duisburg (1981).

[6] Knoop, H.B.: Hermite-Fejér and higher Hermite-Fejér interpolation with boundary conditions. These proceedings (1985).

[7] Knoop, H.B., Stockenberg, B.: On Hermite-Fejér-type interpolation. Preprint 1982.

[8] Locher, F.: On Hermite-Fejér interpolation at Jacobi zeros. J. Appr. Theory (1985), to appear.

[9] Sharma, A., Tzimbalario, J.: Quasi Hermite-Fejér-type interpolation of higher order. J. Approx. Theory 13, 431-442 (1975).

[10] Shisha, O., Mond, B.: The rapidity of convergence of the Hermite-Fejér approximation to functions of one or several variables. Proc. Amer. Math. Soc. 16, 1269-1276 (1965).

[11] Szegö, G.: Über gewisse Interpolationspolynome, die zu den Jacobischen und Laguerreschen Abszissen gehören. Math. Z. 35, 579-602 (1932).

[12] Szegö, G.: Orthogonal polynomials. Amer. Math. Soc. Coll. Publ. vol. 23 (1939). Providence R.I.

[13] De Vore, R.A.: The approximation of continuous functions by positive linear operators, Lect. Notes in Math. vol. 293. Berlin-New York: Springer-Verlag 1972.

Prof. Dr. F. Locher
FB Mathematik und Informatik
Postfach 940
D-5800 Hagen 1

International Series of
Numerical Mathematics, Vol. 75

CUBATURE ERROR BOUNDS USING DEGREES OF APPROXIMATION

Eberhard Luik

Department of Mathematics
University of Tübingen
D-7400 Tübingen

1. Introduction

Error estimates for cubature rules are usually given in terms of partial derivatives (Peano-Sard) or in terms of analyticity properties (Davis-Hämmerlin). The approximation method has found little attention. This method can be refined by using biorthogonal systems (BOGS). We present these BOGS estimates both for cubature rules which are exact for P_m (the space of bivariate polynomials of total degree notgreater than m) and for cubature rules which are exact for $P_{k,l}$ (the space of bivariate polynomials with degree in x notgreater than k and degree in y notgreater than l). As BOGS there will be used bivariate Chebyshev polynomials and the Fourier coefficient functionals. Furthermore, for product rules we get another error bound by reducing the cubature error to the quadrature errors (Nikolskii) and taking the BOGS estimates for quadrature rules. As application we treat Clenshaw-Curtis product rules.

2. General Inequality

We start with a general inequality which holds for continuous linear functionals. Therefore assume we are given a normed vector space X with norm $\|\cdot\|$ and the dual space X', further a normalized biorthogonal system (BOGS)

$$(g_i, L_i)_{i=0,\dots,s} , \qquad g_i \in X \quad \text{and} \quad L_i \in X' ,$$

i. e. we have

$$L_j[g_i] \;=\; \delta_{ij} \qquad \text{for } i,j=0,\dots,s$$

(where δ_{ij} is the Kronecker symbol).

For $f \in X$ let $D_k(f)$ denote the degree of approximation with respect to the subspace $\text{span}(g_0,\dots,g_k)$:

$$D_k(f) \;:=\; \min\{\|f-p\| \;:\; p \in \text{span}(g_0,\dots,g_k)\} \quad .$$

Theorem 1. Let R be a continuous linear functional on X. Then for any $f \in X$ and any $n=0,\dots,s$ the following inequality holds (with $D_{-1}(f) := \|f\|$) :

$$|R[f]| \;\leq\; \|R\|\cdot D_n(f) \;+\; \sum_{i=0}^{n} \|L_i\|\cdot\left(D_{i-1}(f) + D_n(f)\right)\cdot|R[g_i]| \quad .$$

For the proof see Haußmann-Luik-Zeller [2]. In many applications some of the $R[g_i]$ will vanish. Especially, if we have $R[g_i] = 0$ $(i=0,\dots,k)$ for a certain $k \leq s$ we get the

Corollary. The estimate of Theorem 1 reduces to

$$|R[f]| \;\leq\; \|R\|\cdot D_n(f) \;+\; \sum_{i=k+1}^{n} \|L_i\|\cdot\left(D_{i-1}(f) + D_n(f)\right)\cdot|R[g_i]| \quad .$$

We call the above inequalities the BOGS estimates, the g_i the BOGS functions, and the L_i the BOGS functionals. In our context X will be the space of continuous functions, endowed with the maximum-norm, and for R we take the cubature error.

3. Cubature Rules

As domain of integration we take $B := [-1,1]\times[-1,1]$. $C(B)$ denotes the space of continuous functions $h : B \to \mathbb{R}$, which will be endowed with the maximum-norm:

$$\|h\| \quad := \quad \max\{|h(x)| : x \in B\} \quad .$$

Assume we are given a cubature rule of the type

$$\int_{-1}^{1}\int_{-1}^{1} h(x,y)\,dxdy \quad = \quad \sum_{i=1}^{M} w_i h(x_i,y_i) \quad + \quad R[h]$$

with real weights w_i and the nodes $(x_i,y_i) \in B$, or shortly written

$$I[h] \quad = \quad S[h] \quad + \quad R[h] \quad .$$

We can also admit weight functions in the integral expression.

The cubature error $R[\cdot]$ is a continuous linear functional on $C(B)$. That means it is an element of the dual space $C(B)'$, which is endowed with the operator norm

$$\|R\| \quad := \quad \sup\{|R[h]| \ : \ h \in C(B) \text{ and } \|h\| \le 1\} \quad .$$

In the given setting one has

$$\|R\| \quad = \quad \|I\| \quad + \quad \|S\|$$

and therefore

$$\|R\| \quad = \quad 4 \quad + \quad \sum_{i=1}^{M} |w_i| \quad .$$

Regarding the exactness of cubature rules there occur two kinds of bivariate polynomial spaces. The first is the space of polynomials with total degree notgreater than m

$$P_m \quad := \quad \text{span}(x^i y^j \ : \ 0 \le i+j \le m)$$

and the second is the space of polynomials with degree in x notgreater than k and degree in y notgreater than l

$$P_{k,l} \quad := \quad \text{span}(x^i y^j \ : \ 0 \le i \le k,\ 0 \le j \le l) \quad .$$

4. Biorthogonal Systems

We now apply the BOGS estimates both to cubature rules exact for the polynomial space P_m and to cubature rules exact for the polynomial space $P_{k,l}$.

As BOGS functions there will be used the bivariate Chebyshev polynomials

$$T_{i,j}(x,y) \quad := \quad T_i(x) \cdot T_j(y)$$

(where T_l denotes the univariate Chebyshev polynomial of the first kind). As BOGS functionals we take the functionals for the Fourier coefficients ($h \in C(B)$):

$$L_{i,j}[h] \quad := \quad \frac{c_{i,j}}{\pi^2} \cdot \int_{-1}^{1} \int_{-1}^{1} w(x,y) T_{i,j}(x,y) h(x,y) \; dxdy$$

with $\quad w(x,y) \quad := \quad (1-x^2)^{-1/2} \cdot (1-y^2)^{-1/2}$

and $\quad c_{i,j} \quad := \begin{cases} 4 & \text{if } i > 0 \text{ and } j > 0 \\ 2 & \text{if } i > 0,\ j = 0 \text{ or } i = 0,\ j > 0 \\ 1 & \text{if } i = j = 0 \end{cases} \quad .$

For the BOGS estimates the norm of the BOGS functionals is needed. In the above setting we have

$$\| L_{i,j} \| \quad = \begin{cases} 16/\pi^2 & \text{if } i > 0 \text{ and } j > 0 \\ 4/\pi & \text{if } i > 0,\ j = 0 \text{ or } i = 0,\ j > 0 \\ 1 & \text{if } i = j = 0 \end{cases} \quad .$$

Since we have a finite biorthogonal system only many of the integral functionals can be replaced by discrete point functionals. Interesting for us are such point functionals with norm lower than the norm of the above defined coefficient functionals. This will be discussed in a later work.

5. Cubature Rules Exact for P_m

Let $E_k(h)$ denote the degree of approximation to the function $h \in C(B)$ with respect to the polynomial space P_k:

$$E_k(h) \quad := \quad \min\{\|h-p\| \ : \ p \in P_k\} \qquad .$$

Assume that we have $R[p] = 0$ for all $p \in P_m$.

Theorem 2. Let $h \in C(B)$ and $r \in \mathbb{N}$. Then

$$|R[h]| \leq \|R\| \cdot E_{m+r}(h) + \frac{16}{\pi^2} \cdot \sum_{l=1}^{r} \{ (E_{m+r}(h) + E_{m+l-1}(h)) \cdot \sum_{i=0}^{m+l}{}^{*} |R[T_{m+l-i,i}]| \}$$

(where $\sum^*$ means that both the first and the last term are taken with factor $\pi/4$).

Proof. For simplicity we only consider the case $r = 1$. P_m has dimension $d := (m+2)(m+1)/2$. If $D_{d+i}(h)$, $i=1,\ldots,m+2$, denotes the degree of approximation with respect to the space

$$\text{span}(P_m; \ T_{m+1-j,j}, \ j=0,\ldots,i-1)$$

then we have

$$D_{d+i}(h) \leq E_m(h) \ , \qquad i=1,\ldots,m+1 \ ,$$

$$D_{d+m+2}(h) = E_{m+1}(h) \qquad .$$

Using the Corollary and the above mentioned relation for $\|L_{i,j}\|$ we get the assertion. □

Taking $r = 0$ Theorem 2 reduces to

$$|R[h]| \leq \|R\| \cdot E_m(h) \qquad ,$$

which is the well known approximation method.

In a previous paper we have applied the BOGS estimate of Theorem 2 to Romberg cubature (see [4]).

6. Cubature Rules Exact for $P_{m,n}$

By $E_{k,l}(h)$ we denote the degree of approximation to the function $h \in C(B)$ with respect to the polynomial space $P_{k,l}$:

$$E_{k,l}(h) \quad := \quad \min\{\|h-p\| \; : \; p \in P_{k,l}\} \quad .$$

Assume that we have $R[p] = 0$ for all $p \in P_{m,n}$.

Theorem 3. Let $h \in C(B)$ and $r \in \mathbb{N}$. Then

$$|R[h]| \quad \leq \quad \|R\| \cdot E_{m+r,n+r}(h)$$
$$+ \quad \frac{16}{\pi^2} \cdot \sum_{l=1}^{r} \{ \left(E_{m+r,n+r}(h) + E_{m+l-1,n+l-1}(h) \right) \cdot K_l \}$$

with
$$K_l \quad := \quad \sum_{j=0}^{n+l}{}^{+} |R[T_{m+l,j}]| \quad + \quad \sum_{i=0}^{m+l-1}{}^{+} |R[T_{i,n+l}]|$$

($\sum^+$ means that the first term is taken with factor $\pi/4$).

The proof is similar to that of Theorem 2 and will be omitted. Taking $r = 0$ Theorem 3 reduces to

$$|R[h]| \quad \leq \quad \|R\| \cdot E_{m,n}(h) \quad ,$$

which is the ordinary approximation method.

The bivariate degrees of approximation can be estimated by univariate ones (see Scherer-Zeller [7]). Therefore we define

$$E_k^x(h;y) \quad := \quad \min\{\|h_y - p\| \; : \; p \in \Pi_k\}$$

(univariate degree of approximation to $h_y(x) := h(x,y)$ with respect to Π_k, the space of univariate polynomials of degree at most k);

$$E_k^x(h) \quad := \quad \sup\{E_k^x(h;y) \; : \; y \in [-1,1]\} \quad .$$

This is the supremum of a family of univariate degrees of approximation. In a similar way we define

$E_l^y(h;x)$ and $E_l^y(h)$.

Then one has

$$E_{k,l}(h) \le \left(E_k^x(h) + E_l^y(h)\right)\cdot\Lambda_l + E_l^y(h) \quad ,$$

$$E_{k,l}(h) \le \left(E_k^x(h) + E_l^y(h)\right)\cdot\Lambda_k + E_k^x(h) \quad ,$$

where Λ_l are the ordinary Lebesgue constants. There are examples where a logarithmic factor like Λ_l is realistic.

For the special case $h(x,y) := f(x)\cdot g(y)$ (f and g continuous) we get the inequalities

$$E_{k,l}(h) \le E_k(f)\cdot\|g\| + E_l(g)\cdot\|f\| + E_k(f)\cdot E_l(g) \quad ,$$

$$E_{k,l}(h) \ge \max\{E_k(f)\cdot\|g\|,\ E_l(g)\cdot\|f\|\} \quad ,$$

where $E_k(f)$ and $E_l(g)$ are the univariate degrees of approximation with respect to the polynomial spaces Π_k and Π_l, respectively. Lower and upper bound can only differ by a factor at most 3.

<u>Example.</u> We regard the function $h(x,y) := e^{x+y}$. In the following Table I the lower and upper bounds for the bivariate degrees of approximation $E_{k,l}(h)$ are given. The univariate degrees of approximation to $f(x) := \exp(x)$ have been computed by using the Remez exchange algorithm.

Table I.

k	l	lower bound	upper bound
1	1	7.579 (-1)	1.593 (0)
3	3	1.503 (-2)	3.008 (-2)
5	5	1.229 (-4)	2.458 (-4)
7	7	5.432 (-7)	1.086 (-6)
9	9	1.526 (-9)	3.052 (-9)

The upper bounds will be used for the BOGS estimates in a later example.

7. Tensor Product Rules

The tensor product rule is based on two quadrature formulas:

$$\int_{-1}^{1} f(x)\,dx = \sum_{i=1}^{M} a_i f(x_i) + R_x[f] ,$$

$$\int_{-1}^{1} g(y)\,dy = \sum_{j=1}^{N} b_j g(y_j) + R_y[g] .$$

We shortly write

$$I_x[f] = S_x[f] + R_x[f] \quad \text{and} \quad I_y[g] = S_y[g] + R_y[g] .$$

Then the cubature rule

$$\int_{-1}^{1}\int_{-1}^{1} h(x,y)\,dxdy = \sum_{i=1}^{M}\sum_{j=1}^{N} a_i b_j h(x_i,y_j) + R[h]$$

(or shortly $I_x I_y[h] = S_x S_y[h] + R[h]$)

is called the tensor product rule.

Here the cubature error can be described by the two quadrature errors (originally due to Nikolskii, cf. Stroud-Secrest [9], p. 72). We use the following form:

Lemma. In the given setting one has ($h \in C(B)$)

$$|R[h]| \leq \|S_x\| \cdot \|R_y[h]\| + \|I_y\| \cdot \|R_x[h]\|$$

with $\|R_y[h]\| := \sup\{|R_y[h(x,y)]| : x \in [-1,1]\}$,

$\|R_x[h]\| := \sup\{|R_x[h(x,y)]| : y \in [-1,1]\}$.

For the quadrature rules defined above we have

$$\|I_y\| = 2 \quad \text{and} \quad \|S_x\| = \sum_{i=1}^{M} |a_i| .$$

If the degree of exactness of the two quadrature rules is m and n, respectively, then for the tensor product rule there holds $R[p] = 0$ for all $p \in P_{m,n}$ and again we can apply Theorem 3.

Applying the BOGS estimates of Theorem 1 to quadrature rules (see Luik [3]) we'll take as BOGS functions the Chebyshev polynomials of the first kind

$$g_j \ := \ T_j \qquad .$$

For the BOGS functionals L_j there are several choices, in the first place the functionals for the Fourier coefficients. Then one has $\|L_j\| = 4/\pi \quad (j \geq 1)$. Important for us is that we can replace many of them by point functionals of norm 1 :

$$L_k[f] \ := \ \frac{1}{k} \cdot \sum_{i=0}^{k}{}'' (-1)^i f(z_i) \qquad (s/3 < k \leq s)$$

where the z_i are the extremal points of T_k (i. e. $z_i = \cos i\pi/k$) and $\sum''$ means that we have a "trapezoidal sum" (insert the factor 1/2 for i = 0 and for i = k).

Using these point functionals and the above mentioned Lemma we get for tensor product rules the following

Theorem 4. Assume that the quadrature rules have degrees of exactness m and n, respectively. Let $h \in C(B)$ and $q,r \in \mathbb{N}$ with $q \leq 2m$ and $r \leq 2n$. Then we have

$$|R[h]| \leq \|S_x\| \cdot \{\|R_y\| \cdot E^y_{n+r}(h) + \sum_{l=1}^{r} \big(E^y_{n+r}(h) + E^y_{n+l-1}(h)\big) \cdot |R_y[T_{n+l}]|\}$$

$$+ \|I_y\| \cdot \{\|R_x\| \cdot E^x_{m+q}(h) + \sum_{k=1}^{q} \big(E^x_{m+q}(h) + E^x_{m+k-1}(h)\big) \cdot |R_x[T_{m+k}]|\}$$

(for the definition of the occuring degrees of approximation see section 6).

Here we have only univariate degrees of approximation and quadrature remainders of the univariate Chebyshev polynomials. On the contrary to section 6, the logarithmic factors Λ_l do not appear.

Choosing q = r = 0 Theorem 4 leads to the approximation method (cf. Scherer [6])

$$|R[h]| \ \leq \ \|S_x\| \cdot \|R_y\| \cdot E^y_n(h) \ + \ \|I_y\| \cdot \|R_x\| \cdot E^x_m(h) \qquad .$$

8. Clenshaw-Curtis Product Rules

As a first application Clenshaw-Curtis product rules are considered. For simplicity we take the two quadrature rules to be the same, namely the Clenshaw-Curtis rule with an odd number $M \geq 3$ of nodes. The nodes are the extremal points of the Chebyshev polynomials of the first kind and the weights are chosen to be interpolatory (cf. Braß [1]).

For the corresponding product rule we have

$$R[T_{k,l}] = 0 \quad \text{if } k \text{ is odd or } l \text{ is odd .}$$

Using the error representation (cf. Stancu [8])

$$R[T_{k,l}] = R_y[T_l]\cdot I_x[T_k] + I_y[T_l]\cdot R_x[T_k] - R_y[T_l]\cdot R_x[T_k]$$

and the Clenshaw-Curtis quadrature remainder term for the T_j (see Braß [1], p. 145) we get the following

Lemma. For Clenshaw-Curtis product rules we have

$$|R[T_{M+1,2l}]| = |R[T_{2l,M+1}]| = \frac{2}{|4l^2-1|}\cdot\frac{16(M-1)}{(M+2)M(M-2)|M-4|}$$

for $l=0,\dots,(M-1)/2$,

$$|R[T_{M+1,M+1}]| \leq \frac{4}{M(M+2)}\cdot\frac{16(M-1)}{(M+2)M(M-2)|M-4|} + \left(\frac{16(M-1)}{(M+2)M(M-2)|M-4|}\right)^2 .$$

For $M \geq 5$ equality holds.

First we give the BOGS estimate using bivariate degrees of approximation for the case $r = 2$ (cf. Theorem 3).

Theorem 5. Let $h \in C(B)$ and $\bar{M} := (M+1)/2$. Then

$$|R[h]| \leq 8\cdot E_{M+2,M+2}(h) + L_M\cdot\left(E_{M+2,M+2}(h) + E_{M,M}(h)\right)$$

where ($\sum^+$ means that the first term is taken with factor $\pi/4$)

$$L_M := \frac{16}{\pi^2}\cdot\frac{64(M-1)}{(M+2)M(M-2)|M-4|}\cdot\left(\sum_{j=0}^{\bar{M}}{}^{+}\frac{1}{|4j^2-1|} + \frac{4(M-1)}{(M+2)M(M-2)|M-4|}\right)$$

The constant L_M depends only on the number of nodes and can easily be computed. For greater M the constant L_M is very small. For example, we have

$$L_{25} = 0.00968 , \qquad L_{75} = 0.00033 .$$

The BOGS estimate using univariate degrees of approximation (cf. Theorem 4) leads for the case $q = r = 2$ to

Theorem 6. Let $h \in C(B)$. Then

$$|R[h]| \leq 8\cdot\left(E^x_{M+2}(h) + E^y_{M+2}(h)\right)$$

$$+ K_M\cdot\left\{\left(E^x_{M+2}(h) + E^x_M(h)\right) + \left(E^y_{M+2}(h) + E^y_M(h)\right)\right\}$$

with $$K_M := \frac{32(M-1)}{(M+2)M(M-2)|M-4|} .$$

For greater M the constant K_M is very small. For example, we have

$$K_{25} = 0.00236 , \qquad K_{75} = 0.00008 .$$

There are examples such that in Theorem 6 equality holds (take $h(x,y) := T_{M+1,0}(x,y)$).

Example. We take the function $h(x,y) := e^{x+y}$. For the bivariate degrees of approximation the upper bounds of Table I are used. In the following Table II we give the BOGS estimates of Theorem 5 and Theorem 6, the error bound resulting from the approximation method (cf. the remarks to Theorem 4), and the true error (absolutely taken).

Table II.

	M = 5	M = 7
true error	1.270 (-4)	9.659 (-8)
approximation method	1.966 (-3)	8.690 (-6)
BOGS, Theorem 5	1.343 (-3)	9.252 (-7)
BOGS, Theorem 6	3.096 (-4)	2.457 (-7)

References

[1] Braß, H.: Quadraturverfahren. Vandenhoeck & Ruprecht, Göttingen 1977.

[2] Haußmann, W., Luik, E., Zeller, K.: Cubature remainder and biorthogonal systems. Internat. Ser. Numer. Math., Vol. 61 (1982), 191-200.

[3] Luik, E.: BOGS-Methoden bei der Romberg-Integration. ZAMM 64(1984), T415-T417.

[4] Luik, E.: Abschätzung des Kubaturfehlers mittels Approximationsgraden. To appear in ZAMM 65(1985).

[5] Luik, E.: Fehlerabschätzungen bei Quadratur und Kubatur auf der Grundlage von Approximationsgraden. Ph.D. Thesis, University of Tübingen 1984.

[6] Scherer, R.: Über Fehlerschranken bei Produkt-Kubatur. ZAMM 60(1980), T315-T317.

[7] Scherer, R., Zeller, K.: Bivariate polynomial approximation. Proc. of the Internat. Conf. held in Gdańsk, August 27 - 31, 1979, 621-628.

[8] Stancu, D. D.: The remainder of certain linear approximation formulas in two variables. SIAM J. Numer. Anal. 1(1964), 137-163.

[9] Stroud, A. H., Secrest, D.: Gaussian quadrature formulas. Prentice-Hall, Englewood Cliffs, N. J., 1966.

Dr. Eberhard Luik
Department of Mathematics
University of Tübingen
Auf der Morgenstelle 10
D-7400 Tübingen
F.R.G.

International Series of
Numerical Mathematics, Vol. 75

SQUARE FUNCTIONS IN THE THEORY OF CESÀRO SUMMABILITY OF DOUBLE ORTHOGONAL SERIES

F. Móricz

Bolyai Institute, University of Szeged, Hungary

1. Preliminaries

Let (X, F, μ) be a positive measure space, $\{\varphi_i(x): i = 0,1,\ldots\}$ an orthonormal system (in abbreviation: ONS) defined on X, and $\{a_i\}$ a sequence of real numbers (coefficients). We consider the single orthogonal series

$$(1.1) \qquad \sum_{i=0}^{\infty} a_i \varphi_i(x)$$

with partial sums

$$s_m(x) = \sum_{i=0}^{m} a_i \varphi_i(x)$$

and (C,α)-means

$$\sigma_m^\alpha(x) = \frac{1}{A_m^\alpha} \sum_{i=0}^{m} A_{m-i}^\alpha a_i \varphi_i(x) \qquad (\alpha > -1),$$

where

$$A_m^\alpha = \binom{\alpha+m}{m} \qquad (m = 0,1,\ldots).$$

The following square functions play a key role in the study of a.e. $(C,\alpha > 0)$-summability of series (1.1):

$$S(x) = \{ \sum_{p=-1}^{\infty} [s_{2^p}(x) - \sigma^1_{2^p}(x)]^2 \}^{1/2},$$

$$R(x) = \{ \sum_{m=1}^{\infty} m[\sigma^1_m(x) - \sigma^1_{m-1}(x)]^2 \}^{1/2},$$

and

$$Q^\alpha(x) = \{ \sum_{m=0}^{\infty} \frac{1}{m+1} [\sigma^{\alpha-1}_m(x) - \sigma^\alpha_m(x)]^2 \}^{1/2}.$$

Here we make the following convention: for $p = -1$ by 2^p we mean 0.

Theorem A (see, e.g. [1, pp. 109-112, 118-120]). If

(1.2) $$\sum_{i=0}^{\infty} a_i^2 < \infty,$$

then

$$S(x) \in L^2 = L^2(X, F, \mu), \ R(x) \in L^2, \text{ and } Q^\alpha(x) \in L^2 \ (\alpha > 1/2).$$

From here it follows immediately that, under (1.2),

(i) $s_{2^p}(x) - \sigma^1_{2^p}(x) \to 0$ a.e. as $p \to \infty$,

(ii) $\max_{2^p < m \leq 2^{p+1}} |\sigma^1_m(x) - \sigma^1_{2^p}(x)| \to 0$ a.e. as $p \to \infty$,

(iii) $\frac{1}{M+1} \sum_{m=0}^{M} [\sigma^{\alpha-1}_m(x) - \sigma^\alpha_m(x)]^2 \to 0$ a.e. as $M \to \infty$.

These statements are due in turn to Kolmogorov [4], Kaczmarz [2], and Zygmund [10], respectively.

The most important consequence of (i)-(iii) is the following

Corollary B (see, e.g. [1, p. 125]). If the condition

$$\sum_{i=0}^{\infty} a_i^2 [\log \log(i+4)]^2 < \infty$$

is satisfied, then series (1.1) is (C,α)-summable a.e. for every $\alpha > 0$.

The logarithm is to the base 2 in this paper.

Our goal is to extend the above square functions from single orthogonal series to double ones and in this way to obtain the corresponding theorems.

2. Extension of $S(x)$

Denote by $\{\varphi_{ik}(x): i,k = 0,1,\ldots\}$ a double ONS on X and by $\{a_{ik}\}$ a double sequence of real numbers. We consider the double orthogonal series

(2.1) $$\sum_{i=0}^{\infty} \sum_{k=0}^{\infty} a_{ik}\varphi_{ik}(x)$$

and set, for $\alpha,\beta > -1$,

$$\sigma_{mn}^{\alpha\beta}(x) = \sum_{i=0}^{m} \sum_{k=0}^{n} \frac{A_{m-i}^{\alpha}}{A_m^{\alpha}} \frac{A_{n-k}^{\beta}}{A_n^{\beta}} a_{ik}\varphi_{ik}(x).$$

In particular,

$$s_{mn}(x) = \sigma_{mn}^{00}(x) = \sum_{i=0}^{m} \sum_{k=0}^{n} a_{ik}\varphi_{ik}(x)$$

are the rectangular partial sums of (2.1),

$$\sigma_{mn}^{10}(x) = \sum_{i=0}^{m} \sum_{k=0}^{n} (1-\frac{i}{m+1}) a_{ik}\varphi_{ik}(x)$$

are the arithmetic means with respect to m, and

$$\sigma_{mn}^{11}(x) = \sum_{i=0}^{m} \sum_{k=0}^{n} (1-\frac{i}{m+1})(1-\frac{k}{n+1}) a_{ik}\varphi_{ik}(x)$$

are the arithmetic means with respect to m and n.

Part 1: (C,1,0)-summability. The relevant square function is

$$S^{10}(x) = \{\sum_{p=-1}^{\infty} [\sup_{n\geq 0} |s_{2^p,n}(x)-\sigma_{2^p,n}^{10}(x)|]^2\}^{1/2}.$$

Theorem 1. If

(2.2) $$\sum_{i=0}^{\infty} \sum_{k=0}^{\infty} a_{ik}^2 [\log(k+2)]^2 < \infty,$$

then $S^{10}(x) \in L^2$.

An immediate consequence: under (2.2),

$$s_{2^p,n}(x)-\sigma_{2^p,n}^{10}(x) \to 0 \text{ a.e. as } p \to \infty,$$

uniformly in n.

Part 2: (C,1,1)-summability. Since

$$\begin{aligned} & s_{2^p,2^q}(x)-\sigma^{11}_{2^p,2^q}(x) \\ &= [s_{2^p,2^q}(x)-\sigma^{10}_{2^p,2^q}(x)]+[s_{2^p,2^q}(x)-\sigma^{01}_{2^p,2^q}(x)] \\ &-[s_{2^p,2^q}(x)-\sigma^{10}_{2^p,2^q}(x)-\sigma^{01}_{2^p,2^q}(x)+\sigma^{11}_{2^p,2^q}(x)] \\ &= \sum_{i=0}^{2^p}\sum_{k=0}^{2^q}\left(\frac{i}{2^p+1}+\frac{k}{2^q+1}-\frac{ik}{(2^p+1)(2^q+1)}\right)a_{ik}\varphi_{ik}(x), \end{aligned}$$

the appropriate square functions are

$$S_*^{10}(x) = \{\sum_{p=-1}^{\infty}[\sup_{q\geq -1}|s_{2^p,2^q}(x)-\sigma^{10}_{2^p,2^q}(x)|]^2\}^{1/2},$$

$$S_*^{01}(x) = \{\sum_{q=-1}^{\infty}[\sup_{p\geq -1}|s_{2^p,2^q}(x)-\sigma^{01}_{2^p,2^q}(x)|]^2\}^{1/2}$$

and

$$S^{11}(x) = \{\sum_{p=0}^{\infty}\sum_{q=0}^{\infty}[\sum_{i=0}^{2^p}\sum_{k=0}^{2^q}\frac{ik}{(2^p+1)(2^q+1)}a_{ik}\varphi_{ik}(x)]^2\}^{1/2}.$$

Here $S_*^{01}(x)$ is the symmetric counterpart of $S_*^{10}(x)$.

Theorem 2. (i) If

$$\sum_{i=0}^{\infty}\sum_{k=0}^{\infty}a_{ik}^2[\log\log(k+4)]^2 < \infty, \tag{2.3}$$

then $S_*^{10}(x)\in L^2$.

(ii) If

$$\sum_{i=0}^{\infty}\sum_{k=0}^{\infty}a_{ik}^2[\log\log(i+4)]^2 < \infty,$$

then $S_*^{01}(x)\in L^2$.

(iii) If

$$\sum_{i=0}^{\infty}\sum_{k=0}^{\infty}a_{ik}^2 < \infty, \tag{2.4}$$

then $S^{11}(x)\in L^2$.

In the sequel, we do not indicate any statement separately for symmetric counterparts.

The following consequences are obvious:

(i) under (2.3),

$$s_{2^p,2^q}(x)-\sigma^{10}_{2^p,2^q}(x) \to 0 \text{ a.e. as } p \to \infty,$$

uniformly in q;

(ii) under (2.4),

$$\sum_{i=0}^{2^p} \sum_{k=0}^{2^q} \frac{ik}{(2^p+1)(2^q+1)} a_{ik}\varphi_{ik}(x) \to 0 \text{ a.e. as } \max\{p,q\} \to \infty.$$

To sum up, we obtain a Kolmogorov type statement proved in [6].

<u>Corollary</u> 3. If

$$\sum_{i=0}^{\infty} \sum_{k=0}^{\infty} a_{ik}^2 [\log \log(\max\{i,k\}+4)]^2 < \infty, \tag{2.5}$$

then

$$s_{2^p,2^q}(x)-\sigma^{11}_{2^p,2^q}(x) \to 0 \text{ a.e. as } \min\{p,q\} \to \infty.$$

As is shown in [9], Corollary 3 is the best possible in the sense that if log log t in (2.5) is replaced by any function $\lambda(t) = o(\log \log t)$ as $t \to +\infty$, then the conclusion is no longer true in general.

3. <u>Extension of</u> R(x)

<u>Part</u> 1: (C,1,0)-<u>summability</u>. Now the appropriate square function is

$$R^{10}(x) = \{ \sum_{m=1}^{\infty} m[\sup_{n\geq 0} |\sigma^{10}_{mn}(x)-\sigma^{10}_{m-1,n}(x)|]^2\}^{1/2}.$$

<u>Theorem</u> 4. If condition (2.2) is satisfied, then $R^{10}(x) \in L^2$.

Hence it follows that

$$\max_{2^p\leq m\leq 2^{p+1}} |\sigma^{10}_{mn}(x)-\sigma^{10}_{2^p,n}(x)| \leq$$

$$\leq \{ \sum_{m=2^p+1}^{2^{p+1}} m[\sigma_{mn}^{10}(x)-\sigma_{m-1,n}^{10}(x)]^2\}^{1/2} \to 0 \text{ a.e. as } p \to \infty,$$

uniformly in n. Since the condition

$$(3.1) \qquad \sum_{i=0}^{\infty} \sum_{k=0}^{\infty} a_{ik}^2[\log \log(i+4)]^2[\log(k+2)]^2 < \infty$$

implies the a.e. convergence of $s_{2^p,n}(x)$ as $\min\{p,n\} \to \infty$, Theorems 1 and 4 yield

Corollary 5. If condition (3.1) is satisfied, then series (2.1) is (C,1,0)-summable a.e.

This corollary is proved in [6] and it is the best possible result in the same sense as Corollary 3 is (see [8]).

Part 2: (C,1,1)-summability. We use the following identity: for $2^p \leq m \leq 2^{p+1}$ and $2^q \leq n \leq 2^{q+1}$

$$\sigma_{mn}^{11}(x)-\sigma_{2^p,2^q}^{11}(x)$$
$$= [\sigma_{m,2^q}^{11}(x)-\sigma_{2^p,2^q}^{11}(x)]+[\sigma_{2^p,n}^{11}(x)-\sigma_{2^p,2^q}^{11}(x)]$$
$$+[\sigma_{mn}^{11}(x)-\sigma_{2^p,n}^{11}(x)-\sigma_{m,2^q}^{11}(x)+\sigma_{2^p,2^q}^{11}(x)].$$

Accordingly, the relevant square functions are defined as follow

$$R_*^{10}(x) = \{ \sum_{m=1}^{\infty} m[\sup_{q\geq-1}|\sigma_{m,2^q}^{11}(x)-\sigma_{m-1,2^q}^{11}(x)|]^2\}^{1/2},$$

the symmetric counterpart $R_*^{01}(x)$, and

$$R^{11}(x) = \{ \sum_{m=1}^{\infty} \sum_{n=1}^{\infty} mn[\sigma_{mn}^{11}(x)-\sigma_{m-1,n}^{11}(x)$$
$$-\sigma_{m,n-1}^{11}(x)+\sigma_{m-1,n-1}^{11}(x)]^2\}^{1/2}.$$

Since

$$\sigma_{m,2^q}^{11}(x)-\sigma_{m-1,2^q}^{11}(x) = [\sigma_{m,2^q}^{10}(x)-\sigma_{m-1,2^q}^{10}(x)]$$
$$- \sum_{i=0}^{m} \sum_{k=0}^{2^q} \frac{ik}{m(m+1)(2^q+1)} a_{ik}\varphi_{ik}(x),$$

the treatment of $R_*^{10}(x)$ is based on that of $R^{10}(x)$. The treatment of $R^{11}(x)$ is simpler, thanks to the representation

$$\sigma_{mn}^{11}(x)-\sigma_{m-1,n}^{11}(x)-\sigma_{m,n-1}^{11}(x)+\sigma_{m-1,n-1}^{11}(x)$$
$$= \sum_{i=0}^{m} \sum_{k=0}^{n} \frac{ik}{m(m+1)n(n+1)} a_{ik}\varphi_{ik}(x).$$

Theorem 6. (i) If condition (2.3) is satisfied, then $R_*^{10}(x)\in L^2$.

(ii) If condition (2.4) is satisfied, then $R^{11}(x)\in L^2$.

The following consequences are obvious:

(i) under (2.3),

$$\max_{2^p\leq m\leq 2^{p+1}} |\sigma_{m,2^q}^{11}(x)-\sigma_{2^p,2^q}^{11}(x)| \to 0 \text{ a.e. as } p \to \infty,$$

uniformly in q;

(ii) under (2.4),

$$\max_{2^p\leq m\leq 2^{p+1}} \max_{2^q\leq n\leq 2^{q+1}} \left| \sum_{i=0}^{m} \sum_{k=0}^{n} \frac{ik}{m(m+1)n(n+1)} a_{ik}\varphi_{ik}(x) \right| \to 0$$

a.e. as $\max\{p,q\} \to \infty$.

Collecting together, we get a Kaczmarz type statement proved also in [6].

Corollary 7. If condition (2.5) is satisfied, then

$$\max_{2^p\leq m\leq 2^{p+1}} \max_{2^q\leq n\leq 2^{q+1}} |\sigma_{mn}^{11}(x)-\sigma_{2^p,2^q}^{11}(x)| \to 0 \text{ a.e.}$$

as $\min\{p,q\} \to \infty$.

Combining Corollaries 3 and 7 with the statement that if

$$(3.2) \qquad \sum_{i=0}^{\infty} \sum_{k=0}^{\infty} a_{ik}^2 [\log\log(i+4)]^2 [\log\log(k+4)]^2 < \infty$$

then $s_{2^p,2^q}(x)$ converges a.e. as $\min\{p,q\} \to \infty$, we come to the extension of the Menshov-Kaczmarz theorem [3, 5].

Corollary 8. If condition (3.2) is satisfied, then series (2.1) is (C,1,1)-summable a.e.

Corollary 8 is proved in [6]. Both Corollaries 7 and 8 are the best possible. (See [8, 9], respectively.)

4. Extension of $Q^{\alpha}(x)$

Part 1: (C,α,0)-summability. This time the appropriate square function is defined by

$$Q_{10}^{\alpha 0}(x) = \{ \sum_{m=0}^{\infty} \frac{1}{m+1}[\sup_{n\geq 0}|\sigma_{mn}^{\alpha-1,0}(x)-\sigma_{mn}^{\alpha 0}(x)|]^2\}^{1/2}.$$

Theorem 9. If condition (2.2) is satisfied, then $Q_{10}^{\alpha 0}(x)\in L^2$ for every $\alpha > 1/2$.

This implies that

$$\frac{1}{M+1}\sum_{m=0}^{M}[\sigma_{mn}^{\alpha-1,0}(x)-\sigma_{mn}^{\alpha 0}(x)]^2 \to 0 \text{ a.e. as } M \to \infty,$$

uniformly in n, which is the basic relation to obtain the following

Corollary 10. If condition (3.1) is satisfied, then series (2.1) is (C,α,0)-summable a.e. for every $\alpha > 0$.

This corollary is proved in [7].

Part 2: (C,α,β)-summability. We use the following identity:

$$\sigma_{mn}^{\alpha-1,\beta-1}(x)-\sigma_{mn}^{\alpha\beta}(x)$$
$$= [\sigma_{mn}^{\alpha-1,\beta}(x)-\sigma_{mn}^{\alpha\beta}(x)]+[\sigma_{mn}^{\alpha,\beta-1}(x)-\sigma_{mn}^{\alpha\beta}(x)]$$
$$+[\sigma_{mn}^{\alpha-1,\beta-1}(x)-\sigma_{mn}^{\alpha-1,\beta}(x)-\sigma_{mn}^{\alpha,\beta-1}(x)+\sigma_{mn}^{\alpha\beta}(x)].$$

Accordingly, we introduce the square functions

$$Q_{10}^{\alpha\beta}(x) = \{\sum_{m=0}^{\infty} \frac{1}{m+1}(\sup_{N\geq 0} \frac{1}{N+1} \sum_{n=0}^{N} [\sigma_{mn}^{\alpha-1,\beta}(x)-\sigma_{mn}^{\alpha\beta}(x)]^2)\}^{1/2},$$

the symmetric counterpart $Q_{01}^{\alpha\beta}(x)$, and

$$Q_{11}^{\alpha\beta}(x) = \{\sum_{m=0}^{\infty} \sum_{n=0}^{\infty} \frac{1}{(m+1)(n+1)}[\sigma_{mn}^{\alpha-1,\beta-1}(x)-\sigma_{mn}^{\alpha-1,\beta}(x) -\sigma_{mn}^{\alpha,\beta-1}(x)+\sigma_{mn}^{\alpha\beta}(x)]^2\}^{1/2}.$$

Since

$$\sigma_{mn}^{\alpha-1,\beta}(x)-\sigma_{mn}^{\alpha\beta}(x) = [\sigma_{mn}^{\alpha-1,0}(x)-\sigma_{mn}^{\alpha 0}(x)] - \sum_{i=0}^{m} \sum_{k=0}^{n} \frac{A_{m-i}^{\alpha-1}}{\alpha A_m^{\alpha}}(1-\frac{A_{n-k}^{\beta}}{A_n^{\beta}}) i a_{ik}\varphi_{ik}(x),$$

the treatment of $Q_{10}^{\alpha\beta}(x)$ is based on that of $Q_{10}^{\alpha 0}(x)$ and the following two inequalities:

$$\sum_{m=i}^{\infty} [\frac{A_{m-i}^{\alpha-1}}{A_m^{\alpha}}]^2 = O\{\frac{1}{i}\} \qquad (\alpha > \frac{1}{2})$$

and

$$\sum_{n=k}^{\infty} \frac{1}{n}[1-\frac{A_{n-k}^{\beta}}{A_n^{\beta}}]^2 = O\{1\} \qquad (\beta > 0).$$

The first inequality is well-known (see, e.g. [1, p. 110]), while the second one seems to be new [7].

The study of $Q_{11}^{\alpha\beta}(x)$ is simpler, owing to the representation

$$\sigma_{mn}^{\alpha-1,\beta-1}(x)-\sigma_{mn}^{\alpha-1,\beta}(x)-\sigma_{mn}^{\alpha,\beta-1}(x)+\sigma_{mn}^{\alpha\beta}(x) = \sum_{i=0}^{m} \sum_{k=0}^{n} \frac{A_{m-i}^{\alpha-1}}{\alpha A_m^{\alpha}} \frac{A_{n-k}^{\beta-1}}{\beta A_n^{\beta}} ik a_{ik}\varphi_{ik}(x).$$

<u>Theorem</u> 11. (i) If condition (2.3) is satisfied, then $Q_{10}^{\alpha\beta}(x)\in L^2$ for every $\alpha > 1/2$ and $\beta > 0$.

(ii) If condition (2.4) is satisfied, then $Q_{11}^{\alpha\beta}(x)\in L^2$ for every $\alpha > 1/2$ and $\beta > 1/2$.

As an immediate consequence we obtain that in the case of (i)

$$\frac{1}{(M+1)(N+1)} \sum_{m=0}^{M} \sum_{n=0}^{N} [\sigma_{mn}^{\alpha-1,\beta}(x) - \sigma_{mn}^{\alpha\beta}(x)]^2 \to 0 \quad \text{a.e.}$$

as $M \to \infty$, uniformly in N; while in the case of (ii)

$$\frac{1}{(M+1)(N+1)} \sum_{m=0}^{M} \sum_{n=0}^{N} [\sigma_{mn}^{\alpha-1,\beta-1}(x) - \sigma_{mn}^{\alpha-1,\beta}(x)$$

$$-\sigma_{mn}^{\alpha,\beta-1}(x) + \sigma_{mn}^{\alpha\beta}(x)]^2 \to 0 \text{ a.e. as } \max\{M,N\} \to \infty.$$

To sum up, we obtain a Zygmund type statement proved in [7].

Corollary 12. If condition (2.5) is satisfied, then

$$\frac{1}{(M+1)(N+1)} \sum_{m=0}^{M} \sum_{n=0}^{N} [\sigma_{mn}^{\alpha-1,\beta-1}(x) - \sigma_{mn}^{\alpha\beta}(x)]^2 \to 0 \quad \text{a.e.}$$

as $\min\{M,N\} \to \infty$, for every $\alpha > 1/2$, $\beta > 1/2$.

Finally, applying a double version of the Tauberian theorem from [10] yields

Corollary 13. If condition (3.2) is satisfied, then series (2.1) is (C,α,β)-summable a.e. for every $\alpha > 0$, $\beta > 0$.

This corollary is also proved in [7].

References

[1] Alexits, G. (1961) Convergence problems of orthogonal series (Pergamon, Oxford).

[2] Kaczmarz, S. (1925) Über die Reihen von allgemeinen Orthogonalfunktionen. Math. Ann. 96, 148-151.

[3] Kaczmarz, S. (1927) Über die Summierbarkeit der Orthogonalreihen. Math. Z. 26, 99-105.

[4] Kolmogoroff, A.N. (1924) Une contribution à l'étude de la convergence des séries de Fourier. Fund. Math. 5, 96-97.

[5] Menchoff, D.E. (1926) Sur les séries de fonctions orthogonales II. Fund. Math. 8, 56-108.

[6] Móricz, F. (1983) On the a.e. convergence of the arithmetic means of double orthogonal series. Trans. Amer. Math. Soc., submitted.

[7] Móricz, F. (1985) On the (C,$\alpha \geqq 0$,$\beta \geqq 0$)-summability of double orthogonal series. Studia Math., to appear.

[8] Móricz, F. and Tandori, K. (1985) On the a.e. divergence of the arithmetic means of double orthogonal series. Studia Math., to appear.

[9] Tandori, K. (1985) Über die Cesàrosche Summierbarkeit von mehrfachen Orthogonalreihen. Acta Sci. Math. (Szeged), to appear.

[10] Zygmund, A. (1927) Sur l'application de la première moyenne arithmétique dans la théorie des séries de fonctions orthogonales. Fund. Math. 10, 356-362.

Prof. Ferenc Móricz, Bolyai Institute, University of Szeged, 6720 Szeged, Aradi vértanuk tere 1, Hungary.

International Series of
Numerical Mathematics, Vol. 75

GENERALIZED MELKES INTERPOLATION

H. Nienhaus
Lehrstuhl für Mathematik I
University of Siegen , Siegen
West Germany

1. Introduction

An important class of rectangular finite elements are those of reduced Hermite interpolation type. In comparison with the corresponding tensor product interpolation the number of nodes is reduced; only the values of the function f and its derivatives $D_x^i D_y^j f$ $(0 \le i+j \le M)$ in the vertices of the given rectangle are used.

For every $M \in \mathbb{N}_0$ MELKES [4] proved the existence and uniqueness of two interpolants in appropriate polynomial spaces. The elements differ in the degree of conformity, i.e. the maximal degree of derivatives which are continuous when interpolating on a rectangular grid using the scheme several times. Melkes type I - interpolation is $C^{[M/2]}$-conform, Melkes type II C^0-conform. Boolean characterizations with explicit representation formulas are given by DELVOS, POSDORF [2] and BASZENSKI, DELVOS, POSDORF [1] .

The objective of the present paper is to extend these Boolean constructions in order to establish a systematic method of reduced Hermite interpolation which yields besides the two Melkes elements new C^n-conforming schemes for every n between 0 and $[M/2]$.

2. Univariate and parametric interpolation projectors

We first summarize some well known properties of univariate Hermite interpolation.

Let $H_n : C^n[0,1] \to \Pi_{2n+1}$ $(n \in \mathbb{N}_0)$ denote the univariate two point Hermite interpolation projector which is determined by

$$D^i H_n f(u) = D^i f(u) \qquad (f \in C^n[0,1]\,;\ i=0,\dots,n;\ u=0,1)\,.$$

Using the cardinal polynomials

$$\begin{aligned} p_{i,n}^{(0)}(x) &= \frac{x^i}{i!}(1-x)^{n+1} \sum_{s=0}^{n-i} \binom{n+s}{s} x^s \quad \text{and} \\ p_{i,n}^{(1)}(x) &= (-1)^i\, p_{i,n}^{(0)}(1-x) \qquad (i=0,\dots,n) \end{aligned} \tag{2.1}$$

that are orthogonal to the set of interpolation functionals we obtain the representation

$$H_n f = \sum_{i=0}^{n} \sum_{u=0}^{1} D^i f(u)\, p_{i,n}^{(u)} \qquad (\text{cf. PHILLIPS [5]})\,. \tag{2.2}$$

Moreover, we require a second class of one dimensional interpolation projectors.

For $i,n \in \mathbb{N}_0$ with $i \le n$ let $P_{i,n} : C^i[0,1] \to \operatorname{ran} P_{i,n} \subseteq \Pi_{2n+1}$ be defined by

$$P_{i,n} f = \sum_{u=0}^{1} D^i f(u)\, p_{i,n}^{(u)} \qquad (f \in C^i[0,1])\,. \tag{2.3}$$

The polynomial $P_{i,n} f$ satisfies the conditions

$$D^j P_{i,n} f(u) = \delta_{ij}\, D^j f(u) \qquad (i,j \le n;\ u=0,1)\,.$$

With respect to the projector product the absorptive conditions

$$\begin{aligned} P_{i,m} P_{j,k} &= \delta_{ij} P_{i,m} && (i,j \le k;\ i \le m)\,, \\ P_{i,m} H_n &= H_n P_{i,m} = P_{i,m} && (i \le m \le n) \quad \text{and} \\ H_m H_n &= H_n H_m = H_m && (m \le n) \end{aligned} \tag{2.4}$$

are valid.

To use these interpolation schemes for the interpolation of functions on $U = [0,1] \times [0,1]$, we define the projectors H_n^x, H_n^y, $P_{i,n}^x$ and $P_{i,n}^y$ by the method of parametric extension, so that

$$\begin{aligned}
H_n^x f(x,y) &= \sum_{i=0}^{n} \sum_{u=0}^{1} D_x^i f(u,y)\; p_{i,n}^{(u)}(x) ,\\
H_n^y f(x,y) &= \sum_{i=0}^{n} \sum_{u=0}^{1} D_y^i f(x,u)\; p_{i,n}^{(u)}(y) ,\\
P_{i,n}^x f(x,y) &= \sum_{u=0}^{1} D_x^i f(u,y)\; p_{i,n}^{(u)}(x) \quad \text{and}\\
P_{i,n}^y f(x,y) &= \sum_{u=0}^{1} D_y^i f(x,u)\; p_{i,n}^{(u)}(y) \qquad (i \le n;\; f \in C^{(n,n)}(U)) .
\end{aligned} \tag{2.5}$$

Obviously the above properties of the univariate interpolation projectors can be transferred to their parametric extensions.

Thus the projectors

$P_{0,n}^x, \ldots, P_{n,n}^x, H_n^x, \ldots, H_M^x$ and $P_{0,n}^y, \ldots, P_{n,n}^y, H_n^y, \ldots, H_M^y$

$(n \le M)$ commute and generate with respect to the binary operations operator product and Boolean sum $(P \oplus Q = P + Q - PQ)$ and the unary remainder operation $(\overline{P} = I - P)$ a Boolean algebra $\mathcal{A}_{M,n}$ of mutually commuting projectors on $C^{(M,M)}(U)$.
The order relation "$\le$" is defined as

$$P \le Q \;:\Longleftrightarrow\; PQ = QP = P \qquad (P,Q \in \mathcal{A}_{M,n}).$$

The infimum of P, Q is the product $\inf\{P,Q\} = PQ$, their supremum the Boolean sum $\sup\{P,Q\} = P \oplus Q$ (cf. GORDON [3]).

Special elements of the Boolean algebra $\mathcal{A}_{M,n}$ are the product projectors $H_k^x H_{M-k}^y$, $P_{i,n}^x H_{M-i}^y$ and $H_{M-i}^x P_{i,n}^y$ $(k=n,\ldots,M-n;\; i=0,\ldots n)$.
They satisfy just those interpolation conditions which are common to their factors, i.e.,

$$D_x^s D_y^t H_k^x H_{M-k}^y f(u,v) = D_x^s D_y^t f(u,v) \qquad (0 \le s \le k;\; 0 \le t \le M-k) ,$$

$$D_x^i D_y^t P_{i,n}^x H_{M-i}^y f(u,v) = D_x^i D_y^t f(u,v) \qquad (0 \le t \le M-i;\ i \le n), \quad (2.6)$$

$$D_x^s D_y^i H_{M-i}^x P_{i,n}^y f(u,v) = D_x^s D_y^i f(u,v) \qquad (0 \le s \le M-i;\ i \le n)$$

with $u=0,1$ and $f \in C^{(M,M)}(U)$.

3. Boolean characterization and representation formulas

In the sequal let $m = [M/2]$.
The Boolean representations of the projectors

$$\widetilde{Q}_{2M+1} = \bigoplus_{i=0}^{m} P_{i,m}^x H_{M-i}^y \oplus \bigoplus_{j=0}^{m} H_{M-j}^x P_{j,m}^y$$

of Melkes type I - interpolation (cf. [1]) and

$$B_M = \bigoplus_{i=0}^{M} H_i^x H_{M-i}^y = \bigoplus_{i=0}^{m} H_i^x H_{M-i}^y \oplus \bigoplus_{j=0}^{m} H_{M-j}^x H_j^y$$

of Melkes type II - interpolation (cf. [2]) differ in replacing the projectors H_i^x and H_i^y by $P_{i,m}^x$ and $P_{i,m}^y$ $(i=0,\ldots,m)$ in $\widetilde{Q}_{2M+1}$. We will extend this exchange to arbitrary n with $0 \le n \le m$.

<u>Definition 3.1:</u> Assume that $M,n \in \mathbb{N}_0$ and $n \le m$. We define the projector $Q_{M,n}$ of generalized Melkes interpolation as the Boolean sum

$$Q_{M,n} = \bigoplus_{i=0}^{n} P_{i,n}^x H_{M-i}^y \oplus \bigoplus_{k=n}^{M-n} H_k^x H_{M-k}^y \oplus \bigoplus_{j=0}^{n} H_{M-j}^x P_{j,n}^y \, . \qquad (3.1)$$

It is easy to verify that $Q_{M,0} = B_M$ and $Q_{M,m} = \widetilde{Q}_{2M+1}$; i.e., type I and type II - interpolation are special cases of generalized Melkes interpolation.

The construction of $Q_{M,n}$ as a Boolean sum yields the relations

$$P_{i,n}^x H_{M-i}^y Q_{M,n} = P_{i,n}^x H_{M-i}^y \qquad (0 \le i \le n) \ ,$$

$$H_k^x H_{M-k}^y Q_{M,n} = H_k^x H_{M-k}^y \qquad (n \le k \le M-n) \quad \text{and}$$

$$H_{M-j}^x P_{j,n}^y Q_{M,n} = H_{M-j}^x P_{j,n}^y \qquad (0 \le j \le n) \, .$$

Thus the interpolation properties of $Q_{M,n}$ can immediately be derived from the corresponding properties of the product projectors (see (2.6)) and we get

<u>Theorem 3.2:</u> For $f \in C^{(M,M)}(U)$ and $0 \le n \le m$ the interpolant $Q_{M,n}f$ satisfies the interpolation conditions

$$D_x^i D_y^j Q_{M,n} f(u,v) = D_x^i D_y^j f(u,v) \qquad (0 \le i+j \le M; \; u,v=0,1)$$

of reduced Hermite interpolation.

Our next objective is to establish an explicit representation of $Q_{M,n}f$. For this purpose we first determine an expression of $Q_{M,n}$ in terms of sums of the tensor product projectors $P_{i,n}^x H_{M-i}^y$, $H_k^x H_{M-k}^y$ and $H_{M-j}^x P_{j,n}^y$.

Taking into account the identities

$$\bigoplus_{i=0}^{n} P_{i,n}^x H_{M-i}^y = \sum_{i=0}^{n} P_{i,n}^x H_{M-i}^y \, ,$$

$$\bigoplus_{j=0}^{n} H_{M-j}^x P_{j,n}^y = \sum_{j=0}^{n} H_{M-j}^x P_{j,n}^y \quad \text{and}$$

$$\bigoplus_{k=n}^{M-n} H_k^x H_{M-k}^y = \sum_{k=n}^{M-n} H_k^x H_{M-k}^y - \sum_{k=n}^{M-n-1} H_k^x H_{M-k-1}^y$$

and considering the absorptive conditions for the parametrically extended projectors one obtains

$$\begin{aligned} Q_{M,n} = & \sum_{i=0}^{n} P_{i,n}^x H_{M-i}^y + \sum_{j=0}^{n} H_{M-j}^x P_{j,n}^y \\ & + \sum_{k=n}^{M-n-1} H_k^x H_{M-k}^y - \sum_{k=n}^{M-n-1} H_k^x H_{M-k-1}^y - H_n^x H_{M-n}^y \, . \end{aligned} \tag{3.2}$$

We proceed with replacing H_1^x by $\sum_{i=0}^{1} P_{i,1}^x$ and H_1^y by $\sum_{i=0}^{1} P_{i,1}^y$.

Then regrouping the terms of the sum yields

$$
\begin{aligned}
Q_{M,n} = \\
&\sum_{i=0}^{n}\sum_{j=0}^{n}\{ P^x_{i,n}P^y_{j,M-i} + P^x_{i,M-j}P^y_{j,n} - P^x_{i,n}P^y_{j,M-n} \\
&\qquad + \sum_{k=n}^{M-n-1} P^x_{i,k}P^y_{j,M-k} - \sum_{k=n}^{M-n-1} P^x_{i,k}P^y_{j,M-k-1}\} \\
&+ \sum_{i=0}^{n}\sum_{j=n+1}^{M-i}\{ P^x_{i,n}P^y_{j,M-i} + \sum_{k=n+1}^{M-j} P^x_{i,k}P^y_{j,M-k} - \sum_{k=n}^{M-j-1} P^x_{i,k}P^y_{j,M-k-1}\} \\
&+ \sum_{j=0}^{n}\sum_{i=n+1}^{M-j}\{ P^x_{i,M-j}P^y_{j,n} + \sum_{k=i}^{M-n-1} P^x_{i,k}P^y_{j,M-k} - \sum_{k=i}^{M-n-1} P^x_{i,k}P^y_{j,M-k-1}\} \\
&+ \sum_{i=n+1}^{M-n-1}\sum_{j=n+1}^{M-i}\{ \sum_{k=i}^{M-j} P^x_{i,k}P^y_{j,M-k} - \sum_{k=i}^{M-j-1} P^x_{i,k}P^y_{j,M-k-1}\}.
\end{aligned}
$$

Using the explicit representations of $P^x_{s,t}f(x,y)$ and $P^y_{s,t}f(x,y)$ (see (2.5)) we finally get

<u>Theorem 3.3:</u> For $0 \le n \le m$ and $0 \le i+j \le M$ let

$$
\Phi^{M,n}_{i,j}(x,y) :=
\begin{cases}
p^{(0)}_{i,n}(x)p^{(0)}_{j,M-i}(y) + p^{(0)}_{i,M-j}(x)p^{(0)}_{j,n}(y) - p^{(0)}_{i,n}(x)p^{(0)}_{j,M-n}(y) \\
\quad + \sum_{k=n}^{M-n-1} p^{(0)}_{i,k}(x)p^{(0)}_{j,M-k}(y) - \sum_{k=n}^{M-n-1} p^{(0)}_{i,k}(x)p^{(0)}_{j,M-k-1}(y) & (0 \le i,j \le n) \\
p^{(0)}_{i,n}(x)p^{(0)}_{j,M-i}(y) + \sum_{k=n+1}^{M-j} p^{(0)}_{i,k}(x)p^{(0)}_{j,M-k}(y) \\
\quad - \sum_{k=n}^{M-j-1} p^{(0)}_{i,k}(x)p^{(0)}_{j,M-k-1}(y) & (0 \le i \le n < j \le M-i) \\
p^{(0)}_{i,M-j}(x)p^{(0)}_{j,n}(y) + \sum_{k=i}^{M-n-1} p^{(0)}_{i,k}(x)p^{(0)}_{j,M-k}(y) \\
\quad - \sum_{k=i}^{M-n-1} p^{(0)}_{i,k}(x)p^{(0)}_{j,M-k-1}(y) & (0 \le j \le n < i \le M-j) \\
\sum_{k=i}^{M-j} p^{(0)}_{i,k}(x)p^{(0)}_{j,M-k}(y) - \sum_{k=i}^{M-j-1} p^{(0)}_{i,k}(x)p^{(0)}_{j,M-k-1}(y) \\
\qquad & (n+1 \le i \le M-n-1,\ n+1 \le j \le M-i).
\end{cases}
\tag{3.3}
$$

The representation formula for the generalized Melkes interpolant $Q_{M,n}f$ of $f \in C^{(M,M)}(U)$ is given by

$$Q_{M,n}f(x,y) = \sum_{i=0}^{M} \sum_{j=0}^{M-i} \{ D_x^i D_y^j f(0,0) \quad \Phi_{i,j}^{M,n}(x,y)$$
$$+ D_x^i D_y^j f(1,0) \; (-1)^i \quad \Phi_{i,j}^{M,n}(1-x,y)$$
$$+ D_x^i D_y^j f(0,1) \; (-1)^j \quad \Phi_{i,j}^{M,n}(x,1-y)$$
$$+ D_x^i D_y^j f(1,1) \; (-1)^{i+j} \; \Phi_{i,j}^{M,n}(1-x,1-y) \}.$$

4. Remainder projector and function precision

We now establish an explicit formula for the remainder projector $\overline{Q}_{M,n} := I - Q_{M,n}$ (I denotes the identity - operator on $C^{(M,M)}(U)$). It enables us later to construct the function precision ran $Q_{M,n}$ of generalized Melkes interpolation.

In the sum

$$\overline{Q}_{M,n} = I - \sum_{i=0}^{n} P_{i,n}^{x} H_{M-i}^{y} - \sum_{j=0}^{n} H_{M-j}^{x} P_{j,n}^{y}$$
$$- \sum_{k=n}^{M-n-1} H_k^x H_{M-k}^y + \sum_{k=n}^{M-n-1} H_k^x H_{M-k-1}^y + H_n^x H_{M-n}^y$$

(see(3.2)) we substitute $I - \overline{H}_l^x$ for H_l^x and $I - \overline{H}_l^y$ for H_l^y . Then a short calculation leads to

<u>Lemma 4.1:</u> Let $0 \le n \le m$. For the remainder projector $\overline{Q}_{M,n}$ the following representation formula is valid:

$$\overline{Q}_{M,n} = \sum_{i=0}^{n} P_{i,n}^{x} \overline{H}_{M-i}^{y} + \sum_{j=0}^{n} \overline{H}_{M-j}^{x} P_{j,n}^{y}$$
$$- \sum_{k=n}^{M-n-1} \overline{H}_k^x \overline{H}_{M-k}^y + \sum_{k=n}^{M-n-1} \overline{H}_k^x \overline{H}_{M-k-1}^y + \overline{H}_n^x \overline{H}_{M-n}^y \; . \tag{4.1}$$

Since the identity ran $P = \ker \overline{P}$ $(P \in A_{M,n})$ holds, we first study the kernel of $\overline{Q}_{M,n}$ instead of ran $Q_{M,n}$. For this purpose we need

Lemma 4.2: (i) Let $f \in \Pi_{2r+1,2M+1} + \Pi_{2M+1,2s+1}$.

Then $\overline{H}_r^x \overline{H}_s^y f = 0$.

(ii) Assume that $0 \le i \le n \le m$ and $f \in \Pi_{2M+1,2M+1}$ with $D_x^i f(u,.) \in \Pi_{2(M-i)+1}$ $(u=0,1)$. Then $P_{i,n}^x \overline{H}_{M-i}^y f = 0$.

(iii) Assume that $0 \le j \le n \le m$ and $f \in \Pi_{2M+1,2M+1}$ with $D_y^j f(\cdot,u) \in \Pi_{2(M-j)+1}$ $(u=0,1)$. Then $\overline{H}_{M-j}^x P_{j,n}^y f = 0$.

Lemma 4.2 enables us to define a polynomial space which is contained in the kernel of every product projector occuring in the representation formula of the remainder projector $\overline{Q}_{M,n}$.

Definition 4.3: Let $0 \le n \le m$. The polynomial space $T_{M,n}$ is defined as

$$T_{M,n} :=$$

$$\{\alpha(x,y) : \alpha \in \Pi_{2n+1,2M+1} + \Pi_{2M+1,2n+1} + \sum_{i=n+1}^{M-n-1} \Pi_{2i+1,2(M-i)+1} ;$$
$$D_x^k \alpha(u,\cdot),\ D_y^k \alpha(\cdot,u) \in \Pi_{2(M-k)+1} \quad (k \le n;\ u=0,1)\ \}.$$

It is easy to verify that $T_{M,n}$ enjoys the expected properties.

Let $f \in T_{M,n}$. Then we have

$$D_x^i f(u,.),\ D_y^i f(.,u) \in \Pi_{2(M-i)+1} \quad (i \le n;\ u=0,1)$$

and in view of Lemma 4.2

$$P_{i,n}^x \overline{H}_{M-i}^y f = \overline{H}_{M-i}^x P_{i,n}^y f = 0 \quad (i \le n).$$

Moreover, the condition

$$T_{M,n} \subseteq \Pi_{2n+1,2M+1} + \Pi_{2M+1,2n+1} + \sum_{i=n+1}^{M-n-1} \Pi_{2i+1,2(M-i)+1}$$

yields

$$T_{M,n} \subseteq \ker \bar{H}^x_k \bar{H}^y_{M-k-1} \subseteq \ker \bar{H}^x_k \bar{H}^y_{M-k} \qquad (n \le k \le M-n-1).$$

Thus we obtain

$$T_{M,n} \subseteq \ker \bar{Q}_{M,n} \quad (= \operatorname{ran} Q_{M,n}) .$$

It remains to show $\operatorname{ran} Q_{M,n} \subseteq T_{M,n}$, i.e., we have to establish that $\operatorname{ran} Q_{M,n}$ satisfies the two defining conditions of the polynomial space $T_{M,n}$.

I. The relations for $P,Q \in A_{M,n}$

$$\operatorname{ran} P \oplus Q = \operatorname{ran} P + \operatorname{ran} Q, \quad \operatorname{ran} PQ = \operatorname{ran} P \cap \operatorname{ran} Q$$

(cf. GORDON [3, p 230]) imply

$$\begin{aligned}\operatorname{ran} Q_{M,n} &= \operatorname{ran} \bigoplus_{i=0}^{n} P^x_{i,n} H^y_{M-i} \oplus \bigoplus_{k=n}^{M-n} H^x_k H^y_{M-k} \oplus \bigoplus_{j=0}^{n} H^x_{M-j} P^y_{j,n} \\ &= \sum_{i=0}^{n} \operatorname{ran} P^x_{i,n} H^y_{M-i} + \sum_{k=n}^{M-n} \operatorname{ran} H^x_k H^y_{M-k} + \sum_{j=0}^{n} \operatorname{ran} H^x_{M-j} P^y_{j,n} \\ &\subseteq \Pi_{2n+1,2M+1} + \Pi_{2M+1,2n+1} + \sum_{k=n+1}^{M-n-1} \Pi_{2k+1,2(M-k)+1} .\end{aligned}$$

II. Suppose that $f \in \operatorname{ran} Q_{M,n}$, $0 \le s \le n$ and $u=0,1$. Taking into account the interpolation properties of the parametrically extended projectors (2.6) and the representation formula for $Q_{M,n}$ (3.2) we get

$$D^s_x f(u,\cdot) = D^s_x H^y_{M-s} f(u,\cdot) \in \Pi_{2(M-s)+1} \quad \text{and}$$

$$D^s_y f(\cdot,u) = D^s_y H^x_{M-s} f(\cdot,u) \in \Pi_{2(M-s)+1} .$$

Thus we have constructed the space of interpolants $\operatorname{ran} Q_{M,n}$ with the aid of the representation formula for the remainder projector $\bar{Q}_{M,n}$.

<u>Theorem 4.4:</u> Let $0 \le n \le m$. The space of the interpolation functions $\operatorname{ran} Q_{M,n}$ of generalized Melkes interpolation is the polynomial space $T_{M,n}$.

From Theorem 4.4 we immediately obtain

Corollary 4.5: The interpolation scheme, associated with the projector $Q_{M,n}$, has the degree of exactness

$$\gamma(Q_{M,n}) := \max\{k \in \mathbb{N}_0 \mid Q_{M,n} x^i y^j = x^i y^j \quad 0 \le i+j \le k\} = 2M+1-n .$$

5. Conformity

Up to now we have considered the generalized Melkes interpolation for interpolating functions defined on the unit square $U = [0,1] \times [0,1]$. Nevertheless, it makes no difficulties to extend these methods to functions on arbitrary rectangles $S = [a_0, a_1] \times [b_0, b_1]$. All formulas can be adopted if we replace the cardinal polynomials $p_{i,k}^{(0)}(x)$ and $p_{i,k}^{(0)}(y)$ by $(a_1-a_0)^i p_{i,k}^{(0)}((a_1-a_0)^{-1}(x-a_0))$ and $(b_1-b_0)^i p_{i,k}^{(0)}((b_1-b_0)^{-1}(y-b_0))$. This enables us to discuss "global" properties of generalized Melkes interpolation.

Suppose that R is an arbitrary rectangular grid whose sides are parallel to the coordinate axes. Furthermore, let f be a function of class $C^{(M,M)}(R)$. By applying $Q_{M,n}$ to f on each subrectangle we obtain a piecewise polynomial $Q_{M,n}^{(R)} f$.
If $Q_{M,n}^{(R)} f$ and its derivatives $D_x^i D_y^j Q_{M,n}^{(R)} f$ $(0 \le i+j \le k)$ are continuous on R we call the interpolation scheme, associated with $Q_{M,n}$, (at least) C^k-conform.

Lemma 5.1: Let $0 \le n \le m$. The interpolation scheme, associated with the projector $Q_{M,n}$, is at least C^n-conform.

Proof: Assume that $U = [0,1] \times [0,1]$ and $f \in C^{(M,M)}(U)$. It is sufficiant to show that on each side of U the functions $D_x^i D_y^j Q_{M,n} f$ $(0 \le i+j \le n)$ are uniquely determined merely by the values of $D_x^i D_y^j f$ $(0 \leq i+j \leq M)$ in the two vertices lying on the side under consideration (cf. MELKES [4]).

Let us consider the side $x \equiv u$, $u \in \{0,1\}$.
For $0 \leq s \leq n$ we define the polynomial $g(y) := D_x^s Q_{M,n} f(u,y)$.
In view of the properties of $T_{M,n}$ g is an element of $\Pi_{2(M-s)+1}$ and therefore uniquely determined by the $2(M-s)+2$ interpolation conditions $D_y^t g(v) = D_x^s D_y^t f(u,v)$ $(0 \leq t \leq M-s;\ v=0,1)$.
It is proved by differentiation that also the derivatives $D_x^s D_y^t Q_{M,n} f(u,y)$ $(1 \leq t \leq n-s)$ are uniquely determined by the above values.

In a similar way we can show the same result for the other sides of U. □

Suppose now that the rectangular grid R is of the form $R = R_{0,0} \cup R_{1,0}$ with $R_{0,0} = [0,1]\times[0,1]$ and $R_{1,0} = [1,2]\times[0,1]$.
Furthermore, let f be a function of class $C^{(M,M)}(R)$ satisfying the conditions

$$f(0,0) = 1 ,$$

$$D_x^i D_y^j f(0,0) = 0 \quad (1 \leq i+j \leq M), \qquad D_x^i D_y^j f(0,1) = 0 \quad (0 \leq i+j \leq M),$$

$$D_x^i D_y^j f(u,v) = 0 \quad (0 \leq i+j \leq M;\ u=1,2;\ v=0,1).$$

For the interpolant $Q_{M,n}^{(R)} f$ we get

$$Q_{M,n}^{(R)} f \,|R_{0,0} \equiv \Phi_{0,0}^{M,n} \quad \text{and} \quad Q_{M,n}^{(R)} f \,|R_{1,0} \equiv 0 \quad (\text{see } (3.3)).$$

Since $D_x^{n+1} \Phi_{0,0}^{M,n}(1,.) \not\equiv 0$ we obtain that $D_x^{n+1} Q_{M,n}^{(R)} f$ is not continuous on R. This yields

<u>Theorem 5.2:</u> Let $0 \leq n \leq m$. The interpolation scheme of generalized Melkes interpolation, associated with the projector $Q_{M,n}$, is exactly C^n-conform.

In account of Corollary 4.5 we finally obtain the

Corollary 5.3: Let $0 \leq n \leq m$. For the interpolation scheme, associated with the projector $Q_{M,n}$, the degree of conformity and the degree of exactness yield together the value $2M+1$.

To given interpolation data we are now able to choose that interpolation scheme of reduced Hermite interpolation which has the appropriate degree of conformity for the particular problem. But you have to consider that a higher degree of conformity implies a lower degree of exactness.

In order to illustrate the different degrees of conformity of the interpolation schemes, defined by the projectors $Q_{4,0}$ (Melkes type II), $Q_{4,1}$ and $Q_{4,2}$ (Melkes type I), we present plots of the derivatives $D_y Q_{4,n}^{(R)} f$ $(n = 0,1,2)$ with

$f(x,y) = \exp((x-0.3)(y+1.7))$ and $R = \bigcup_{i,j=0}^{1} [i-1,i] \times [j-1,j]$.

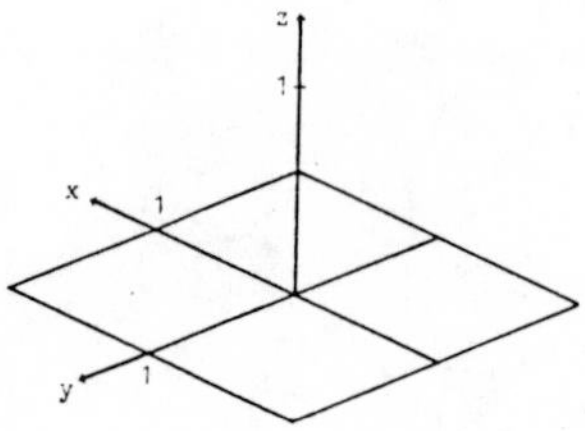

Fig. 1: Grid R

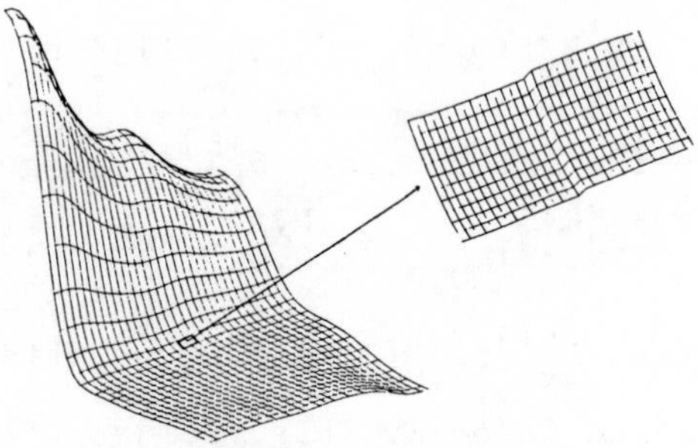

Fig. 2: $0.5\ D_y Q_{4,0}^{(R)} f$

The discontinuity of $D_y Q_{4,0}^{(R)} f$ (Fig.2) follows from the C^0-conformity of the Melkes type II element. Since the interpolation scheme, associated with $Q_{4,1}$, is C^1-conform, the piecewise polynomial $D_y Q_{4,1}^{(R)} f$ is continuous (Fig. 3). The smoothness of $D_y Q_{4,2}^{(R)} f$ (Fig. 4) results from the C^2-conformity of the Melkes type I element.

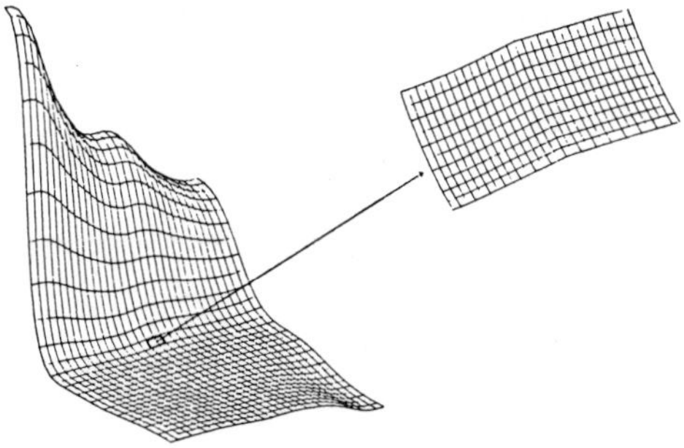

Fig. 3: $0.5\ D_y Q_{4,1}^{(R)} f$

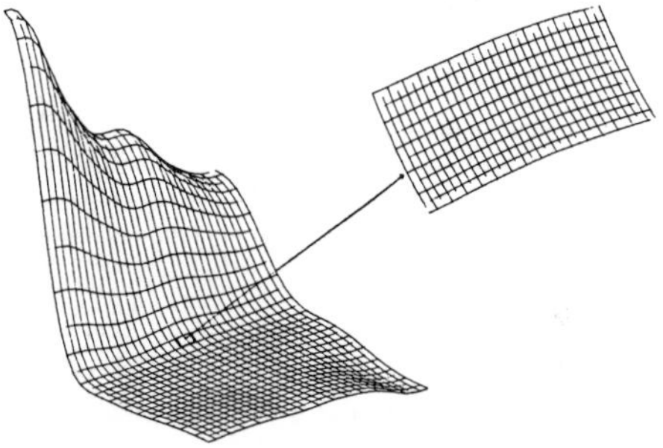

Fig. 4: $0.5\ D_y Q_{4,2}^{(R)} f$

References

1. Baszenski, G., Delvos, F.J., Posdorf, H., "Representation formulas for conforming bivariate interpolation". In: Approximation theory III. Ed. E. W. Cheney, Academic Press (1980), 193-198.

2. Delvos, F.J., Posdorf, H., "A representation formula for reduced Hermite interpolation". In: Numerische Methoden der Approximationstheorie, Bd. 4. Eds.: L. Collatz, G. Meinardus, H. Werner. ISNM 42 (1978), 124-137.

3. Gordon, W.J., "Distributive lattices and approximation of multivariate functions". Proc. Symp. Madison (Wisc.) (1969), 223-277.

4. Melkes, F., "Reduced piecewise bivariate Hermite interpolation". Num. Math. 19 (1972), 326-340.

5. Phillips, G.M., "Explicit Forms for certain Hermite approximations". BIT 13 (1973), 177-180.

Dipl.-Math. Helmut Nienhaus, Lehrstuhl für Mathematik I, Universität - Gesamthochschule Siegen, Hölderlinstr. 3, 5900 Siegen (West Germany)

International Series of
Numerical Mathematics, Vol. 75

APPROXIMATION THEORY AND ANALYSIS OF SPECTRAL METHODS (*)

Alfio Quarteroni

1. Introduction

In this paper we present some Jackson-type results concerning approximation by polynomials. They involve best approximation errors, interpolation errors, and errors arising from the truncation of Fourier expansions, in the maximum norm as well as in the norms of the weighted Sobolev spaces.
The application of these results is primarily conceived to the convergence analysis of *spectral methods*. Spectral methods (e.g., [11], [21], [15]) are today a largely used technique for the numerical approximation of (initial) boundary-value problems. They allow to achieve very high accuracy for smooth solutions, for the numerical spectral solution is a finite expansion of infinitely smooth functions over the whole physical domain.

We introduce now some basic notations. We define $\Omega = I^n$ where $I = (-1,1)$, $n \geq 1$, and we denote by $w(x) = w(x_1)w(x_2)...w(x_n)$ a weight function over Ω which is n-times the product of a given function $w(\xi)$ which is a positive integrable function on I.

We denote by $C(\overline{\Omega})$ the Banach space of continuous functions on $\overline{\Omega}$. Moreover, for any real $p \in [1,\infty)$ we set:

$$L^p_w = \{v(x) \text{ measurable on } \Omega \mid \|v\|_{L^p_w} = (\int_\Omega |v(x)|^p w(x)dx)^{1/p} < \infty\}$$

(For convenience of notation, the dependence on Ω has been dropped in this definition). If $p = 2$, L^2_w is a Hilbert space whose norm $\|.\|_w$ is induced by the inner product

$$(u,v)_w = \int_\Omega u(x)v(x)w(x)dx .$$

(*) - This research has been sponsored in part by the U.S. Army through its European Research Office under contract No. DAJA-84-C-0035.

As usual we set

$$L^\infty = \{v(x) \; measurable \; on \; \Omega \mid \|v\|_\infty = \underset{x \in \Omega}{ess\,sup} |v(x)| < \infty\}$$

For any integer $m \geq 0$ we introduce now the weighted Sobolev space (see, e.g., [20])

$$W_w^{m,p} = \{v \in L_w^p \mid D^j v \in L_w^p, \; |j| \leq m\}$$

where $j = (j_1,...,j_n)$ is a multiindex, $|j| = j_1 + \cdots + j_n$ and

$$D^j v = \frac{\partial^{|j|} v}{\partial x_1^{j_1} \cdots \partial x_n^{j_n}}$$

is the distributional derivative of order j of v (see [18]). The norm of $W_w^{m,p}$ is defined by

$$\|v\|_{m,p,w} = \Big(\sum_{|j| \leq m} \|D^j v\|_{L_w^p}^p \Big)^{1/2},$$

When $p = 2$, then $H_w^m \equiv W_w^{m,2}$ is a Hilbert space whose norm will be denoted by $\|\cdot\|_{m,w}$.

For real m, the spaces $W_w^{m,p}$ are defined by the interpolation method (e.g., [12], [2]).

Throughout this paper, $\mathbf{P}_N$ will denote the space of algebraic polynomials of degree not greater than N in each variable x_i , for $i = 1,...,n$. Moreover, C will denote a constant, independent of N, which may differ in the different contexts.

An outline of the paper is as follows. In section 2 a spectral collocation approximation to a linear model problem is reviewed. Its basic properties of accuracy and stability are investigated. This is done on the purpose of motivating the results of the approximation theory which will be presented in the forthcoming sections. In sections 3 and 4 it is shown how to get error estimates from the abstract results of section 2. To this end, several Jackson-type inequalities are given for the norms of the Sobolev spaces previously introduced. The effects on the error estimates of using the pseudo-spectral differencing technique are also discussed. This technique, which consists of replacing a function with its interpolant in $\mathbf{P}_N$ before differentiating, is the most relevant feature of any spectral collocation method.

2. Accuracy and convergence properties of spectral methods

We present here an example of numerical approximation by spectral methods of the boundary-value problem:

$$Lu = f \quad in \ \Omega \equiv I^n \ ; \ Bu = 0 \ on \ \partial\Omega_b \tag{2.1}$$

Here L is a linear differential operator in Ω, B is a linear boundary operator on $\partial\Omega_b$ which is a part (proper or not) of the boundary $\partial\Omega$ of Ω.
It will be assumed that, for some given weight function $w(x)$ of Ω, L is an unbounded operator in $X = L^2_w(\equiv L^2_w(\Omega))$ and its domain of definition $D(L)$ is a dense subspace of X. If we set

$$D_B(L) = \{v \in D(L){:}Bv = 0 \ on \ \partial\Omega_b\} \, ,$$

and if we assume that $f \in X$, then (2.1) can be restated as follows:

$$u \in D_B(L){:} \ Lu = f \ in \ X \tag{2.2}$$

Several kinds of spectral approximations can be resorted for this problem. We will focus on the ***spectral collocation*** method, which is undoubtedly more efficient than other methods such as Galerkin and Tau methods (see [11], [7],[21]). For this, we are given a family of linear operators L_N, depending on a parameter $N \in \mathbf{N}$. Tipically, L_N is obtained from L by replacing any derivative with the corresponding pseudo-spectral derivative. Each L_N maps a finite dimensional subsapce X_N of $C(\overline{\Omega})$ into $C(\overline{\Omega})$. If $f \in C(\overline{\Omega})$, then a spectral collocation approximation to (2.2) is:

$$u_N \in X_N{:} \ (L_N u_N - f, v)_N = 0 \ \ for \ all \ \ v \in Y_N \tag{2.3}$$

Here Y_N is the space of ***test functions*** and $dim \ Y_N = dim \ X_N$, while $(.,.)_N$ is a ***discrete inner product*** which approximates the inner product of L^2_w. Customarily the space of the trial functions X_N is the subset of $\mathbf{P}_N$ of those functions v for which $Bv = 0$ on $\partial\Omega$. Y_N is also a subset of $\mathbf{P}_N$, which may coincide with X_N. Let x_j and $w_j, j \in J$ (a set of multiintegers) be the nodes and the weights of a Gaussian formula in Ω, which is obtained as the n-product of a given Gaussian formula using $N + 1$ nodes in the interval I. Then, setting

$$(u,v)_N = \sum_{j \in J} u(x_j)v(x_j)w_j \tag{2.4}$$

it follows that [10]

$$(u,v)_N = (u,v)_w \ \ if \ \ u\,.\,v \in \mathbf{P}_{2N-1} \tag{2.5}$$

Problem (2.3) is then equivalent to the collocation problem:

$$\begin{cases} L_N u_N(x_j) = f(x_j) & \textit{for all } j \in J : x_j \in \bar{\Omega}\backslash\partial\Omega_b \\ Bu_N(x_k) = 0 & \textit{for all } k \in J : x_k \in \partial\Omega_b \end{cases} \tag{2.6}$$

Efficient numerical methods to solve the linear algebraic system (2.6) are based on the use of iterative techniques with preconditioning, and also multigrid techniques (see, e.g., [21],[8],[22]).

To discuss the properties of accuracy of the scheme (2.6), we confine for simplicity to one dimension, hence $\Omega = I$ from now on.

Let $\{\varphi_k\}_{k=0}^{\infty}$ be an orthonormal Hilbert basis of $L^2_w(I)$. Then the solution u of (2.2) can be written as follows:

$$u(x) = \sum_{k=0}^{\infty} \hat{u}_k \varphi_k(x), \quad \hat{u}_k = (u, \varphi_k)_w \tag{2.7}$$

Similarly, we can expand the spectral solution to (2.3) as

$$u_N(x) = \sum_{k=0}^{N} a_k \varphi_k(x), \quad a_k = (u_N, \varphi_k)_w .$$

It will be assumed that the φ_k's are the eigenfunctions of a *singular Sturm-Liouville problem* of the form:

$$-(p\,\varphi'_k)' = \lambda_k w \varphi_k \quad -1 < x < 1 , \; k \geq 0$$

where p is a differentiable function such that $p(-1) = p(1) = 0$.
If $u \in C^\infty(I)$ then (e.g. [9])

$$k^s |\hat{u}_k| \to 0 \quad \textit{as } k \to \infty, \; \textit{for all } s > 0,$$

i.e., $\hat{u}_k$ tends to zero ***faster than algebraically*** if u is infinitely smooth. If u has a finite regularity, e.g. if $u \in H^{2m}_w(I)$ for some $m \geq 1$, then (see [7])

$$(\lambda_k)^m \; |\hat{u}_k| \to 0 \quad \textit{as } k \to \infty$$

This holds provided that $pu'_{(m-1)} \to 0$ as $x \to \pm 1$, where $u_{(0)} = u$ and $u_{(m)} = \frac{1}{w}(-pu'_{(m-1)})'$. We stress that this is merely a regularity assumption on u, and does not prescribe any specific boundary condition for u. (On the contrary, if p would not vanish at the boundary, i.e., if the φ'_ks were the eigenfunctions of a ***regular Sturm-Liouville problem***, then the above requirement would give a set of unnatural boundary conditions for the function u).

Since $\lambda_k \sim k^2$ (see [9]) then

$$k^{2m} \, |\hat{u}_k| \to as \;\; k \to \infty$$

As it will be seen in next section, this entails that the remainder of order N of the series (2.7) vanishes as N^{-s} provided $u \in H_w^s$. Hopefully, this behaviour will be enjoyed by the spectral error $u - u_N$, too, under the only assumption that $u \in H_w^m$ and $Bu = 0$ on $\partial\Omega_b$.

If we want the φ_k's to be polynomials, then necessarily [7]

$$w(x) = (1-x)^{\alpha}(1+x)^{\beta} \text{ and } p(x) = (1-x)^{\alpha+1}(1+x)^{\beta+1} \, , -1 \leq \alpha,\beta \leq 1 \, .$$

Thus, the Jacobi polynomials are the only polynomials to be eigenfunctions of a singular Sturm-Liouville problem.
Among the family of Jacobi polynomials, the Chebyshev polynomials:

$$T_k(x) = \cos(k \arccos x) \, , \;\; k = 0,1,\ldots$$

which correspond to take $w(x) = (1-x^2)^{-\frac{1}{2}}$, are the most fruitful to be used in the framework of spectral approximations. Indeed, if $u_N(x) = \sum_{k=0}^{N} a_k \, T_k(x)$, an efficient numerical algorithm which uses the Fast Fourier Transform can be devised to solve the spectral problem (2.3).

In the multidimensional case, i.e. if $\Omega = I^n$ for $n \geq 2$, then the basis for $L_w^2(\Omega)$ will be given by the tensor product of the functions φ_k's. For instance for the Chebyshev polynomials we will have

$$u_N(x) = \sum_k a_k \, T_{k_1}(x_1) \ldots T_{k_n}(x_n) \, , \;\; k = (k_1, \ldots, k_n), \; 0 \leq k_i \leq N$$

The results we shown in one dimension can be generalized in the obvious way to this case.

A *convergence result* for $u - u_N$ can be established under very general assumptions on the operators L and L_N. We follow here the same approach as in [1] and [5].

Let W and V be two Hilbert spaces which are subspaces of $L_w^2(\Omega)$, and assume moreover that W is a dense subspace of $D(L)$. Typically, W is a subspace (proper or not) of H_w^k, for $k = 0$ or $k = 1$, however the theory below is fairly general.
We assume that there exist two positive constants α and β such that:

$$\sup_{u \in D_B(L)} (Lu, v)_w > 0 \;\; for \; all \;\; v \in V \, ,$$

$$\alpha \|u\|_W \le \sup_{\substack{v \in V \\ v \ne 0}} \frac{(Lu,v)_w}{\|v\|_V} \quad for\ all \quad u \in D_B(L) \ ,$$

$$|(Lu,v)_w| \le \beta \|u\|_W \|v\|_V \quad for\ all\ u \in D_B(L)\ and\ v \in V$$

Under these assumptions there is a unique solution of problem (2.2). (This is essentially an application of the closed range theorem of Banach). Furthermore, it will be assumed that there is a constant $\gamma > 0$ such that

$$\gamma \|u\|_W \le \sup_{\substack{v \in Y_N \\ v \ne 0}} \frac{(L_N u,v)_N}{\|v\|_V} \quad for\ all \quad u \in X_N$$

Then problem (2.3) has a unique solution u_N whose norm $\|u_N\|_W$ is uniformely bounded, and the following convergence result holds:

$$\|u - u_N\|_W \le (1 + \frac{\beta}{\gamma}) \|u - R_N u\|_W + \sup_{\substack{v \in Y_N \\ v \ne 0}} \frac{|(LR_N u,v)_w - (L_N R_N u,v)_N|}{\|v\|_V} + \sup_{\substack{v \in Y_N \\ v \ne 0}} \frac{|(f,v)_w - (f,v)_N|}{\|v\|_V} \tag{2.8}$$

In the above inequality $R_N u$ is any function of X_N. To get an error bound we need to investigate the behaviour of the terms on the right side of (2.8) as $N \to \infty$.

3. Truncation and best approximation errors

An optimal choice of the function $R_N u$ in (2.8) is undoubtedly that for which the inequality

$$\|u - R_N u\|_W \le C \inf_{v \in X_N} \|u - v\|_W \tag{3.1}$$

is fulfilled with a constant C independent of N. For W is a Hilbert space, taking $R_N u$ as the orthogonal projection of u upon X_N with respect to the inner product of W which induces the norm $\|.\|_W$ (or another equivalent norm) will yield (3.1). In the scale of the spaces H^r_w the best approximation error can be bounded as follows

$$\inf_{v \in X_N} \|u - v\|_{r,w} \le C N^{r-s} \|u\|_{s,w} \quad for\ all \quad r,s : 0 \le r \le s \tag{3.2}$$

where $C = C(r,s)$ (see [14] and [13]). In one dimension, the above inequality can be extended to the scale of spaces L^p_w for $p : 2 \le p < \infty$ as follows:

$$\inf_{v \in \mathbf{P}_N} \|u - v\|_{L^p_w} \le C N^{-s} \|u\|_{s,p,w} \quad \textit{for all} \quad s \ge 0 \tag{3.3}$$

C is a constant which depends on p and s. Both results (3.2) and (3.3) hold either for the Chebyshev weight and for the Legendre weight $w(x) \equiv 1$ [16]. In this latter case (3.3) can be stated for the maximum norm too, i.e., with $p = \infty$.

If (3.1) holds, then the above estimates can be used to bound the first term on the right side of (2.8).

Using (2.5) the last term of (2.8) can be controlled by the inequality [6]

$$\sup_{\substack{v \in Y_N \\ v \ne 0}} \frac{|(f,v)_w - (f,v)_N|}{\|v\|_V} \le C(\|f - P_{N-1}f\|_w + \|f - I_N f\|_w) \tag{3.4}$$

For any positive integer N, we have denoted with P_N the *orthogonal projection operator* from L^2_w upon $\mathbf{P}_N$, i.e., for any $u \in L^2_w$, $P_N u$ is the truncated of order N of the series (2.7) of u. Further, I_N is the *interpolation operator* at the Gaussian nodes x_j, $j \in J$, i.e., for any $u \in C(\overline{\Omega})$, $I_N u \in \mathbf{P}_N$ and $(I_N u)(x_j) = u(x_j)$ for all $j \in J$.

Concerning the truncation error, the following estimate holds (with $C = C(s)$)

$$\|u - P_N u\|_w \le C N^{-s} \|u\|_{s,w} \quad \textit{for all} \quad s \ge 0 \tag{3.5}$$

Similar estimates are available for higher order norms, precisely

$$\|u - P_N u\|_{r,w} \le C N^{e(r,s)} \|u\|_{s,w} \quad \textit{for all} \quad r,s : 0 \le r \le s \tag{3.6}$$

where $C = C(r,s), e(r,s) = \frac{3}{2}r - s$ if $r \le 1$ while $e(r,s) = 2r - s - \frac{1}{2}$ otherwise (see [4]).

For one space dimension and for the Chebyshev weight only, we also have

$$\|u - P_N u\|_{L^p_w} \le C N^{-s} \|u\|_{s,p,w} \quad \textit{for all} \quad s \ge 0 \textit{ and } p \in (1,\infty) \tag{3.7}$$

The above inequality holds for $p = 1$ and $p = \infty$ also (and $w \equiv 1$), provided the right hand side is multiplied by $\log N$ [16].

4. Interpolation error and pseudo-spectral differencing

Going back to the inequality (2.8), two terms are still to be bounded. The first is the interpolation error $\|f - I_N f\|_w$, which shows up in (3.4), and the latter is the second supremum on the right side of (2.8). In the scale of the spaces H^r_w we have for both Chebyshev and Legendre weights [4]

$$\|u - I_N u\|_{r,w} \le C N^{2r-s} \|u\|_{s,w} \quad \text{for } all \;\; r,s : 0 \le r \le s \,,\; s > \frac{n}{2} \tag{4.1}$$

For $r = 0$, this provides an optimal error bound for $\|f - I_N f\|_w$. The above inequality holds for all Gauss nodes, including Radau and Lobatto ones.

We are proving now how to get an estimate of the *maximum norm* of the interpolation error. We focus for instance on one space dimension and on the Chebyshev weight. Assume that $u \in H^1_w(-1,1)$, and let $R_N u$ be its orthogonal projection upon $\mathbf{P}_N$ with respect to the inner product of $H^1_w(-1,1)$. The triangle inequality gives:

$$\|u - I_N u\|_{L^\infty} \le \|u - R_N u\|_{L^\infty} + \|R_N u - I_N u\|_{L^\infty} \tag{4.2}$$

The Bernstein inequality [16]

$$\|v\|_{L^\infty} \le C\sqrt{N}\, \|v\|_w \quad \textit{for all} \;\; v \in \mathbf{P}_N$$

joined with (4.1) yields

$$\|R_N u - I_N u\|_{L^\infty} \le C\sqrt{N}\, \|R_N u - I_N u\|_w \le$$

$$C\sqrt{N}\,(\|u - I_N u\|_w + \|u - R_N u\|_w) \le C N^{\frac{1}{2}-s} \|u\|_{s,w} \quad \textit{for all} \;\; s \ge 1$$

The norm $\|u - R_N u\|_w$ has been bounded using (3.1), (3.2) and a duality argument [14]. By the Sobolev inequality we have also

$$\|u - R_N u\|_{L^\infty} \le C \|u - R_N u\|_w^{\frac{1}{2}} \|u - R_N u\|_{1,w}^{\frac{1}{2}} \le C N^{\frac{1}{2}-s} \|u\|_{s,w}$$

for all $s \ge 1$, hence we conclude that

$$\|u - I_N u\|_{L^\infty} \le C N^{\frac{1}{2}-s} \|u\|_{s,w} \quad \textit{for all} \;\; s \ge 1 \tag{4.2}$$

As it has been mentioned in section 2, for a spectral-collocation scheme the operator L_N differs from L since the derivatives are replaced by the pseudo-spectral derivatives. Thus, a control of the second term on the right side of (2.8) will be effective if a control of the error

$$D_i(u) \equiv \frac{\partial u}{\partial x_i} - \frac{\partial}{\partial x_i}(I_N u) \quad i = 1,\dots,n$$

is available. Indeed, using in a proper way the results on $u - R_N u$ and the assumptions on L and L_N allows to bound the second term on the right side of (2.8) by a constant time $\|\nabla u - I_N(\nabla u)\|_w$ (see [7]). To this purpose, a straighforward use of (4.1) yields:

$$\|D_i(u)\|_{r,w} \leq C N^{2(r+1)-s} \|u\|_{s,w} \; for\ all\ r,s : 0 \leq r \leq s\ ,\ s > \frac{n}{2} + 1$$

In one space dimension, following the same guideline for proving (4.2), it can be stated that

$$\|u' - (I_N u)'\|_{L^\infty} \leq C N^{\frac{5}{2}-s} \|u\|_{s,w} \; for\ all\ s > \frac{3}{2}$$

If u is an analytic function in $[-1,1]$ then the above error decays exponentially, precisely like $exp(-\delta N)$. Here $\delta = log r$, where r is the sum of the semiaxis of the regularity ellipse of u [19].

Remark Other Jackson-type estimate in the framework of approximation by either algebraic and trigonometric polynomials are given in references [4],[13],[16],[19],[3],[17].

References

[1] I. BABUSKA, A.K. AZIZ, Survey lectures on the mathematical foundations of the finite element method, in *The Mathematical Foundations of the Finite Element Method with Applications to Partial Differential Equations* (A.K. AZIZ, Editor), Academic Press (New York), 1972, 3-359

[2] J. BERGH, J. LOFSTROM, *Interpolation Spaces: An Introducton*, Springer, Berlin and New York, 1976.

[3] C. CANUTO, Y. MADAY, A. QUARTERONI, Analysis for the combined finite element and Fourier interpolation, *Numer. Math.*, 39, (1982), 205-220.

[4] C. CANUTO, A. QUARTERONI, Approximation results for orthogonal polynomials in Sobolev spaces, *Math. Comp*, 38, (1982), 67-86.

[5] C. CANUTO, A. QUARTERONI, Variational methods in the theoretical analysis of spectral approximations, 55-78 in reference 21.

[6] C. CANUTO, A. QUARTERONI, Spectral and pseudo-spectral methods for parabolic problems with nonperiodic boundary conditions, *Calcolo*, 18, (1981), 197-218.

[7] C. CANUTO, A. QUARTERONI, Numerical analysis of spectral methods for partial differential equations, *Publ. n. 418 of I.A.N.*, Pavia.

[8] C. CANUTO, A. QUARTERONI, Preconditioned minimal residual metods for Chebyshev spectral calculations, to appear in *J. Comput. Phys.*

[9] R. COURANT, D. HILBERT, *Methods of Mathematical Physics*, vol. I, Wiley-Interscience, New York, 1953.

[10] P. J. DAVIS, P. RABINOWITZ, *Methods of Numerical Integrations*, Academic Press, New York, 1975.

[11] D. GOTTLIEB, S.A. ORSZAG, *Numerical Analysis of Spectral Methods: Theory and Applications*, CBMS Regional Conference Series in Applied Mathematics 26, SIAM, Philadelphia, 1977.

[12] J.L. LIONS, J. PEETRE, Sur une classe d'éspaces d'interpolation, *Publ. Math. I.H.E.S.*, Paris, 19, (1954), 5-68.

[13] Y. MADAY, Analysis of spectral operators in one dimensional domains, *ICASE report*, 1985.

[14] Y. MADAY, A. QUARTERONI, Legendre and Chebyshev spectral approximations of Burgers' equation, *Numer. Math.*, 37, (1981), 321-332.

[15] R. PEYRET, T.D. TAYLOR, *Computational Methods for Fluid Flow*, Springer, New York, 1983.

[16] A. QUARTERONI, Some results of Bernstein and Jackson type for polynomial approximation in L^p-spaces, *Japan J. Appl. Math.*, 1, (1984), 173-181.

[17] A. QUARTERONI, Blending Fourier and Chebyshev interpolation, submitted to *J. Approx. Theory.*

[18] L. SCHWARTZ, *Théorie des Distributions*, Herrmann, Paris, 1973.

[19] E. TADMOR, The exponential accuracy of Fourier and Chebyshev differencing methods, to appear in *S.I.A.M. J. Numer. Anal.*

[20] H. TRIEBEL, *Interpolation Thwory, Functions Spaces, Differential Operators*, North-Holland, Amsterdam, 1978.

[21] R.G. Voigt, D. Gottlieb and M.Y. Hussaini, Eds., *Spectral Methods for Partial Differential Equations*, SIAM, Philadelphia, 1984.

[22] T.A. ZANG, Y.S. WONG, M.Y. HUSSAINI, Spectral multigrid methos for elliptic equations, *J. Comput. Phys.*, 48, (1982), 485-501.

Alfio Quarteroni
Istituto di Analisi Numerica del C.N.R.
C.so Carlo Alberto, 5
27100 Pavia, Italy

International Series of
Numerical Mathematics, Vol. 75

ON MULTIVARIATE POLYNOMIAL L^1 - APPROXIMATION TO ZERO AND RELATED COEFFICIENT INEQUALITIES

Heinz-Joachim Rack

I. Introduction : It is well known (cf. TIMAN /12/, pp.66) that among all monic univariate polynomials of degree n the n-th normalized orthogonal polynomial with respect to the weight function w_p, given by $w_p(x) = (1-x^2)^{1/p-1/2}$, is the best approximation to zero on $I = [-1,1]$ in the L^p-sense, $p \in \{1,2,\infty\}$. It is also true that among all polynomials of degree $\leq n$ with second leading coefficient equal to 1 the corresponding monic orthogonal polynomial of degree n - 1 deviates least from zero on I in the L^p-sense.

These extremal properties imply sharp inequalities for the leading and second leading coefficient of a polynomial P_n in its power form,

(1) $$P_n(x) = \sum_{k=0}^{n} a_k x^k \quad \text{(cf.e.g. SCHÖNHAGE /11/, Satz 1.2):}$$

p = 1 : Let $\|P_n\|_1 = \int_{-1}^{1} |P_n(x)|\,dx \leq 1$, then

(2) $$|a_n| \leq 2^{n-1},$$

(3) $$|a_{n-1}| \leq 2^{n-2} \qquad (n \geq 2).$$

Equality holds if $P_n = U_n/2$ resp. $P_n = U_{n-1}/2$, where U_n denotes the n-th Chebyshev polynomial of the second kind. This result is originally due to KORKINE and ZOLOTAREFF /4/; see also GERONIMUS /2/ and VAN DER CORPUT and VISSER /14/ and the references given therein.

p = 2 : Let $\|P_n\|_2 = \left(\int_{-1}^{1} (P_n(x))^2\,dx\right)^{1/2} \leq 1$, then

(4) $$|a_n| \leq 2^{-n} \binom{2n}{n} \left(\frac{2n+1}{2}\right)^{1/2},$$

(5) $$|a_{n-1}| \leq 2^{1-n} \binom{2n-2}{n-1} \left(\frac{2n-1}{2}\right)^{1/2} \qquad (n \geq 2).$$

Equality holds if $P_n = \left(\frac{2n+1}{2}\right)^{1/2} L_n$ resp. $P_n = \left(\frac{2n-1}{2}\right)^{1/2} L_{n-1}$, where L_n denotes the n-th Legendre polynomial.This result is sometimes attributed to TOEPLER /13/.

$p = \infty$: Let $\|P_n\|_\infty = \max_{x \in I} |P_n(x)| \leq 1$, then

(6) $$|a_n| \leq 2^{n-1} \quad ,$$

(7) $$|a_{n-1}| \leq 2^{n-2} \qquad (n \geq 2).$$

Equality holds if $P_n = T_n$ resp. $P_n = T_{n-1}$, where T_n denotes the n-th Chebyshev polynomial of the first kind.Inequality (6) is originally due to CHEBYSHEV, inequality (7) goes back to MARKOV (cf. SCHÖNHAGE /11/, Satz 6.12).

II.Statement of the Problem : We put forward the task to extend these classical best approximation properties and related coefficient inequalities to multivariate polynomials of total degree $\leq n$, replacing the unit interval I by the unit cube $I^r = [-1,1]^r$, $r \geq 2$.

Let $P_{n,r}$ with

(8) $$P_{n,r}(\underline{x}) = \sum_{|\underline{k}| \leq n} A_{\underline{k}} \, \underline{x}^{\underline{k}}$$

denote a polynomial in r variables of total degree $\leq n$, where

$$\underline{k} = (k_1,\dots,k_r) \in \mathbb{N}_0^r \quad , \quad |\underline{k}| = k_1 + \dots + k_r \quad ,$$

$$\underline{x} = (x_1,\dots,x_r) \in \mathbb{R}^r \quad , \quad \underline{x}^{\underline{k}} = x_1^{k_1} \cdots x_r^{k_r} \quad \text{and } A_{\underline{k}} \in \mathbb{R}.$$

Set

(9) $$\|P_{n,r}\|_1 = \int_{I^r} |P_{n,r}(\underline{x})| \, d\underline{x}$$

and denote the space of polynomials $P_{n,r}$ in (8) by $\mathbb{P}_{n,r}$, i.e.,

$$\mathbb{P}_{n,r} = \operatorname{span}\left\{ \underline{x}^{\underline{l}} : |\underline{l}| \leq n \, , \, \underline{l} \in \mathbb{N}_0^r \right\} .$$

What should be considered the "leading coefficient" resp. the "second leading coefficient" of $P_{n,r}$? Of course, every $A_{\underline{k}}$ with $|\underline{k}| = n$ resp. $|\underline{k}| = n-1$. But since, in the univariate case, a_n is the value at $x = 1$ of the n-th parabola F_n given by $F_n(x) = a_n x^n$, we may as well consider the homogeneous part of degree n resp. n-1 of $P_{n,r}$, evaluated at $\underline{x} = (1,\dots,1)$, as an extension of the concept of leading resp. second leading coefficient, i.e.,

$$(10) \qquad \sum_{|\underline{k}|=n} A_{\underline{k}} \qquad \text{resp.} \qquad \sum_{|\underline{k}|=n-1} A_{\underline{k}} \quad .$$

With this interpretation in mind we are going to establish, in particular, two generalizations both of inequality (2) and (3). The solution for the case $p = 2$ (extension of inequalities (4) and (5)) has appeared in RACK /10/; the case $p = \infty$ (extension of inequalities (6) and (7)) is treated in RACK /7/, /8/.

III. Statement of Results : One of the first contributions to the multivariate Korkine-Zolotareff theorem seems to be FROMM /1/:

THEOREM 1A

For a given $\underline{k} \in \mathbb{N}_0^r$ with $|\underline{k}| = n$, zero is the (unique) best L^1-approximation over I^r to $\bar{U}_{n,r,\underline{k}} \in \mathbb{P}_{n,r}$ (here, $\bar{U}_{n,r,\underline{k}}(\underline{x}) = \prod_{q=1}^{r} 2^{-k_q} U_{k_q}(x_q)$) from the space $\mathbb{P}_{n-1,r}$. ∎

This result can slightly be refined:

THEOREM 1B (RACK /6/; KROÒ /5/, Theorem 3)

For a given $\underline{k} \in \mathbb{N}_0^r$ with $|\underline{k}| = n$, zero is the (unique) best L^1-approximation over I^r to $\bar{U}_{n,r,\underline{k}}$ from the space $\tilde{\mathbb{P}}_{n,r} = \operatorname{span}\{\underline{x}^{\underline{l}} : |\underline{l}| \leq n,\ \underline{l} \neq \underline{k}\} \supset \mathbb{P}_{n-1,r}$.

THEOREM 2 (RACK /6/)

For a given $\underline{k} \in \mathbb{N}_0^r$ with $|\underline{k}| = n-1 \geq 1$, zero is the (unique) best L^1-approximation over I^r to $\bar{U}_{n-1,r,\underline{k}} \in \mathbb{P}_{n-1,r}$ from the space $\tilde{\mathbb{P}}_{n,r}$. ∎

Theorems 1B and 2 imply the following sharp inequalities for the leading coefficients of $P_{n,r}$ (cf.e.g. SCHÖNHAGE /11/, Satz 1.2):

COROLLARY 1

For each $\underline{k}$ with $|\underline{k}| = n$,

$$(11) \qquad |A_{\underline{k}}| \leq 2^{n-\bar{r}} \, \|P_{n,r}\|_1$$

with equality if $P_{n,r}(\underline{x}) = U_{n,r,\underline{k}}(\underline{x}) = \prod_{q=1}^{r} U_{k_q}(x_q)$. ∎

Here, and in what follows, $\bar{r}$ denotes the number of non-zero coordinates of $\underline{k}$.

COROLLARY 2

For each $\underline{k}$ with $|\underline{k}| = n-1$,

$$(12) \qquad |A_{\underline{k}}| \leq 2^{n-\bar{r}-1} \, \|P_{n,r}\|_1 \qquad (n \geq 2)$$

with equality if $P_{n,r} = U_{n-1,r,\underline{k}} \in \mathbb{P}_{n-1,r}$. ∎

We now turn to estimates for the sum of leading coefficients of $P_{n,r}$, see (10).

THEOREM 3

$$(13) \qquad \left| \sum_{|\underline{k}|=n} A_{\underline{k}} \right| \leq 2^{n-r} \binom{n+r-1}{r-1} \|P_{n,r}\|_1$$

with equality if $P_{n,r} = \sum_{|\underline{k}|=n} U_{n,r,\underline{k}}$.

THEOREM 4

$$(14) \qquad \left| \sum_{|\underline{k}|=n-1} A_{\underline{k}} \right| \leq 2^{n-r-1} \binom{n+r-2}{r-1} \|P_{n,r}\|_1 \qquad (n \geq 2)$$

with equality if $P_{n,r} = \sum_{|\underline{k}|=n-1} U_{n-1,r,\underline{k}} \in \mathbb{P}_{n-1,r}$.

Observe that inequalities (11) and (13) reduce to (2), and inequalities (12) and (14) to (3), in case of $r = 1$.

IV. Proofs : Since Theorems 1B and 2 are proved in /5/, /6/, we confine ourselves to Theorems 3 and 4. But the proof of Theorem 4 is similar to that of

Theorem 3 (see Remark i below) so that it suffices to prove Theorem 3 only. It should be pointed out, however, that the proof of Theorem 3 as given below offers also an alternative approach to inequality (11) (see Remark ii below).

We start we three lemmas, of which Lemma 3 contains the main part of the proof of Theorem 3.

LEMMA 1

(15) $$\sum_{R=0}^{2n-1} (-1)^R \sin v(t + R\pi/n) = \begin{cases} 2n \sin vt , & \text{if } v \equiv n \mod 2n \\ 0 & \text{otherwise} \end{cases} .$$

Proof : Consider the value of the (finite) scaled geometric series $e^{ivt} \sum_{R=0}^{2n-1} e^{Ri\pi(v/n - 1)}$ and split into real and imaginary parts. ∎

LEMMA 2

Set $x_q = \cos t_q$ for $q = 1,\ldots,r$. Then the expression $P_{n,r}(\cos t_1,\ldots,\cos t_r) \prod_{q=1}^{r} \sin t_q$ constitutes a r-variate sine-polynomial $S = S_{n+r,r}$ of degree $n + r$ given by

(16) $$S(\underline{t}) = \sum_{\substack{1 \leq h_1,\ldots,h_r \leq n+1 \\ r \leq |\underline{h}| \leq n+r}} B_{\underline{h}} \prod_{q=1}^{r} \sin h_q t_q \qquad (\underline{t}=(t_1,\ldots,t_r))$$

with coefficients $B_{\underline{h}}$ satisfying $(\underline{h}=(h_1,\ldots,h_r))$

(17) $$B_{\underline{h}} = 2^{-n} A_{\underline{k}}$$

provided

(18) $$|\underline{h}| = n + r \text{ and } \underline{k} = (h_1-1,\ldots,h_r-1) .$$

Proof : The inductive verification of identity (16) and of the bijective coefficient relation (17) involves some lengthy calculations with trigonometric identities and will therefore be omitted. ∎

LEMMA 3

$$(19)\qquad \int_{[0,\,2\pi]^r} |S(\underline{t})|\, d\underline{t} \geq 2^{2r-n} \binom{n+r-1}{r-1}^{-1} \left| \sum_{|\underline{k}|=n} A_{\underline{k}} \right| .$$

Proof : Let $\underline{h}' = (h_1',\dots,h_r')$ with $|\underline{h}'| = n+r$ be given. The following identities hold in view of (15), (16), (17), and (18):

$$(20)\qquad \sum_{R_1=0}^{2h_1'-1} \cdots \sum_{R_r=0}^{2h_r'-1} (-1)^{R_1+\dots+R_r} \; S(\tilde{\underline{t}}) =$$

$$(\tilde{\underline{t}}=(t_1+R_1\pi/h_1',\dots,t_r+R_r\pi/h_r'))$$

$$= \sum_{R_1=0}^{2h_1'-1} \cdots \sum_{R_r=0}^{2h_r'-1} (-1)^{R_1+\dots+R_r} \sum_{\underline{h}} B_{\underline{h}} \prod_{q=1}^{r} \sin h_q(t_q+R_q\pi/h_q')$$

$$= \sum_{\underline{h}} B_{\underline{h}} \prod_{q=1}^{r} \sum_{R_q=0}^{2h_q'-1} (-1)^{R_q} \sin h_q(t_q + R_q\pi/h_q')$$

$$= \sum_{\underline{h}} B_{\underline{h}} \prod_{q=1}^{r} \begin{cases} 2h_q' \sin h_q t_q & , \text{ if } h_q \equiv h_q' \mod 2h_q' \\ 0 & \text{otherwise} \end{cases}$$

$$= B_{\underline{h}'} \prod_{q=1}^{r} 2h_q' \sin h_q' t_q$$

$$(21) \quad = 2^{r-n} A_{\underline{k}'} \prod_{q=1}^{r} h_q' \sin h_q' t_q \qquad (\underline{k}'=(h_1'-1,\dots,h_r'-1)).$$

Thus we have (20) = (21). Integrating both sides of this equation with respect to $\underline{t}$ over the parallelepiped $\prod_{q=1}^{r} [0,\pi/h'_q]$ one obtains , on the one hand,

$$\sum_{R_1=0}^{2h'_1-1} \cdots \sum_{R_r=0}^{2h'_r-1} \int_0^{\pi/h'_1} \cdots \int_0^{\pi/h'_r} (-1)^{R_1+\ldots+R_r} S(\underline{\tilde{t}})\, d\underline{t} =$$

(Substituting $b_q = t_q + R_q\pi/h'_q$ for $q = 1,\ldots,r$)

$$(22) = \sum_{R_1=0}^{2h'_1-1} \cdots \sum_{R_r=0}^{2h'_r-1} \int_{R_1\pi/h'_1}^{(1+R_1)\pi/h'_1} \cdots \int_{R_r\pi/h'_r}^{(1+R_r)\pi/h'_r} (-1)^{R_1+\ldots+R_r} S(\underline{b})\, d\underline{b}$$

$(\underline{b}=(b_1,\ldots,b_r))$

and, on the other hand,

$$2^{r-n} A_{\underline{k}'} \prod_{q=1}^{r} (h'_q \int_0^{\pi/h'_q} \sin h'_q t_q\, dt_q) =$$

$$(23) = 2^{2r-n} A_{\underline{k}'} \qquad \left(\text{since } \int_0^{\pi/u} \sin ut\, dt = 2/u\right).$$

Hence we get (22) = (23), and this equation holds for any multi-index $\underline{h}'$ with the property $|\underline{h}'| = n + r$. Summing up over all such $\underline{h}' = \underline{h}$ and taking the absolute value in (22) and (23) yields the estimate

$$2^{2r-n} \left| \sum_{|\underline{h}|=n+r} A_{(h_1-1,\ldots,h_r-1)} \right| = 2^{2r-n} \left| \sum_{|\underline{k}|=n} A_{\underline{k}} \right| \leq$$

$$(24) \quad \leq \sum_{|\underline{h}|=n+r} \sum_{R_1=0}^{2h_1-1} \cdots \sum_{R_r=0}^{2h_r-1} \int_{R_1\pi/h_1}^{(1+R_1)\pi/h_1} \cdots \int_{R_r\pi/h_r}^{(1+R_r)\pi/h_r} |S(\underline{b})| \, d\underline{b}.$$

Note that the integration in (24) is performed over disjoint parallelepipeds which constitute a partition of $[0,2\pi]^r$, so that the upper bound (24) actually equals

$$(25) \quad \sum_{|\underline{h}|=n+r} \int_{[0,2\pi]^r} |S(\underline{b})| \, d\underline{b} = \binom{n+r-1}{r-1} \int_{[0,2\pi]^r} |S(\underline{t})| \, d\underline{t} ,$$

and this gives (19). ▰

We are now in a position to prove Theorem 3,

$$\|P_{n,r}\|_1 = \int_{I^r} |P_{n,r}(\underline{x})| \, d\underline{x}$$

$$= \int_{[0,\pi]^r} \left|P_{n,r}(\cos t_1,\ldots,\cos t_r) \prod_{q=1}^{r} \sin t_q \right| d\underline{t}$$

$$= 2^{-r} \int_{[0,2\pi]^r} |S(\underline{t})| \, d\underline{t} \geq \qquad \text{(Invoking Lemma 3)}$$

$$\geq 2^{-r}\, 2^{2r-n} \binom{n+r-1}{r-1}^{-1} \left| \sum_{|\underline{k}|=n} A_{\underline{k}} \right| ,$$

so that (13) holds true.

Equality in (13) occurs if $P_{n,r} = \hat{P}_{n,r} = \sum_{|\underline{k}|=n} U_{n,r,\underline{k}}$ as is seen by examining the estimate (24). Note in this connection that in the one-dimensional case $U_n(\cos t) = (\sin (n+1)t)/\sin t$ and hence the (n+r)-dimensional sine-polynomial S corresponding to $\hat{P}_{n,r}$ reads

$$S(\underline{t}) = \sum_{|\underline{k}|=n} \prod_{q=1}^{r} \sin (k_q+1)t_q \quad . \blacksquare$$

V. Closing Remarks : (i)

The proof of Theorem 4 is quite analogous to that of Theorem 3 and makes use of the one-to-one correspondence

$$(17') \qquad B_{\underline{h}} = 2^{1-n} A_{\underline{k}}$$

provided

$$(18') \qquad |\underline{h}| = n + r - 1 \text{ and } \underline{k} = (h_1-1,\ldots,h_r-1) \text{ , i.e., } |\underline{k}| = n-1.$$

Such a bijective relation does not hold if $|\underline{h}| \leq n + r - 2$.

(ii)

An alternative proof of (11) which does not depend on known best approximations consists in deducing, similarly as before, from the equation (23)= (22) the estimate

$$(26) \qquad 2^{2r-n} |A_{\underline{k}'}| \leq \int_{[0,2\pi]^r} |S(\underline{t})| \, d\underline{t} = 2^r \, \|P_{n,r}\|_1 \quad .$$

(iii)

Theorems 1B and 2 can slightly be modified by considering polynomial spaces supported by subsets of $\mathbb{N}_0^r$ which satisfy the so-called S-property, cf. /5/.

(iv)

In the univariate case, it is not true that U_n resp. L_n ($n \geq 3$), normalized so that their third leading coefficient is equal to 1, deviates least from zero on I in the L^p-sense ($p = 1$ resp. $p = 2$) among all P_n with the same property. But in the case $p = \infty$, the scaled polynomial T_n does keep that property as it follows from Markov's theorem (cf.e.g. SCHÖNHAGE /11/, Satz 6.12). A generalization of this fact to multivariate polynomials $P_{n,r}$ and their coefficients $A_{\underline{k}}$ with $|\underline{k}| = n - 2$ fails, as the counterexample in RACK /8/ shows. Yet Markov's theorem can completely be extended to several variables if polynomials of bounded single degrees rather than of bounded total degree are considered, see RACK /9/.

(v)

Further aspects of multivariate polynomial L^1-approximation are covered by HAUSSMANN and ZELLER /3/ and KROÓ /5/, and in the references given therein.

VI. References :

/1/ Fromm, J.: L_1-approximation to zero, Math.Z. 151 (1976), 31-33.

/2/ Geronimus, J.: On some extremal properties of polynomials, Ann.of Math. 37 (1936), 483-517.

/3/ Haußmann, W. and Zeller, K.: Blending interpolation and best L^1-approximation, Arch.Math.(Basel) 40 (1983), 545-552.

/4/ Korkine, A. and Zolotareff, G.: Sur un certain minimum, Nouv.Ann.Math.(2) 12 (1873), 337-355.

/5/ Kroó, A.: On the unicity of best L_1-approximation by polynomials of several variables, Acta Math.Hung. 42 (1983), 309-318.

/6/ Rack, H.-J.: Doctoral Dissertation, Universität Dortmund, 1982.

/7/ Rack, H.-J.: A generalization of an inequality of V.Markov to multivariate polynomials, J.Approx.Theory 35 (1982), 94-97.

/8/ Rack, H.-J.: A generalization of an inequality of V.Markov to multivariate polynomials II, J.Approx.Theory 40 (1984), 129-133.

/9/ Rack,H.-J.: Koeffizientenabschätzungen bei Polynomen in mehreren Variablen, Z.Angew.Math.Mech. 63 (1983), no.5, T371-T372.

/10/ Rack,H.-J.: On multivariate polynomial L^2-approximation to zero, Anal. Math. 10 (1984), 241-247.

/11/ Schönhage,A.: "Approximationstheorie", W.de Gruyter, Berlin, 1971.

/12/ Timan,A.: "Theory of approximation of functions of a real variable", Pergamon,Oxford, 1963 (Translated from Russian).

/13/ Toepler,A.: Notiz über eine bemerkenswerthe Eigenschaft der periodischen Reihen, Anz.Österr.Akad.Wiss.Math.-Natur.Cl.(Wien) 13 (1876), 205-209.

/14/ Van der Corput,J. and Visser,C.: Inequalities concerning polynomials and trigonometric polynomials, Indag.Math. 8 (1946) 239-247.

Dr.Heinz-Joachim Rack, Universität Dortmund, Abteilung Mathematik, Postfach 500500, D-4600 Dortmund 50 (FRG).

International Series of
Numerical Mathematics, Vol. 75
© 1985 Birkhäuser Verlag Basel

Abschätzungen von Lagrange-Quadratsummen für die Sphäre mit Hilfe gewisser Eigenwerte

M. Reimer

Wir betrachten rotationsinvariante N-dimensionale Unterräume $\mathbb{P}$ des Raumes

$$\mathbb{P}_\mu^r = \mathbb{P}_\mu^r(S^{r-1})$$

aller reellen sphärischen Polynomfunktionen in r Veränderlichen, den wir mit dem Skalarprodukt

$$\langle F,G\rangle := \int_{|x|=1} F(x)\, G(x)\, dx$$

versehen. Zum Beispiel kann $\mathbb{P}$ einer der Räume

$$\mathbb{P}_\mu^r,\ \overset{*}{\mathbb{P}}{}_\mu^r,\ \mathbb{H}_\mu^r,\ \overset{*}{\mathbb{H}}{}_\mu^r \quad (\text{mit } \mathbb{H}_\mu^r = \mathbb{P}_\mu^r)$$

d. h. der Polynome, homogenen Polynome, harmonischen Polynome bzw. homogen-harmonischen Polynome vom Grade μ auf der Sphäre sein. Der reproduzierende Kern von $\mathbb{P}$ ist dann eine zonale Funktion, d.h. es gilt für jedes Orthonormalsystem $S_1,\dots,S_N$ in $\mathbb{P}$

$$\sum_{j=1}^{N} S_j(t)\, S_j(x) = P(tx) \qquad \text{für } t,x \in S^{r-1} \tag{1}$$

mit einem geeigneten Polynom $P \in \mathbb{P}_\mu^1$. Man beweist dies mit einem von C. Müller [1] für den Raum $\mathbb{P} = \overset{*}{\mathbb{H}}{}_\mu^r$ angegebenen Verfahren. Die Kerne der Räume $\mathbb{P}_\mu^r$, $\overset{*}{\mathbb{P}}{}_\mu^r$ und $\overset{*}{\mathbb{H}}{}_\mu^r$ sind auf Grund der Beziehungen

$$\overset{*}{\mathbb{P}}{}_\mu^r \oplus \overset{*}{\mathbb{P}}{}_{\mu-1}^r = \mathbb{P}_\mu^r = \mathbb{H}_\mu^r = \bigoplus_{\nu=0}^{\mu} \overset{*}{\mathbb{H}}{}_\nu^r$$

explizit bekannt, sie lassen sich mit Hilfe gewisser Gegenbauer-Polynome ausdrücken (M. Reimer [3]).

Ein Knotensystem

$$T = (t_1,\ldots,t_N) \ , \ t_j \in S^{r-1}$$

heiße ein Fundamentalsystem für $\mathbb{P}$, wenn die Punktfunktionale

$$\mathbb{P} \ni Q \to Q(t_j) \in \mathbb{R} \ , \quad j = 1,\ldots,N,$$

linear unabhängig sind.

Für jedes Knotensystem setzen wir

$$S := S(T) = S(t_1,\ldots,t_N) = \begin{pmatrix} S_1(t_1),\ldots,S_1(t_N) \\ \ldots \quad \ldots \\ S_N(t_1),\ldots,S_N(t_N) \end{pmatrix}$$

und

$$P := P(T) = P(t_1,\ldots,t_N) = \begin{pmatrix} P_{11},\ldots,P_{1N} \\ \ldots \quad \ldots \\ P_{N1},\ldots,P_{NN} \end{pmatrix}$$

mit

$$P_{jk} := P_j(t_k) = P(t_j t_k) \ ,$$

$$P_j(x) := P(t_j x) \quad \text{für} \quad x \in S^{r-1} \ .$$

Aus (1) ergibt sich dann

$$P = S^T S \ . \tag{2}$$

Also ist P positiv semidefinit und dabei definit genau dann, wenn T ein Fundamentalsystem ist. Insbesondere ist P stets diagonalisierbar, das heißt, zu jedem T gibt es eine orthogonale Matrix A mit

$$\begin{aligned} APA^T &= \Lambda = \operatorname{diag}(\lambda_1,\dots,\lambda_N), \\ 0 \leq \lambda_{min} &:= \lambda_1 < \lambda_2 < \dots < \lambda_N := \lambda_{max}, \end{aligned} \tag{3}$$

und es gilt

$$\lambda_{min} > 0 \Leftrightarrow T \text{ ist ein Fundamentalsystem.}$$

Ist T ein Fundamentalsystem, so sind die Lagrangeelemente $L_j \in \mathbb{P}$ wohl definiert durch

$$L_j(t_k) = \delta_{jk} \quad \text{für} \quad j,k=1,\dots,N \ .$$

Die Lebesgue-Funktion

$$\sum_{j=1}^{N} |L_j(x)| \quad , \ x \in S^{r-1}$$

kann über die Schwarz-sche Ungleichung mit Hilfe der Lagrange-Quadratsumme

$$\sum_{j=1}^{N} L_j^2(x) \ , \quad x \in S^{r-1} \ , \tag{4}$$

abgeschätzt werden. Dies führt dann zu einer Abschätzung des zugehörigen Interpolationsoperators $\mathcal{L} : C(S^{r-1}) \to \mathbb{P}$ in der Form

$$\|\mathcal{L}\|_\infty^2 \leqq N \cdot \max\{\sum_{j=1}^{N} L_j^2(x) \mid x \in S^{r-1}\} \ . \tag{5}$$

Aus diesem Grunde sind wir an der Abschätzung von (4) interessiert.

Dazu setzen wir

$$L := (L_1,\dots,L_N)^T$$

und definieren

$$Q = (Q_1,\dots,Q_N)^T$$

durch

$$Q := AL \,.$$

Dann gilt jedenfalls $Q_j \in \mathbb{P}$ für $j = 1,\dots,N$ und

$$\sum_{j=1}^{N} Q_j^2(x) = \sum_{j=1}^{N} L_j^2(x) \quad \text{für } x \in S^{r-1} \,.$$

Andererseits ist

$$P(xy) = \sum_{j=1}^{N} L_j(x)P(t_jy) = \sum_{j=1}^{N} L_j(x) \sum_{k=1}^{N} P(t_jt_k)L_k(y)$$

oder wegen (3)

$$P(xy) = L^T(x)PL(y) = L^T(x)A^T \Lambda AL(y) = Q^T(x)\Lambda Q(y) \,.$$

Es gilt also

$$P(xy) = \sum_{j=1}^{N} \lambda_j Q_j(x)Q_j(y) \quad \text{für} \quad x,y \in S^{r-1} \,,$$

und hieraus ergibt sich für $x = y$ der

<u>Satz.</u> Sei T ein Fundamentalsystem für $\mathbb{P}$ und $\mathbb{P}$ rotationsinvariant. Dann gilt

$$P(1)\lambda_{max}^{-1} \leq \sum_{j=1}^{N} L_j^2(x) \leqq P(1) \cdot \lambda_{min}^{-1} \,. \tag{6}$$

<u>Korollar.</u> Ist $\lambda_1 = \lambda_2 = \dots = \lambda_N = \lambda$, so gilt

$$\sum_{j=1}^{N} L_j^2(x) = 1 \quad \text{für} \quad x \in S^{r-1} \,,$$
$$\|\mathcal{L}\|_\infty \leqq \sqrt{N} \,. \tag{7}$$

Beweis: Es gilt

$$N \cdot \lambda = \sum_{j=1}^{N} \lambda_j = \text{spur } P = N \cdot P(1) .$$

Bemerkung. Aus (7) folgt

$$\| L_j \|_\infty = 1 \quad \text{für} \quad j = 1,\ldots,N , \tag{8}$$

diese Normen sind also minimal, die L_j bilden eine extremale Basis (M. Reimer [2]).

Diese Situation tritt auf, wenn die t_j äquidistant auf einem Kreis verteilt liegen oder die Ecken eines regelmäßigen (projektiven) Polyeders sind. Im Falle r = 2 führt dies auf eine bekannte Abschätzung für trigonometrische Polynome, für die B. Sündermann [4] einen besonders schönen Beweis gegeben hat.

Allgemein sind wir wegen (6) und (5) in der Lage, zu jedem Fundamentalsystem eine obere und eine untere Schranke für die entsprechende Lebesgue-Konstante zu bestimmen, und zwar unter Vermeidung der äußerst aufwendigen Berechnung der Norm der entsprechenden Lebesgue-Funktion.

Für den Raum $\mathbb{P} = \overset{*}{\mathbb{H}}{}^3_\mu$ haben wir so z. B. Knoten gefunden, für welche folgende Abschätzungen gelten:

$$\overset{*}{\mathbb{H}}{}^2_2 \; : \; \sum_{j=1}^{5} L_j^2(x) \leqq \frac{11+\sqrt{21}}{10} = 1.558257\ldots \quad \text{(statt 5)}$$

$$\overset{*}{\mathbb{H}}{}^2_3 \; : \; \sum_{j=1}^{7} L_j^2(x) \leqq \frac{5}{336}\left(73 + 19\sqrt{\frac{13}{5}}\right) = 1.542211\ldots \quad \text{(statt 7).}$$

Beide Schranken liegen deutlich unter dem Wert von dim $\overset{*}{\mathbb{H}}{}^2_\mu = 2\mu+1$, den man für extremale Fundamentalsysteme stets garantieren kann. Die Knoten liegen ganz in der Nähe der Knoten, mit deren Hilfe B. Sündermann [5] allgemein eine äußerst günstige $O(N^{3/4})$-Abschätzung für die Lebesgue-Konstanten erzielte.

Literatur

[1] C. Müller : Sperical harmonics.
Springer: Berlin, Heidelberg, New York 1966

[2] M. Reimer : Extremal bases for normed vector spaces.
In E. W. Cheney (ed.), Approximation Theory, Academic Press: New York 198o, 723 - 728

[3] M. Reimer : Interpolation on the sphere and bounds for the Lagrangian square sums.
Ergebnisbericht Nr. 72 der Lehrstühle III und VIII (Angewandte Mathematik) der Universität Dortmund 1985

[4] B. Sündermann: On a minimal property of trigonometric interpolation at equidistant nodes.
Computing 27 (1981) 371 - 372

[5] B. Sündermann: Projektionen auf Polynomräume in mehreren Veränderlichen.
Diss. Dortmund 1983

International Series of
Numerical Mathematics, Vol. 75

ON GABOR INFORMATION CELLS

Walter Schempp
Lehrstuhl fuer Mathematik I
University of Siegen
Siegen

This paper presents a group-theoretic approach to the Whittaker-Shannon-Kotel'nikov sampling theorem of digital signal processing. This approach is based on harmonic analysis on the compact Heisenberg nilmanifold $A(\mathbf{Z})\setminus\tilde{A}(\mathbf{R})$, to wit, the differential principal fiber bundle over the two-dimensional compact torus group $\mathbf{T}^2$ with structure group isomorphic to the one-dimensional center C of the reduced real Heisenberg nilpotent Lie group $A(\mathbf{R})$. In this geometric framework, the projection of a fundamental domain for $A(\mathbf{Z})\setminus\tilde{A}(\mathbf{R})$ in the direction of the fiber C forms the Gabor information cell of the time-frequency integer lattice $\mathbf{Z} \oplus \mathbf{Z}$ in the information plane $\mathbf{R} \oplus \mathbf{R}$.

1. Introductory Discussion of Sampling

Let f denote a smooth complex-valued function on the real line of period 1 in the variable $t \in \mathbf{R}$. We may consider f as defined on the one-dimensional compact torus group in the variable $\dot{t} \in \mathbf{T}$, i.e., as an element of the complex vector space $\mathscr{C}^{\infty}(\mathbf{T})$. In the following we adopt the signal theoretic point of view by considering the time t and the frequency ω as Fourier dual ("conjugate") variables in the information plane $\mathbf{R} \oplus \mathbf{R}$ (cf. Gabor [2]). If $(\hat{f}(\nu))_{\nu \in \mathbf{Z}}$ denotes the sequence of Fourier coefficients

$$\hat{f}(\nu) = \int_{\mathbf{T}} f(\dot{t}).\bar{\chi}_{\nu}(\dot{t})d\dot{t}$$

of the periodic signal f where $(\chi_\nu)_{\nu \in \mathbf{Z}}$ forms the discrete dual (or character) group of **T**, we obtain the time-frequency lattice $\mathbf{Z} \oplus \mathbf{Z}$ of Gabor information cells of unit area in the information plane $\mathbf{R} \oplus \mathbf{R}$ displayed below.

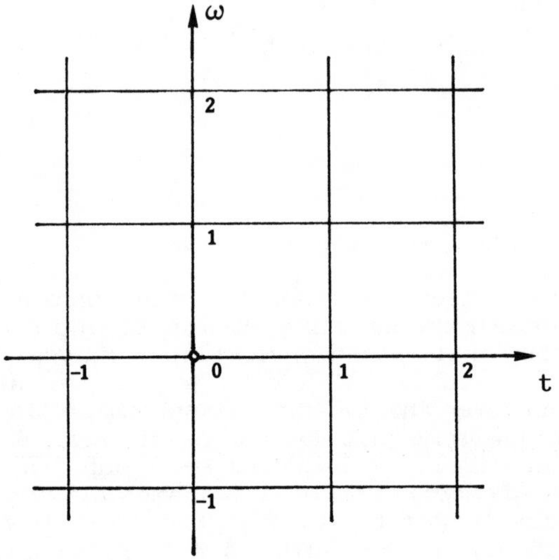

The problem of reconstructing the value f(t) for every time $t \in \mathbf{R}$ by the data $(\hat{f}(\nu))_{\nu \in \mathbf{Z}}$ arranged along the vertical frequency axis leads to the Fourier series of f:

$$f = \sum_{\nu \in \mathbf{Z}} \hat{f}(\nu)\, \chi_\nu$$

with summation over the equally spaced frequency variable $\nu \in \mathbf{Z}$. Sweeping out a 90° yields the analogous problem of reconstructing the value f(t) for every time $t \in \mathbf{R}$ and suitable signals f on **R** by means of their values $(f(\mu))_{\mu \in \mathbf{Z}}$ at the discrete times $\mu \in \mathbf{Z}$. The Whittaker-Shannon-Kotel'nikov sampling theorem states that a bandlimited signal f can be completely represented by and recoverable from knowledge of its instantaneous values ("samples") $(f(\mu))_{\mu \in \mathbf{Z}}$ equally spaced on the time axis (see, for instance, Petersen [5] and the papers [7], [8]). Much of the importance and usefulness of the sampling theorem lies in its rôle as a bridge between continuous-time signals and discrete-time signals. In many contexts, processing of discrete-time signals is more flexible and is often preferable to processing of continuous-time signals, in part because of the increasing availability of inexpensive, light-weight, programmable and easily reproducible digital and discrete-time systems. This technology also offers the possibility of exploiting the concept of sampling to convert a continuous-time signal to a discrete-time signal. After processing the discrete-time signal using a discrete-time system, we can then convert back to continuous time.

The time-frequency integer lattice $\mathbf{Z} \oplus \mathbf{Z}$ in the information plane $\mathbf{R} \oplus \mathbf{R}$ suggests to apply harmonic analysis on the two-dimensional compact torus group $\mathbf{T}^2$. In view of the parallels between quantum mechanics and signal theory, however, it is advantageous to look at $\mathbf{T}^2$ as the basis of a differential principal circle bundle, the so-called Heisenberg nilmanifold $A(\mathbf{Z})\backslash\widetilde{A}(\mathbf{R})$ admitting the one-dimensional center C of the reduced Heisenberg nilpotent Lie group $A(\mathbf{R})$ as its structure group (cf. Auslander-Tolimieri [1]). We will show that this principal circle bundle forms the natural geometric framework for establishing the Whittaker-Shannon-Kotel'nikov sampling theorem of digital signal processing. In this way, the present paper completes the recent article by Higgins [3].

2. The Compact Heisenberg Nilmanifold

The real Heisenberg group is the three-dimensional real Lie group $\widetilde{A}(\mathbf{R})$ of unipotent matrices

$$\begin{pmatrix} 1 & x & z \\ 0 & 1 & y \\ 0 & 0 & 1 \end{pmatrix} = (x,y,z)$$

with real entries x,y,z (cf. Auslander-Tolimieri [1], the papers [6], [8], and the monograph [9]). The center $\tilde{C} = \{(0,0,z) \mid z \in \mathbf{R}\}$ of $\tilde{A}(\mathbf{R})$ is isomorphic to the additive group $\mathbf{R}$ and the descending central series as well as the derived series of $\tilde{A}(\mathbf{R})$ are given by the descending filtration

$$\tilde{A}(\mathbf{R}) \hookleftarrow \tilde{C} \hookleftarrow \{1\}_{\tilde{A}(\mathbf{R})}.$$

Thus $\tilde{A}(\mathbf{R})$ is a connected, simply connected, two-step nilpotent, three-dimensional, real Lie group with one-dimensional center and this property characterizes $\tilde{A}(\mathbf{R})$ within isomorphy. It forms the universal covering group of the reduced real Heisenberg nilpotent Lie group $A(\mathbf{R})$ with center C isomorphic to the one-dimensional compact torus group $\mathbf{T}$. The reduced real Heisenberg Lie group $A(\mathbf{R})$ has $\mathbf{R} \times \mathbf{R} \times \mathbf{T}$ as its underlying differential manifold and admits the group law

$$(x_1, y_1, \zeta_1)(x_2, y_2, \zeta_2) = (x_1+x_2, y_1+y_2, \zeta_1 \zeta_2 e^{2\pi i x_1 y_2})$$

(cf. [7]). $A(\mathbf{R})$ forms in a sense the simplest non-abelian Lie group.

It is not easy to visualize geometrically the action of the real Heisenberg nilpotent Lie group $\tilde{A}(\mathbf{R})$. However, it will be useful to consider $\tilde{A}(\mathbf{R})$ as the differential principal fiber bundle over the two-dimensional polarized cross-section $P = \{(x,y,0) \mid x \in \mathbf{R},\ y \in \mathbf{R}\}$ to $\tilde{C}$ in $\tilde{A}(\mathbf{R})$ with structure group isomorphic to $\tilde{C}$.

$$\begin{array}{ccc} \tilde{C} & \longrightarrow & \tilde{A}(\mathbf{R}) \\ & & \downarrow \\ & & P \end{array}$$

The Lie algebra $\mathfrak{n}$ of $\tilde{A}(\mathbf{R})$ which is also the Lie algebra of $A(\mathbf{R})$ is formed by the nilpotent matrices

$$\begin{pmatrix} 0 & a & c \\ 0 & 0 & b \\ 0 & 0 & 0 \end{pmatrix}$$

with real entries a, b, c. The matrices

$$X = \begin{pmatrix} 0 & 1 & 0 \\ 0 & 0 & 0 \\ 0 & 0 & 0 \end{pmatrix}, \quad Y = \begin{pmatrix} 0 & 0 & 0 \\ 0 & 0 & 1 \\ 0 & 0 & 0 \end{pmatrix}, \quad E = \begin{pmatrix} 0 & 0 & 1 \\ 0 & 0 & 0 \\ 0 & 0 & 0 \end{pmatrix}$$

form a basis of the three-dimensional real Heisenberg nilpotent Lie algebra $\mathfrak{n}$ and satisfy the canonical commutation relations of Heisenberg

$$[X,Y] = XY - YX = E, \quad [X,E] = 0, \quad [Y,E] = 0$$

whence the name of $\mathfrak{n}$, $\widetilde{A}(\mathbf{R})$, and $A(\mathbf{R})$. The exponential map

$$\exp_{\widetilde{A}(\mathbf{R})}: \mathfrak{n} \longrightarrow \widetilde{A}(\mathbf{R})$$

gives rise to a global diffeomorphism of $\mathfrak{n}$ onto $\widetilde{A}(\mathbf{R})$ which maps the center $\mathfrak{z} = \mathbf{R}.E$ of $\mathfrak{n}$ onto $\widetilde{C}$. The figure displayed below illustrates the situation in $\mathfrak{n}$ and $\widetilde{A}(\mathbf{R})$, respectively.

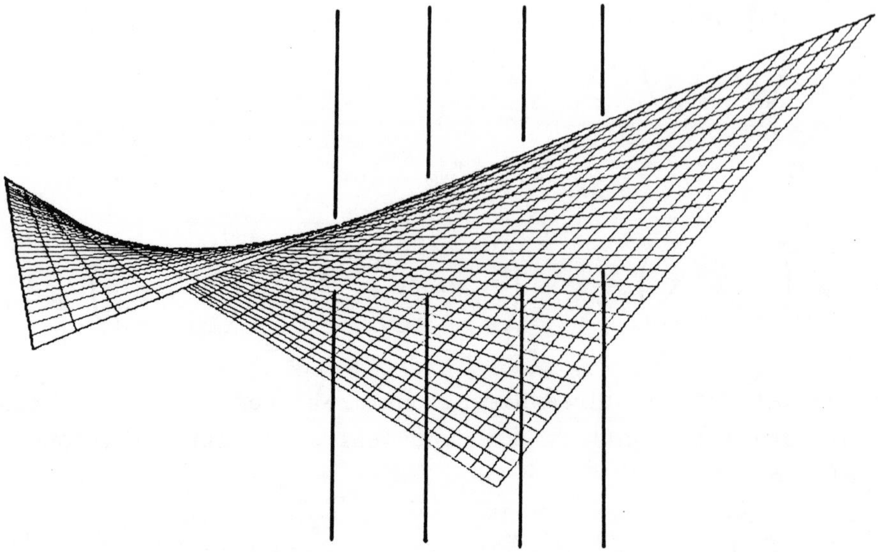

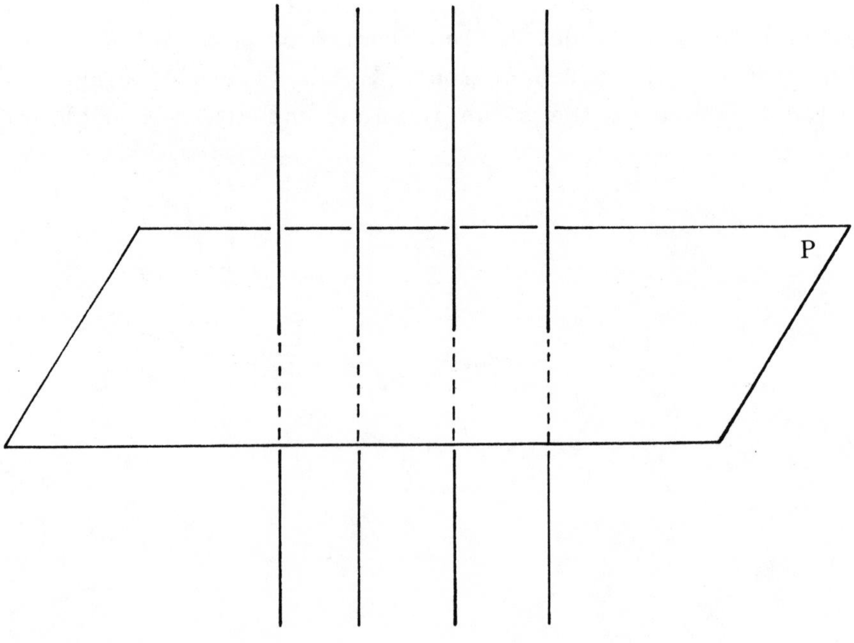
P

In $\widetilde{A}(\mathbf{R})$ we consider the arithmetic subgroup $A(\mathbf{Z})$ defined by x, y, $z \in \mathbf{Z}$. The quotient $A(\mathbf{Z})\backslash\widetilde{A}(\mathbf{R})$ of right cosets modulo $A(\mathbf{Z})$ forms a compact two-step nilmanifold, the Heisenberg nilmanifold. It forms a differential principal circle bundle over the two-dimensional compact torus group $\mathbf{T}^2$.

$$\begin{array}{ccc} \widetilde{C} & \longrightarrow & A(\mathbf{Z})\backslash\widetilde{A}(\mathbf{R}) \\ & & \big\downarrow \\ & & \mathbf{T}^2 \end{array}$$

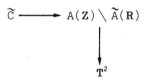

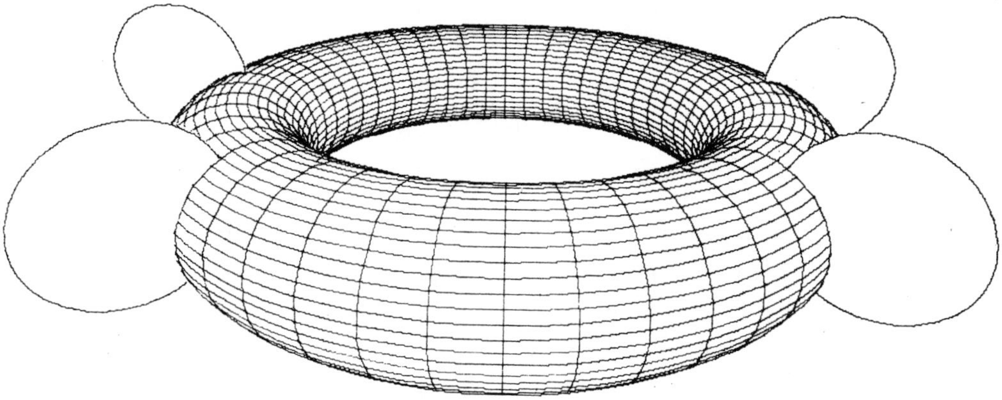

The projection of a fundamental domain for $A(\mathbf{Z})\backslash\tilde{A}(\mathbf{R})$ in the direction of the fiber C forms a Gabor information cell of the time-frequency lattice $\mathbf{Z} \oplus \mathbf{Z}$ in the information plane $\mathbf{R} \oplus \mathbf{R}$.

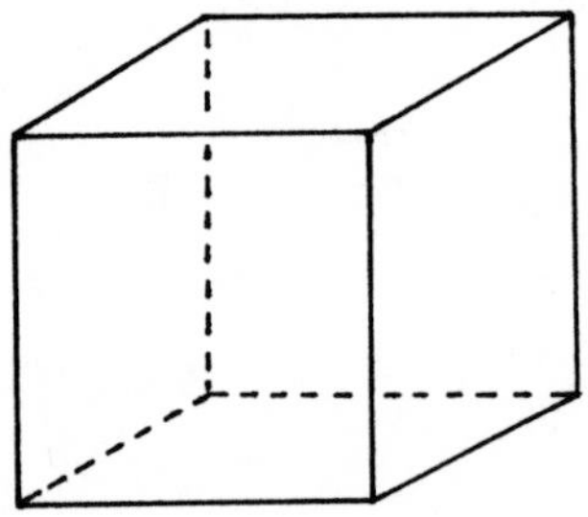

3. The Linear Lattice Representation of $\tilde{A}(\mathbf{R})$

Let

$$\chi_1 : \tilde{C} \ni (0,0,z) \rightsquigarrow e^{2\pi i z} \in \mathbf{T}$$

be the basic character of $\tilde{C}$. Then we have the following version of the Stone-von Neumann uniqueness theorem (cf. von Neumann [4]).

Theorem 1. The monomial representation $\mathrm{Ind}_{\tilde{C}}^{\tilde{A}(\mathbf{R})}\chi_1$ is an isotypic, continuous, unitary, linear representation of $\tilde{A}(\mathbf{R})$. Its isotypic component U is the only topologically irreducible, continuous, unitary, linear representation of $\tilde{A}(\mathbf{R})$ with central character χ_1.

The preceding result shows the "central" importance of the center $\tilde{C}$ for harmonic analysis on $\tilde{A}(\mathbf{R})$. For details, see the monograph [9]. The linear Schrödinger representation U of $\tilde{A}(\mathbf{R})$ acting in the complex Hilbert space $L^2(\mathbf{R})$ admits various rather different looking realizations. Extend the central character χ_1 from $\widetilde{C}$ to the closed normal subgroup

$$L = (\mathbf{Z} \oplus \mathbf{Z}) \times \widetilde{C}$$

of $\widetilde{A}(\mathbf{R})$ in the trivial way and form the monomial representation

$$V = \mathrm{Ind}_L^{\widetilde{A}(\mathbf{R})} \chi_1$$

of $\widetilde{A}(\mathbf{R})$. Then the Weil-Brezin isomorphism

$$w: \mathscr{S}(\mathbf{R}) \ni f \rightsquigarrow ((x,y,z) \rightsquigarrow e^{2\pi i z} \sum_{\mu \in \mathbf{Z}} f(\mu+x) e^{2\pi i \mu y})$$

forms an intertwining operator between the linear Schrödinger representation U and the linear lattice representation V of $\widetilde{A}(\mathbf{R})$. It follows

Theorem 2. The linear lattice representation V is a topologically irreducible, continuous, unitary linear representation of $\widetilde{A}(\mathbf{R})$.

Let the group $SL(2,\mathbf{R})$ act on $\widetilde{A}(\mathbf{R})$ in the natural as a group of automorphisms of $\widetilde{A}(\mathbf{R})$ leaving $\widetilde{C}$ pointwise fixed. Consider the Weyl element

$$J = \begin{pmatrix} 0 & 1 \\ -1 & 0 \end{pmatrix}$$

of $SL(2,\mathbf{R})$. Of course, the automorphism J of $\widetilde{A}(\mathbf{R})$ may be considered as a rotation of 90° in the polarized cross-section P to $\widetilde{C}$ in $\widetilde{A}(\mathbf{R})$ which transforms the time-frequency lattice $\mathbf{Z} \oplus \mathbf{Z}$ of Gabor information cells into itself. The metaplectic Lie group homomorphism maps the Fourier cotransform $\overline{\mathscr{F}}_{\mathbf{R}}$ which acts as an automorphism on the complex Hilbert space $L^2(\mathbf{R})$ onto J. From this fact we conclude

Theorem 3. The Fourier cotransform considered as an automorphism of the standard Hilbert space $L^2(\mathbf{R})$ admits the Poisson-Weil factorization

$$\overline{\mathscr{F}}_{\mathbf{R}} = W^{-1} \circ J \circ W.$$

The preceding result allows to interpret the Poisson summation formula in a geometric way.

4. Sampling

It is immediate that the Fourier cotransform of the signal

$$f(t) = \begin{cases} 1 & \text{for } |t| \leqq \frac{1}{2} \\ 0 & \text{for } |t| > \frac{1}{2} \end{cases}$$

is given by the function

$$\operatorname{sinc}(\omega) = \begin{cases} \frac{\sin \pi\omega}{\pi\omega} & \text{for } \omega \neq 0 \\ 1 & \text{for } \omega = 0 \end{cases}$$

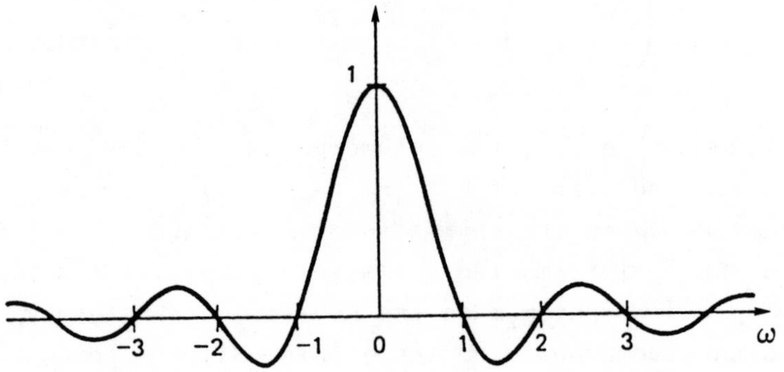

Notice that f forms one side of the fundamental domain of the compact Heisenberg nilmanifold $A(\mathbf{Z})\setminus\tilde{A}(\mathbf{R})$ shown in Section 2 supra.

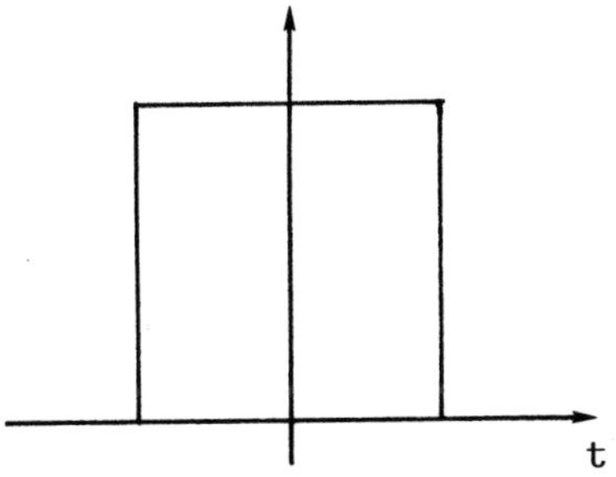

If $PW(\mathbf{C})$ denotes the Paley-Wiener space of all entire functions of exponential type at most π that are square integrable on the real line $\mathbf{R}$, an application of Theorem 3 supra furnishes

Theorem 4. Each function $f \in PW(\mathbf{C})$ admits the cardinal series expansion

$$f(z) = \sum_{\mu \in \mathbf{Z}} f(\mu)\operatorname{sinc}(z-\mu)$$

for all $z \in \mathbf{C}$. The convergence of the cardinal interpolation series is uniform on the compact subsets of $\mathbf{C}$.

This result may be interpreted in two ways, each of which has found important apllications in signal theory.

(1) Every signal of finite energy and bandwidth $W = 1/2$ Hz may be completely recaptured, in a simple way, from a knowledge of its samples taken at the rate $2W = 1$ per second (Nyquist rate). Moreover - indispensable for any implementation in practice - the recovery is stable, in the sense that a small error in reading the sample values produces only a correspondingly small error in the recaptured signal.

(2) Every square-summable sequence of complex numbers my be transmitted at the rate of $2W = 1$ per second

over an ideal channel of bandwidth W = 1/2 Hz, by being represented as the samples at the integer points $\mu \in \mathbf{Z}$ of an easily reconstructed bandlimited signal of finite energy.

Thus the Whittaker-Shannon-Kotel'nikov sampling theorem as stated above serves as a basis for the interchangeability of analog representations of signals and their representations in digital sequences. For instance, the recently developed CD (=**C**ompact **D**isc) technology forms a very efficient practical application of the digital signal representation. The fact that in general the cardinal series converges slowly is overcome by the oversampling principle of digital/analog conversion. The figures displayed below show the structures of a cross-section and the surface of a CD.

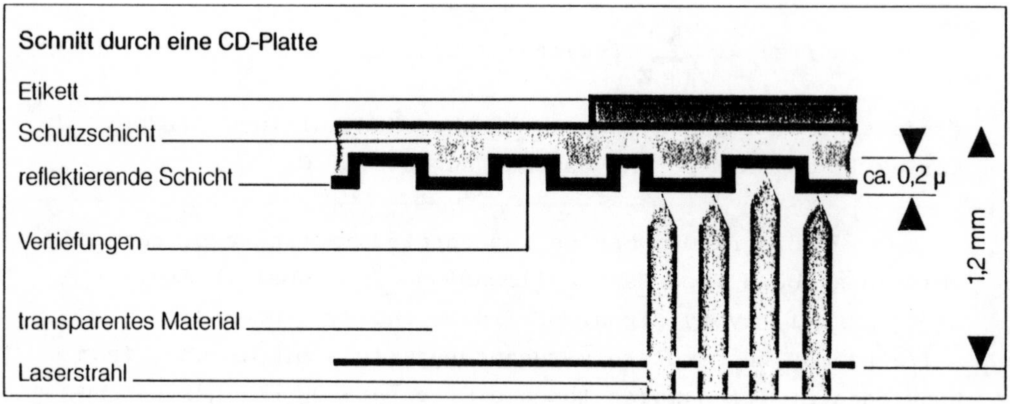

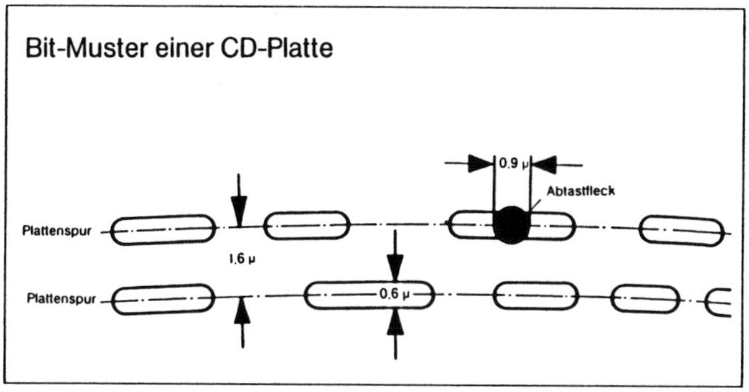

The sequence of digital signals located on the surface of the CD are transformed by means of a laser beam, a corresponding sensor and a digital-to-analog (D-to-A) converter into analog electrical signals. Finally, it is the task of the loudspeakers to convert as electrico-acoustical transducers these electrical signals into corresponding sound waves (cf. [8]).

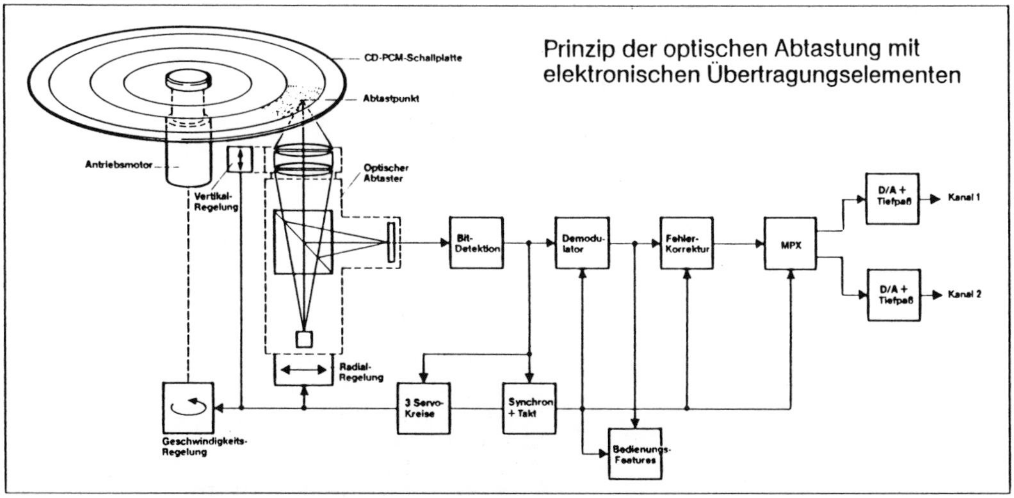

Other examples for the application of the Whittaker-Shannon-Kotel'nikov sampling theorem are the digital typography, the medical computerized tomography, the digital holography, and the seismic exploration. For applications of the sampling theorem to optical signals, the reader is referred to Soroko [10].

References

1. Auslander, L., Tolimieri, R.: Abelian harmonic analysis, theta functions and function algebras on a nilmanifold. Lecture Notes in Math., Vol. **436**. Berlin-Heidelberg-New York: Springer 1975
2. Gabor, D.: Communication theory and physics. Phil. mag. **41** (1950), 1161-1187
3. Higgins, J.R.: Five short stories about the cardinal series. Bull. (New Series) Amer. Math. Soc. **12** (1985), 45-89
4. Neumann, J.v.: Die Eindeutigkeit der Schrödingerschen Operatoren. Math. Ann. **104** (1931), 570-578
5. Petersen, B.E.: Introduction to the Fourier transform and pseudo-differential operators. Monographs and Studies in Mathematics, Vol. **19**. Boston-London-Melbourne: Pitman Advanced Publishing Program 1983
6. Schempp, W.: Drei statt einer reellen Variablen? In: Multivariate Approximation Theory II, pp. 331-341. W. Schempp and K. Zeller, eds. ISNM **61**. Basel-Boston-Stuttgart: Birkhäuser 1982
7. Schempp, W.: Gruppentheoretische Aspekte der Signalübertragung und der kardinalen Interpolationssplines I. Math. Meth. in the Appl. Sci. **5** (1983), 195-215
8. Schempp, W.: Analog radar signal design and digital signal processing - a Heisenberg nilpotent Lie group approach. In: Lie Methods in Optics. K.B. Wolf, ed. Lecture Notes in Physics. Berlin-Heidelberg-New York-Tokyo: Springer (in print)
9. Schempp, W.: Harmonic analysis on the Heisenberg nilpotent Lie group, with applications to signal theory. Boston-London-Melbourne: Pitman Advanced Publishing Program (in preparation)
10. Soroko, L.M.: Holography and coherent optics. New York-London: Plenum Press 1980

Prof.Dr. Walter Schempp
Lehrstuhl fuer Mathematik I
University of Siegen
Hoelderlinstrasse 3
D-5900 Siegen
Federal Republic of Germany

International Series of
Numerical Mathematics, Vol. 75

EIN BEITRAG ZUR FLÄCHENAPPROXIMATION ÜBER UNREGELMÄSSIG VERTEILTEN DATEN

Rita Schmidt

Hahn-Meitner-Institut für Kernforschung GmbH
Berlin, FRG

It is shown how surface splines are used to fit scattered data in the least squares sense. There are two main points which make them useful in practical applications: Neither boundary conditions nor regular grids are necessary.

1. Einleitung

Meinguet hat in [2-4] eine Funktionenklasse angegeben, die zur Interpolation diskreter Daten im $\mathbb{R}^n$ geeignet ist. Dabei dürfen die Stützstellen der zu interpolierenden Daten beliebig angeordnet sein. Das ist in praktischen Anwendungen vorteilhaft, weil die Lage der Stützstellen nicht immer frei gewählt werden kann. Im vorliegenden Beitrag wird diese Funktionenklasse verwendet, um für fehlerbehaftete Daten, die über unregelmäßig verteilten Stützstellen in der Ebene liegen, eine Ausgleichsfläche nach der Methode der kleinsten Abweichungsquadratsumme zu bestimmen.

2. Die Funktionenklasse

In [2-4] ist das lineare Interpolationsproblem für diskrete Datenmengen beliebiger Dimension durch Einführung nichtlinearer Nebenbedingungen in eleganter Weise gelöst worden. Für den vorliegenden Spezialfall, eine Fläche im R^3 zu bestimmen, ergibt sich die Interpolationsfunktion als Linearkombination aus zwei Funktionenfamilien, den Abstandsfunktionen $d(r) = r^{2m} \ln r$ mit $r^2 = x^2+y^2$ und den bivariaten Polynomen des totalen Grades m-1. Die rotationssymmetrischen Abstandsfunktionen haben die Form

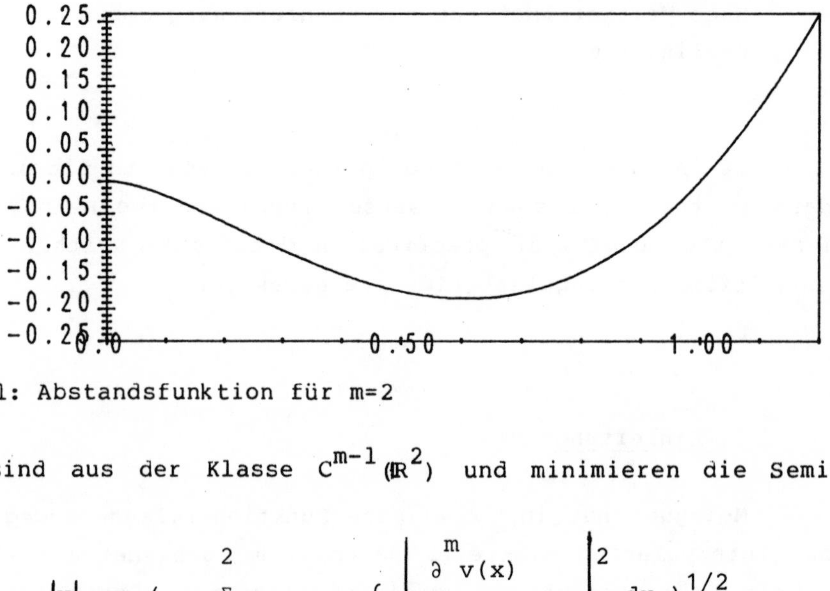

Bild 1: Abstandsfunktion für m=2

Sie sind aus der Klasse $C^{m-1}(\mathbb{R}^2)$ und minimieren die Seminorm

$$|v|_m := \left(\sum_{i_1,\dots,i_m=1}^{2} \int_{\mathbb{R}^2} \left| \frac{\partial^m v(x)}{\partial x_{i_1} \cdots \partial x_{i_m}} \right|^2 dx \right)^{1/2}$$

Die so definierte Fläche ist über der ganzen Ebene regulär mit Ausnahme derjenigen Punkte, die als Zentrum der Abstandsfunktionen verwendet werden. Dort erfolgt wegen der logarithmischen Singularität ein Regularitätsabfall auf die Ordnung m-1. Diese Ausnahmepunkte werden als Knoten der Fläche bezeichnet. In [2-4] werden die Stützstellen der Datenpunkte als Knoten verwendet. Der Interpolationsfall hat auch eine physikalische Bedeutung.

Für m=2 ist das Polynom eine Ebene, die physikalisch als unendlich ausgedehnte dünne Platte interpretierbar ist. Die Abstandsfunktionen beschreiben die Verbiegung der Platte unter Aufwendung minimaler Biegeenergie und zwar so, daß diese in den Knoten vorgeschriebene Werte annimmt. Der Vorteil dieser Behandlung liegt in der unendlichen Ausdehnung des Gebietes und der endlichen Anzahl von Randbedingungen.

Für die Interpolationsaufgabe gilt also: Durch die Datenmenge $D:=\{(x_i,y_i,z_i),i=1,\dots,N\}$ ist für jeden Punkt $P\in\mathbb{R}^2$ eindeutig die Interpolationsfunktion

$$u(P) = p(P) + \sum_{i=1}^{N} \gamma_i \, d(\|Q_i-P\|)$$

mit den Knoten $\{Q_i:=(x_i,y_i),i=1,\dots,N\}$ und dem Polynom

$$p(P) = p(x,y) = \sum_{j=o}^{m-1} \sum_{k=o}^{j} a_{j-k,k} x^{j-k} y^k$$

definiert. Die Parameter $\{\gamma_i, a_{j-k,k}\}$ sind durch die Interpolationsforderungen $u(Q_i)=z_i$, $i=1,\dots,N$, eindeutig bestimmt.

3. Die Ausgleichsfläche

Für mittlere Datenmengen ($N \simeq 250$) ist die Methode gut geeignet, Interpolationsflächen für diskrete Daten zu bestimmen, wenn für diese keine Modellfunktionen vorliegen. Sind die Daten jedoch fehlerbehaftet, so wird oft eine Ausgleichsfläche nach der Methode der kleinsten Abweichungsquadratsumme die angemessenere Beschreibung sein. Deshalb wurde probeweise die obige Interpolationsfunktion als Ansatzfunktion verwendet, um für eine gegebene Datenmenge $D:=\{(x_j,y_j,z_j),j=1,\dots,M\}$ diejenige Fläche zu bestimmen, für die die Fehlernorm

$$f(\gamma,a) := \sum_{j=1}^{M} \left(z_j - \left(p(P_j) + \sum_{i=1}^{N} \gamma_i d(\|Q_i - P_j\|)\right)\right)^2$$

minimal wird im Parameterraum $\gamma \varepsilon R^N, a \varepsilon R^{m(m+1)/2}$. Als freie Parameter treten hier die Knoten $\{Q_i\}$ auf. Numerische Experimente haben gezeigt, daß es am günstigsten ist, sie "gleichmäßig" auf die Stützstellenmenge zu verteilen. Damit entfällt das bei Tensorproduktansätzen auftretende Lückenproblem [5].

4. Beispiele

Für die gewählten Beispiele liegen keine Modellfunktionen zugrunde. Das erste Beispiel zeigt die Verteilung der Regenmengen während eines Unwetters in Berlin am 8.8.1982. Die Meßpunkte häufen sich im Zentrum der Regenfront und nehmen zu den Rändern hin stark ab. Bild 2 zeigt die 51 Stützstellen. Die aus der Interpolation gewonnenen Isolinien (20(10)80 l/m^2) im Bild 3 stimmen sehr gut mit den handgezeichneten der amtlichen Wetterkarte überein. Daß auch die Ausgleichsfläche den Sachverhalt noch gut widerspiegelt, zeigt Bild 5, das unter Verwendung der Knoten im Bild 4 entstanden ist. Die Knoten bilden ein deformiertes 4x4 Produktgitter, das an die Stützstellenmenge angepaßt wurde. Es hätte auch jede andere Knotenverteilung gewählt werden können. Im zweiten Beispiel werden Niederschlagsmessungen in der Sahelzone behandelt. Es liegen 655 Meßstellen vor, die ebenfalls nach der Stärke der Niederschläge verteilt sind (Bild 6). Auch das deformierte 10x10 Produktgitter im Bild 7 zeigt noch eine Häufung der Knoten. Für die Berechnung der Fläche, deren Isolinien (0(500)1000(100)1600(200)2400(300)3000(500)4000(1000)7000) im Bild 8 dargestellt sind, wurde das Gebiet auf das Einheitsquadrat [0,1]x[0,1] transformiert.

Die zur Herstellung der Bilder verwendeten Programme werden im Rahmen der Software-Werkzeuge [1] angeboten.

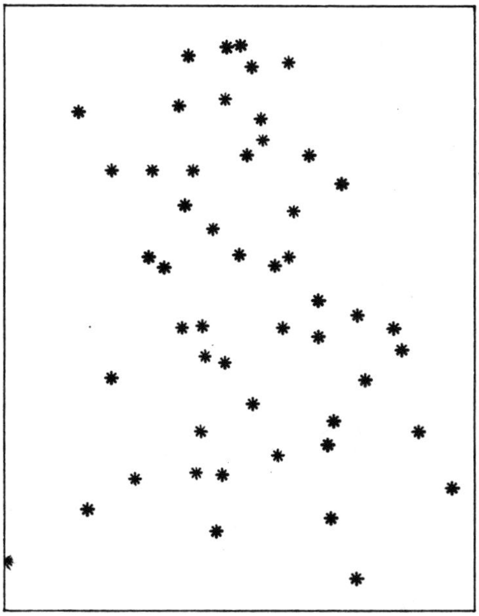

Bild 2: Stützstellen für Regenmessungen in Berlin

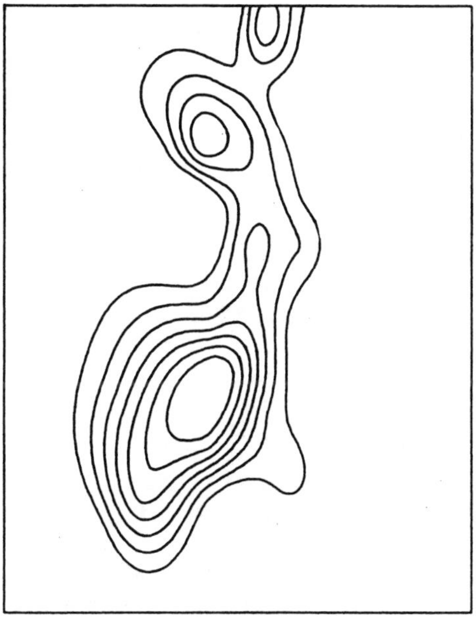

Bild 3: Isolinien auf der Interpolationsfläche

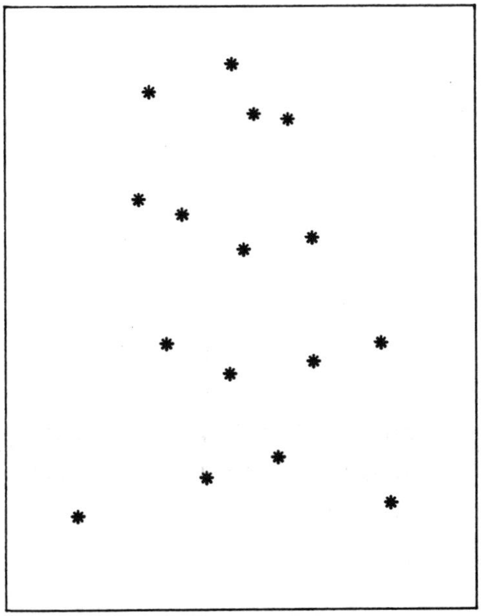

Bild 4: Knoten für die

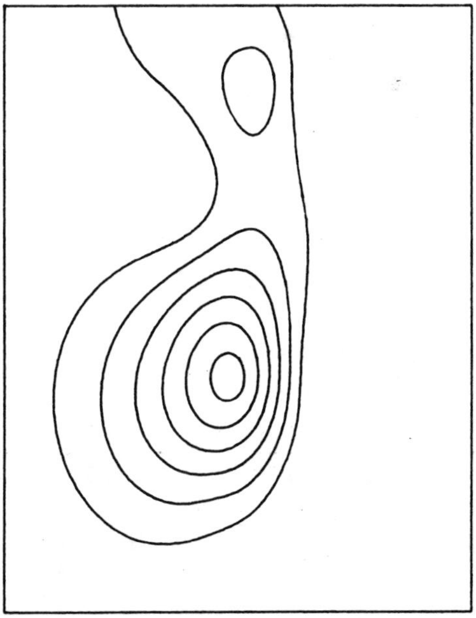

Bild 5: Isolinien auf der

Ausgleichsfläche

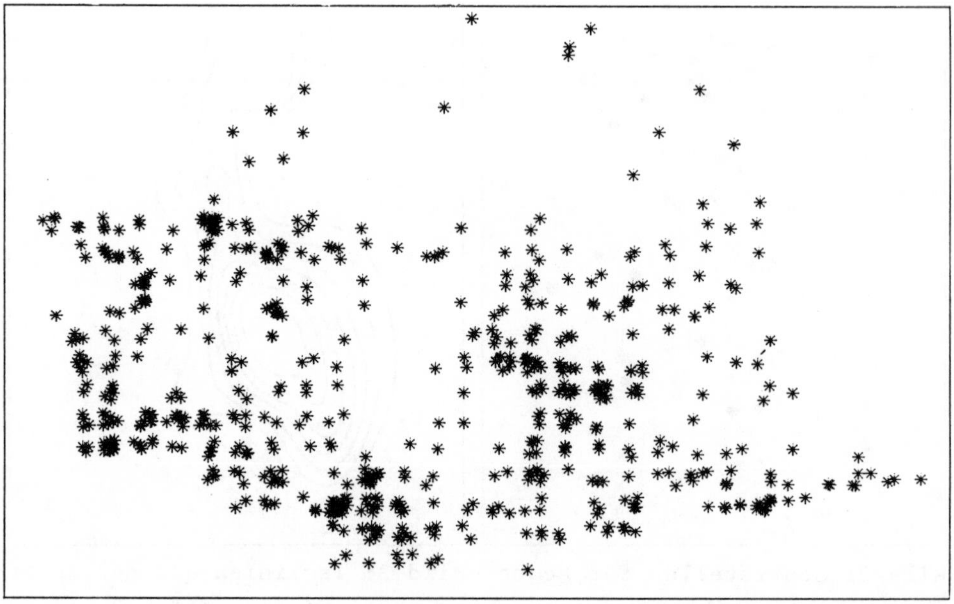

Bild 6: Stützstellen für Niederschlagsmessungen in der Sahelzone

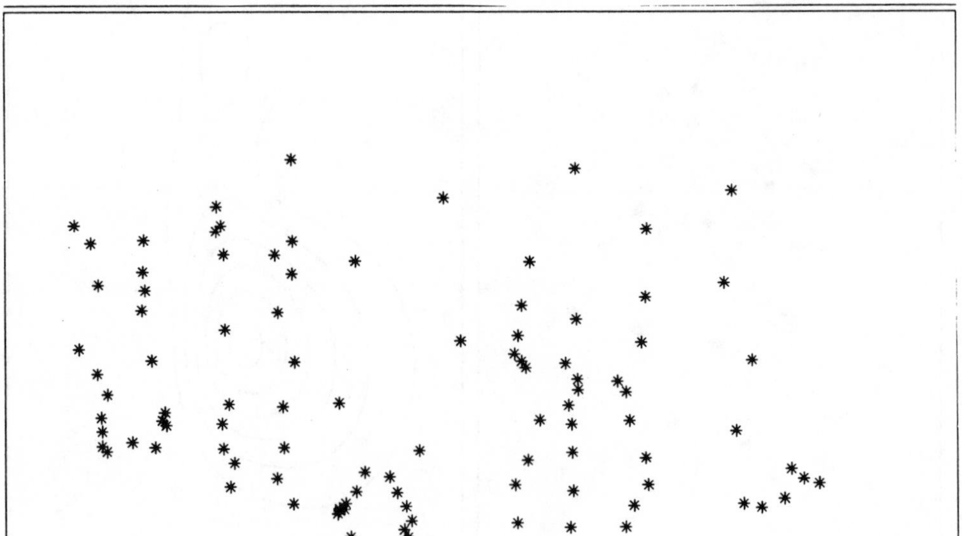

Bild 7: Knoten für die Ausgleichsfläche

Bild 8: Isolinien auf der Ausgleichsfläche

Literaturverzeichnis

1. Hoffmann-Schulz, G. und R.M. Schmidt (1985) Software-Werkzeuge für Fitprobleme. HMI-B 421, Berlin

2. Meinguet, J. (1979) An Intrinsic Approach to Multivariate Spline Interpolation at Arbitratry Points, in Badri N. Sahney (ed.), Polynomial and Spline Approximation, D. Reidel Publishing Company, 163-190

3. Meinguet, J. (1979) Multivariate Interpolation at Arbitrary Points Made Simple. ZAMP 30, 292-304

4. Meinguet, J. (1979) Basic Mathematical Aspects of Surface Interpolation, in G. Hämmerlin (ed.), Numerische Integration, ISNM 45, Birkhäuser, Basel, 211-220

5. Schmidt, R.M. (1983) Fitting Scattered Surface Data with Large Gaps, in R.E. Barnhill, W.Boehm (eds.), Surfaces in CAGD, North-Holland Publishing Company, 185-189

Dr. R. Schmidt, Bereich Datenverarbeitung und Elektronik, Hahn-Meitner Institut für Kernforschung GmbH, Glienicker Str. 100, D-1000 Berlin 39, Germany

International Series of
Numerical Mathematics, Vol. 75

THE BASIS AND MOMENT PROBLEMS OF SOME SYSTEMS OF ANALYTIC FUNCTIONS

Xie-Chang Shen

Department of Mathematics
Peking University, China

The basis, completeness, interpolation and moment problems have its closed connection with each other. In this paper I would like to introduce some results about these problems for some systems of analytic functions which have been obtained in last year.

1. The characteristic properties of some incomplete systems.

Let G be a domain bounded by a closed rectifiable Jordan curve Γ in the complex plane, G_∞ be a complement of $\bar{G}$.

We denote the function conformally mapping G_∞ onto $|w| > 1$ by $w = \Phi(z)$, $\Phi(\infty) = \infty$, $\Phi'(\infty) > 0$ and $\Psi(w)$ is its inverse function.

<u>Definition.</u> (Shen 1980[1]) The domain G is said to belong to class K_q, $q > 1$, if for any function $f(\xi) \in L_q(\Gamma)$ the integral of Cauchy type

$$F(z) = \frac{1}{2\pi i} \int_\Gamma \frac{f(\xi)}{\xi - z} d\xi$$

determines a function $F(z) \in E_q(G)$ (or $E_q(G_\infty)$, $F(\infty) = 0$, we denote the class of functions by $E_q^0(G_\infty)$).

Let $\{b_k\}$ be a given sequence in G_∞, the element of which can be coincided with each other. We denote by s_k the number of appearance of b_k in $\{b_1, b_2, \ldots, b_k\}$ and by p_k the number of appearance of b_k in whole sequence $\{b_j\}$.

It is known (Shen 1980 [1]) that if $G \in K_q$, $q > 1$, then the necessary and sufficient condition for the completeness of $\{(z-b_k)^{-s_k}\}$ in $E_p(G)$, $\frac{1}{p} + \frac{1}{q} = 1$ is

$$(1.1) \quad \sum_{k=1}^{+\infty} (1 - |a_k|) = +\infty, \quad a_k = \overline{\Phi(b_k)^{-1}} .$$

If the condition (1.1) is not valid, i.e.,

$$(1.2) \quad \sum_{k=1}^{+\infty} (1 - |a_k|) < +\infty , \quad a_k = \overline{\Phi(b_k)^{-1}} ,$$

then the closure of $\{(z-b_k)^{-s_k}\}$ is a subspace in $E_p(G)$ which we denote by $R_p(G;b_j)$. We are interested in the characteristic properties of $R_p(G;b_j)$.

Let

$$(1.3) \quad \eta_k(w) = \frac{(s_k-1)!w^{s_k-1}}{(1-\bar{a}_k w)^{s_k}} , \quad a_k = \overline{\Phi(b_k)^{-1}} , \quad k = 1,2,\ldots,$$

and $m_k^{(1/p)}(z)$ be the principal part of $\eta_k[\Phi(z)]\Phi'(z)^{1/p}$ at its poles $z = b_k$, $k = 1,2,\ldots$, $1 < p < +\infty$. Obviously, the closure of $\{m_k^{(1/p)}(z)\}$ is the $R_p(G;b_j)$ too.

Hereafter we suppose

$$(1.4) \quad \sup s_k = \sup p_k = p < +\infty$$

Consider the Blaschke product (under the condition (1.2))

$$(1.5) \quad B(w) = \prod_{k=1}^{+\infty} \frac{a_k - w}{1-\bar{a}_k w} \frac{|a_k|}{a_k} , \quad a_k = \overline{\Phi(b_k)^{-1}} ,$$

$$(1.6)\qquad \frac{(w-a_k)^{p_k}}{B(w)} = \sum_{\nu=0}^{+\infty} \alpha_\nu(a_k)(w-a_k)^\nu, \quad k = 1,2,\ldots,$$

and

$$(1.7)\qquad \Omega_k(w) = \frac{(w-a_k)^{s_k}}{(s_k-1)!}\,\frac{B(w)}{(w-a_k)^{p_k}} \sum_{\nu=0}^{p_k-s_k} \alpha_\nu(a_k)(w-a_k)^\nu,$$

$$k = 1,2,\ldots .$$

Dzarbajian [2] proved that $\{\eta_k(w)\}$ and $\{\Omega_k(w)\}$ are biorthogonal systems on $|w| = 1$, i.e.

$$(1.8)\qquad \frac{1}{2\pi}\int_{|w|=1} \eta_k(w)\,\overline{\Omega_n(w)}\,|dw| = \frac{1}{2\pi}\int_{|w|=1} \overline{\eta_k(w)}\,\Omega_n(w)\,|dw| = \delta_{k,n}$$

$$k = 1,2,\ldots, \quad n = 1,2,\ldots .$$

From $\Omega_k(w)$, $k = 1,2,\ldots$, we construct

$$(1.9)\qquad \rho_k^{(1/p)}(z) = \frac{\Phi'(z)}{\Phi(z)}^{1/p}\,\overline{\Omega_k\left(\frac{1}{\overline{\Phi(z)}}\right)}, \quad k = 1,2,\ldots .$$

It can be proved (Shen 1984 [3]) that

$$\frac{1}{2\pi i}\int_\Gamma m_n^{(1/p)}(\xi)\rho_m^{(1/p)}(\xi)\,d\xi = \delta_{n,m},$$

$$n = 1,2,\ldots, \quad m = 1,2,\ldots .$$

(For special case $p = 2$ see H.M. Hairapetian 1975 [4] ; for different $\{b_j\}$ see H.M. Hairapetian 1974 [5] and M.M. Dzarbajian 1973 [6]).

Definition. The $\{b_k\}$ (or $\{a_k\}$, $a_k = \overline{\Phi(b_k)^{-1}}$, $k=1,2,\dots$) is said to belong to $\Delta(P,\delta)$, if it satisfies condition (1.4) and condition

$$(1.10)\quad \inf_k \prod_{a_j \neq a_k} \left| \frac{a_j - a_k}{1-\bar{a}_j a_k} \right| \geq \delta > 0, \quad a_k = \overline{\Phi(b_k)^{-1}}, \; k=1,2,\dots .$$

Theorem 1 (Shen 1984[3]) Suppose $\{b_k\} \in \Delta(P,\delta)$, then every function $f(z) \in E_p(G)$, $p > 1$ has the representation:

$$(1.11)\quad f(z) = \sum_{k=1}^{+\infty} l_k(f) m_k^{(1/p)}(z)$$

$$+ \frac{1}{2\pi i} \int_{|t|=1} \frac{f[\Psi(t)]\,\Psi'(t)^{1/p}}{t\,B(t)} \gamma(\tfrac{1}{t};z)\,dt, \quad z \in G$$

where

$$(1.12)\quad l_k(z) = \frac{1}{2\pi i} \int_\Gamma f(\xi)\,\rho_k^{(1/p)}(\xi)\,d\xi, \quad k=1,2,\dots,$$

$$\gamma(w;z) = \frac{1}{2\pi i} \int_{|t|=1} \frac{B(t)\Psi'(t)^{1/q}}{\Psi(t)-z} \frac{dt}{1-tw} \in H_q(|w|<1),$$

$$\frac{1}{q} + \frac{1}{p} = 1.$$

Definition. The function $f(z)$ is said to belong to $\lambda_p(G;b_j)$ if

1° $\quad f(z) \in E_p(G)$, $\quad p > 1$;

2° $$\frac{1}{2\pi i} \int_{|t|=1} \frac{f[\Psi(t)]\Psi'(t)^{1/p}}{t\,B(t)} \gamma(\tfrac{1}{t};z)\,dt \equiv 0, \quad z \in G.$$

It is obvious, $m_k^{(1/p)}(z) \in \lambda_p(G;b_j)$, $k=1,2,\ldots$.

<u>Theorem 2</u> (Shen 1984[3]) Let $G \in K_q \cap K_p$, $\frac{1}{p} + \frac{1}{q} = 1$, $p > 1$, $\{b_j\} \in \Delta(P,\delta)$, then for any given $f(z) \in \lambda_p(G;b_j)$ the series

$$(1.13) \qquad \sum_{k=1}^{+\infty} l_k(f) m_k^{(1/p)}(z) = f(z)$$

converges in $L_p(\Gamma)$ strongly.

<u>Remark</u> By the condition of above theorem it is easy to see

$$(1.14) \qquad R_p(G;b_j) = \lambda_p(G;b_j).$$

Consequently, system $\{m_k^{(1/p)}(z)\}$ is the basis in its closure $R_p(G;b_j)$.

We would like to characterize the class $R_p(G;b_j)$ by the following theorem.

<u>Theorem 3</u> (Shen 1984[3]) Under the condition of Theorem 2, the class $R_p(G;b_j) = \lambda_p(G;b_j)$, $p > 1$ can be characterized as follows:

1° $\quad f(z) \in E_p(G)$,

2° $\quad f(z) = B[\Phi(z)]F(z)$, $z \in G_\infty$, $F(z) \in E_p^\circ(G_\infty)$,

where $B(w)$ is the Blaschke product (see (1.5)).

3° $\quad$ The boundary values of $f(z)$ from inside and outside Γ are identical almost everywhere.

Now we are going to consider another system $\{\rho_k^{(1/p)}(z)\}$.

Theorem 4 (Shen[7]) Let $G \in K_p$, $p > 1$ and the sequence $\{b_k\}$ in G_∞ satisfying the condition (1.2), then the system $\{\rho_k^{(1/p)}(z)\}$ is out complete in $E_q^o(G_\infty)$, $\frac{1}{q} + \frac{1}{p} = 1$.

Thus the space $Q_p(G_\infty; b_j)$ produced by the system $\{\rho_k^{(1/p)}(z)\}$ is a real subspace in $E_q^o(G_\infty)$, so we are interested in its characteristic properties.

Theorem 5 (Shen[7]) Let $G \in K_q \cap K_p$, $p > 1$, $\frac{1}{q} + \frac{1}{p} = 1$, $\{b_k\} \in \Delta(P, \delta)$, then every function $g(\xi) \in E_q^o(G_\infty)$ possesses the following representation

$$(1.15) \quad g(\xi) = \sum_{k=1}^{+\infty} h_k(g)\rho_k^{(1/p)}(\xi)$$

$$+ \frac{\Phi'(\xi)^{1/q}}{B[\Phi(\xi)]} \frac{1}{2\pi i} \int_\Gamma f(z)Q(z;\xi)dz, \quad \xi \in G_\infty,$$

where $B(w)$ is the Blaschke product (see (1.5)),

$$(1.16) \quad h_k(g) = \frac{1}{2\pi i} \int_\Gamma g(\xi) m_k^{(1/p)}(\xi)d\xi, \quad k=1,2,\ldots,$$

and

$$(1.17) \quad Q(z;\xi) = \frac{1}{2\pi i} \int_\Gamma \frac{B[\Phi(\eta)]\Phi'(\eta)^{1/p} \, d\eta}{(\eta - z)(\Phi(\xi) - \Phi(\eta))}, \quad z \in G, \quad \xi \in G_\infty.$$

Definition. The function $g(\xi)$ is said to belong to $M_q(G_\infty; b_j)$ if

1° $\quad g(\xi) \in E_q^o(G_\infty)$,

2° $\quad \frac{1}{2\pi i} \int_\Gamma g(z)Q(z;\xi)dz \equiv 0, \quad \xi \in G_\infty$.

Theorem 6(Shen[7]) Suppose $G \in K_q \cap K_p$, $q > 1$, $\frac{1}{p} + \frac{1}{q} = 1$, $\{b_k\} \in \Delta(P,\delta)$. If function $g(\xi) \in M_q(G_\infty; b_j)$, then the series

$$(1.18) \qquad \sum_{k=1}^{+\infty} h_k(g)\rho_k^{(1/p)}(\xi) = g(\xi)$$

converges in $L_q(\Gamma)$ strongly.

Remark By the condition of the above theorem it is easy to see

$$(1.19) \qquad Q_q(G_\infty; b_j) = M_q(G_\infty; b_j).$$

Consequently system $\{\rho_k^{(1/p)}(\xi)\}$ is the basis in its closure $Q_q(G_\infty; b_j)$.

We would like to characterize the class $Q_q(G_\infty; b_j)$ by the following theorem.

Theorem 7 (Shen[7]) Under the condition of Theorem 6, the necessary and sufficient condition for $g(\xi) \in M_q(G_\infty; b_j) = Q_q(G_\infty; b_j)$ is that there exists a function $G(\tau) \in H_q(|\tau| < 1)$ such that

$$G(\tau) = g[\Psi(\tau)]B(\tau)\Psi'(\tau)^{1/q}, \quad |\tau| = 1$$

holds almost everywhere where $B(\tau)$ is defined by (1.5) and $\Psi(\tau)$ is a mapping function.

2. Moment problem

For the system $\{\rho_k^{(1/p)}(\xi)\}$ we can pose the moment problem: for any given sequence $\{g_k\}$ of complex numbers can we find a function $f(z) \in E_p(G)$, $p > 1$ such that

$$(2.1) \qquad \frac{1}{2\pi i} \int_\Gamma f(\xi)\rho_k^{(1/p)}(\xi)d\xi = g_k, \quad k=1,2,\ldots ?$$

Theorem 8 (Shen[8]) Let $G \in K_q \cap K_p$, $p > 1$, $\frac{1}{q} + \frac{1}{p} = 1$, $\{b_k\} \in \Delta(P,\delta)$, then the necessary and sufficient condition for solving the moment problem (2.1) in $E_p(G)$ is

$$(2.2) \quad \|g_k\|^{\{b_j\}} := \{\sum_{k=1}^{+\infty} (1-|a_k|)^{-ps_k+1} |g_k|^p\}^{1/p} < +\infty,$$

$$a_k = \overline{\Phi(b_k)^{-1}}, \qquad k=1,2,\ldots,$$

and in the case of existence of solution it can be expressed as follows:

$$(2.3) \qquad f(z) = \sum_{k=1}^{+\infty} g_k m_k^{(1/p)}(z), \qquad z \in G.$$

The series (2.3) converges in $L_p(\Gamma)$ strongly and converges in the interior of G uniformly. Besides $f(z) \in \lambda_p(G;b_j)$.

Furthermore

$$(2.4) \qquad \|f\|_{L_p(\Gamma)} \le C \|g_k\|^{\{b_j\}},$$

where C is a constant.

Theorem 9 (Shen[8]) Under the condition of Theorem 8, if (2.2) is valid, then all the solution of moment problem (2.1) $f(z) \in E_p(G)$, $p > 1$ can be expressed as follows:

$$f(z) = f_1(z) + f_2(z),$$

where $f_1(z) \in \lambda_p(G;b_j)$,

$$(2.5) \qquad f_1(z) = \sum_{k=1}^{+\infty} g_k m_k^{(1/p)}(z) = \sum_{k=1}^{+\infty} l_k(f_1) m_k^{(1/p)}(z),$$

where $l_k(f_1)$ is defined by (1.12) and the series (2.5) converges in $L_p(\Gamma)$, $f_2(z) \in E_p(G)$ and the function

$$F_2(w) = \frac{1}{2\pi i} \int_{|\tau|=1} \frac{f_2[\Psi(\tau)]\Psi'(\tau)^{1/p}}{\tau - w} d\tau \in H_p(|w|<1)$$

possesses the expression

$$F_2(w) = B(w)\tilde{F}_2(w), \quad \tilde{F}_2(w) \in H_p(|w|<1).$$

Theorem 10 (Shen[8]) Suppose $G \in K_p \cap K_q$, $p > 1$, $\frac{1}{q} + \frac{1}{p} = 1$. For any given $\{g_k\}$ satisfying (2.2) the necessary and sufficient condition for the moment problem (2.1) with a solution $f(z) \in E_p(G)$ is $\{b_k\} \in \Delta(P,\delta)$.

Now for any given function $f(z) \in E_p(G)$, $p > 1$ define g_k according to (2.1), then introduce an operator:

$$M_p : f \in E_p(G) \to \{(1 - |\Phi(b_k)|)^{-s_k+1/p} g_k\}.$$

From Theorem 8 we know that if $\{b_k\} \in \Delta(P,\delta)$, then $M_p(E_p(G)) \subset l_p$. But by combining Theorems 8 and 10 we can directly obtain the following theorem.

Theorem 11 (Shen[8]) Let $G \in K_q \cap K_p$, $q > 1$, $\frac{1}{p} + \frac{1}{q} = 1$, and sequence $\{b_k\}$ satisfies the conditions (1.4) and (1.2), then the necessary and sufficient condition for $M_p(E_p(G)) = l_p$ is $\{b_k\} \in \Delta(P,\delta)$.

References

(1) X.C. Shen: On the approximation by rational functions in certain class of domains. Scienta sinica 11 (1980), 1029-1039 (Chinese), (English translation 24:8(1981), 1033-1046).

(2) M.M. Dzarbasjan: Biorthogonal systems and the solution of interpolation problem based on the nodes with bounded multiplicity in class H_2, Izv. Akad. Nauk Armjan SSR Ser. Math. 9:5 (1974), 339-373 (Russian).

(3) X.C. Shen: On the basis of rational functions in a certain class of domains. Journal of Approximation Theory and its Applications, 1:1 (1984), 123-140.

(4) H.M. Hairapetian: On the basis of biorthogonal systems in complex plane, Izv. Akad. Nank Armjan SSR Ser. Math. 10:2 (1975), 133-152 (Russian).

(5) H.M. Hairapetian: On the basis of rational functions in the subspace of classes $E_p(1 < p < +\infty)$, Izv. Akad. Nauk Armjan SSR Ser. Math. 9:3 (1974), 171-184.

(6) M.M. Dzarbasjan: Biorthogonal systems of rational functions and representation of Cauchy kernel, Izv. Akad. Nauk Armjan SSR Ser. Math. 8:5 (1973), 384-406 (Russian).

(7) X.C. Shen: On the incompleteness basis of a system of analytic functions, Scienta Sinica (to appear).

(8) X.C. Shen: On the moment problem of a system of analytic functions, Proceedings of Approximation Theory and its Applications, held in St. Johns, Newfoundland, Canada 1984, (to appear).

Prof. Xie-Chang Shen, Department of Mathematics, Peking University, Beijing, China

International Series of
Numerical Mathematics, Vol. 75

NORMEN VON PROJEKTIONEN IN MEHREREN VERÄNDERLICHEN

Burkhard Sündermann

Es sei $K \subset \mathbb{R}^r$ kompakt, $C(K)$ der Raum der stetigen reellwertigen Funktionen auf K und $\mathbb{P} \subset C(K)$ ein endlichdimensionaler Teilraum von $C(K)$. Wir nennen eine lineare Abbildung $L: C(K) \to \mathbb{P}$ eine Projektion von $C(K)$ auf $\mathbb{P}$, falls L surjektiv ist und $L \circ L = L$ gilt. Ferner sei

$$||L|| := \max \{ ||Lf||_\infty \mid f \in C(K),\ ||f||_\infty = 1 \}$$

mit

$$||f||_\infty := \max \{ |f(x)| \mid x \in K \} .$$

Die Projektionskonstante $\Lambda(\mathbb{P})$ des Teilraumes $\mathbb{P}$ (bzgl. $C(K)$) ist definiert durch

$$\Lambda(\mathbb{P}) := \inf \{ ||L|| \mid L \text{ ist Projektion von } C(K) \text{ auf } \mathbb{P} \} .$$

Im folgenden betrachten wir eine Folge $\{\mathbb{P}_n\}$ von Teilräumen $\mathbb{P}_n$, $n \in \mathbb{N}$, von $C(K)$ mit den Eigenschaften

$$\mathbb{P}_n \subset \mathbb{P}_{n+1} \quad \text{für } n \in \mathbb{N} \quad \text{und} \quad \overline{\bigcup_{n \in \mathbb{N}} \mathbb{P}_n} = C(K) .$$

Es sei ferner eine Folge von Projektionen $L_n: C(K) \to \mathbb{P}_n$ gegeben sowie $f \in C(K)$. Wir beschäftigen uns hier mit der Frage, unter welchen Bedingungen

$$L_n f \to f \tag{1}$$

gilt. Es sei

$$\operatorname{dist}(f,\mathbb{P}) := \min \{ ||f-p||_\infty \mid p \in \mathbb{P} \}$$

die Minimalabweichung von f in $\mathbb{P}$.

Dann gilt die bekannte Ungleichung

$$\|f - L_n f\|_\infty \leq (1 + \|L_n\|)\cdot \mathrm{dist}(f,\mathbb{P}_n) . \qquad (2)$$

Wählt man für die Räume $\mathbb{P}_n$ geeignete Polynomräume, so lassen sich unter Benutzung bekannter Sätze vom "Jackson-Typ" (vgl. [7-9]) Aussagen über die Konvergenzordnung von $\mathrm{dist}(f,\mathbb{P}_n)$ in Abhängigkeit von Regularitätsaussagen über f machen.
Die Untersuchung der Gültigkeit von (1) reduziert sich damit auf die Bestimmung der Normen $\|L_n\|$, die in diesem Zusammenhang auch Lebesgue-Konstanten genannt werden. Natürlich gilt stets $\|L_n\| \geq \Lambda(\mathbb{P}_n)$, und zur Konstruktion "guter" Operatoren ist es notwendig, die Projektionskonstanten $\Lambda(\mathbb{P}_n)$ oder zumindest ihr asymptotisches Wachstum zu bestimmen sowie eine geeignete Folge $\{L_n\}$, für die dieses Wachstum erreicht wird.
Ein erstes Ergebnis im Fall trigonometrischer Polynome stammt von Berman (vgl. z.B. M.W. Müller [6]). Eine Verallgemeinerung findet man bei Daugavet [1], der den Raum $\mathbb{H}_\mu^r$ der harmonischen Polynome in r Veränderlichen des Grades μ eingeschränkt auf die Einheitssphäre $S^{r-1} := \{x \in \mathbb{R}^r \mid |x| = 1\}$ betrachtet.
Daugavet zeigt, daß Teilsummen von Lagrange-Entwicklungen Projektionen mit minimaler Norm liefern. Das asymptotische Wachstum der Lebesgue-Konstanten dieser Operatoren ist bekannt, vgl. [1].
Es ist naheliegend, neben dem Raum $\mathbb{H}_\mu^r$ den Raum $\mathbb{P}_\mu^r$ der Polynome vom Grad μ in r Veränderlichen eingeschränkt auf die Einheitskugel $B^r := \{x \in \mathbb{R}^r \mid |x| \leq 1\}$ zu betrachten. Im Fall r=1 läßt sich mit Bermans Methode das asymptotische Wachstum der Projektionskonstanten $\Lambda(\mathbb{P}_\mu^1)$ angeben. In diesem Fall sind ebenfalls Operatoren mit optimalem Wachstum der Lebesgue-Konstanten bekannt, allerdings keine Projektionen mit minimaler Norm. Im Fall $r \geq 2$ gibt Daugavet [1] eine untere Schranke für die Projektionskonstanten an, die, wie wir zeigen werden, jedoch nicht scharf ist.

Wir verwenden eine andere, in einem Spezialfall bereits von Faber [2] benutzte konstruktive Methode, mit der man sowohl Daugavets Ergebnis wie auch genaue asymptotische Aussagen über das Wachstum der Projektionskonstanten der Räume $\mathbb{P}_\mu^r$ erhält. Projektionsoperatoren mit entsprechendem Wachstum der Lebesgue-Konstanten sind ebenfalls bekannt.

Um das Prinzip der von uns benutzten Methode zu verdeutlichen, betrachten wir zunächst einen Spezialfall, der bereits im Ergebnis von Daugavet enthalten ist.

Satz 1

Es sei $r \geq 2$. Dann existiert eine reelle Zahl $c_r > 0$, so daß für alle $\mu \in \mathbb{N}$ und jeden Interpolationsoperator L von $C(S^{r-1})$ auf $\mathbb{H}_\mu^r$ gilt:

$$||L|| \geq c_r \cdot \begin{cases} \log \mu & \text{für } r=2 \\ \mu^{\frac{r-2}{2}} & \text{für } r\geq 3 \end{cases} .$$

Beweis

Im Fall $r=2$ ist $\mathbb{H}_\mu^2$ isomorph zum Raum der trigonometrischen Polynome des Grades μ. Hier ist der Satz seit langem bekannt, vgl. z.B. Faber [1].

Es sei jetzt $r \geq 3$. Zur Abkürzung schreiben wir $n := \dim \mathbb{H}_\mu^r$. L sei ein Interpolationsoperator von $C(S^{r-1})$ auf $\mathbb{H}_\mu^r$, $x^{(1)}, x^{(2)}, \ldots, x^{(n)}$ die zugehörigen Knoten. Der Satz ist natürlich bewiesen, falls man ein $h \in \mathbb{H}_\mu^r$ und $c_r > 0$ angeben kann mit

$$|h(x^{(j)})| \leq 1, \; j=1,\ldots,n \quad \text{und} \quad ||h||_\infty \geq c_r \cdot \mu^{\frac{r-2}{2}} .$$

Ein solches Polynom h wird im folgenden konstruiert.

Es sei $T_{\mu+1}$ das Tschebyscheff-Polynom 1. Art vom Grad $\mu+1$ sowie $P_j^r := C_j^{\frac{r-2}{2}} / C_j^{\frac{r-2}{2}}(1)$, $j=0,\ldots,\mu+1$, wobei C_j^λ das Gegenbauerpolynom vom Grad j mit Index λ bezeichnet. Wir entwickeln $T_{\mu+1}$ nach den P_j^r:

$$T_{\mu+1} = \sum_{j=0}^{\mu+1} a_j \cdot P_j^r \quad .$$

$T_{\mu+1}$ hat den Höchstkoeffizienten 2^μ und $P_{\mu+1}^r$ den Höchstkoeffizienten $\frac{\Gamma(r-1)\cdot\Gamma(\mu+1+r/2)\cdot 2^{\mu+1}}{(2\mu+r)\cdot\Gamma(\mu+r-1)\cdot\Gamma(r/2)}$ (vgl. C. Müller [5]).

Also ist $\quad a_{\mu+1} = \frac{(2\mu+r)\cdot\Gamma(\mu+r-1)\cdot\Gamma(r/2)}{\Gamma(r-1)\cdot\Gamma(\mu+1+r/2)\cdot 2} \quad .$

Unter Benutzung bekannter asymptotischer Darstellungen für die Γ-Funktion ergibt sich hieraus die Existenz eines $c_r > 0$ mit

$$a_{\mu+1} - 1 \geqq c_r \cdot \mu^{\frac{r-2}{2}} \quad \text{für alle hinreichend großen } \mu.$$

$l_j \in \mathbb{H}_\mu^r$, $j=1,\ldots,n$, seien die Lagrange-Polynome zum Operator L, d.h. es gilt $l_j(x^{(k)}) = \delta_{jk}$.

Wir definieren $\quad I := \int_{S^{r-1}} \sum_{j=1}^{n} l_j(x)\cdot P_{\mu+1}^r(x\cdot x^{(j)}) \, dx \quad .$

$P_{\mu+1}^r(x\cdot x^{(j)})$ stimmt auf S^{r-1} mit einem homogenen harmonischen Polynom des Grades $\mu+1$ überein. Wegen $l_j \in \mathbb{H}_\mu^r$ ist daher $I = 0$. Infolgedessen existiert ein $y \in S^{r-1}$ mit

$$\sum_{j=1}^{n} l_j(y)\cdot P_{\mu+1}^r(y\cdot x^{(j)}) = 0 \quad .$$

$h \in \mathbb{H}_\mu^r$ sei nun definiert durch

$$h(x) := a_{\mu+1} \cdot \sum_{j=1}^{n} l_j(x)\cdot P_{\mu+1}^r(y\cdot x^{(j)}) + \sum_{j=0}^{\mu} a_j \cdot P_j^r(x\cdot y) \quad .$$

Dann ist $|h(x^{(j)})| = |T_{\mu+1}(y\cdot x^{(j)})| \leqq 1$, $j=1,\ldots,n$,
und

$$h(y) = a_{\mu+1}\cdot \sum_{j=1}^{n} l_j(y)\cdot P^r_{\mu+1}(y\cdot x^{(j)}) + \sum_{j=0}^{\mu} a_j\cdot P^r_j(y\cdot y)$$

$$= \sum_{j=0}^{\mu} a_j\cdot P^r_j(1) \quad .$$

Wegen $T_{\mu+1}(1) = P^r_{\mu+1}(1) = 1$ gilt daher

$$|h(y)| \geqq a_{\mu+1} - 1 \geqq c_r\cdot\mu^{\frac{r-2}{2}} \quad .$$

Der Satz ist damit für alle hinreichend großen μ bewiesen. Wegen $||L|| \geqq 1$ gilt er dann auch für alle $\mu \in \mathbb{N}$.

Der Beweis von Satz 1 scheint auf Interpolationsoperatoren zugeschnitten zu sein. Es ist jedoch möglich, ihn auf den Fall allgemeiner Projektionen zu übertragen. Einen ausführlichen Beweis findet man in [10]. Es gilt also auch

Satz 1'

Es sei $r\geqq 2$. Dann existiert eine reelle Zahl $c_r>0$, so daß für alle $\mu \in \mathbb{N}$ und jeden Projektionsoperator L von $C(S^{r-1})$ auf $\mathbb{H}^r_\mu$ gilt:

$$||L|| \geqq c_r\cdot \begin{cases} \log\mu & \text{für } r=2 \\ \mu^{\frac{r-2}{2}} & \text{für } r\geqq 3 \end{cases}$$

Wie bereits erwähnt, läßt sich die von uns benutzte Methode auch auf die Räume $\mathbb{P}^r_\mu$, $r\geqq 2$, übertragen. Der Beweis ist in diesem Fall technisch aufwendiger und erfordert einige Hilfsmittel über spezielle Funktionen, vgl. hierzu [10] und [11].

Satz 2

Es sei $r \in \mathbb{N}$. Dann existiert eine reelle Zahl $c_r > 0$, so daß für alle $\mu \in \mathbb{N}$ und jeden Projektionsoperator L von $C(B^r)$ auf $\mathbb{P}^r_\mu$ gilt:

$$||L|| \geq c_r \cdot \begin{cases} \log \mu & \text{für } r=1 \\ \mu^{\frac{r-1}{2}} & \text{für } r \geq 2 \end{cases} .$$

Satz 2 gibt untere Schranken für die Projektionskonstanten $\Lambda(\mathbb{P}^r_\mu)$. Man stellt sich natürlich die Frage, wie genau diese Schranken sind. Im Fall r=1 liefern Orthogonalentwicklungen nach Tschebyscheff-Polynomen Projektionsoperatoren, deren Lebesgue-Konstanten von der Ordnung $\log \mu$ wachsen. Analog kann man für $r \geq 2$ Partialsummen von Entwicklungen nach Orthogonalpolynomen bzgl. des Skalarproduktes

$$\langle f,g \rangle := \int_{B^r} (1-x^2)^{-1/2} \cdot f(x) \cdot g(x) \, dx$$

betrachten. Die Lebesgue-Konstanten der zugehörigen Projektionsoperatoren wachsen von der gleichen Ordnung wie die in Satz 2 angegebenen unteren Schranken (vgl. Kogbetliantz [3]). Diese Schranken sind daher, bis auf eine genaue Bestimmung der Konstanten, scharf. Wir sind damit in der Lage, die exakte Ordnung der Projektionskonstanten $\Lambda(\mathbb{P}^r_\mu)$ anzugeben.

Korollar 1

Es sei $r \geq 2$. Dann existieren Konstanten $0 < b_r \leq c_r$, so daß für alle $\mu \in \mathbb{N}$ für die Projektionskonstanten $\Lambda(\mathbb{P}^r_\mu)$ der Räume $\mathbb{P}^r_\mu$ gilt:

$$b_r \cdot \mu^{\frac{r-1}{2}} \leqq \Lambda(\mathbb{P}_\mu^r) \leqq c_r \cdot \mu^{\frac{r-1}{2}} .$$

Nach Korollar 1 kennt man das genaue Wachstum der Projektionskonstanten, ohne allerdings Projektionen mit minimaler Norm zu kennen. Dabei ist jedoch zu beachten, daß selbst im Fall r=1 bis auf wenige Ausnahmen keine Minimalprojektionen bekannt sind (siehe hierzu Morris und Cheney [4]).

Die von uns benutzte Methode zur Konstruktion unterer Schranken von Projektionskonstanten läßt sich auf eine Reihe weiterer Polynomräume, z.B. Räume homogener harmonischer Polynome auf der Einheitssphäre oder Räume gewisser Orthogonalpolynome auf der Einheitskugel, anwenden. In vielen Fällen lassen sich ebenfalls Projektions- oder sogar Interpolationsoperatoren mit asymptotisch minimalem Wachstum angeben. Für Einzelheiten verweisen wir auf [10].

LITERATUR

[1] Daugavet, I.K.: Some applications of the Marcinkiewicz-Berman identity. Vestnik Leningrad Univ. Math. 1, 321 - 327 (1974)

[2] Faber, G.: Über die interpolatorische Darstellung stetiger Funktionen. Jahresbericht DMV 23, 192 - 210 (1914)

[3] Kogbetliantz, E.: Recherches sur la sommabilité des séries ultrasphérique par la méthode des moyennes arithmétique. Journal de Mathématique (9), 3, 125 - 196 (1924)

[4] Morris, P.D., Cheney, E.W.: On the existence and characterization of minimal projections. J. Reine Angew. Math. 270, 61 - 76 (1974)

[5] Müller, C.: Spherical harmonics. Berlin, Heidelberg, New York: Springer 1966

[6] Müller, M.W.: Approximationstheorie. Wiesbaden: Akademische Verlagsgesellschaft 1978

[7] Newman, D.J., Shapiro, H.S.: Jackson's theorems in higher dimensions. Proc. Conf. Appr. Theory Oberwolfach 1963. Basel: Birkhäuser 208 - 219, 1964

[8] Ragozin, D.L.: Polynomial approximations on compact manifolds and homogeneous spaces. Trans. Amer. Math. Soc. 150, 41 - 53 (1970)

[9] Ragozin, D.L.: Constructive polynomial approximation on spheres and projective spaces. Trans. Amer. Math. Soc. 162, 157 - 170 (1972)

[10] Sündermann, B.: Projektionen auf Polynomräume in mehreren Veränderlichen. Dissertation, Dortmund 1963

[11] Sündermann, B.: On projection constants of polynomial spaces on the unit ball in several variables. Math. Z. 188, 111 - 117 (1984)

Dr. Burkhard Sündermann
Universität Dortmund
Abteilung Mathematik
Postfach 500 500
D-4600 Dortmund 50
Bundesrepublik Deutschland

International Series of
Numerical Mathematics, Vol. 75

THE SOLUTION OF GENERALIZED LEAST SQUARES PROBLEMS

G.A. Watson

Department of Mathematical Sciences, University of Dundee

1. Introduction

A problem frequently encountered in empirical sciences is that of establishing a causal relationship between experimental variables. This involves firstly the selection of a suitable model for the process under consideration containing a number of free parameters, and secondly the choice of values of these parameters to give a best fit, in an appropriate sense, to the available data. The usual procedure is to treat one of the problem variables as being the 'dependent' variable, and to attribute errors to the observed values of that variable. The parameters are then chosen so as to make these errors small in some sense: for example a commonly used method is to minimize the sum of squares.

In this conventional approach, there is an implicit assumption that values of the 'independent' variables are exact (or contain negligible errors). In many situations, however, this is an oversimplification, and use of the usual least squares method may lead to bias in the estimated parameter and variance values (see, for example [10], [11]). It is then necessary to take proper account of errors in all variable values, and this is the motivation behind the idea of generalized least squares. For a general treatment of some problems of this kind, see [15].

The purpose of this paper is to suggest some ways of solving generalized least squares problems. It will be assumed that a suitable choice of model has already been made, and also that the least squares criterion (with weighting if necessary) is an appropriate one. Let $x \in R^k$ be the vector of problem variables, let $x_i \in R^k$, $i = 1,2,\dots,m$, be the observed values of these, and let $W_i \in R^{k\times k}$, $i = 1,2,\dots,m$ be positive diagonal weighting matrices. Then if the underlying relationship is given by

$$f(a,x) = 0 \tag{1.1}$$

where $f: R^n \times R^k \to R$, the corresponding generalized least squares problem may be stated as

$$\begin{aligned} &\text{minimize} \quad \sum_{i=1}^{m} e_i^T W_i e_i \\ &\text{subject to } f(a, x_i + e_i) = 0,\ i = 1,2,\dots,m. \end{aligned} \tag{1.2}$$

We will consider two distinct general classes of problems of this kind, in Sections 3 and 4. First, however, we introduce a rather special generalized least squares problem which turns out to be equivalent to a problem whose solution is known.

2. Fitting a linear manifold

Let $x_i \in R^k$, $i = 1,2,\dots,m > k$ be observed data and consider the problem of fitting to this data an n-dimensional linear manifold, where $1 \le n \le k-1$. If unit weights are assumed, the corresponding generalized least squares problem is to find $p \in R^k$, $Z \in R^{k\times n}$ with rank n to minimize $\sum_{i=1}^{m} e_i^T e_i$ subject to

$$x_i + e_i = p + Zt_i,\ i = 1,2,\dots,m, \tag{2.1}$$

where $t_i \in R^n$ are parameter vectors, or equivalently to minimize

$$\sum_{i=1}^{m} (p + Zt_i - x_i)^T (p + Zt_i - x_i) \ . \tag{2.2}$$

In particular, at a minimum we must have

$$p = \bar{x} - Z\bar{t} \ ,$$

where $\bar{x}$ and $\bar{t}$ are means. Without loss of generality, we may assume that the columns of Z are orthonormal, and that $[Y \vdots Z]$ is a $k \times k$ orthogonal matrix. It follows from (2.1) that

$$Y^T(x_i - \bar{x}) + Y^T e_i = 0 \ , \quad i = 1,2,\ldots,m,$$

so that defining matrices $X, E \in R^{m\times k}$ by requiring that X^T, E^T have i^{th} column $x_i - \bar{x}$, e_i respectively, $i = 1,2,\ldots,m$, the problem may be restated:

$$\begin{aligned} &\text{find} \quad E \in R^{m\times k}, \ Y \in R^{k\times(k-n)} \quad \text{to minimize} \quad \sum_{i=1}^{m} e_i^T e_i \\ &\text{subject to} \quad (X+E)Y = 0 \\ &\qquad\qquad\quad Y^T Y = I \ . \end{aligned} \tag{2.3}$$

In this form the problem has a known solution. Let the $(k-n)$ smallest eigenvalues of X^TX be $\lambda_1, \lambda_2, \ldots, \lambda_{k-n}$ with corresponding orthonormal eigenvectors $y_1, y_2, \ldots, y_{k-n}$. Then (2.3) is solved by taking Y to be the matrix with columns y_i, $i = 1,2,\ldots,k-n$, and setting $E = -XYY^T$; the minimum value of the sum of squares is $\sum_{i=1}^{k-n} \lambda_i$ (see, for example [6], [12]).

<u>Remark</u> The above problem may be interpreted as that of minimizing the sum of squares of orthogonal distances from the data points to the manifold: see [14].

3. Explicit models

We return now to the general problem of Section 1. It is usually the case that one of the variables may be split off from the others so that it can be made the subject of the relationship (1.1), and so plays the traditional role of the dependent variable. It is convenient to think now of the total number of variables as $(k+1)$, and of (1.1) being replaced by the relation

$$y = f(a,x), \qquad (3.1)$$

where $y \in R$, $x \in R^k$ and $f:R^n \times R^k \to R$, with f assumed to be a C^2 function of its parameters. Then if $w_i > 0$, $i = 1,2,\ldots,m$ are given weights (1.2) is replaced by

$$\begin{aligned} &\text{minimize} \quad \sum_{i=1}^{m} w_i r_i^2 + \sum_{i=1}^{m} e_i^T W_i e_i \\ &\text{subject to } y_i + r_i = f(a,x_i+e_i),\ i = 1,2,\ldots,m. \end{aligned} \qquad (3.2)$$

Before proceeding, it is helpful to have some additional notation: let

$z_i = x_i + e_i$, $i = 1,2,\ldots,m$,

$r \in R^m$ have i^{th} component r_i, $i = 1,2,\ldots,m$,

$d_i \in R^k$ be the vector $\nabla_x f(a,z_i)$, $i = 1,2,\ldots,m$,

$A \in R^{m\times n}$ have i^{th} row $\nabla_a f(a,z_i)^T$, $i = 1,2,\ldots,m$,

$D \in R^{m\times mk}$ have i^{th} row $[\underbrace{0\ldots0}_{\leftarrow(i-1)k\rightarrow}\ d_i^T\ \underbrace{0\ldots0}_{\leftarrow(m-i)k\rightarrow}]$, $i = 1,2,\ldots,m$,

$W_y = \text{diag}\{w_1,w_2,\ldots,w_m\} \in R^{m\times m}$,

and $W_x = \text{diag}\{W_1,W_2,\ldots,W_m\} \in R^{mk\times mk}$.

Then (3.2) is equivalent to the unconstrained problem:

$$\begin{aligned} &\text{minimize} \quad \phi = \tfrac{1}{2} r^T W_y r + \tfrac{1}{2}\sum_{i=1}^{m}(z_i-x_i)^T W_i (z_i-x_i) \\ &\text{where} \quad y_i + r_i = f(a,z_i),\ i = 1,2,\ldots,m. \end{aligned}$$

This problem can be solved by the direct application of a conventional least squares method. However, it is important to exploit the special structure of ϕ, and in particular the fact that the variables a and z (where $z^T = (z_1^T,z_2^T,\ldots,z_m^T)$) can be treated separately. We have, in an obvious notation

$$\phi' = \begin{bmatrix} \phi_a \\ \phi_z \end{bmatrix} \quad \begin{bmatrix} A^T W_y r \\ w_1 r_1 d_1 + W_1(z_1-x_1) \\ \vdots \\ w_m r_m d_m + W_m(z_m-x_m) \end{bmatrix}, \qquad (3.3)$$

$$\phi'' = \begin{bmatrix} \phi_{aa} & \phi_{az} \\ \phi_{za} & \phi_{zz} \end{bmatrix} = \begin{bmatrix} A^T W_y A & A^T W_y D \\ D^T W_y A & D^T W_y D + W_x \end{bmatrix} + \text{second derivative terms} . \tag{3.4}$$

An approximate Newton's method for solving $\phi' = 0$ is given by Powell and Macdonald [9] who include the second derivative terms in (3.4) but replace ϕ_{az} (and ϕ_{za}) by zero, thus permitting separation of the variables in a straightfoward manner. The approach is an extension of a method due to O'Neill, Sinclair and Smith [8] valid when $k = 1$ and $f(a,x)$ is a polynomial in x. We prefer to approximate the Hessian matrix by the matrix displayed on the right hand side of (3.4), a procedure which corresponds to the use of the Gauss-Newton method. Again it is possible to separate the variables, and we use a method based on the approach taken by Ruhe and Wedin [13]. For example if f is an affine function of a, then keeping the other variables fixed the solution of $\phi_a = 0$ is a linear least squares calculation, and it is then possible to proceed by regarding a as a function of z_i, $i = 1,2,\ldots,m$, and performing Gauss-Newton steps in the mk components of z_i, $i = 1,2,\ldots,m$. Because n is likely to be very small compared with mk, and because we are primarily interested in problems which are nonlinear in a, we consider a similar procedure but with the roles of the variables reversed. Then, for each i, $1 \le i \le m$, and fixed a,

$$w_i r_i d_i + W_i (z_i - x_i) = 0 \tag{3.5}$$

is a system of k equations in the k components of z_i, which may be solved by Newton's method or the (damped) Gauss-Newton method (with initial approximation $z_i = x_i$) applied to the minimization of

$$\tfrac{1}{2} w_i r_i^2 + \tfrac{1}{2} (z_i - x_i)^T W_i (z_i - x_i) .$$

Let

$$\psi(a) = \phi_a(a, z(a)) = A^T W_y r.$$

Then using the approximations obtained by ignoring second derivative terms in (3.4),

$$\psi_a(a) \approx A^T W_y A - A^T W_y D(D^T W_y D + W_x)^{-1} D^T W_y A$$
$$= A^T V A, \quad \text{say},$$

where

$$V = \text{diag}\{w_i - w_i^2 d_i (W_i + w_i d_i d_i^T)^{-1} d_i,\ i = 1,2,\ldots,m\}$$
$$= \text{diag}\{w_i/(1+w_i(d_i^T W_i^{-1} d_i)),\ i = 1,2,\ldots,m\}$$

using the Sherman-Morrison formula. The Gauss-Newton step s in the variables a is now obtained by solving the linear least squares problem

$$\text{minimize} \| V^{\frac{1}{2}} As + V^{-\frac{1}{2}} W_y r \|_2 . \tag{3.6}$$

If A has full rank, then s in a descent direction for ϕ at the current point, and the incorporation of a line search can lead to a globally convergent algorithm, corresponding to a (damped) separated Gauss-Newton method. Each iteration of the method involves the separate solution of m minimization problems with k unknowns, and one linear least squares problem of dimension $m \times n$. The fact that each of the problems (3.5) is not finite is an unsatisfactory feature. However some computational savings can be achieved by initially ignoring the errors in x_i, $i = 1,2,\ldots,m$ and just applying the Gauss-Newton method to the usual least squares problem in a (i.e. setting $V = W_y$ in (3.6)). After reasonable reduction in ϕ has been achieved, the current approximation can be used as starting point for the procedure outlined above.

A version of the method has been coded in Algol for the DEC 10 of the University of Dundee (single precision). A simple line search was used, based on an initial trial step length of one, with subsequent halving (if necessary) until a Goldstein-type test was satisfied with $\sigma = 10^{-4}$. Progress of the method was monitored by the size of the directional derivative of ϕ in the Gauss-Newton direction, and the switch from the usual to the generalized least squares method made when this quantity became less than 0.1 in modulus.

Example

The relationship defined by

$$y = a_1(10)^{a_2x/(a_3+x)}$$

connects pressure and temperature in saturated steam. Table 1 shows the progress of the algorithm using data given in [4] p.518 (m=14), with unit weights. The asterisk shows the first value of ϕ calculated from the whole objective function of (3.2).

i	a_1	a_2	a_3	ϕ
1	4	10	300	$4.685_{10}5$
2	4.8780	9.5127	322.60	$1.756_{10}4$
3	5.1753	8.5629	294.111	938.907
4	5.2645	8.5628	294.852	859.118
5	5.2674	8.5652	295.001	9.42594*
6	4.8594	7.6598	247.570	8.05522
7	4.4748	7.1252	218.694	7.68299
8	4.4887	7.1891	221.885	7.63142
9	4.4879	7.1882	221.840	7.63141

Table 1

Pressure of space prevents the inclusion here of further examples which have been treated using the algorithm described above. Some further numerical results may be found in [16].

4. Implicit models

For some problems it is inconvenient, or indeed impossible, to rewrite (1.1) in the form (3.1), and so the techniques of the previous section are no longer appropriate. Retaining previous notation, the problem now to be considered may be written as the constrained problem

$$\begin{aligned} &\text{minimize} \quad \tfrac{1}{2}\sum_{i=1}^{m}(z_i-x_i)^T W_i (z_i-x_i) \\ &\text{subject to } f(a,z_i) = 0, \quad i = 1,2,\ldots,m . \end{aligned} \tag{4.1}$$

A standard approach to the solution of equality constrained optimization problems is through the solution of a sequence of quadratic programming problems, formed by making quadratic approximations to the objective function and linear approximations to the constraints (see, for example [5]). Let $f \in R^m$ denote the vector with components $f(a,z_i)$, $i = 1,2,\ldots,m$ and let $\delta_i \in R^k$, $i = 1,2,\ldots,m$, $s \in R^n$, with $\delta \in R^{mk}$ such that $\delta^T = [\delta_1^T\delta_2^T\ldots\delta_m^T]$. Then the appropriate quadratic programming problem is

$$\begin{aligned} &\text{minimize} \quad \sum_{i=1}^{m}\delta_i^T W_i (z_i-x_i) + \tfrac{1}{2}[\delta^T s^T]B\begin{bmatrix}\delta\\ s\end{bmatrix} \\ &\text{subject to } f + [D\,\vdots\,A]\begin{bmatrix}\delta\\ s\end{bmatrix} = 0, \end{aligned} \tag{4.2}$$

where B is an $(mk+n) \times (mk+n)$ symmetric matrix. Now define the Lagrangian function

$$L = \tfrac{1}{2}\sum_{i=1}^{m}(z_i-x_i)^T W_i (z_i-x_i) + \lambda^T f \tag{4.3}$$

where $\lambda \in R^m$. Then if B is chosen to be the Hessian matrix $\nabla^2 L$ of L with respect to the components of z_i, $i = 1,2,\ldots,m$ and a, the solution of (4.2) is just the Newton step for the solution of the system of equations $\nabla L = 0$. If B is chosen as $\nabla^2 L$ with the second derivative terms ignored then it is easily seen that

$$B = \begin{bmatrix} W_x & 0 \\ 0 & 0 \end{bmatrix}$$

and in this case (4.2) may be rewritten

$$\begin{aligned} &\text{minimize} \quad \sum_{i=1}^{m} \delta_i^T W_i (z_i - x_i) + \tfrac{1}{2} \sum_{i=1}^{m} \delta_i^T W_i \delta_i \\ &\text{subject to } f + [D \vdots A] \begin{bmatrix} \delta \\ s \end{bmatrix} = 0 \ . \end{aligned} \tag{4.4}$$

Let $c \in R^m$ have i^{th} component $d_i^T(z_i - x_i)$, $i = 1,2,\ldots,m$ and define

$$X = \text{diag}\{d_i^T W_i^{-1} d_i, \ i = 1,2,\ldots,m\} \ .$$

Assume further (without loss of generality) that at the current point

$$d_i = 0, \ i = 1,2,\ldots,q \ ,$$

and let the following quantities be partitioned into q and $(m-q)$ elements (or rows):

$$f = \begin{bmatrix} f_1 \\ f_2 \end{bmatrix} \quad c = \begin{bmatrix} c_1 \\ c_2 \end{bmatrix} \quad A = \begin{bmatrix} A_1 \\ A_2 \end{bmatrix} \quad X = \begin{bmatrix} X_1 & \\ & X_2 \end{bmatrix} .$$

<u>Theorem 1</u>

Let $s \in R^n$ solve the problem

$$\begin{aligned} &\text{minimize} \quad \tfrac{1}{2} s^T A_2^T X_2^{-1} A_2 s + (f_2 - c_2)^T X_2^{-1} A_2 s \\ &\text{subject to} \quad f_1 + A_1 s = 0 \end{aligned} \tag{4.5}$$

and let $\mu_1 \in R^q$ be a vector of Lagrange multipliers. Let

$$\mu_2 = X_2^{-1}(f_2 - c_2 + A_2 s), \ \mu = \begin{bmatrix} \mu_1 \\ \mu_2 \end{bmatrix},$$

$$\delta_i = -(z_i - x_i), \ i = 1,2,\ldots,q \ ,$$

$$\delta_i = -\mu_i W_i^{-1} d_i - (z_i - x_i), \ i = q+1,\ldots,m \ .$$

Then s, δ_i, $i = 1,2,\ldots,m$ solve (4.4), with μ a Lagrange multiplier vector.

<u>Proof</u> This follows by straightfoward manipulation of the Kuhn-Tucker conditions for (4.4). □

If $q = 0$ (the usual case) then (4.5) is an unconstrained problem, and a solution may be obtained by solving the linear least squares problem

$$X^{-\frac{1}{2}}As = X^{-\frac{1}{2}}(c-f) \ . \tag{4.6}$$

If $q > 0$, then standard techniques for (4.5) based on the QR factorization of A_1 may be used to reduce (4.5) to an unconstrained problem [5]; again this may be solved as a linear least squares problem because of the structure of the objective function.

If δ_i, $i = 1,2,\ldots,m$ and s are regarded as increments in the current values of z_i, $i = 1,2,\ldots,m$ and a, respectively, then the resulting iterative process is equivalent to the algorithm suggested by Britt and Luecke [2], and the presentation given here may be regarded as a stable and efficient way of implementing that method. There is no guarantee, however, that this algorithm will converge, and the development given here has the further advantage that it shows how the process may be globalized in a straightforward manner. Because the matrix B is positive semi-definite, it follows from standard analysis that the vector $\begin{bmatrix}\delta \\ s\end{bmatrix}$ is a descent direction at the current point for the exact ℓ_1 penalty function

$$P = \tfrac{1}{2}\sum_{i=1}^{m}(z_i-x_i)^T W_i(z_i-x_i) + \theta\|f\|_1$$

provided that $\theta > |\mu_i|$, $i = 1,2,\ldots,m$. The incorporation of a line search then permits progress to be made towards the minimum of P. The eventual rate of convergence will depend primarily on how close the matrix B is to the true Hessian matrix $\nabla^2 L$, and it is easy to see that if $\lambda_i = 0$, $i = 1,2,\ldots,m$, then $B = \nabla^2 L$. Also at a solution to (4.1)

$$W_i(z_i-x_i) + \lambda_i d_i = 0, \quad i = 1,2,\ldots,m \ .$$

Thus if $d_i \neq 0$,

$$\lambda_i = \frac{\| W_i(z_i - x_i) \|}{\| d_i \|} ,$$

so that, as in the usual Gauss-Newton method, the eventual rate of convergence essentially depends on the size of the errors. In particular if $\| d_i \| \neq 0$, $z_i = x_i$, $i = 1,2,\ldots,m$, then $\begin{bmatrix} \delta \\ s \end{bmatrix}$ is just the Newton step for solving $\nabla L = 0$, and so the algorithm can converge at a second order rate.

A version of the algorithm described here has been implemented, with line search strategy as in the previous section. The initial value of θ was chosen to be 1, and this was increased to $\max|\mu_i|$ if necessary.

Example The hyperbolic model defined by

$$f = x_1^2 x_2^2 - a_1$$

is considered in [2], with data for $m = 10$. Taking initially $a_1 = 0$, $z_i = x_i$, $i = 1,2,\ldots,m$ except for $z_{11} = 0.1$, the algorithm described above converged in 11 interations to $a_1 = 126.7971$, with objective function value 3.768530, and penalty function directional derivative in the last direction calculated -0.000008.

For more details and another example see [16].

5. Concluding remarks

The methods of Sections 3 and 4 are based on the Gauss-Newton method, and therefore possess the same disadvantages as that method has in the usual nonlinear least squares situation. In particular, there will certainly be problems for which better approximations of the Hessian matrix will be required for satisfactory performance. A number of methods are now available for nonlinear least squares calculations which achieve these better approximations through the use of quasi-Newton techniques (see, for example, [1], [3], [7]), and for the problems of Section 3 at least it would appear that appropriate modifications of these ideas could be developed. A feature of those methods is the important role which the basic Gauss-Newton method continues to play, and in view of this it is hoped that the methods described here represent some further progress towards the goal of developing efficient numerical methods for the solution of generalized least squares problems.

References

1. Al-Baali, M. and Fletcher, R. Variational methods for nonlinear least squares, Journal of the Oper. Res. Soc. (to appear).

2. Britt, H.I. and Luecke, R.H. The estimation of parameters in nonlinear, implicit models, Technometrics 15 (1973), 233-247.

3. Dennis, J.E. Jr., Gay, D.M. and Welsch, R.E. An adaptive nonlinear least squares algorithm, A.C.M. Trans. Math. Software 7 (1981), 348-368.

4. Draper, N.R. and Smith, H. Applied Regression Analysis (Second Edition), Wiley, New York (1981).

5. Fletcher, R. Practical Methods of Optimization, Vol. II, Constrained Optimization, Wiley, Chichester (1981).

6. Golub, G.H. Least squares, singular values and matrix approximations, Aplikace Mathematiky 13 (1968), 44-51.

7. Nazareth, L. An adaptive method for minimizing a sum of squares of nonlinear functions, IIASA Report WP-83-99 (1983).

8. O'Neill, M., Sinclair, I.G. and Smith, F.J. Polynomial curve fitting when abscissas and ordinates are both subject to error, The Computer Journal 12 (1969), 52-56.

9. Powell, D.R. and Macdonald, J.R. A rapidly convergent iterative method for the solution of the generalized nonlinear least squares problem, The Computer Journal 15 (1972), 148-155.

10. Macdonald, J.R. Review of some experimental and analytical equations of state, Rev. Mod. Phys. 41 (1969), 306-349.

11. Macdonald, J.R. and Powell, D.R. Discrimination between equations of state, J. Res. Nat. Bur. Stand. Series A 75A (1971), 441-453.

12. Rao, C.R. Matrix approximations and reduction of dimensionality in multivariate statistical analysis, in Multivariate Analysis V (ed. P.R. Krishnaiah) North Holland (1980).

13. Ruhe, A. and Wedin, P.-Å. Algorithms for separable nonlinear least squares problems, SIAM Rev. 22 (1980), 318-339.

14. Späth, H. Orthogonal least squares fitting with linear manifolds, preprint (1984).

15. Tarantola, A. and Valette, B. Generalized nonlinear inverse problems solved using the least squares criterion, Rev. Geo. and Space Phys. 20 (1982), 219-232.

16. Watson, G.A. The solution of generalized least squares problems, University of Dundee, Department of Mathematical Sciences Report N.A./86 (1985).

Dr G. Alistair Watson,
Department of Mathematical Sciences,
University of Dundee,
Dundee DD1 4HN,
Scotland.